A WRETCHED
AND PRECARIOUS
SITUATION

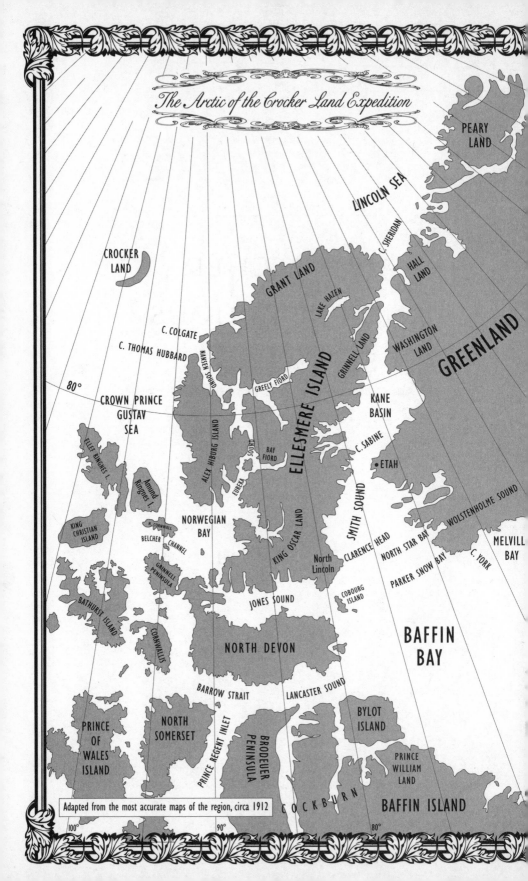

The Arctic of the Crocker Land Expedition

PEARY LAND

CROCKER LAND

LINCOLN SEA

C. SHERIDAN

HALL LAND

GRANT LAND

LAKE HAZEN

GREENLAND

C. COLGATE

C. THOMAS HUBBARD

NANSEN SOUND

GRINNELL LAND

WASHINGTON LAND

GREELY FIORD

ELLESMERE ISLAND

KANE BASIN

80°

CROWN PRINCE GUSTAV SEA

ALEX HIBURG ISLAND

BAY FIORD

C. SABINE

• ETAH

ELLEF RINGNES I.

EUREKA

SMITH SOUND

Amund Ringnes I.

WOLSTENHOLME SOUND

KING CHRISTIAN ISLAND

NORWEGIAN BAY

N. CORNWALL

KING OSCAR LAND

MELVILL BAY

BELCHER CHANNEL

CHANNEL

North Lincoln

CLARENCE HEAD

NORTH STAR BAY

C. YORK

GRINNELL PENINSULA

PARKER SNOW BAY

BATHURST ISLAND

CORNWALLIS

JONES SOUND

COBOURG ISLAND

BAFFIN BAY

NORTH DEVON

BARROW STRAIT

LANCASTER SOUND

BYLOT ISLAND

PRINCE OF WALES ISLAND

NORTH SOMERSET

PRINCE REGENT INLET

BRODEUER PENINSULA

PRINCE WILLIAM LAND

Adapted from the most accurate maps of the region, circa 1912

100°

90°

COCKBURN

80°

BAFFIN ISLAND

A WRETCHED

—— AND ——

PRECARIOUS
SITUATION

In Search of the Last Arctic Frontier

DAVID WELKY

W. W. NORTON & COMPANY

INDEPENDENT PUBLISHERS SINCE 1923

NEW YORK · LONDON

For information about permission to reproduce selections from this book,
write to Permissions, W. W. Norton & Company, Inc.,
500 Fifth Avenue, New York, NY 10110

For information about special discounts for bulk purchases, please contact
W. W. Norton Special Sales at specialsales@wwnorton.com or 800-233-4830

Manufacturing by LSC Communications Harrisonburg
Book design by Lisa Buckley
Production manager: Anna Oler

ISBN 978-0-393-25441-9

W. W. Norton & Company, Inc., 500 Fifth Avenue, New York, NY 10110
www.wwnorton.com

W. W. Norton & Company Ltd.,
15 Carlisle Street, London W1D 3BS

1 2 3 4 5 6 7 8 9 0

To H:
For reminding me what's most important.

_____

And to A, J, and K:
For being what's most important. *Asannittumik.*

CONTENTS

——— BOOK 2 ———

Not here: The White North hath thy bones;
And thou, heroic sailor-soul,
Art passing on thine happier voyage now
Toward no earthly pole.

—Alfred, Lord Tennyson,
epitaph for Rear Admiral Sir John Franklin, Arctic explorer

A NOTE ON NAMES
AND WORDS

ONE OF THE GREAT CHALLENGES of writing about the far north is figuring out who you are writing about. The Polar Inuit tribe of northwest Greenland had no written language at the time of the Crocker Land expedition. Visiting Westerners who transcribed what they heard therefore recorded many variants of a single person's name. To give but one example, a man named Qisuk appears in explorers' notes as Kishu, Kissuk, Kessuh, Kubliknik, Qissuk, and Kusshan. When reading multiple accounts from the same time period, it becomes easy for a historian to inadvertently combine two people with similar names into one person, or to turn a single person into two or more people.

Throughout *A Wretched and Precarious Situation*, I have done my best to regularize the names of members of the Polar Inuit tribe, also known as the Inughuit ("Inuk" means "person" and "Inughuit" means "people") in accordance with current official Greenlandic orthography. Except for a few clearly marked points in the text, I have silently modified names appearing in quoted material to conform with proper spellings. I have done the same with Inuktun words (Inuktun is the language of the Inughuit), again with a few exceptions. To avoid confusion, I use the conventional "kayak" instead of "qajaq." The settlement of "Iita" has been consistently referred to as "Etah" for more than a century, so I have again opted for the westernized spelling. Finally, I have changed the plural form of some Inuktun words for the sake of Western sensibilities. The plural of *qamutit* (sledge), for example, is also *qamutit*, but I have added an "s" for ease of reading. The word *kamik* (boot) has two plurals: *kamiik* (a pair of boots), and *kamiit* (three or more boots). Instead of having people put a *kamiik* on their feet, I use *kamiks* when referring to multiple boots, despite it being grammatically incorrect.

INTRODUCTION

"MINE BY THE RIGHT
OF DISCOVERY"

APRIL 21, 1906. NAVY COMMANDER Robert E. Peary, the world's most famous explorer, had failed again.

An uninformed observer might disagree. Swaddled in furs against temperatures that sometimes reached −60 degrees Fahrenheit even when the wind was calm, as it was today, Peary appeared confident as he strode across the thick ice encrusting the polar sea. His most recent navigational sightings told him that he was standing at 87° 6′ north latitude.* At that moment he and his men were more than the northernmost people on the planet; they were farther north than any humans had ever been.

Peary was in the ultimate no man's land. The nearest piece of solid ground lay over 350 miles to the south. His goal, the North Pole, lay 174 nautical miles in front of him, roughly the distance from Boston to New York—half again as far as he had already traveled.† He squinted at the expanse before him, plotting the smoothest route through the jumble of ice blocks spiking up from the

---

* Some of Peary's detractors claim, with good reason, that he made it only to 86° 30′.
† A nautical mile is about 1.15 standard miles, or 1.85 kilometers.

frozen surface. Over the past few decades he had earned a well-deserved reputation as the most determined, the most resourceful, and the most gifted leader in the history of Arctic exploration. If there was any way to get to the top of the Earth, he was the man to do it.

Then again, the travails the explorer had endured on his way to 87° 6′ would have killed an uninformed observer. Peary envisioned nature as a relentless, almost demonic foe bent on thwarting his dreams. On this frigid morning, four and a half years into Theodore Roosevelt's presidency and eight years before the phrase "world war" had any real meaning, the enemy had defeated him again.

Peary's men had suffered a series of delays during their six weeks on the polar sea. One hundred miles out, after days of battering their sledges into unforgiving walls of uneven ice, the team had encountered a wide band of open water, called a lead, slashing across their path. Although common, leads were one of the great banes of dogsled travel. Native drivers prodded east and west for a way around but found no solid ice. No matter how much the commander stomped and fumed, he could not cross what he called the river Styx until that mythological boundary of Hades literally froze over.

Peary was losing the Pole. His entire campaign relied on his precise calculations of weight, distance, and time. Sled dogs could haul only so much food and vital equipment such as stoves and alcohol fuel. There was no hope of resupply this far out. Peary had set off with a large party and sledges packed full of supplies. Members sacrificed themselves for the good of the mission, consuming the supplies they carried until they were forced to peel away from the main group and return to safety. Having ensured Peary's further progress toward "ninety north," their job was complete and they were expendable. But no amount of planning could restrain the seasons. Every day wasted before the river Styx increased the chance that climbing temperatures would break up the ice, stranding and eventually drowning the expedition. It was a paradox unfamiliar to other Americans: warmth meant death.

The men waited for an excruciating week before a rubbery strip of new ice created a bridge over the Styx. Not long after the crossing, the frustrated commander called another halt when the weather turned rotten. More precious days slipped away while the "hell-born music" of an Arctic blizzard battered the forlorn camp.

Peary then ran headlong into a maze of jagged rafters, the huge piles of ice heaved skyward when currents drove massive floes together in an aquatic version of the tectonic collisions that created mountain chains. The men muscled their sledges, or *qamutits*, over miles of frozen chaos. Inch by inch they pushed and pulled, often slowing their pace to a literal crawl as they nudged northward.

Each degree of latitude exacted a greater emotional and physical toll. Exhaustion marked the team's wind-scarred faces. Even the heartiest among them looked half dead. Frostbite blotched Peary's left cheek. Agonizing blisters enveloped his feet. His toes—eight of them mere stumps, having been amputated seven years previously because of frostbite —throbbed with pain. Food was running low.

The dogs whined with hunger. Peary had the six weakest ones killed and fed to the others. There was no game within 300 miles, no walruses or seals or caribou, so starvation would certainly claim more of the beasts. Fewer dogs meant slower travel, and slower travel meant death. The natives muttered doubts about ever seeing their families again.

All those weeks of suffering brought Peary here, to 87° 6'. He pondered whether he should cast caution aside and barrel toward the Pole, or withdraw and save his team. The bristling landscape would hinder any further progress, as would several small leads he saw waiting ahead. Each break in the ice might slow him down by an hour, or a day, or more, depending on the temperature and wind conditions. Peary could control neither. He hated anything he could not control.

Time had run out. Peary had "cut the margin as narrow as

could reasonably be expected." Dejected, he slipped a mittened hand under his fur coat and unwound a silk American flag from his waist. His wife had given him the flag fifteen years ago as a trophy he could one day raise at the top of the world. With that dream postponed, he clipped out a square and stuffed it into a bottle along with a brief message summarizing his journey. Dropping the bottle on the ice, he took a last look toward the Pole before turning away.

"It was the first and only time in all my Arctic work that I felt doubtful as to the outcome," Peary admitted. Retreat became a grim march for survival. Party members burned sledges for fuel and slaughtered dogs for food. By the time Peary reached his ship, the *Roosevelt*, only 41 of his original 120 dogs were still alive. Snow-blind and despondent, the commander hurled his stinking fur clothes onto the quarterdeck, bathed, ate, and collapsed in his bunk.

Photographs of three men glared from the walls of his stateroom, their stern poses conveying an impression of perpetual disapproval. The ship's namesake, Theodore Roosevelt; Morris Jesup, the financier who had bankrolled him for fifteen years; Charles Darling, the assistant secretary of the navy, who had arranged Peary's most recent sabbatical from the fleet so he could dash north. Darling gave him explicit orders. "The attainment of the Pole should be your main objective," he said. "Nothing short will suffice."

Peary had come up short. Instead of rewarding his backers with the Pole, he merely advanced the farthest north line from 86° 34', the mark the Italian explorer Umberto Cagni reached in 1900, to 87° 6'. Forty-three nautical miles. Some of the hardest miles he had ever traveled, to be sure, but less than his supporters expected, and less than what the world was waiting for.

"To think that I have failed once more, that I shall never have a chance to win again," Peary moaned. He tossed and turned in his bunk, unable to sleep more than a few hours at a time and spending listless days moping around the *Roosevelt*. His legs and feet swelled. His appetite vanished. Events from the past few months spooled through his mind as he probed for the cause of his misfortune. It had taken him fifteen years to refine his techniques, and to get the exact ship and crew he wanted. He had spent months planning what he assumed would be his final assault on the polar sea. No detail had escaped his attention—who to take with him, where to cache supplies, which dogs to bring, how many pounds of this and ounces of that to pack.

With his polar dreams dashed, Peary set about plotting his next move. A noose of pack ice held the *Roosevelt* at Cape Sheridan, a spit of brown-gray rubble thrusting from the northeast corner of Ellesmere Island, a 500-mile-long, question-mark-shaped chunk of ice, glaciers, and toothy rock west of northwest Greenland. It would be a few months before the summer thaw freed the ship. Suddenly faced with an abundance of time, Peary scoured his mental index of polar history for some achievement, no matter how insignificant, that he could present to his supporters.

An unexplored sliver of territory 90 miles west of Cape Sheridan offered a tempting opportunity for discovery. Setting this untrammeled place as his target, Peary gathered a small team, some *qamutits*, and his remaining dogs, and set out on June 2. "Surely he is a wonderful and great man," one amazed crewman remarked. "Just returned from the ice, being nearly starved to death, and now starts off for another land trip."

A week of slogging through wet, mushy snow brought the party to Cape Columbia, a forlorn promontory at the northern peak of Ellesmere's question mark. Peary, following established explorer etiquette, ordered his men to erect a cairn of stones as proof he had reached that spot.

"I am very much below par," he noted in his journal. Every part of his body hurt. But poor health had never stopped him before, and it wouldn't stop him now. Westward went his team, passing Cape Nares, Cape Alexandra, and Cape Discovery. Peary saw this journey as a trip across time as well as space. Each landmark he passed aroused memories of the brave, sometimes foolhardy men who first sighted these places. He knew their adventures backward and forward, having scoured their writings for any insights that might advance his quest for the Pole.

Peary's black mood lifted as he regained his sense of comfort and control. Food was plentiful and the winds benevolent. His sledges swept past Cape Aldrich and into virgin territory. "What I see before me in all its splendid, sunlit savageness is *mine*," he enthused. "Mine by the right of discovery, to be credited to me, and associated with my name generations after I have ceased to be."

Taking the silhouette of a faraway mountain as a reference point, the commander pushed his guides through several days of soupy weather. Thick fog obscured their surroundings. Snowstorms whipped crystals into their eyes. Peary felt his fifty-year-old body getting stronger despite the poor weather. The swelling in his legs eased, and he slept better in his canvas tent than he had on the *Roosevelt*.

Fair skies on June 24 unveiled the hill they had chased for the past 50 miles. "As fine and clear as could be desired," Peary observed in his journal. He hungered for the vistas its summit would offer. "I felt this was an opportunity not to be lost," he said, as "the elevation would enable me to see what there was beyond."

Beyond. For nearly twenty years the idea of pushing beyond existing limits of human knowledge had compelled him to go farther north, farther onto the polar ice, farther from the safety of home. In his mind, a monomaniacal thirst for what lay beyond was what separated him from other people, from the ordinary people history would soon forget. Above all else, Robert Peary wanted to be remembered.

Iggiannguaq and Ulloriaq, the native Greenlanders accompanying Peary, brewed a pot of tea and boiled some cornmeal mush. Then they led the explorer up the 2,000-foot peak. He dubbed it Cape Colgate, in honor of his financial backer James Colgate.

"The view was more than interesting," Peary crowed. Looking east, he could trace the long path leading back to the *Roosevelt*.

To the south and west lay Nansen Strait, the 20-mile-wide lane of ice separating Ellesmere from Axel Heiberg Island, a bean-shaped mass of fiords and glaciers nestled inside Ellesmere's question-mark curve. Turning north, he contemplated his tormentor of so many years, the frozen sea.

Dialing his binoculars into focus, he espied a line of snow-clad hills rising from the ice far to the northwest. Iggiannguaq and Ulloriaq, battling the glare, confirmed his conclusion: this was undiscovered land. Peary had lost the Pole, but he might have snagged a different prize worthy of his enormous reputation.

He wanted more information. After descending from Cape Colgate, the party sledged across Nansen Strait and onto the eastern shores of Axel Heiberg Island. Peary pointed his *qamutit* toward a far-off line of heights overlooking the northern shore.

Even as a new conquest beckoned, Peary found himself wrestling with old demons. "Twenty years last month . . . since I began," he wrote in his journal, "and yet I have missed the prize. . . . It seems as if I deserved it." The vitality and recuperative powers of his youth were distant memories. He believed he had blown his last chance at the Pole.

Following three days of heavy snowshoeing, the team reached the hills cresting the northeast corner of Axel Heiberg Island late on the evening of June 27. No human had ever stood in that place. Peary named the spot Cape Thomas Hubbard to honor yet another financial backer. He brewed coffee and flailed at swarms of blue flies while his two assistants fed the dogs pemmican, a nutrient-rich amalgam of dried meat, fat, flour, vegetables, sugar, and raisins compressed into low-weight, high-calorie blocks and packed into tins. Iggiannguaq shot two deer, a welcome change from the preserved eggs the men had lived on for the past five days.

At 11 p.m., with the summer sun hanging low in the sky, Peary strung his binoculars over his shoulder and ordered his team's sledges up the slope. A blanket of snow provided traction for their runners until it petered out a third of the way up. Tying off their dogs, Peary, Iggiannguaq, and Ulloriaq began scrambling up the last 1,000 vertical feet. Tufts of grass and purple saxifrage reminded them of summer's imminent arrival. Recognizing that this climb might mark his final moment of discovery, Peary paused several times on the way up to snap a photograph.

For ninety minutes they climbed, encountering alternating strips of snow and bare ground. At the top the terrain devolved into a field of loose rocks about the size of dinner plates. Geology held no interest for the commander at this moment. The ice-covered polar sea extended out as far as he could see. Peary pointed his binoculars toward the northwest horizon.

There it was, 50 or 75 miles in the distance. Right where it was supposed to be. Snowcapped hills filled Peary's binoculars, more vivid and detailed than before. His "heart leaped the intervening miles of ice" as he "looked longingly at this land and in fancy trod its shores and climbed its summits." Unanswerable questions raced through his mind. What was this place? How big was it? What kinds of creatures lived there?

Romanticism collided with practicality. Much as his heart yearned for those peaks, his mind told him to turn back. Rising temperatures were punching holes in the Arctic ice sheet. Although the dogs were probably healthy enough to deliver him to this new land, he and his men would get stranded there, hundreds of miles from the nearest rescuers, if the melting continued at its present rate. It was too risky. This land, tantalizing as it was, must wait for someone else.

Peary, Iggiannguaq, and Ulloriaq piled rocks into a waist-high, cone-shaped cairn. The commander stashed a note and another square from his American flag inside. Taking a last look at the enigma beyond the ice, they began their descent. Dogs and men huffed into camp at 4 a.m.

"Out of my new domain, and back into the known world again," the commander lamented when he recrossed Cape Aldrich two weeks later, this time traveling from west to east. So far as he believed, his door to the Arctic was closing forever.

Peary climbed back aboard the *Roosevelt* on July 30, weary from his fifty-eight-day round trip. His face was haggard, and his clothes hung in tatters. His sealskin boots clanked on the deck; when they started rotting away in the field, he had resoled them with sheets of tin snipped from pemmican containers. All the suffering he endured during what he assumed was his final Arctic ordeal was for a good cause. He wasn't bringing home *the* prize, but he was bringing home *a* prize.

Robert Peary organized his life around two goals: reaching the North Pole, and raising enough money for another assault on the North Pole. Four trips over a twenty-year span had taught him as much about massaging potential donors as about surviving extreme conditions. Monuments to his supporters dotted maps of the Arctic. Each cape, glacier, and fiord bearing a backer's name served as both an eternal testament to past generosity and an implicit request for future contributions. Claiming geographical prizes was an ongoing process; the explorer identified new landmarks in need of titles throughout his trip. "Name the —— Sea," he reminded himself in his diary. "Name the glacial fringe."

As he contemplated whether he could make a fifth and certainly final push for the top of the world, he had another honor to bestow on some lucky patron. He thought of George Crocker, a San Francisco banker who had donated $50,000 toward this most recent expedition.

Whatever Peary had twice seen, whether island or continent, would henceforth and forever be known as Crocker Land.

Commander Peary's discovery confirmed centuries' worth of folklore, rumors, and science indicating that at least one large, undiscovered landmass was still hiding somewhere in the vast and little-explored Arctic Ocean. The Greek historian Herodotus recorded stories of a frozen northern land nearly 2,500 years before Peary marched up Cape Colgate. Other ancient Greeks described a fertile paradise, which they called Hyperborea, located beyond the birthplace of the north wind. Some medieval Christian theologians claimed the Antichrist inhabited a gloomy realm in the far north. Norse legends placed both Hel (the underworld) and Niflheim (home of Yggdrasil, or the "world tree," meeting place of the gods) in the high latitudes. Gerardus Mercator's 1567 world map featured a large *Terra Septentrionalis Incognita* sprawling over the North Pole. This continent, which many took to be real, was a product of Mercator's desire for aesthetic equilibrium rather than any actual knowledge; he wanted to balance the equally speculative *Terra Australis Incognita* he drew in the southern latitudes.

Magical, missing, or lost islands, Atlantis being the most famous, have long intrigued humans. Mankind cannot live in the sea, so islands strike many people as hospitable oases in a watery desert. They are perceived as exotic and unusual, inspiring fantastic dreams of shipwrecks, buried treasure, and vanished civilizations. Authors from Alexandre Dumas (*The Count of Monte Cristo*), to Jules Verne (*The Mysterious Island*), to H. G. Wells (*The Island of Dr. Moreau*) have exploited our fascination with these places. Marco Polo called any place he had heard about but not visited an "island."

Many ancient seafaring cultures set their most extraordinary myths on islands. King Arthur had his Avalon, where Excalibur was forged and the sorceress Morgan le Fay wove her spells. Chinese mythologists wrote about Peng-Lai, home of the immortals. The *Arabian Nights* described El-Wák-Wák, three strange islands lush with trees whose fruit resembled women's heads hanging by their hair. "Wák-wák!" the fruits cried, falling silent only when someone plucked them.

The age of legends had passed by the time Peary spotted Crocker Land, but the era of discoveries in the far north had not. Whalers, shipwreck survivors, and adventurers had outlined only the fringes of the Arctic's 11,000,000-square-mile expanse. "We know less about [the Arctic] than any such extensive region on the planet Mars," amateur scientist Henry Mellen Prentiss declared in 1897. In 1906, the same year Peary reached 87° 6', William Reed claimed in his *Phantom of the Poles* that holes at 90° north and south accessed a paradise inside the Earth peopled by a humanlike race. Reed was wrong, of course, but the Arctic is still yielding new finds; in 2007 an expedition led by American Dennis Schmitt discovered tiny Stray Dog West Island off Greenland's northeast shore.

By 1906 there were few blank spaces left on the world map. Central Africa, the Amazon River basin, the high Himalayas, and Antarctica still had some uncharted areas. Unlike Crocker Land, none of those places held the possibility of a new continent with unidentified animals, plants, and perhaps even humans living on it. Outsiders had not stumbled across northwest Greenland's Polar Inuit, or Inughuit, the small tribe that produced Iggiannguaq, Ulloriaq, and the other people who kept Peary alive during his years in the north, until 1818. Why couldn't someone else be out there, waiting to be found? Whoever unlocked Crocker Land's secrets would join the pantheon of Christopher Columbus, Captain Cook, Lewis and Clark, and other legendary explorers.

Peary's sighting confirmed earlier signs of undiscovered land. On previous trips, the commander spotted fox and deer tracks hundreds of miles from any known landmass and tracked icebergs with sand mixed into their surface. Peary's contemporary, Danish explorer Ejnar Mikkelsen, watched migratory birds flying over Franz Josef Land, north of Russia, toward some northern destination. Inuit in both Alaska and Greenland told stories about islands somewhere north of the Canadian coast. Some of them said they had visited these places, or had ancestors who had visited them.

In 1904, Dr. Rollin A. Harris, an expert in ocean tides employed by the United States Geodetic and Coastal Survey, laid out the scientific argument for an undiscovered Arctic continent in his *National Geographic* article "Some Indications of Land in the Vicinity of the North Pole." Harris built his case on several pieces of qualitative and quantitative evidence. Sailors' reports of thick, old ice floes north of Alaska and the Canadian Yukon implied that a large landmass was blocking their path to warmer waters. Unexpectedly low levels of tidal activity throughout the Arctic suggested that something was inhibiting the ocean's predicted rise and fall.

Harris clinched his case by tracing the drift of ships that had become trapped in pack ice over the years. Their courses convinced him that two currents dominated the Arctic Ocean. One flowed from west to east (or counterclockwise, if viewed from high above the North Pole) above Alaska and northern Canada before entering the Atlantic Ocean east of Greenland. A second also began north of Alaska but proceeded from east to west (clockwise) around Siberia and the northern edge of Scandinavia before dumping into the Atlantic. This divergence between two currents originating from the same place suggested "a large tract of land," probably something similar in size to Greenland, forcing them apart. Greenland is the largest island in the world.

Crocker Land had to be there because its presence was the best way of explaining the facts accumulated by eyewitnesses. It was in this sense an early-twentieth-century version of the Higgs boson, a particle whose existence physicists had predicted through the use of computer models and mathematical formulas decades before a powerful atom smasher confirmed its presence. Cartographers, certain that Crocker Land existed but unsure of its exact borders, began representing the newest continent with either a circle or an inexact shoreline in an otherwise blank expanse.

In 1906, Robert Peary literally put Crocker Land on the map. Scientists, explorers, and journalists would spend the next several years wondering what it was, and what secrets it might hold. Was it an island, an archipelago, or something larger, as Harris and others insisted? Some dared ask whether people lived there. As "the last great geographical problem left to the world for solution," it symbolized the conclusion of the global journey of exploration begun

many thousands of years ago when a few hundred bipedal hominids living in east Africa set out to learn what lay over the horizon.

Peary himself seemed the natural candidate to unravel Crocker
Land's mysteries, yet not even an unexplored continent could cool
the commander's North Pole fever. Two of his acolytes eventually
took up the challenge. Their quest to solve the puzzle brought triumph, frustration, joy, infighting, betrayal, and murder to one of
the harshest environments on the planet.

But, as with any story involving Peary, the North Pole must
come first, along with two young men who helped him get there.

BOOK
1

1

THE TENDERFEET

ONE DAY IN MAY 1908, eighteen months after Peary returned to the United States, a thirty-three-year-old French, math, and physical education teacher was swimming in the white-tiled pool on the campus of Worcester Academy, a prep school in Massachusetts. Students splashed one another and sprang from the diving board while their coach imagined himself boating in the deep blue Atlantic the moment the school year ended.

A Western Union delivery boy barreled through the door of the natatorium. "Donald MacMillan!" he shouted. Roused from his reverie, the teacher paddled over to accept the telegram. In the water he looked unremarkable, with a prematurely diminishing crop of sandy-brown hair and the soft, skeptical expression of a man who spent his days bouncing between guiding schoolboys' intellectual development and keeping them from getting into too much trouble.

A different figure emerged once MacMillan hoisted himself onto the edge of the pool. A naturally gifted athlete, he had always been a little bit faster, a little bit stronger, and a little bit nimbler than everyone else. Beneath his modest, two-piece swimsuit was a taut, lean body sculpted by hundreds of hours of gymnastics and calisthenics. Barely an ounce of fat disrupted his muscular frame. MacMillan enjoyed performing feats of strength for his delighted students, who used the teacher's exploits as motivation to improve their own fitness. One of his favorite stunts was leaping straight up and out of a chest-high barrel.

MacMillan accepted the yellow envelope and thanked the boy. Tearing it open, he read the terse message with wide eyes:

IF YOU ARE STILL INTERESTED IN ARCTIC EXPLORATION, COME TO SEE ME AT ONCE. GRAND UNION HOTEL, NEW YORK CITY, PEARY.

Professor MacMillan leapt from the water and started banging the gong that signaled the end of swimming time. He had a train to catch.

Peary began planning his next shot at ninety north while sledging back to the *Roosevelt* following his Crocker Land sightings. "Biscuits of compressed grape nuts?" he penciled in his field notebook. "A little pea flour?" He filled pages of his journal with possible modifications to sledges, ideas for enhancing the nutritional value of pemmican, and potential fundraising schemes. (Why not carry a miniature globe to the Pole, he asked. "There is something in the idea and it should appeal to some wealthy man.") Sweating out the details made him feel happy and in control. "Shade caps for another expedition to be red white and blue, with a spread eagle on outside of visor," he decided as his dog team mushed down the trail.

"Certain it is, the lure of the North, the 'Arctic fever' as it has been called, entered my veins," he realized, "and I came to have a feeling of fatality, a feeling that the reason and intent of my existence was the solution of the mystery of the frozen fastnesses of the Arctic." Peary needed the Pole. Striving for it, and for the notoriety that came with it, gave his life meaning. "I *must* have fame," he told his mother, "and I cannot reconcile myself to years of commonplace drudgery." His obsession with a point on the map compelled him to endure frostbite and starvation, to abandon his family for years at a time, and to destroy anyone who stood between him and his ultimate purpose.

Peary tried to mount a northern expedition in 1907, but postponed it when his principal supporters balked at covering the enormous cost of repairing the *Roosevelt*. Desperate, the commander turned to George Crocker. "You will note that I have attached your name to the distant new land observed by me . . . as a slight indication of my deep appreciation of your invaluable assistance," Peary wrote to him in April 1907. Crocker wouldn't take the bait. "I am sorry that I can do nothing for you in your next trip to the North Pole," he replied.

The next year found the explorer no less determined, and in no better financial shape. Even so, rumors that he was assembling another team loosed a torrent of eager applicants who were long on bluster and short on experience. Ambitious young men orbited him like a galaxy of juvenile Theodore Roosevelts, boasting about their good morals, unswerving loyalty, and superhuman strength. These would-be adventurers offered Peary their lives because his patronage offered a means of escaping the confines of modern life and attaining immortality.

Early-twentieth-century Americans were replacing frontier hardships and homestead farming with urban comforts and white-collar bureaucracies. Cities throbbed with the gaudy syncopations of ragtime music. Electric lights turned night into day. Live-entertainment experiences such as vaudeville, with its vibrant lineup of animal acts, comedians, dancers, and singers, were giving way to mass-culture spectacles emanating from the budding motion picture industry. Telephones enabled instantaneous communication, and a maturing network of streetcars, interurban trains, and locomotives slashed commute times and fused the United States into a single interconnected market. Factories converted a seemingly limitless bounty of raw materials into an ever-expanding array of consumer goods designed to remove inconvenience from everyday life. Success in this modernizing world came from climbing a corporate ladder, not from claiming new realms in the name of progress and civilization. Many in this ambitious, restless generation recoiled at having so few opportunities to prove their manliness, at least in the traditional, time-tested ways. Their grandfathers related stories of hacking out homesteads from a wilderness teeming with dangerous animals and even more dangerous Indians. Their fathers had sacrificed themselves for their country, whether Union or Confederacy, in the fiery cauldron of the Civil War. What would the boys of the 1900s tell their children? Tales of their ascent to middle management?

With the frontier closed and the country at peace, Arctic exploration became a way for educated boys from prosperous families to engage in the kind of manly struggle that shaped their forefathers. Recent conflicts such as the Spanish-American War and the Philippine War sparked divisive debates about racial hierarchy and overseas imperialism. In contrast, adventurers in the far north could reinvigorate old-fashioned models of masculinity by civilizing the wilderness, discovering untapped natural resources, and westernizing native peoples without ruffling the feathers of a domesticated society.

In an era of intensifying media competition, Peary and other publicity-savvy explorers became national heroes in part because their feats occurred at such an incredible geographical and psychological distance from the tame world of office desks and telephones. Fully cognizant of this appeal, the commander and his ghostwriters crafted travel narratives that served more as promotional tools than scientific contributions. *Northward over the Great Ice* (1898) and *Nearest the Pole* (1907) held much greater appeal for enthusiastic romantics bursting with dreams of adventure than they did for oceanographers and geologists.

Peary's mass-market aspirations were part of a larger trend. Over the past few decades explorers' memoirs and public lectures had evolved from stuffy treatises into macho adventure stories. "This book is not a record of scientific investigations," explained Elisha Kent Kane in his best-selling *Arctic Explorations* (1856). Instead, Kane, a U.S. Navy medical officer whose 1853–55 expedition had mapped parts of Ellesmere Island and established a new farthest north, targeted "the general reader."

Like oil paintings emerging from blank canvases, the heart-pounding Arctic stories of Peary, Kane, and their peers breathed life into what most readers saw as a remote realm of empty whiteness. Imaginative readers with a taste for excitement could envision themselves zipping across the far north behind a team of half-wild sled dogs. *Arctic Explorations, Nearest the Pole,* and the other red-blooded travel books even infected a tiny percentage of readers with a full-blown case of Arctic fever.

One of those people had just evicted a pool full of schoolboys.

Donald MacMillan hopped off the New York train at Grand Central within several hours of receiving Peary's message. Hustling across the street to the Grand Union Hotel, he learned from a clerk that the commander had retired for the evening. A note from Peary was waiting for him at the desk: "I'll see you at breakfast in the morning."

MacMillan believed his whole life had been building toward that meal. One of his earliest memories was of constructing a snow house outside his home in Provincetown, Massachusetts, a fishing village at the tip of Cape Cod. "Thrilled, I crept in through the half-oval door and sat there as within a crystal palace, entirely surrounded by glittering white blocks," he remembered, "and there I stubbornly remained until forcibly removed by my somewhat anxious mother." As a preschooler, MacMillan (family members called him "Dan" to avoid confusing him with his uncle Donald) hopped across ice pans that drifted from their Arctic spawning grounds into Provincetown Bay. One of his favorite boyhood activities, and one that nearly drowned him on multiple occasions, was to drill a hole through a small floe, insert an oar, and scull around the harbor.

The MacMillans' house on Commercial Street faced Provincetown's bustling docks. Young Dan could smell the pungent odors of salted fish and fresh paint from inside his home. The ringing thuds of caulking mallets became symphonies in his mind. In the afternoons he lurked in the back room of Kibbie Cook's grocery store, listening with rapt attention while grizzled fishermen spun tales about Pacific headhunters, grass-skirted women, and Arctic storms. MacMillan couldn't wait until he was old enough to tell his own sea stories. For a Provincetown boy, choosing a career meant either joining the West Indies run for oranges, bananas, and coconuts or, like MacMillan's father, Captain Neil, signing on with the northern whaling fleet.

Infatuated with the sea, MacMillan began devouring Arctic narratives almost as soon as he could read. Every new development thrilled him: a new farthest north, an innovation in shipbuilding, a mystery like Crocker Land. This sense of awe continued into adulthood. Students at Worcester sat spellbound as he unfurled maps of the Arctic, pointing out blank spaces awaiting some gifted explorer who could reveal their secrets. Perhaps he might be that person, if only someone would give him a chance.

Two acts of heroism in July 1904 made the schoolteacher a local celebrity and changed the course of his life. MacMillan spent his summers at Camp Wychmere, an adventure camp for boys located on Maine's Bustins Island. One evening, he noticed a commotion about a mile offshore. Peering into the distance, he saw six black dots bobbing on the surface. Along with a friend, he commandeered a dory and began rowing toward the scene. A strong southwesterly shoved the boat forward until the dots grew into people hugging the rail of an overturned yacht.

"Take this woman, she's nearly done," one of the survivors gasped. Dan hauled her aboard before circling back for the others.

"How many have you?" one of them asked once everyone was in the boat.

"Six," MacMillan replied. "How many were there?"

"Seven," came the answer.

A boy was missing. Even though he was probably dead, MacMillan dove into the sea. He found the boy underwater, tangled in the rigging. Cutting him free and dragging him to the surface, MacMillan administered artificial respiration but could not revive him.

Still shaken by the incident, Dan was startled a few nights later by shouts coming from the water: two women's desperate cries. He ran to the dock and jumped into a flat-bottomed punt. Following their voices, he rowed until he spotted a rowboat capsized in the waves. One woman clung to the bow, another to the stern. A man floated amidships.

Dan pulled the women on board. He wasn't sure what to do about the man in the water, because the punt couldn't hold four people without swamping. Fortunately, a fisherman arrived on the scene. MacMillan left the last victim in his care and rowed the other grateful survivors back to shore.

In less than a week he had saved eight or nine lives. Such bravery brought a measure of fame, along with a most unexpected letter from one of his heroes, Robert Peary, who owned an estate on nearby Eagle Island. The commander wondered whether the heroic camp director would teach Robert Peary, Jr., how to swim, shoot, and row—all the things the absentee father had never taught his son.

MacMillan and Peary's initial face-to-face encounter occurred when they bumped into each other at the Portland ferry terminal. "Don't wait for opportunity; make it," MacMillan had written in his diary two years earlier. This was his chance. The teacher lured the reticent explorer into a conversation by demonstrating an intimate familiarity with pretty much every book ever written about the Arctic, including Peary's *Northward over the Great Ice*. MacMillan's bookshelves at the academy groaned with well-thumbed Arctic narratives, Jack London's *The Sea Wolf,* and such turgid tomes as *American Merchant Ships and Sailors.* Had Peary let him, he could have gone on for hours about Kane or some other explorer.

His knowledge—or perhaps his flattery—impressed the commander. MacMillan opened up as their dialogue progressed, revealing that his father had captained fishing vessels off the Greenland coast before being lost at sea when Dan was a boy. This revelation exposed a crack in MacMillan's sunny façade. He had traveled a bumpy road since those bucolic early years in Provincetown, but he almost never discussed the dark times. MacMillan's confession touched some chord in Peary, who had lost his father to pneumonia when he was only two years old. The explorer "stood there apparently deep in thought for a moment," MacMillan remembered, "then turned and walked down the dock toward the boat."

Interpreting this inscrutable reaction as encouragement, in the summer of 1905 MacMillan applied for a position with Peary's upcoming polar expedition, the same one that would discover Crocker Land.

Nervous days passed before he saw a delivery boy pedaling a bicycle around the Worcester campus. The messenger dismounted and handed over a telegram. Inside the envelope was a characteristically blunt message:

HAVE PLACE FOR YOU ON NORTH POLE TRIP. WHEN CAN YOU
MEET ME IN PORTLAND.

"Do you want to send an answer, sir?" the boy asked.

MacMillan thought for a few seconds, then told the boy he'd wire a response later.

The rest of the day passed in a fog of classes and meetings. That evening, MacMillan weighed his options while jogging around the school's quarter-mile cinder track. He wanted to go more than he had ever wanted anything. But loyalty tugged at his conscience. Worcester had just renewed his contract. Breaking it would leave the school in the lurch. Devastated, he went to the local Western Union office and filled in a telegram blank: "Sorry, but unable to accompany you this year. MacMillan." His heart sank as he handed over the sheet. He had declined what would probably be his only chance to follow in the footsteps of his heroes.

MacMillan visited Portland one blustery day to call on the explorer. No one could find the commander. With his principal mission aborted, MacMillan began poking around the *Roosevelt*. Drenched, he escaped the rain by descending into the ship's hold, where he scratched his name on a timber, claiming a tiny piece of the ship, and its upcoming adventures, for himself.

MacMillan returned to Worcester and his mundane life in the classroom. Peary still haunted him. He consumed every available scrap of information about the commander's journey, the one he could have joined had he not been so loyal to the school. When the *Roosevelt* returned, he renewed his slender relationship with the adventurer. "My interest in Arctic exploration is even stronger than . . . a year ago," he informed Peary in December 1906. "It is my earnest desire to become a member of your next expedition." Unsure whether the commander remembered him, he again recited his qualifications: never smoked or drank, vacationed in the rugged outdoors, exercised every day. "My life has been almost a life of training for such work," he stressed.

"Will gladly meet all personal expenses and will contribute more, if necessary," MacMillan promised. Looking for any angle, he added "Bowdoin '98" after his signature. Both he and Peary had attended Maine's Bowdoin College.

Several months passed without encouragement.

All that prodding resulted in the breakfast at the Grand Union Hotel. Peary's sheer presence overwhelmed MacMillan, who committed every detail of the explorer's appearance to memory, as if it were a divine revelation. The fine, double-breasted suit. The broad shoulders, delicate hands, and bushy eyebrows. The lines etched into his face by years of exposure. And the eyes: MacMillan felt those blue-grey eyes most of all.

Peary was studying MacMillan too. His mouth smiled, but those steely eyes remained flat while they inspected the teacher with the clinical detachment of a tailor sizing up a client. Peary was indeed imagining him in different clothes—the furs of an Arctic explorer.

Peary approached his pursuit of the Pole like a grandmaster preparing for a chess match. Mother Nature played white, beginning each contest with the advantage of moving first. The commander would have to play a perfect game if he hoped to win. To checkmate the enemy he must arm himself with the best equipment, the optimal schedule, and the ideal route. His Eskimos—and he viewed the Inughuit as *his* Eskimos—served as pawns who shielded him, the king, from his opponent.

Kings needed other pieces on the board. Right now he was gauging whether MacMillan might become a useful rook, knight, or bishop.

Peary stocked his expeditions with "young men, of first-class physique, perfect health, education, and attainment." Being strong wasn't enough. Successful candidates must embody all of his stringent standards. Heavyset men tended toward clumsiness and were more likely to crash through fresh ice. They required more clothing material, ate more food, and took up more space in an operation where a few additional cubic inches could mean the difference between life and death. Thin men, on the other hand, were too frail, or lacked sufficient insulation to withstand the Arctic's punishing cold. Peary preferred "wiry" underlings who weighed between 2 and 2.5 pounds per inch of height. MacMillan weighed 2.39 pounds per inch.

Peary's breakfast companion struck him as an intelligent, upbeat, and self-reliant man who respected his authority and would follow orders without question. This last point was crucial, as he believed that "the success of any expedition depends upon the magnetism and force of its leader." Moreover, MacMillan's dogged pursuit of Peary's attention over the past several years demonstrated the kind of persistence and single-mindedness essential for any would-be explorer.

"MacMillan," Peary sighed, "I am fifty-two years old. This is probably the last attempt of my life. I want you to be in command of one of my supporting parties."

The teacher was so excited he could barely eat. Peary invited him upstairs to his luxurious quarters. The commander led the way with an odd, shuffling gait—a result of his abbreviated feet. MacMillan entered the suite, which resembled "a veritable curiosity shop" for explorers. Oil- and alcohol-burning stoves sat everywhere, as did coils of rope, samples of wood, and items so bizarre that not even the Arctic scholar could identify them. It was glorious chaos. It was everything MacMillan dreamed of.

Peary gave MacMillan two weeks to consider his offer. Dan didn't need them. As soon as he arrived back in Worcester, he marched into the office of the president of the Board of Overseers with his resignation letter in hand.

"I'm going to the North Pole," he said.

"Very interesting," came the reply. "How long do you expect to be gone?"

"One year, perhaps two," he answered. "It may be that we shall never come back."

Rather than lose one of its best instructors, Worcester granted MacMillan a leave of absence. He packed up his possessions and relocated to New York City.

MacMillan's pronouncement was premature. He wasn't going anywhere unless the commander scraped together some more money. Desperate for funds, Peary used Crocker Land as a fundraising carrot, mentioning in the presence of reporters that he might dispatch a squadron to its shores after he bagged the Pole. The mysterious continent "might entirely change all preconceived notions in regard to the unknown polar area," he declared.

Peary accumulated sufficient funds by early June. George Crocker did not contribute a dime. With the season growing late, Peary assembled his crew in a hurry. Three veterans of the 1905–06 trip returned to the fold: ship captain Robert Bartlett, longtime assistant Matthew Henson, and secretary Ross Marvin. Dr. John Goodsell signed on as expedition surgeon. With MacMillan on board, one more "tenderfoot" would round out the group.

Personnel issues lay beyond MacMillan's domain. He was a cataloger at heart, a list-maker who recognized the value of minutiae and took joy in doing a job completely right. These traits, along with his unswerving devotion and peerless work ethic, made him Peary's ideal gofer. The commander was too busy handling publicity and other big-picture issues to spend time tracking down the exact supplies his expedition required. He trusted his new hire to follow his precise specifications.

That was fine with MacMillan, who reveled in detail work. If Peary needed four-by-seven-inch field notebooks, bound at the top, a half inch thick, "with light, substantial, flexible covers," he would find them. He ran around New York City pricing aluminum kettles, sprucewood oars, and twenty-gallon milk tins, and locating the exact gauge of wire Peary wanted, at the specific price Peary would pay. MacMillan had chased this opportunity for years, and he was not about to jeopardize it by displeasing his boss. "You are doing good work," the explorer told him in a rare compliment.

"Young Geo. Borup is to occupy room with you," Peary scrawled on one of the myriad notes he sent MacMillan during the frenetic summer of 1908. MacMillan had no problem sharing a room with a stranger. He had no problem with anything the commander asked of him.

Twenty-two-year-old George Borup was a last-second addition, the final piece on Peary's board. In many ways he epitomized the flock of go-getters who pestered the explorer for a chance at glory. Borup was a recent graduate of Yale University, where he excelled at track, golf, and wrestling. He was an outdoor enthusiast, a tightly packed bundle of energy willing to walk a thousand miles for a clear shot at a moose. He was also a well-to-do naïf who lacked even a shred of Arctic experience. Peary had met a hundred just like him.

Borup cracked Peary's inner circle only because of his father's relentless determination to get him there. Retired U.S. Army Colonel Henry Dana (H. D.) Borup served nearly thirty years as an ordnance officer and military attaché in posts across the United States and around Europe. Giving orders was part of his nature. A single parent since his wife Mary's death in 1897, H. D. dominated his only son's world. He raised George like an industrial-age Spartan, imposing a rigorous physical training regimen and preaching the value of manly courage at every opportunity.

H. D. wanted to focus his beloved child's restless ambition by giving him the opportunity of a lifetime. For sixteen months the colonel badgered Peary for an audience. When the commander ignored his letters, he convinced mutual acquaintances such as Peary's brother-in-law, Emil Diebitsch, to press his case. Still, Peary said nothing. So the colonel tried again. "My son . . . is dead set on accompanying you on your next Polar Expedition," he explained. "He is an honest, merry, fearless boy, very strong and athletic, does not smoke or drink, and I hence can recommend him. I would like very much for you to see him so that you may judge for yourself." Peary ignored his request. H. D. tried again, and again, and again, until Peary broke down and agreed to meet George at the Grand Union Hotel, if for no other reason than to get the persistent colonel off his back.

Much to his surprise, Peary liked what he saw in his young, grey-suited visitor, who arrived at the door with his father in tow. George Borup stood five feet eight inches tall—four inches shorter than his host—and tipped the scales at a sturdy 158 pounds, or 2.3 pounds per inch. Dark, wavy hair and heavy eyebrows set off a face that was intriguing rather than classically handsome. Borup's broad nose made his mouth seem small. Soft brown eyes conveyed a joyful innocence absent from the commander's icy glare.

Peary felt an instant, almost paternal connection with the boy. Borup said that he was moldering away in Altoona, where he held a job his father had secured for him in the Pennsylvania Railroad's machine shop. Adventure called. Imbued with the colonel's teachings about bravery and honor, he yearned for a test of his manly credentials. Sensing George's intelligence, optimism, and loyalty, the commander had placed him on his mental shortlist by the time he ushered the Borups from his rooms.

George Borup intrigued Peary, but the commander worried the boy might be too delicate for the hard road ahead. Perhaps he could bring him north on a trial basis, he suggested in a letter, and send him back on a supply ship if he couldn't hack it. George demurred. "My father went to a great deal of trouble in securing me my present position and I do not think it fair to him to give it up without the *certainty* of being selected," he explained.

This show of defiance impressed Peary. "Glad to have you join expedition unconditionally," he telegrammed on June 14.

A few days later Borup signed Peary's standard contract, the same one MacMillan had signed. In exchange for seventy-five dollars a month, he pledged "to obey the directions of Commander Peary." Any "disobedience or insubordination" would result in his immediate termination. Peary retained legal control over all of Borup's notes, photographs, and diaries. The recent college graduate had in essence signed over his life to a man he knew solely by reputation.

MacMillan grew up around boats, so he appreciated how carefully Peary had designed the vessel that would carry them north. Appropriating the best elements of Scottish whalers and other veterans of the Arctic Ocean, the *Roosevelt* was the finest ship ever sent into the ice fields. Planks of white oak and dense greenheart—an evergreen tree from the laurel family imported from Guiana—protected its sides during collisions. Steel plates in the bow deflected bergs and pans. Its reinforced propeller and shaft repelled clawing ice. A stubby footprint made the steamer more of a stout egg than a sleek shark. Rather than getting crushed between squeezing floes, the pressure simply lifted the ship until it rested atop the ice on its bowl-shaped hull. It was, in sum, an exploring craft worth every penny that Morris Jesup and Thomas Hubbard had contributed toward its construction.

Moored at the pier jutting from East Twenty-fourth Street into the East River, the *Roosevelt* buzzed with activity. Stevedores in shirtsleeves complained about the scorching heat as they lowered cases into the hold. Coiled lines lay here and there. Heaps of folded canvas spilled across the deck. Molasses, oil, tomatoes, lumber, tin, and wire came on board, as did eight tons of flour, two tons of codfish, two hundred cases of beans, one hundred cases of brown bread, and boxes containing rifles, ammunition, hammers, shovels, and brooms.

MacMillan found evidence of Peary's foresight and rigorous preparation wherever he looked. Every incoming crate had the same dimensions. If the *Roosevelt* burned or got crushed by ice, survivors could construct shelters from the brick-like containers. Dashes of paint indicated each box's contents. Suppliers were not allowed to simply stencil "tea" or "canned fruit" on the outside, because the Polar Inuit could not read. Neither could some of the sailors. Peary had his dog pemmican shipped in tins as wide as a sledge so they would form a floor for the vehicle. Pemmican for people came in tins scored in such a way that a man could pop off a one-pound serving with a knife. Six tons of ship's biscuit, or hardtack, a tooth-breaking cracker made from flour, salt, and water, arrived in rectangular blocks divided sixteen to a pound for easy rationing. "These things may seem trivial," Peary conceded, "but every movement and operation which can be eliminated and every minute that can be saved under the trying accompaniments of cold, wind, hunger, and fatigue, which are inevitable in polar travel, make for the conservation of the energy, vitality, and morale of the members of the party." Awed by Peary's precision, MacMillan filed away these lessons for future use.

MacMillan was splitting his time between the ship and last-second supply matters when Borup arrived from Altoona. The youngest member of Peary's team wandered the teeming vessel with wide eyes and a broad grin. Afraid of appearing useless, he started loading crates without knowing what he was doing. Matt Henson, the commander's right-hand man, cast a skeptical eye on the newcomer. "I have seen too many enthusiastic starters, and I am sorry to say some of them did not finish well," he said.

MacMillan and Borup, Peary's two tenderfeet, seemed a mismatched pair. Eleven years separated the two. As a child, MacMillan had shimmied up the masts of big schooners moored across the street from his house. Borup had never been beyond sight of land. With the *Roosevelt* preparing for departure, both men were too busy to do much more than exchange pleasantries. They could get to know each other later. Roommates in a 4-by-8-foot cabin couldn't keep many secrets.

2

THE BEST YEAR

ON JULY 6, 1908, thousands of well-wishers gathered at the East Twenty-fourth Street pier to watch the *Roosevelt* depart for the far north. It was a sweltering day. Men wore their thinnest suits and tugged at sweaty collars. Ladies in beribboned hats and neck-to-ankle dresses fanned themselves and sheltered beneath parasols. Wild cheers erupted when Peary, just late enough to be dramatic, strode across the gangplank. "Surely no ship ever started for the end of the earth with more heart-stirring farewells," the commander declared. Josephine, his long-suffering wife, shepherded their children, Robert Jr. and Marie, around the bustling deck. Crewmen wound the mooring lines. MacMillan ran through supply lists in his head. George Borup waved at the crowd while H. D., who insisted on accompanying his son on this leg of the journey, stood close by.

With a blast from its siren, the *Roosevelt* pulled from its berth. Tugs and ferries tooted as the brawny cruiser steamed up the East River.

The next day, Captain Bob Bartlett moored the ship at President Theodore Roosevelt's Oyster Bay estate. Roosevelt stormed aboard with his customary enthusiasm, scaling his namesake's rope ladder like a boy entering a treehouse. First Lady Edith trailed behind with three of their sons. Resplendent in a black linen suit, the president picked through cargo crates and pumped the crew's hands, scouring the vessel from stem to stern while rattling off facts about seamanship, Greenland, dogsleds, and whatever else crossed his encyclopedic mind.

"It's ninety or nothing, the North Pole or bust this time," Bartlett said when Roosevelt descended the ladder.

"Good-bye captain, good-bye boys," the president replied. "Good luck to you all. I believe you'll get there this time."

"Good luck, Peary," he bellowed, doffing his hat.

Roosevelt was "a HIT," Borup declared.

Bartlett guided the *Roosevelt* back into Long Island Sound, past Cape Cod, and into the wide Atlantic, where he set a course for Sydney, a fishing village on the tip of Nova Scotia that was a popular layover for Arctic voyagers.

MacMillan absorbed the steamer's pitches and rolls by assuming the wide-legged stance of an experienced sailor. Borup's stomach heaved as he wobbled around the deck. Peary recommended crackers and champagne as a remedy for intestinal woes. Charlie Percy, the ship's grizzled steward, convinced the newbie that a tall glass of seawater would settle his insides.

Sydney represented both a landmark and a moment of parting. This was as far as Jo Peary was going. Bracing herself for another year or more without her husband, she guided her children onto a waiting tug to begin their return home. Young Robert mustered a chipper "Come back soon, Dad." Unbeknownst to her father, the lovely, blue-eyed, fifteen-year-old Marie left her portrait with George Borup. The two had huddled together like co-conspirators throughout the brief voyage. George hid the photograph in his diary.

Much as H. D. Borup wanted to stay, it was also time for him to leave. For the next fourteen months, another stern, authoritarian, and at times overbearing father figure would supervise his son.

———

"If you fellows want to see an iceberg, you had better get up," Charlie Percy roared on the third morning after the *Roosevelt* left Sydney. Rushing to the rail, MacMillan and Borup gawked at what was by Arctic standards a modest berg. Rising some 60 feet above the surface, it glowed pure white. Vivid green reflections shimmered beneath the waterline. "The lure of the North is a strange and a powerful thing," Peary observed. Indescribable emotions overwhelmed the commander's two young protégés as they watched the iceberg glide along an inexorable path to its own destruction. Arctic fever gripped their souls. Neither man wanted a cure.

If Borup was getting a surrogate father in Peary, he was also getting a big brother. MacMillan—everyone on the expedition called him Mac, instead of Dan, except for Peary, who preferred the more formal "Mr. MacMillan"—doubted the young Yalie's abilities. "He was not especially interested in any branch of Arctic [work] or in [any] branch of Science," he said of Borup. "He simply wanted to go." MacMillan, a child of the sea who treated Arctic narratives like holy texts, found himself sharing a compartment with a gentleman scholar who had never heard of the great American explorer Elisha Kent Kane. Their contrasting backgrounds might prove contentious.

Oddly enough, the pairing worked. Borup's charisma, stamina, and enthusiasm charmed MacMillan. Their tiny quarters, which they called the Chamber of Horrors, became a mutual joke. Borup laughed that "the cabin was so small when we went in the lights went out." Ammunition, books, field glasses, clocks, thermometers, barometers, and photography equipment cluttered the shelves. Snowshoes hanging from the ceiling served as additional shelving. A gun rack carried three Winchesters and two Remingtons. Clothes and furs swayed from hooks on the walls. A tin pail on the floor held water for bathing and shaving.

A comfortable familiarity settled over the pair. Borup was the more outgoing of the two, prone to cracking jokes while they performed the mindless task of sorting through the hundreds of donated magazines in the lazarette, or aft storage area. Mac played it closer to the vest but got off some good barbs when the stench of rotting whale meat in the rear hold made his new friend retch. Borup guffawed whenever a roll sent Mac careening into a stack of crates. Somehow, MacMillan didn't mind.

Mac's natural reserve fell away when the *Roosevelt* slid past Newfoundland's Bay of Islands. Sorrowful memories clouded his mind. He unburdened himself to Borup with a trust born from their immediate bond. In November 1883, he explained, Captain Neil, his father, was offered a commission to haul a load of New-foundland herring. It was late in the season for a northern voyage, and Sarah MacMillan worried that her husband's ship would get trapped in the ice. Neil, never one to reject a contract, decided the risk was worth it. Nine-year-old Dan watched his father pilot the *Abbie Brown*, its hull shining with a new coat of black paint, out of Provincetown. He wished he could be on board. Although Dan resembled his mother, he inherited his father's spirit of adventure and love of the sea. He wanted to join him on big fishing trips, if only to perform grunt labor, such as cutting the tongues out of cod.

Weeks passed without word of the *Abbie Brown*. Every day, Sarah donned her heavy shawl and climbed Miller's Hill to watch for her husband's return. Dan started hearing chatter at school. "He's lost," his friends whispered, "lost with all hands." Captains spoke in hushed tones whenever the boy walked the docks. "Neil probably drove her under; he was a perfect devil for carrying sail," they muttered. Dan heard their whispers. There were only two Neils in Provincetown, and Neil Ross was in the West Indies.

MacMillan never saw his father again, nor did he ever discover where the *Abbie Brown* went down. For all he knew, the *Roosevelt* was passing over the wreck while he was speaking with Borup.

Neil's death sent the family into a tailspin. Sarah took in laun-dry but could not afford to feed her five children while keeping up with the rent. She moved the family from their white-shingled cottage into a hovel. Dan did whatever he could to help make ends meet. While other kids his age were playing, he dove for pennies off Railroad Wharf, sold clumps of pond lilies, and hawked a dubious history of Provincetown (among other howlers, it warned visitors that a 300-foot-long sea serpent with six eyes and two-foot-long fangs lived off the coast). It wasn't enough. Bills piled up. Sarah sent two of Dan's siblings to live with friends. By 1886 the family was surviving on handouts from neighbors.

Sarah died that same year. Her eleven-year-old son stood before her open grave, wondering what to do next. Dan considered quitting school so he could work full-time. A friend's family took him in for a few months before shuffling him off to another family. Two years later he moved in with his oldest sister, Letitia, in Freeport, Maine, a sleepy community of 3,000 people that was as dependent on shoemaking as Provincetown was on fishing.

MacMillan's early years revolved around the water. But in Freeport he could no longer see the waves or hear the surf. It was all gone, leaving only a hazy yearning for the ocean, the ice, and a father figure. Peary offered him all three.

MacMillan credited his mother for his love of science and literature, and for a cautious disposition that tempered the impulsiveness inherited from his father. Careful yet bold, level-headed yet confident, he pushed forward through obstacles that would have derailed most children his age. MacMillan starred on Freeport High School's football, baseball, track, tennis, and gymnastics teams, as well as in the classroom. Excellent grades got him a scholarship to Bowdoin College, ten miles up the road in Brunswick. Too poor to board near campus, he commuted from Freeport, limiting his daily expenses to a 22-cent round-trip train ticket and 19 cents worth of frankfurters.

MacMacillan seemed content with this threadbare existence, which at least held the promise of a better future. Summer jobs at resort hotels barely covered tuition and transportation for the next term. Then, right before his senior year, he contracted typhoid fever. The illness kept him out of school for the fall semester. The following spring he spent an aimless stretch working as a timekeeper for a construction company. Again he pulled himself together, reenrolling at Bowdoin and completing his degree in June 1898. MacMillan spent his graduation day working in a farmer's hayfield. The job paid four dollars, too much money to pass up.

MacMillan is "a man of good character and scholarship," Bowdoin president William DeWitt Hyde wrote. "He has an unusual degree of energy, force, and executive ability; and gives promise of marked success." The new graduate toyed with the prospect of medical school before rejecting it as too expensive. With Hyde's recommendation letter in hand, he accepted a teaching job in North Gorham, Maine. Two years later he joined the faculty at Swarthmore Prep, a Quaker school outside of Philadelphia. Then it was on to Worcester Academy, and dreams of the far north.

As the *Roosevelt* slid past Newfoundland, George Borup gained a new appreciation of the forces driving MacMillan. Perfect strangers not long ago, the bunkmates were on their way to becoming the closest of friends. They understood each other. They shared the pain of losing a parent. Borup admired MacMillan's modesty, his ambition, and his resolve. He grasped that this journey marked the culmination of the older man's dreams. Mac's passion made it a mutual dream, and they would be partners in achieving it.

Northward went the *Roosevelt*, over the *Abbie Brown*, past the Bay of Islands, and toward the Arctic Circle.

"Land!" came the cry from the bow on July 27, exactly three weeks into the *Roosevelt*'s journey. Greenland's towering black cliffs, some of them 8,000 feet high, rose to the northeast. Dense fog cloaked the shore. Mac and Borup were ecstatic even though they could barely discern the imposing wall of rock through the haze. "It was almost impossible to realize that I was on an Arctic Expedition, and that the land in sight was Greenland," Borup later wrote. "I couldn't feel thankful enough for being on this wonderful trip."

"*Kissa Tikeri-Unga!*" Peary shouted in his accented, ungrammatical Inuktun. "I'm arriving, for a fact!" His declaration was unnecessary, as the native hunters at Cape York, the southern limit of the Polar Inuit's range, had already spotted the *Roosevelt*. Spilling from their *tupeqs*, tents made from skins, several Inughuit began paddling toward the ship. Their arrival on board delighted Borup, who thought the short, fur-clad natives resembled overgrown foxes. His only reservation was that he could "smell 'em a hundred yards" away. "Good Lord!" he cried to Mac, "have we got to live with that bunch?"

Peary loaded Borup, MacMillan, and a crate of hardtack into a whaleboat, and they rowed ashore. The commander laughed as he dumped the food on the beach. "Men, women, and children hurl[ed] themselves on the biscuits like dogs," an Inuk man remembered decades later. "That scene tells very well how [Peary] considered this people—my people—who were, for all of that, devoted to him." The Inughuit sometimes called him Piulerriaq, "the great Peary." At other times, and never when he was around, they grumbled about "the great tormentor."

In 1891, when Peary first met the Polar Inuit, he handed out gifts of glass beads and other trinkets. These useless items failed to impress their recipients. He, too, was wary, as his understanding of the natives came from such disdainful predecessors as Elisha Kane, who had called them "a declining—almost obsolete—people."

Peary changed his mind once he grasped that his fortunes depended on their favor. The commander believed that "the Almighty had put the little tribe in this particular place for the express purpose of assisting [me] to win the pole." They deserved his respect, but not his affection. He never learned the Inuktun language beyond some basic nouns and verbs, and never really grasped their culture. "On the whole," he decided, "these people are much like children, and should be treated as such." They were "his" Eskimos, much as the icy highway running from Smith Sound to the polar sea was "his" route to ninety north.

Peary created a new economy based on exchanging Western goods for labor and for exotic furs that would fetch a handsome price from buyers in the United States. American blades, hatchets, files, and saws revolutionized everyday life for the 250-person tribe. Metal was practically nonexistent before the commander arrived. One hunter proposed trading "his wife and two children for a shining knife." A woman offered "everything she had for a needle."

Inughuit craftsmen traditionally made sledges and tool handles from bits of driftwood, bone, and anything else they could find in their resource-poor environment. Peary brought more wood than they imagined possible. None of them had ever seen a tree, or any plant more than a few inches high. One man promised the explorer "his dogs and sledges and all his furs for a bit of board as long as himself." Peary also transformed Inughuit hunting techniques. The Inughuit acquired a few firearms in the mid-nineteenth century but still relied on harpoons and other weapons. Peary distributed guns as gifts. As the number of rifles among the Inughuit grew, so did their importance. They became essential for survival. Ammunition ran so low between Peary's visits that desperate hunters carved bullets out of bone.

Until 1818, when British explorer John Ross chanced upon them, the Inughuit believed they were alone in the world. By 1908 they were dependent on occasional infusions of products from an alien culture. Men shifted from stockpiling meat for their families to stockpiling meat for Americans. Women made clothes for Peary's men rather than for their husbands.

Peary had arrived again, bringing more supplies and new faces. MacMillan exploited his career as a physical education and language teacher by coaxing some rudimentary grammar lessons in exchange for a series of nifty cartwheels and somersaults. Borup seemed more suspicious, but soon decided the Inughuits did not smell "as bad as whale meat several weeks old." It took him longer to accept their casual nudity. "I imagine they are somewhat like the French," he concluded, having never been to France.

Hunting was a distraction from immodesty. Mac and Borup scampered up a hill with a long-handled net borrowed from an Inuk. They were pursuing auks, the small birds that blanketed northwest Greenland with flocks so thick that their droppings fertilized the green hills beneath their nesting sites. Borup snared dozens with barely any effort. MacMillan knocked one from the sky with his hat.

Peary rounded up the Inughuit he wanted to take with him and pushed the *Roosevelt* farther up the coast. Borup kept a look-out for more challenging prey. His opportunity came when the northbound vessel passed a pod of walruses basking on an ice pan. Peary encouraged the first-timers to join the natives' hunt. Walrus meat made excellent dog food, and it would take several tons of it to sustain their growing pack.

"Look out, they may be and can be dangerous," Peary warned. Borup nodded as he loaded his Sauer. Mac fumbled with his .351 automatic, which he could barely use.

Native hunters rowed the whaleboat toward their targets. MacMillan pondered explorer Otto Sverdrup's advice on handling the 10-foot-long, 2,000-pound beasts: "If an infuriated walrus gets his tusks over the rail of the boat, do not frighten him," Sverdrup wrote. "Grasp the tusks gently in the hands and lift him back into the water." Mac wondered whether an interpreter had mistranslated the Norwegian's words.

They closed to 50 yards. Walruses surfaced, noised vigorous "ook, ook"s, and sank back below the surface. They crept to 20 feet, keeping a close eye on the pile of sleeping animals. Mac motioned for his guides to throw their harpoons. They demurred, offering their guests the first shot. More heads broke the surface, adding their "ook, ook"s to the chorus. Mac and Borup crouched in the bow. "Take the big one at the left, George," Mac whispered, "I'll take the one at the right."

Mac opened fire as a big male roused from its slumber. Borup joined in an instant later. "What do you know about that!" Borup exclaimed, eyes wide with exhilaration. Natives issued war cries and hurled harpoons. Two hulking bulls hooked their tusks over the starboard rail. Neglecting Sverdrup's suggestion, Borup blasted one of the walruses in the face. The other worked itself free and dove beneath the waves. Bloody foam sprinkled with clamshells released from dead walruses' stomachs covered the water's surface. It was, Borup said, "one writhing mass of merry Hades let loose."

Then the waters stilled. Entrails sloshed knee-deep in the boat. Peary would be proud of his boys. The dogs would eat.

An Inughuit boy's first walrus kill signified his transition to manhood. The tenderfeet had graduated.

The *Roosevelt* plowed northwest from Cape York, crossing what Peary called "the dividing line between the civilized world . . . and the Arctic world." Ironically, the ship grew more chaotic the farther it got from the bedlam of New York City. Peary called numerous stops to gather families from various camps along the way. Eventually a few dozen Inughuit set up atop the ship's cabin house and forecastle. Down on deck, 112 yowling dogs used their teeth and claws to sort out their status within the pack hierarchy.

Etah, a tiny Inughuit camp on Greenland's northwestern tip, was the expedition's final stop before it turned west for its winter quarters on Ellesmere Island. With its sheltered harbor and abundant game, Etah was an ideal stopover for Arctic travelers. "Everywhere is historic ground," exclaimed MacMillan, whose hunting trips with Borup often became impromptu history classes. From Etah they could see where Dr. Isaac Israel Hayes's *United States* had overwintered in 1860. A short walk brought them to where Charles Francis Hall's *Polaris* ran aground in 1872. On clear days they gazed across Smith Sound to Pim Island, the site of Adolphus Greely's wind-blasted starvation camp, where nineteen men died during the winter of 1883–84. Borup dutifully absorbed Mac's lessons between taking shots at geese, ducks, and walruses.

Mac and Borup also encountered a bedraggled, scurvy-ridden adventurer named Rudolph Franke, who had overwintered alongside Peary's companion from a previous voyage, Dr. Frederick A. Cook. Peary fumed when Franke confirmed his suspicion that several months earlier Cook had left with some of "his" Eskimos and "his" dogs to make a mad dash for the North Pole. Much as Peary despised his former friend turned competitor, he dismissed Cook as a nuisance who was either dead or holed up on Ellesmere Island. Peary seized the fox furs and narwhal tusks Cook had stashed at Etah and arranged for Franke's passage home on his supply ship.

Fog enshrouded the *Roosevelt* on August 18 as it began its 350-mile trip from Etah to Cape Sheridan, on Ellesmere Island. Peary warned that the real work was about to begin. These were dangerous waters. As if confirming his point, the ship collided with a small berg. Rain pounded the deck. Ice pans battered the hull. With its burden of 70 tons of whale meat and a small mountain of coal, the steamer was riding dangerously low in the water.

Borup stumbled out of his cabin when conditions got thick so he could listen to the natives beseech their ancestors for assistance. His own personal deliverer, Captain Bartlett, shouted directions from the crow's nest through a four-foot-long megaphone. "Rip 'em, Teddy!" Bartlett urged the *Roosevelt* as the ice closed in. "Bite 'em in two!"

Mac walked through crowds of Inughuit, asking, *"Qanoq atinga?"* ("What is that?") and recording the answers in a notebook. Borup's halting attempts at communication inspired peals of laughter from the women sewing clothes on deck.

It took two long weeks of clanging into floes, sneaking around bergs, and slipping between pans before Cape Sheridan came into view. The *Roosevelt* had carried the men to 82° 30', farther north than any ship traveling under its own power.* Peary could go no farther this year. It was early September. Winter was closing in. It was time to find a snug harbor and wait out the season's round-the-clock darkness before setting out for the Pole when the faint sunlight of the returning spring arrived in early 1909.

Borup wanted to get off the boat almost as much as the dogs did. MacMillan was bedridden with the flu, so the young man adjusted to Arctic living on his own. Everything was strange. Spooky groans emanated from the ice pack as floes ground out their constant struggle for supremacy. His fur clothes felt uncomfortable. Barking dogs rattled his nerves.

Borup could not be useful until he mastered the complex art of handling a team of those dogs. On his first attempt at driving a 400-pound sledge, the dogs pulled him for less than a mile before slowing to a halt. He screamed at them, to no effect. Snapping his 25-foot walrus-skin whip, he nicked himself in the face. His second try knocked his hat to the ground. His third swing flicked an Inuk. His fourth effort tangled the whip around a trace. Finished with subtleties, he beat the animals with a snowshoe until they lurched forward again.

Once MacMillan escaped his sickbed, the two friends arranged a pile of empty biscuit tins in the shape of a sledge, laid out eight frozen, dead dogs about 20 feet in front of it, and practiced whipping until they routinely nicked their desired target.

Borup and MacMillan revised their understandings of space and place. The Americans had grown up in a world of city grids and railroad schedules timed to the minute; traveling required a precise awareness of hours, minutes, or miles. But these lessons were irrelevant in the trackless Arctic. At first it struck them as a wasteland in need of accurate charting. Slowly they learned that

---

* During his 1893–96 expedition, Fridtjof Nansen purposely iced in his ship, the *Fram*, and allowed the current to carry it above 86°.

the Polar Inuit understood geography in their own way. Their maps existed in their heads, although they were capable of drawing accurate charts for curious Westerners. Prominent glaciers, rocks, and fiords acted as landmarks, as did an area's prevailing winds, tides, and snow patterns. Distances were measured in sleeps or marches. If a typical traveler slept twice while covering a certain route, the length of that route was "two sleeps." Or, if getting from one place to another took three good hikes, the distance was "three marches."

Cape Sheridan's extreme latitude meant twenty-four-hour sunshine during the summer. In the winter, however, the disappearing sun cast the *Roosevelt* into several months of night. "The influence of this long, intense darkness was most depressing," Elisha Kane said of the winter of 1854. "In the darkness and consequent inaction, it was almost in vain that we sought to create topics of thought, and by forced excitement to ward off the encroachments of disease." Peary himself experienced "uncontrollable nightmares of apprehension" during the winter of 1901.

Determined to keep everyone too busy for nightmares, Peary dispatched his men on supply runs during full moons. When not on duty they amused themselves with cards, checkers, dominoes, books, and phonograph records. The *Roosevelt*, which served as their quarters, always needed tidying. Mac and Borup scraped the ice from the floor of their cabin, practiced building igloos, and copied native techniques for keeping their furs dry. Borup experimented with taking photographs in low light. MacMillan tasted polar bear. "Very tender and pleasant," he decided.

On Christmas Day MacMillan organized a series of morale-boosting physical challenges. A brilliant aurora flung pale white streamers across the sky as Borup and Peary hacked out a track from the ice, then lined it with enough lanterns to illuminate Broadway. Inughuit children ran the 75-yard course first, followed by the men, then women carrying babies in their hoods. Fur-clad northerners puffed through −23-degree temperatures toward a finish line bathed in artificial light at two o'clock in the afternoon. For the Americans it was a joyful if surreal moment.

Clean shirts, neckties, a linen tablecloth, and silver place settings gave their dinner of musk ox a hint of elegance. The commander's team opened boxes of candy Mrs. Peary had packed. Then Mac, his belly full and spirits high, rallied the troops for some wrestling.

Busy as MacMillan and Borup were, they sought out opportunities to pepper Peary with questions about his exploits, or to pry oft-told stories from him. Crocker Land must have come up at some point during those months. MacMillan, an avid reader of Arctic travelogues, was no doubt aware of the commander's find and eager for additional information. Although Borup had a slighter grasp of Arctic history, he probably had heard of the new continent too, considering his close proximity to both Mac and Peary.

We cannot know how Peary answered their questions, or even what questions they asked. None of the three mentioned Crocker Land in their reminiscences about those months; it simply wasn't their top priority. It also lay some 600 miles to the west, so far away that there was no point in even thinking about going there. Peary's focus on reaching the North Pole was total. Little else mattered, except perhaps his own reputation and the safety of his men. His intensity inspired Mac and Borup. They couldn't wait to get on the polar sea, the frozen highway to ninety north. Everything else could wait until they proved themselves under Peary's withering gaze.

In February 1909, with the first reddish smear of the returning sun tinting the horizon, Peary gave the order: time to go. Captain Bartlett gathered Mac, Borup, and Ross Marvin in his igloo a few hours before their departure. Warmed by a kerosene stove running at full blast, the young men listened while the veterans dissected the dangerous journey ahead.

Bartlett suggested they lift the mood with some college songs.

The captain couldn't contribute much, having spent most of his brief matriculation at Methodist College in St. John's, Newfoundland, on the waterfront instead of in class. After an hour of selections from Bowdoin, Yale, and Cornell, Marvin's alma mater, they clasped hands for a final tune. *"Amici usque ad aras* [a friend to the last degree]," they sang, "Deep graven on each heart, / Shall be found, unwavering, true, / When we from life shall part."

As the song reached its emotional conclusion, Borup recalled something Peary had recently said: "When you say good-bye to a friend here, the Lord only knows when you'll meet him again."

Borup guided his dogs onto the trackless Arctic ice the next morning, February 28, 1909. He saw positive omens everywhere. Although the thermometer stood at –30 degrees, the air was calm. Wind posed a greater danger than cold for men clad in protective furs. Smooth ice spreading out as far as the eye could see promised perfect travel conditions, at least for the moment. And today was his sister Yvette's birthday.

Mac was having stomach troubles but was otherwise happy. A Bowdoin flag crafted from a black velvet curtain and a scrap of bandage fluttered from his sledge.

Most Americans would have imagined Peary's sledge whizzing due north across a glasslike pane of ice. Actually, he bent his course slightly northwest to compensate for the ice's eastward drift. Moreover, the surface of the polar sea existed in three rather than two dimensions. Intense pressure from currents and waves rippled the ice pack like a piece of paper being pushed from opposite edges, throwing up imposing blockades of rugged white hills. Mac and Borup took turns leading the "pickax brigade" that smoothed this lumpy façade in advance of the main party. Borup also served as a pack mule ferrying up supplies from caches in the rear. It was a brutally tough duty. It was also his job, so there was no point in complaining. Borup's role was to exhaust himself and his team so Peary and his dogs could remain as fresh as possible.

Borup's absences left MacMillan and Peary as frequent travel companions. The commander appreciated Mac's gift for jollying a grumpy Inuk or dispelling dark moments with a joke. One night, while sitting in a snow house, Peary said he was thinking about conquering the South Pole, too. Perhaps his fellow Bowdoin grad might earn a spot on the team. MacMillan could not believe that Peary was contemplating another grueling journey. His admiration for his leader deepened with every passing day.

As the party pushed farther north—83°, 84°—MacMillan sensed trouble among the Inughuit. None of the natives saw the point of visiting the Pole, where there was neither land nor food. All they wanted were Peary's rifles, knives, tobacco, and wood, and not even those wonders were worth their lives. Small groups started wandering out of earshot for private conversations. Talk of evil spirits rattled around camp. Inughuit started complaining about sore chests and other ailments. Panippak, one of Peary's companions in 1906, grumbled about his aching shoulder and moaned about his son, Ittukusuk, who had gone off with Cook and might well be dead. Pualuna was also claiming illness.

MacMillan nearly torpedoed the expedition at this crucial moment with an error born from kindness. Howling winds were battering the camp, so he invited Uisaakassak and Tautsiannguaq into his igloo for some tea. He lit his alcohol-burning stove without first opening its chimney flue, a rookie mistake. Poisonous fumes filled the airtight chamber. Tautsiannguaq's breathing grew irregular. Uisaakassak fell unconscious. MacMillan's head reeled. His ears rang.

Snapping to life, Mac kicked away the snowplug sealing the entrance and stumbled into the night. After inhaling a few gasps of clean air, he dove back into the snow house for the others. Peary noticed the commotion. Checking to make sure no one was watching, the commander helped drag the senseless men from their tomb. MacMillan covered their mouths so the others wouldn't hear their groans. Uisaakassak and Tautsiannguaq regained consciousness. MacMillan told them that they had fallen asleep. They accepted his story, or at least appeared to.

"This was one of those opportunities which circumstances give a man silently to prove the mettle of which he is made," Peary noted. It had been a narrow escape. Had either Uisaakassak or Tautsiannguaq died, their compatriots would probably have abandoned the mission.

MacMillan redeemed himself by sharing his concerns about the natives' flagging spirits with Peary, who quashed the budding insurrection by dismissing Panippak and Pualuna. MacMillan then boosted morale with another series of athletic contests, including "a running broad jump, a standing jump, a high jump, a wrestling match and a fifty-yard dash, also a rope pull, [and] a tug-of-war between the white men and the Huskies." Peary approved. MacMillan was back in the commander's good graces.

"I am finding it a bit difficult to walk without considerable pain," MacMillan wrote in his diary on the same day he nearly asphyxiated Uisaakassak and Tautsiannguaq. His feet were in bad shape, but he held his tongue for fear of disrupting Peary's plans. A frostbitten face or hand was an inconvenience. Frostbitten feet, as the two-toed commander had often reminded him, could halt an expedition in its tracks.

MacMillan grimaced through his work. It wasn't ambition keeping him quiet; he wasn't going all the way to the Pole. He and Borup were merely two prongs of a slingshot designed to propel Peary as far north as possible. They would turn back once their usefulness had passed. Rather, Mac's sense of duty propelled him forward. He had volunteered for suffering. Quitting would disappoint the man who had become his surrogate father.

He wrapped his foot, but the pulling bandages kept his wounds open and oozing. After limping along for a week, he consulted Matt Henson, who took one look at his numb, purplish heel before sending him to the boss. Peary gave MacMillan's foot a cursory inspection. It was obvious he could not go on. Mac begged the commander to let him continue. "You are to go back at once and have that heel attended to by the doctor," the commander replied. MacMillan's trip ended at 84° 29′ north, 330 nautical miles from the Pole.

Borup, drained from a punishing two-week supply run, rejoined the group that evening. He found Mac slumped in Peary's igloo. Borup's heart fell when his friend explained the situation. Fortune was pulling them in opposite directions at the moment of reunion. Borup starting singing "Amici usque." Mac joined in. They broke down before finishing.

The next day, March 15, was a nasty one. Temperatures hovered between −45 and −50 degrees. A sharp wind screamed from the west. The grinding ice emitted ominous cracking sounds.

Mac could walk only a short distance before pain overwhelmed him. He posed for a photograph with Peary, and one with Borup, before stacking his possessions onto a sledge. Peary offered a few words of condolence. Marvin and Bartlett said their goodbyes before marching off with pickaxes over their shoulders. MacMillan climbed aboard the qamutit that would carry him and two Inughuit south. With a "Huk! Huk!" from MacMillan, the dogs leaned into the traces. Borup receded into a black speck on the blinding white polar sea.

MacMillan reached the Roosevelt ten days later. He bathed for the first time in over a month, slathered his heel in musk ox tallow, tucked into some baked beans and brown bread, and wondered where his companions were.

Peary hated losing his assistant so soon but concluded that Mac's premature departure "did not affect the main proposition." For him, "the men, like the equipment, were interchangeable." Four days after MacMillan left, the commander gathered his remaining soldiers for a mission update. Borup would go south with the weakest natives and dogs the next day. Marvin would follow five marches later (with the sun an unreliable determinant of diurnal and nocturnal periods, visitors to the Arctic often adopted the Inughuit method of operating in terms of "sleeps" and "marches" rather than in twenty-four-hour days). Bartlett would go next, leaving only Peary, Henson, and an elite cadre of Inughuit for the final assault on the Pole.

"I would have given my immortal soul to have gone on," Borup wrote. Peary was all business, doling out last-minute advice during their final walk together. Watch out for young ice. Never let your guides get ahead of you, because if you get in trouble they will not come back for you. Joined by three ailing Inughuit—Avatannguaq, Inukittoq, and Qulatannguaq—Borup hitched up sixteen dogs ("all bum ones," he complained) and waved goodbye. His North Pole trip ended at 85° 23′.

On April 3, MacMillan was pacing the *Roosevelt*'s deck when he saw Inukittoq approaching from the north. The Inuk handed over a two-week-old letter in Borup's handwriting addressed to "Prof D. B. MacMillan, Cape Sheridan." Beneath the signature was written "Collect postage at other end am broke."

MacMillan read the other side. "[Inukittoq] on bum coming in with swollen balls," Borup had written. "Hope your heel is o.k. . . . Also that you can decipher this."

Mac and Borup celebrated their reunion eight days later. Both men were aching and exhausted. They spent several quiet days developing photographs, most of which turned out poorly. As their strength returned, they began taking short hikes with no purpose other than to enjoy the scenery. Arctic life was never easy, but this was as good as it got.

The only sour note came when Ross Marvin's Inughuit guides returned to the *Roosevelt* without their charge. Borup rushed out to meet Qillugtooq. "Marvin gone," the Inuk said. "Young ice. I tol' him look out." Marvin ignored his warnings and crashed through a thin skin of ice covering the frigid sea. The Inughuit could not save him.

Devastated, MacMillan and Borup rifled their compatriot's papers for insight into his final days. They unearthed a bundle of postdated letters from home, the most recent of which consisted of four blank sheets of paper. It was dated April 1, 1909—April Fool's Day.

According to Peary's grand plan, MacMillan and Marvin were supposed to lay a string of caches along the north coast of Greenland in case the commander drifted farther east than expected on his return from the Pole. Borup offered to take Marvin's place.

The rugged rhythms of Arctic travel distracted the two men from their sorrows. Amber goggles shielded their eyes from the blazing sun. Mac took the extra precaution of lampblacking his face. Borup called him "a darned old chimney sweep." Hummocks ripped at their sledges. Fences of ice hemmed their path. Borup deemed the trip "worse than what Sherman said war was . . . although a dandy sporting proposition." They amused themselves by setting the Inughuit against each other. "Mac would tell his men they were much better than mine," Borup wrote, "and I'd tell my huskies that they made Mac's huskies look like thirty cents, and each bunch was naturally anxious to beat the other." Borup giggled at how often his dogs urinated.

Spring was coming, softening the snow and widening leads. On the warmest days Borup ran alongside his sledge with his pants off. This was their last taste of the wild Arctic life, and they were bent on enjoying it for all they could.

"George, this is better than teaching school," Mac shouted from his *qamutit*.

"Yes, Mac, and better than working in the Altoona Machine Shop," Borup replied.

They were at Cape Morris Jesup when they saw a smudge in the distance. It slowly grew into the Inuk Qaarqutsiaq. Peary was on the *Roosevelt*, he said. He has traveled a great distance.

Qaarqutsiaq handed over a note from the commander dated April 28, ten days earlier. "Arrived on board yesterday," it read. "Northern trip entirely satisfactory. . . . Remember me to Borup and say to him that if his inclinations are that way, and his plans for his immediate future permit, there will be room for him in the Great National Antarctic Expedition." Borup and Mac screamed Yale and Bowdoin war cries until they went hoarse. Peary had reached the Pole.

That night the tenderfeet—now a term of affection rather than of status—discussed their future inside a tent festooned with college flags. Neither the classroom nor the railroad could satisfy them any more. "We were going to go together somewhere," they decided from atop a warm pile of musk ox hides. Mac would study anthropology. Borup would master geology. Zoology, botany, meteorology, magnetism—there was so much to learn before they could lead their own expedition.

They had almost talked themselves to sleep when Qajuuttaq and Qillugtooq burst through the flap. We killed sixteen musk oxen, they said. Dreams of future glory could wait. There was meat.

Although Peary's note freed them from laying caches, they still had scientific duties to perform. Peary wanted some tidal observations. Borup hated making tidal observations. Sitting in a hut watching water rise and fall against a gauge was as dull as working in the Altoona Machine Shop. But it must be done. It took two days of chipping through ice before they struck water. Borup set up the marker and waited. And waited some more.

MacMillan relieved Borup several hours later. After recording his first observation, he flipped to the "Remarks" page of their notebook. There, in indelible pencil (ink would freeze at these temperatures), Borup had written, "I do not know whether the God damn tide is going up or down." MacMillan stomped off to their tent. "Mac," Borup explained, "that was the page for remarks and that's where I put them."

Mac and Borup returned to the *Roosevelt* on May 31. With their time in the north running short, Peary dispatched them on their final tasks. Borup went off hunting musk ox. Peary sent MacMillan, along with Qillugtooq and *Roosevelt* crewman Jack Barnes, 60 miles south to Fort Conger for another round of tidal observations.

Borup romped through his trip. Mac also had fun. Science was all well and good, but the prospect of walking in his predecessors' footsteps was positively thrilling. George Nares had spent the winter of 1875 at Fort Conger with his British Arctic Expedition, and Adolphus Greely had camped there in 1881 and 1882. MacMillan had worshipped Greely ever since reading *Three Years of Arctic Service* as a boy. Peary had also visited Fort Conger; his expedition surgeon had amputated his toes there in 1899.

Fort Conger was a clump of three decrepit cabins that Peary had built out of wide boards salvaged from Greely's barracks. MacMillan and Qillugtooq treated the camp like their own personal playground. Detritus from the Greely party littered the site. Finding some old clothes in a chest, Qillugtooq paraded around in full army regalia, including sword, epaulets, swallow-tailed coat, and blue cap. MacMillan opened tins of potatoes and cans of perfectly preserved rhubarb. He grabbed a plate and a few of Greely's calling cards as souvenirs. He found a stove stuffed with skulls, presumably deposited there at some point by Inughuit. Boxes of specimens, a comic cartoon of a Prussian general, an advertisement for Pennyroyal Pills with a pretty lady engraved on it. Poems clipped from newspapers, including Wordsworth's "The World Is Too Much With Us," Robert Browning's "The Guardian Angel," and "How My Boy Went Down," a mother's lament for her dead son. MacMillan pocketed them, along with two playing cards—a nine of spades and a nine of diamonds. Collectively, these treasures symbolized the totality of Arctic life: a few creature comforts, fragments of inspiration, death's looming shadow, and a generous dose of Lady Luck.

A festive atmosphere consumed the *Roosevelt*'s crew as Captain Bartlett steered the ship away from Cape Sheridan. Drunk with thoughts of home, the men blasted away at every seal and narwhal that blundered into their sights.

Mac and Borup kept the hilarity going while the *Roosevelt* nosed southward between Ellesmere Island and Greenland. One day, Mac was luxuriating in a warm bath when he decided to take a cold one. "Close the pores of the skin," he reasoned. Stripping off his clothes, he was about to plunge into the ocean when he heard "Wait for me!" A pink flash resembling a naked Borup streaked past. Mac followed him into the 29-degree water. The natives watched in horror. None of them had seen a man swim, at least not on purpose. "Mr. Mac *pivlerortoq* [crazy]! Borup *pivlerortoq*!" they exclaimed. "We had always done things together," MacMillan explained, "and so we did this."

The *Roosevelt* deposited Inughuit at various settlements on its way south. Mac and Borup spread the word among the disembarking passengers: We'll be back, perhaps as early as next summer.

MacMillan awoke one morning in the Chamber of Horrors, exhausted from the previous day's hunt. Dropping from his bunk, he started dressing for breakfast. "Mac, don't get up," Borup yawned. "We can't do any shooting today. It's raining and blowing; look out of the porthole."

Mac crawled into bed, nestling his back against the wall and his head on his left hand. Then a shot rang out. George Wardwell, Peary's strapping chief engineer, rumbled in a moment later, shouting, "Well, well! Who have I killed now?" His levity faded when he saw MacMillan writhing in a pool of blood.

"She's loaded," MacMillan had warned when he gave Peary his Winchester .40-82 the previous evening. The commander turned it over to Wardwell the next morning for cleaning. While ejecting the cartridges, the engineer accidentally hit the trigger. The bullet ripped through a one-and-a-half-inch pine partition, over a sleeping bosun, and through a second partition. From there it zipped past where Matt Henson's head had been a few minutes earlier before penetrating the Chamber of Horrors. It passed clean through Mac-Millan's back, grazed his eyebrow, bisected his left radius and ulna, bounced off the opposite wall, and skittered across the floor until coming to rest. The bullet missed a major artery by about half an inch.

Ever the trooper, Mac was soon on his feet again, though a severed tendon kept his left thumb locked against his palm for some time. Not even multiple gunshot wounds could keep him from enjoying his final days in the Arctic. He and Borup watched the waves break against the prow. They remembered bone-chilling nights, lugging heavy sledges over uneven ice, and wrestling with snarling dogs. Nostalgia was setting in before they crossed the Arctic Circle.

"Gee, whiz!" Borup wrote to his father, "I've had a wonderful trip, and wish in many ways we had been stuck up here for another year." MacMillan declared it "the best year of my life." Veterans of the north, they hungered for another war. Although their decision to become traveling partners emerged from joint conversation, it was probably MacMillan who set their next objective. Convincing Borup was easy enough; he was game for anything. Ninety north was in the bag. A different prize would soon top every Arctic explorer's wish list.

Weeks before they made it home from the adventure of a lifetime, Mac and Borup were planning their next trip. They were going to Crocker Land.

"I WISH I WERE
THERE NOW"

As the Roosevelt steamed past the southern Greenland village of Uummannaq (meaning "heart-shaped," a reference to the twin-peaked cliff looming over the settlement), MacMillan and Borup were sprawled on their bunks in the Chamber of Horrors absorbing their first news from home in a year. Each page from the bundle of newspapers, magazines, and letters that had just come on board contained a new wonder. The explorers in training read about William Howard Taft's election to the White House, a terrible earthquake in Italy, and Ernest Shackleton's trek to 88° 23′ south—111 miles from the South Pole.

Borup started squirming. He couldn't find the one piece of information he really wanted. He tore open another envelope. When he scanned the page, his heart broke.

"Well, well!" he sighed. "Oh! My! Isn't it too bad?"

Mac looked up from his own mail. Perhaps Borup's father had died, he thought.

"What is the matter, George?" he ventured. "Tell me."

"Why, Harvard has beaten Yale!" Borup moaned.

Mac shared the story with the Roosevelt's hardnosed crew, who ragged Borup all the way down the Newfoundland and Nova Scotia coasts.

Reporters started boarding the ship when the party entered the temperate latitudes. Mac and Borup reveled in the attention. Journalists found them to be affable interview subjects and treated them as two halves of a single, Mac-and-Borup whole. MacMillan was articulate, precise, and wise beyond his years. Borup, glib and handsome, was the epitome of enthusiastic youth. Reporters loved their vivid accounts of walruses and rare birds, of battling rough ice, and of nights cold enough to freeze whiskey. MacMillan explained the intricacies of the Inuktun language. Borup described natives going "bughouse" in a blizzard.

MacMillan presented himself as a serious scientist intent on advancing the fields of ethnography, sociology, and linguistics. At the same time, he infused his yarns with crowd-pleasing elements of high adventure. MacMillan never mentioned Crocker Land, lest he steal the limelight from Peary and alert potential rivals of his plans, but the strange place was clearly on his mind. "It is hard to explain what a fascination there is up there," he told a knot of pressmen. "The mystery of it attracts one. Unexplored territory lies ahead of you, and you cannot help feeling awed by the immensity of it." His account of Greely's starvation camp could have packed a vaudeville theater. He stretched a story about riding out a storm in an old trunk, producing a button from Greely's coat at precisely the right dramatic moment. Even his description of Ross Marvin's demise had panache. "Death is a factor with which one is ever face to face in the Arctic," he informed the scribbling journalists.

"I don't know just what it is," MacMillan told a *New York Tribune* reporter. "It's pushing out," he said, gesturing toward the ocean, "the fiords and mountains."

"And unexplored, too," Borup interjected.

"Yes," MacMillan agreed, searching for words. "It's the mystery of it, perhaps, and then the—the—vastness of it all up there."

Mac made good copy, but Borup's dark-eyed charm proved irresistible to reporters seeking marketable heroes. "Bully!" he exclaimed when a newsman asked about a possible return to the Arctic. "I'd go back fast as a bullet. I wish I were there now." His omnipresent smile, adolescent outbursts, and can-do spirit made him an exemplar of the all-American boy. Respectful toward his elders yet fluent in youthful slang, his appeal transcended both generations and social classes. As a Yale graduate, he had elite bona fides. In conquering the frozen wilderness, he proved that modern Americans were tough enough to survive in a premodern environment.

The *Roosevelt*'s triumphant arrival in New York was marred by recent reports of the long-lost Dr. Frederick Cook's sudden appearance in Europe. The doctor insisted that he reached the Pole before Peary. Sailors from other vessels jeered the *Roosevelt* when the steamer maneuvered into its berth. Cook was the true champion and Peary a fraud, they shouted.

With the taunts ringing in their ears, Mac and Borup retreated belowdecks to pack their duffels. A round of goodbyes followed. Then came a brief ride through an alien world of trees and mild breezes, skyscrapers and noise. Most of the apartment buildings they passed sheltered more people than lived in all of northwest Greenland. Then on to Grand Central, so they could board trains that traveled more miles in an hour than a sledge did in a day. It was all so normal, and so unsatisfying.

The friends shook hands before parting. Borup was returning to Altoona and the Pennsylvania Railroad. MacMillan was heading to Maine to see his family.

Their trains chugged in different directions. Each revolution of the clattering wheels increased the distance between the inseparable mates, who weren't planning on being apart for long.

Borup's steady job with the railroad gave him no pleasure. It is "best characterized by a short snappy word of 4 letters," he groused. He seized every chance for escape, dropping into New Haven for Yale football scrimmages and joining Mac at New York's Hippodrome Theater to attend a lecture by Peary's assistant Matt Henson.

While Borup stewed, MacMillan pressed Peary, ever so gently, for a sliver of the action. Perhaps Peary might allow him to give some talks, even though his contract prohibited him from discussing the expedition. "I am not after the money," he insisted. Rather than book the big-city venues that were paying Peary between $1,000 and $7,500 a night, he would tour small-town churches, schools, and YMCAs, clearing each lecture opportunity with Peary and doing only "whatever you think best." Peary consented so long as MacMillan limited himself to New England, submitted his script for vetting, and abstained from showing photos of the North Pole.

MacMillan and Borup maintained their total devotion to Peary. Although the commander was almost unbelievably self-centered, he also possessed a magnetic charisma. For a certain kind of person, his aloofness became magisterial, his single-mindedness a sign of otherworldly resolve. MacMillan and Borup were young, eager, and willing to take orders. For them, Peary was a stern father who delivered extraordinary adventures in exchange for unquestioning servitude.

Both Cook and Peary faced skeptics who insisted they had not reached the North Pole (most modern researchers share similar doubts). Mac and Borup harbored no such reservations about their leader. "Damn Cook!" MacMillan exclaimed. "And damn every man who has ever been in the Arctic and knows conditions who says he believes in him." "He lied like hell," Borup hissed after hearing Cook speak. When in New York, the pair conducted undercover pro-Peary operations. They prowled the Grand Union Hotel's lobby, butting into strangers' conversations about the Cook–Peary dispute in order to dismantle arguments favoring the usurper's claim to the Pole.

Peary had given the men a taste of fame. In defending him, they promoted their own future. Genuine as their loyalty was, MacMillan and Borup understood that Peary stood astride the gates of Crocker Land. His sponsorship gave them credibility within scientific and exploration circles, along with access to an extensive network of wealthy men with a history of contributing to Arctic expeditions. Without money and support from some credible institution, the two young men in a hurry were going nowhere.

Peary was the key to achieving everything MacMillan and Borup desired. Discovering a continent would bring celebrity and probably a considerable fortune. Future generations would celebrate them as great explorers. They could be the next—and presumably last—Columbus, or Magellan, or da Gama, bold men who with a single act of courage redrew the map of the world. The lost continent of Atlantis had gripped imaginations for centuries. Imagine being the person who actually *found* Atlantis!

At the same time, MacMillan and Borup were earnest souls who saw Crocker Land as their best chance at making a great contribution to science, or perhaps even to opening whole new fields of scientific inquiry. Revealing Crocker Land's secrets would also please their surrogate father, Peary, while rounding out what they saw as his life's work. Crocker Land was more than the adventure of a lifetime. It promised enough adventure for several lifetimes. Like so many of their generation, MacMillan and Borup celebrated romanticized notions of pitting oneself against nature, of challenging the wildest of wildernesses, of escaping civilization for a place where life and death were real and omnipresent. Crocker Land provided all of those things.

Borup's dissatisfaction with the nine-to-five lifestyle intensified in late 1909. His only connection with the north came through Peary's frequent requests for information about their recent expedition. The commander, as it turned out, kept rather spotty field journals, so he relied on his apprentice for details he could use in his book manuscript, or in the lucrative magazine articles ghost-writers were producing under his name. On what date did we leave Cape Morris Jesup for the *Roosevelt*? How many marches did that trip take? How many marches did it take you to return from your farthest north?

Borup hoped a trip with his father to London might lift his spirits. His sister Yvette was there on an extended visit, and he was eager to see her. Without telling his son, Colonel Borup dropped in on Peary before sailing to borrow a few photographic slides in case some prominent Englishman asked about the North Pole.

George was settling onto the Belgian steamer *Lapland* when he remembered a piece of incomplete business. He dashed around looking for a bit of stationery so he could fire off a note to Mac before the ship cleared port. "Wish to hell you were aboard," he said. "Lonely as hell. . . . So long old man."

In London, Borup plied the normal tourist circuit in the hope of stumbling across something half as interesting as a walrus hunt. England's drizzly winter weather left him feeling depressed (he confessed the hypocrisy of complaining about a soggy British wind when he had sang away −60-degree nights in an igloo). A cursory inspection tour of the Great Western Railway's machine shops reminded him of the boredom waiting in Altoona. Borup did perk up when he saw Madame Tussaud's excellent wax representation of Peary wearing Arctic furs. He ignored the statue of Dr. Cook standing nearby.

Great Britain had been the center of Arctic exploration until Americans such as Peary, Charles Francis Hall, and Adolphus Greely, along with the Norwegian Fridtjof Nansen, took over the field. Britain's fascination with the far north had blossomed in 1815, when the country's immense navy found itself underemployed following the end of the Napoleonic Wars with France. A succession of ministries solved the dilemma by dispatching fleets in search of the North Pole or a northwest passage to Asia. Most of these displays of British grit fell far short of expectations. British voyagers advanced the art of exploration by experimenting with folding canvas boats and alcohol-fueled stoves. Their rigid, militaristic mind-sets, however, discouraged them from adopting native methods of survival, negating any positive impact from their innovations in equipment. In a ludicrous display of stubbornness, officers wore Royal Navy uniforms instead of furs, ate tinned food instead of fresh meat, slept in tents instead of snow houses, and pulled sledges by hand instead of using dog teams. Such obstinacy resulted in a string of futile expeditions and over 100 deaths during the mid-nineteenth century.

Borup wanted to drink tea and swap stories with these greybeards. Colonel H. W. Feilden, a friend of Peary's who had served as a naturalist on George Nares's 1875–76 Arctic expedition, provided the desired introductions. Borup sat in rapt attention while Nares, still sharp at age seventy-eight, described his unsuccessful bid for the North Pole. Nares's second in command, now-Admiral Albert Markham, recounted leading a sledge party to 83° 20', a farthest north record that survived for two decades. George Bras talked about discovering Cape Sheridan, Borup's home during the winter of 1908–09. Captain Robert Falcon Scott and Sir Ernest Shackleton shared their opinions on how to reach the South Pole. They "seemed like fairy characters," Borup exclaimed to a reporter who tracked him down in London. "For me to come here and meet them in flesh and blood—it was grand."

On the voyage home, Borup celebrated his seaworthy stomach ("Touchdown!!") and pondered his next adventure. "You have got to go to Crocker Land," Feilden advised him, underlining the words for emphasis. "The man who accomplishes that will make a mark." Borup agreed but made no public comment lest a competitor—whether Nansen, or the Canadian Vilhjalmur Stefansson, or someone else—organize his own Crocker Land trip. He told the journalists who met the SS *Baltic* in New York that he would join an American expedition to the South Pole if he could persuade Peary to lead it.

MacMillan was thinking along the same lines, momentarily waffling on his commitment to Crocker Land. While Borup was overseas, he and Captain Bob Bartlett hatched a plan to transport some Polar Inuit from Greenland for a run at the bottom of the world. Borup would come too, of course.

Borup was skeptical when they filled him in on their scheme. He doubted they could raise enough money. He was right. MacMillan could not interest the National Geographic Society in his proposal. Peary would neither offer a donation nor solicit his wealthy friends. "You know you can always count on my moral support and sympathy," he said, but "frankly I do not think there is one chance in a hundred of your success."

MacMillan switched targets, asking Borup whether they should head for Crocker Land in the summer of 1910—less than six months away. Without a ship, equipment, or money, he could do little more than talk. Borup insisted on postponing the expedition until 1911. MacMillan agreed.

Borup began pursuing another potential sponsor. "This Museum seems to me the best place in the world for a fellow," he wrote to E. O. Hovey, the curator of the American Museum of Natural History. "Do you think, Sir, that if I were to study and work like the dickens three or four years I could get a job there?"

Located on New York City's Upper West Side, the AMNH, the largest privately owned museum in the United States, had financed expeditions to the Congo, central Asia, and other remote locations. Many of its directors were tied in with Peary, who had donated a mountain of Arctic artifacts over the years in exchange for their patronage. The museum had prestige and money, two things that Borup and MacMillan needed before they could go anywhere.

Hovey tendered an encouraging reply without making any promises. Borup kept lobbying him throughout the first half of 1910. The curator found himself torn between competing impulses. A scientist himself, Hovey could not in good conscience entwine the museum's fate with a man of no formal scientific training, even if Borup was, like him, an alumni of Yale. For all his doubts, Hovey saw the vigorous and photogenic Borup as a potential catch for the museum. With some polish and guidance, he might even replace the aging Peary as America's leading explorer. Borup was a rotten public speaker whose propensity for slang diminished his credibility with learned audiences. Then again, Peary, with his remote demeanor and wooden delivery, was no great orator himself. Borup's charisma, like Peary's, shone through in face-to-face encounters. His modesty, soulful eyes, and eminent quotability made him a newspaperman's dream.

Hovey decided to give Borup a chance. Calling in some favors with the United States Geological Survey, he got the would-be explorer a spot with a four-man team slated to spend the summer and fall of 1910 surveying the area around the lonely mining town of Price, Utah. Amid magnificent peaks and aggressive rattle-snakes, Borup could develop the topographical, cartographic, and geological skills required to chart a new continent.

Borup jumped at this opportunity. It meant escape from the machine shop. Climbing mountains with a pack full of surveying equipment interested him far more than railway schedules and London museum crawls. Borup headed west in July, trading the Allegheny highlands around Altoona for the dramatic plateaus of central Utah. To his delight, some of the locals were almost as exotic as Inughuit hunters. "He calls the outfit his 'kingdom,'" Borup informed MacMillan after meeting a twenty-seven-year-old Mormon who had three wives and eleven children, "but to hear the cheering section of 11 kids all under 5 going full blast I'd term it by a word of 4 letters."

Between his lessons in topography and mapmaking, Borup found his mind wandering northward—no matter that he was more than 3,000 miles from Greenland. During quiet hours in camp he flipped through a sheaf of Arctic photographs which his father had sent him. "By the great hornspoon," he wrote, while watching a caterpillar crawl past, "what a time a man would have in the Arctic if he had 100 cold feet at once."

MacMillan headed north around the same time Borup went west. Lacking a patron and having nothing better to do, he accepted a local missionary's invitation to spend a few months mapping the Labrador coast. Some charts of the region were a century old and horribly inaccurate.

A conversation and with some fellow passengers on the north-bound steamer changed his agenda. Vermont-born explorer William Cabot and two medical students, Scoville Clark and George Howe, were heading into the interior of Labrador to map Naskapi Innu trading routes. MacMillan struck Cabot as a strong and intelligent man. He asked whether the polar veteran wanted to join them. MacMillan accepted. "Here were three men after my own heart," MacMillan enthused, "men of the great out-of-doors, men who loved to rough it, men who wanted to learn something of the unknown Labrador, and for this willing to sacrifice comfort and ease."

The month-long journey convinced the exploration community that MacMillan was more than an athletic schoolteacher who had lucked into an apprenticeship with Peary. Using his Labrador trek as a small-scale dry run for Crocker Land, MacMillan took charge of the expedition's geographical and ethnographical work, mapping many previously undiscovered lakes and tributaries and gaining a basic understanding of the native peoples of central Labrador.

Cabot recognized his new recruit's physical prowess and stuck MacMillan with the unenviable job of portaging their 75-pound canoe through the thick forests of central Labrador. Food supplies ran short. Buzzing flies and bloodthirsty mosquitoes tormented the men. Smudgy campfires repelled enough of the insects clogging their mouths and nostrils to save the party from suffocation.

MacMillan proved he could survive tough conditions without Peary's supervision. When the summer ended, he signed up for courses in astronomy, anthropology, geology, and mineralogy at Harvard University, exactly as he and Borup had planned atop their pile of furs. He kept his face before the Arctic community, maintaining a correspondence with Peary and commuting into Boston whenever a veteran of the north came into town. From them he learned about recent births and deaths among the Inughuit. MacMillan also heard about Knud Rasmussen, a half Danish, half Inuit explorer who was manning some kind of "large, concrete observatory" in northwest Greenland. "Rasmussen is going to explore the world!" MacMillan told Peary, half in jest and half in fear of losing his prize.

"Look here, Dan," Borup wrote a few weeks into the semester, "for God's sake don't go out for the Harvard football team, as you, altho a star of the 1st magnitude, would strike something worse than that pressure ridge off [Cape] Morris Jesup when you hit the Yale line. . . . For the sake of Crocker Land behave yourself."

Borup roughed it in Utah until December, then charted a leisurely route home, stopping in Washington DC for a visit with the Pearys before heading to Cambridge to see Mac. The friends sat in MacMillan's rented quarters near the Harvard campus, reminiscing about the *Roosevelt*, sled dogs, and their favorite Inughuit. Last year's Arctic odyssey was "old times." It was time to forge new memories together.

MacMillan shared his outline for a summer 1911 expedition to Crocker Land. A four-man team would take a sealing ship north and establish winter quarters on the north coast of Ellesmere Island. After spending the dark winter laying supply caches along their route, in early 1912 the group would sledge west to Cape Thomas Hubbard, where Peary had got his second and better view of Crocker Land, before striking out across the polar ice for the new continent. MacMillan anticipated finding ruins from ancient human settlements and, perhaps, "new species of animal life."

Although Borup was tempted, the junior partner found himself in the unusual position of cooling his friend's excitement. Mac-Millan's ambitious timetable left them only a few months to raise money and buy equipment. A 1911 departure would also jeopardize Borup's chances of getting hired by the American Museum of Natural History. The museum was much more likely to support their endeavor once he was officially in the fold. We should wait until 1912, he said. MacMillan disagreed. Rasmussen, Stefansson, or possibly even Shackleton might grab Crocker Land if we delay, he said.

Borup boarded a train for New Haven before they resolved the question. Yale was holding a spot for him in its Sheffield Scientific School. While he was off mapping the West, Hovey, in consultation with Colonel Borup, had plotted a course of study in preparation for George's future life as an explorer.

Borup settled into his quarters in Yale's Divinity Hall and started catching up on the three months of graduate-level school-work he had missed while in Utah. MacMillan, still enrolled at Harvard, took charge of keeping their dream alive. Like Borup, he saw the AMNH as a potential sponsor. MacMillan opted for a direct approach. "I have plans for an expedition to the north this year in which you might possibly be interested," he wrote to AMNH president Henry Fairfield Osborn in February 1911. Labeling Crocker Land "the last important work in the line of exploration," he asked for $15,000 toward a two-year expedition. "This work should be done at once while we have the field to ourselves and while it can be done at small cost," he explained, because "another year will set other expeditions in the field."

MacMillan exuded confidence. "I am going to give [Osborn] a chance to come in on it or say that the exploration of an unknown land is of no interest to such a big society," he told a friend.

A few days later he received a cursory response from New York. "I am, as you know, greatly interested in exploration," Osborn wrote, "but our exploring work is already mapped out for the coming twelve months."

With this avenue apparently closed, MacMillan redoubled his wooing of Peary. "Borup and myself, familiar with your methods and equipment, can do this work and a word from you to that effect will go a long ways," he implored.

H. W. Feilden, Borup's acquaintance in London, was telling Peary the same thing. "Make use" of Borup, he advised. "Send him to finish off *your* Crocker Land." That would be "very nice," Peary replied, refusing to say more.

Peary's weak endorsement kept the Crocker Land proposal in limbo until Colonel Borup forced a resolution. He supported his beloved only son's expansive vision but wanted him and MacMillan to get more experience before embarking on such an ambitious campaign. Rather than confront George directly, he interrupted his preparations for a vacation in Berlin to ask "the Great Discoverer" to do it for him.

"As you know you have no more loyal adherent than George," he reminded Peary. "His one ambition is to follow in your footsteps, and as you know, he is trying to fit himself mentally for such work.

"MacMillan and he have long had it in their heads to make a try for Crocker Land," the colonel continued. "I am very much opposed to the trip this year." The boys were too raw. They must be patient. George should finish his graduate studies and secure his future with the museum. If he quit mid-semester to plan an Arctic trip, he would have "nothing to fall back on upon his return.

"When this damned ant hill we call the Earth solidified," the colonel concluded, "Crocker Land possibly appeared, which event may have been a few million years ago, and I think it may possibly be trusted to remain where it is for a short time longer." Couldn't Peary convince MacMillan to postpone "this wretched folly"?

The colonel's plea produced results. Peary shared his concerns with E. O. Hovey when the AMNH curator called on the explorer in Washington. The newly minted admiral gave his blessing to a Crocker Land trip, yet questioned whether his acolytes could assemble a worthwhile expedition in just a few months. George should complete his studies before becoming an explorer.

Hovey concurred. The scientist envisioned George as his apprentice-in-waiting but could not hire him until he possessed the necessary academic credentials. Once young Borup was on the payroll, the museum could support a project certain to attract abundant publicity and scientific glory.

The two men shook hands, having decided Borup and Mac-Millan's future, although Mac was an afterthought in their conversation.

Rather than go straight home, Hovey changed trains in New York and rode on to New Haven. Despite his recent deal-making, he wanted additional evidence of Borup's potential. Hovey was a cautious man who wouldn't bet the museum's resources, and his own prestige, on anything less than a sure thing.

Entering the Yale campus, he strolled toward the Gothic tower capping his alma mater's magnificent Peabody Museum of Natural History. Hovey knocked on office doors and quizzed Borup's professors about their student. Their plaudits convinced him that his instincts were sound. From there he walked the few blocks to Borup's rooms. Finding him at home, Hovey asked him to finish the current semester, then devote the first part of the summer to fieldwork before assuming an internship under him at the museum.

Borup considered it "a dandy way to put in the summer to great advantage." In accepting this offer, he nullified any chance of heading north in 1911, as Hovey and Peary had intended. And with Borup in his pocket, Hovey ensured that none of his institutional rivals, such as the American Geographical Society or the Peary Arctic Club, would get the Borup–MacMillan Crocker Land expedition for themselves.

MacMillan was outraged when Borup told him about the revised schedule. Hovey assured him that the museum would probably sponsor a Crocker Land trip the following year and invited him to New York to discuss the proposition. MacMillan refused, saying he was too busy to leave Cambridge.

Borup eventually mollified MacMillan. Again working in unison, they implored the AMNH to announce their mission. Explorer etiquette discouraged competitors from entering a field once a team claimed it for themselves. Time was running short; Colonel Borup was passing along rumors from Europe, probably baseless but frightening nonetheless, that Shackleton would soon announce his own Crocker Land trip.

Hovey had been preaching patience. Now he acted like a man in a hurry. The curator pitched the project at an AMNH board meeting. With the board's approval, he called a press conference for May 13, 1911 to introduce the museum's upcoming expedition. "It is an unturned page in world discovery," he told reporters, and "Borup and MacMillan have agreed to take [it] upon themselves to turn that page."

Although he presented them as co-leaders, "Borup and MacMillan" was no accident. Hovey saw the younger man as the more equal of the equal partners. In his conversation with reporters he emphasized Borup's rigorous scientific training while saying almost nothing about MacMillan's equally impressive qualifications.

Hovey said the expedition would likely last four or five years and cost upward of $25,000. According to a recap in the *New York Times*, the journey would be "the most ambitious ever undertaken by any scientific institution for the purpose of discovery." The curator deflected questions about who was covering the costs, mostly because he wasn't sure himself. Instead he promised magnificent discoveries and remarkable new specimens; Borup and MacMillan would bring home everything that wasn't "nailed down."

MacMillan was in Cambridge at the time, having learned what Hovey was doing only from a telegram Borup sent him right before the press conference. The prime mover was now on the outside.

No matter how much Hovey's machinations displeased him, there was no point in squawking. In the end he had what he wanted: a voyage of discovery with Borup.

"Come on Dan, we can do it," Borup exclaimed. "We will have to work like HELL but we can push it thru." Their idle talk on the southbound *Roosevelt* nearly two years earlier had borne fruit. They were going to Crocker Land.

COMMANDER BORUP?

On July 17, 1911, George Borup stood on a New York City sidewalk contemplating the granite and pink brownstone exterior of the American Museum of Natural History. Its vast façade and impressive twin towers rose five stories above Seventy-seventh Street. A low, heavy arch spanned the entrance. Passersby enjoyed an unusually mild and lovely day, with temperatures hovering in the low seventies. Storm clouds in the distance suggested rain was coming.

Borup was probably the building's most famous visitor that day. Newspaper reporters, with some prodding from the museum, had ditched the "Mac-and-Borup" pairing of 1909. MacMillan was on the publicity sidelines. Journalists reshaped Borup into a clean-living, clean-thinking exemplar of America's pioneering ethos. Press coverage portrayed him as a young Theodore Roosevelt, an articulate outdoorsman, a well-bred urbanite with the heart of Natty Bumppo. He offered living proof that adventure could coexist with modernity.

Borup's recently released first book, *A Tenderfoot with Peary*, cemented his popular image. A child of the yellow journalism era, Borup wrote in the voice of an eager storyteller spinning yarns around a campfire. Reviewers hailed "the 'kid' of the Peary Arctic Expedition" as a Mark Twain for the coming generation. "You feel all the time that it is a real, live American boy who is letting you into his confidence," the *Newark Call* exclaimed. "His enthusiasm stirs you and you follow him eagerly, tirelessly." Publisher Frederick A. Stokes ordered a third printing by the end of the year.

Although the clouds outside the museum were darkening, Borup saw a bright future for himself. His service alongside the world's most famous explorer gave him an unparalleled education in Arctic survival techniques. E. O. Hovey's patronage had allowed him to supplement his year in the north with on-site studies in both Utah and Virginia, where he had completed six weeks of geological fieldwork as part of a team of students from Yale. Today he was reporting for his first day of work at one of the world's most prestigious scientific institutions. And he was only twenty-five years old.

Borup hustled under the museum's arch, past the uniformed guard behind the information desk, and into the cavernous Memorial Hall.* The stone visage of former AMNH president Morris K. Jesup contemplated him from its marble chair on the far wall. Busts of such great scientists as Louis Agassiz, John James Audubon, and Benjamin Franklin peered from niches.

Robert Peary's presence haunted the room. His most massive prize, Ahnighito ("the tent"), the largest known meteorite in the world, hulked atop a concrete platform on Borup's left. Ahnighito was the Polar Inuit's primary source of iron until 1897, when Peary constructed the first railroad in Greenland for the sole purpose of transporting it to a ship bound for New York.

Walking through the AMNH's corridors was like perusing a department store that catered to anyone interested in populating a virgin planet. Hundreds of display cases bursting with preserved birds, fish, mammals, reptiles, and invertebrates made the museum

---

* Memorial Hall is now the Grand Gallery, best known for the 63-foot-long Great Canoe suspended from the ceiling. Today, the main entrance is on Central Park West, around the corner from where visitors entered in 1911.

the intellectual offspring of Noah's Ark and Madame Tussaud's. It housed a literal ton of Pearyana, including some of his sledges, Inughuit gear, stuffed sled dogs, musk oxen, caribou, and foxes. These "donations" were the price of Morris Jesup's lavish patronage.

Borup was here to work, not gawk. He ascended to Hovey's fifth-floor office, where he found the curator sitting behind neat stacks of fossils, eying him through wire-rimmed, oval glasses. Hovey's hair mixed sandy and grey, as did his moustache, and was parted neatly to the left. Hale and dignified at forty-six, in appearance he resembled a mild-mannered banker.

A scientist he was, though. As a youth Hovey had followed his father, a Presbyterian minister and amateur geologist who loved caves almost as much as he did his parishioners, across Illinois and Missouri before returning to his birthplace of New Haven, Connecticut, for college. He graduated from Yale, then taught in Minnesota for a few years before retuning to his alma mater for graduate school, completing his PhD in geology in 1889.

Hovey's big break came in 1893 when the state of Missouri hired him to develop its minerals exhibit for the Chicago World's Fair. His arrangement of lead, zinc, coal, and clay attracted attention from the AMNH, which brought the budding scholar into its fold. In 1910 he became the curator of the museum's geology department.

Hovey was a prolific researcher who earned respect from his peers. He was also a prickly personality better suited to coexisting with rocks than with other people. Although volcanoes were his latest passion, his personality ran on the cool side. Hovey was blunt, calculating, and harsh. His skeptical eyes assessed their target as if it were a lab specimen. His self-confidence often crossed into arrogance. Hovey liked things to be done his way, and he had little patience with anyone who questioned his opinions.

With input from Colonel Borup, Hovey facilitated George's journey from Arctic trailbreaker to promising scholar. He decided that Borup would become his assistant curator once the young man had completed his two-month museum internship and his program at Yale. From there it would be on to Crocker Land, and fame.

Borup needed to become a scientist before he became a hero. Hovey presented the man who had sledged across the polar sea with an unprocessed collection of fossilized plants and insects. Get to work, he said.

Borup made a smooth transition from geology in the wild to science in the city. Old hands like ornithologist Frank Chapman and AMNH director Frederic Lucas took him under their wings. Assistant curator of mammals Roy Chapman Andrews became a reliable lunch companion and tennis partner. Andrews had just returned from an eighteen-month whaling cruise. His prize specimens, seven massive skeletons, filled a ditch behind the museum's tennis court. Borup tolerated their stink, even when he had to root through the pile looking for mishit balls, because it reminded him of the stench aboard the *Roosevelt*.

Meanwhile, Hovey pondered Crocker Land. The museum had declared its intentions for fear of losing the continent to someone else, but its officers had no idea how much the trip would cost, or how to pay for it. Some back-of-an-envelope figuring convinced Hovey that $15,000 from the museum, plus a matching sum from Borup and MacMillan, should cover the team's expenses. In exchange for its money the museum would get all the geological, paleontological, ethnological, botanical, and animal specimens the pair collected. The two adventurers would receive "all possible credit, glory and other reward from the expedition."

"Crocker Land offers what is considered by many authorities to be the one great geographical problem left for solution," Hovey advised museum president H. F. Osborn. Borup and MacMillan would "make the expedition thoroughly scientific in all respects, eliminating adventure and sport from their calculations. . . .

Young Borup in particular is thoroughly imbued with the scientific spirit." A $15,000 contribution seemed a small price for tremendous scientific advances, to say nothing of the attention those advances would bring the museum.

Osborn hesitated. Hovey was asking for a lot of money at a time when the museum had little to give. It was already funding fifty-one field parties around the world, it had recently spent $300,000 on a new south wing, and it was on the verge of appropriating another $300,000 for exhibition spaces devoted to astronomy, geography, and the whale bones moldering out back. Staffers could not keep up with the collections accumulating in storage. In addition, because the Crocker Land trip was "largely geographical," Osborn doubted it would provide "a full equivalent in specimens." Director Lucas seconded Osborn's skepticism, casting doubt over the entire endeavor.

"What are we going to do about the expedition?" a frustrated Hovey asked Osborn in November 1911, following several months without progress. Borup was back at Yale, and MacMillan was hanging around Freeport, Maine, waiting for news. Colonel Borup was busy gathering information on Arctic essentials as if the money was already in hand.

Hovey had staked his personal reputation on the expedition and was determined to make a go of it. "We can have . . . all the credit attaching thereto, if we come forward *now* with the financial and moral support indicated," he beseeched Osborn.

His badgering convinced Osborn and Lucas, who persuaded the AMNH's trustees to appropriate $6,000, far below Hovey's original request. To sweeten the deal, the museum's board officially tapped Borup as Hovey's assistant curator in the geology and invertebrate paleontology department. For the moment, the post carried no salary, but the title nevertheless improved the young man's chances of raising the additional money he and MacMillan needed. "Hurray! Hurroo! Yea! Touchdown!" Borup exclaimed.

———

"We cannot have a division of command," Osborn warned Hovey. "Some *one* must be Commander, and that person seems to me to be Borup." Not surprisingly, Hovey concurred. He probably shared the verdict with Borup in mid-November, when he visited New Haven for the Yale–Princeton football game. MacMillan remained ignorant of the museum's decision.

The leadership issue detonated when MacMillan, Borup, and Peary's former captain Bob Bartlett gathered in Dr. Lucas's office on the morning of December 8. Hovey dominated the conversation, which focused on potential donors. Bartlett, who had played almost no role in planning but wanted to go, talked up his relationships with the commander's wealthy benefactors. Borup, nursing a bruised head from a falling icicle (his derby hat perished in the accident), described his communications with the Crocker family. MacMillan confessed to knowing no one worth approaching.

Bartlett fidgeted in his chair as if swallowing a question. "Who is to be the leader of the expedition?" he asked.

Lucas sat silent. The board of trustees wants Borup in charge, Hovey explained.

Bartlett exploded. He reminded everyone that he had far more Arctic experience than Borup and MacMillan combined, and that he had been farther north than either of them. A subordinate role was out of the question. MacMillan looked shocked, too. Not only was he older than Borup and better versed in Arctic history, this trip was largely his idea. He and Borup were supposed to be equal partners in a joint venture.

Borup bit his tongue. Hovey held firm. MacMillan could share the accolades with Borup, but he could not share command.

The group reconvened after breaking for lunch. Much to Hovey's relief, Bartlett pulled out of the expedition. MacMillan, although furious at Hovey and suspicious of Borup, stayed on.

Borup and MacMillan talked out their differences that evening. The next morning they trooped into Hovey's office demanding joint leadership. Hovey proposed a compromise, and produced a contract naming them as "equal sharers in the responsibilities, labors and risks of the undertaking and similarly equal sharers in the credit accruing on account of geographical explorations accomplished." A subsequent clause nullified this statement by reserving the museum's right to name "the individual who is to be held ultimately responsible for the welfare of the expedition." The contract confirmed the museum's $6,000 contribution. It assumed no liability for injuries or deaths.

Borup signed, then MacMillan. Crocker Land was a go.

The two men had only five months to finalize their plans, solicit funds, charter a ship, hire a team, and purchase supplies. MacMillan anticipated applying his experience as Peary's executive gofer. His mind ran to details, organization, and preparations. He was a list-maker, a letter-writer, a comparison shopper. Borup preferred the big picture over minutiae but promised to do whatever he could for the team, including canvassing Yale alumni for donations.

Although Hovey and possibly even MacMillan did not know it, Borup was also planning something quite different from an Arctic expedition.

Two weeks earlier, he had asked Marie Peary to marry him.

Borup had never been in love or had a serious girlfriend, never even kissed a woman except for his mother and sister.

The adventurer's hail-fellow-well-met demeanor masked an anxious soul desperate for affection. Borup's mother had died when he was twelve, taking with her much of the joy from his life. He spent holidays putting on a happy face at a social club or at the home of some relative he barely knew. Although he never complained to his demanding father, he longed for a stable family life. He felt incomplete.

Marie had enthralled him since they first met during the hectic days preceding the North Pole trip. "We were just like two boys really, Great Friends and chums," he recalled.

Love was the farthest thing from their minds in 1908. Marie was nearly a decade younger than George and the daughter of one of the country's most famous men—a man Borup worshipped. She had been a public figure since before she could remember. Americans knew her as the "Snow Baby," the white girl born in Greenland's most remote reaches. Newspaper readers had admired pictures of her as an infant in her mother's arms, wrapped in an American flag. *Snow Baby*, Josephine Peary's 1901 bestselling picture book about her daughter's childhood, inspired a rage for Snow Baby dolls in the United States.

Marie's photograph had inspired George during Arctic blizzards and grueling marches. In his mind he began creating an idealized romance. Tentatively at first, then with increasing conviction, he imagined Marie as more than a chum.

Once he was home, Borup visited Marie at every opportunity. Before starting his internship at the AMNH, he spent a joyous week at the Pearys' compound on Maine's Eagle Island. Admirers rather than lovers, they strolled through the island's forest of beech, birch, maple, and spruce trees. She read him her poem about Casco Bay. They discussed her literary efforts and his future. Although the seventeen-year-old girl played it coy, Borup left Maine convinced that Marie was the one for him.

But the hero of the north was too timid to plead his case. An insecure suitor, he studded his letters with the "Bully!"s and "Touchdown!"s expected of a confident man while at the same time insisting that she was too good for him. He mooned around the fringes of her existence, writing lighthearted notes and leaping at chances to see her in New York, Washington, or Maine.

Marie intimidated him. So did her father. "I respect him *so* much," Borup told her. The notion of asking the commander for his daughter's hand terrified him.

Crocker Land offered a means to matrimonial ends. "I must win out," he said of his upcoming expedition. "Otherwise you'd not think much of me." As the conqueror of a new continent, Borup would be worthy of Marie's delicate hand. He could approach Peary as one lion to another.

Borup screwed up his courage in late November, a few days after Hovey put him in charge of the expedition. Intense negotiations with the Peary family netted him an entire day alone with Marie in Portland. It was unseasonably warm, so the couple went for a wander through the woods outside town. Borup rehearsed his question, waiting for the perfect moment. He had faced down blizzards and wrestled snarling wolf-dogs, but could not ask his dark-haired girl to marry him.

The ferry to Eagle Island was waiting at the dock when George proposed. Marie accepted.

Borup was happier than he could remember. He installed Marie's portrait over his desk and carried her letters in his pocket. "You're everything to me," he wrote in one of his daily missives. "I love you more than anybody on earth, sister, father or mother."

Yet doubts troubled him. Perhaps Marie was too young for a lifelong commitment, especially to a man in his circumstances. On Peary's recommendation, they kept their engagement a secret. Reporters would go crazy if they learned of the Snow Baby's engagement to the Tenderfoot. In George's absence, the press would turn Marie into the prototypical lonely woman pacing her widow's walk, straining for a glimpse of her man's ship on the horizon. George didn't want her to become a human-interest story.

George and Marie sustained the "just friends" fiction by limiting themselves to one visit per month. Harried with endless Crocker Land meetings and terrified that Marie's interest might waver during his lengthy exile in the north, Borup's carefree persona crumbled. He lost weight and started punching out his frustrations at a gym. Black moods consumed him whenever a day passed without a letter from Marie. "Do you love me still?" he asked in a fit of self-pity.

"I only wish I had known how you felt before I got mixed up in this Expedition," he wrote in January 1912. Borup considered breaking his contract with the museum but felt duty-bound to uphold everyone's confidence in him. "Not only would I despise myself, but you would too," he realized. "I'll push the darn thing through to success, and then My Dearest, what happiness will be mine if you want."

Borup completed his exams at Yale a few days before Christmas, then rode a train to New York for the annual dinner of the Boone and Crockett Club, a gathering of upscale hunter–conservationists. Forester and political activist Gifford Pinchot was in attendance, as was eugenicist and AMNH board member Madison Grant. Borup circulated, smiling and shaking hands. His reserve fell when he glimpsed the real star of the night, club founder Theodore Roosevelt.

Borup revered the once and perhaps future president almost as much as he did Peary. Maneuvering through the cigar-smoke-filled hall, he stuck out his hand to greet the hunter–explorer–author–politician. Much to his surprise, Roosevelt rattled off a precise narrative of Borup's exploits with Peary in his rapid-fire, high-pitched voice, at a volume loud enough for everyone to hear. Then he inquired into the upcoming Crocker Land venture.

Borup got another thrill later that evening. The gathering was winding down, and Roosevelt was on his way out. Suddenly he paused. His myopic eyes scanned the room until they lit on the young explorer. Changing direction, he offered his hand and a hearty good night. It was a personal benediction, a Rooseveltian blessing conferred upon the Crocker Land expedition.

"It was some event for me," Borup gasped.

Roosevelt further boosted the upcoming expedition by composing a testimonial endorsing Borup and MacMillan as "scientific men of the best out of doors type, scientific men who are equally good in the laboratory and in the field and at the same time able to take the lead in hazardous ventures." They were, in other words, Theodore Roosevelts in the making. Drawing from his oversized sense of masculinity, he commanded "every man able to appreciate and to admire daring" to "feel his blood stir when thinking of what they intend to do."

"It would be a fine thing for America if the discovery of Crocker Land could be placed to our credit as a nation," Roosevelt continued. This imperialistic message suited a nation that was stretching its wings yet wary of militarism. The Spanish-American War of 1898 raised the divisive issue of whether to colonize Asian and Caribbean peoples, and the subsequent Philippine War devolved into a morass of atrocities, guerrilla warfare, and civilian deaths. Arctic exploration offered victory without messiness, national aggrandizement without international controversy.

Borup and MacMillan welcomed Roosevelt's emotional support as a valuable tool for winning financial support. On top of the museum's $6,000, Hovey wrangled a $6,000 commitment from the American Geographical Society and $1,000 from Yale. Another $17,000 was needed before the expedition could charter a ship and start purchasing supplies.

Contributions dribbled in throughout early 1912. A few of Peary's old backers wrote sizable checks. Borup solicited funds from his college classmates. New York state senator Franklin Delano Roosevelt mailed in $15. The young politician had been a few years ahead of Borup at the elite Groton prep school.

MacMillan scored a few contributions, including $300 from Worcester Academy, where he had technically been on leave since 1908. He also acted as the expedition's corporate liaison. At his urging, the country's largest grocery wholesaler, Austin, Nichols & Company, agreed to feed the party at cost. "There is a little pride and glory attached to an order of this kind that more than compensates us for any loss in the way of profit," one company official explained. Boston's Samuel Ward Company donated seventy-two 8-by-10½-inch record books, their covers embossed with "Crocker Land Expedition of the American Museum of Natural History and the American Geographical Society, 1912–1914."

One expected source of cash came up dry. Robert Peary recommended some potential donors but asked his acolytes to withhold his name in their conversations with them. After much prodding, he promised $500 toward the expedition. Claiming a cash shortage, he deferred payment until some unspecified future date.

George Crocker had died of stomach cancer in late 1909. Borup solicited his family without success. His brother, William H. Crocker, who had "a vague idea of some almost unknown region that had been christened 'Crocker Land,'" declined Borup's entreaties, as did his philanthropist nephew, Charles T. Crocker, who cited his losses in the great San Francisco earthquake, six years earlier, as the cause of his reluctance.

Desperate for cash, the expedition launched a publicity blitz. At Hovey's behest, Borup, with assistance from his sister Yvette, produced a masterpiece of "slanguage" for the Sunday, February 18, edition of the *New York Times*. "To Solve the World's Last Big Geographical Problem" repackaged the dangerous mission as an enjoyable romp across the ice. "I won't bother the reader with the details of the scientific work we hope to do on Crocker Land," Borup promised. "Gee whiz!" he continued. "You bet it's going to be some trip. Good time? Holy smoke! We'll have the time of our young lives." A large, romanticized drawing of Borup in furs dominated the small photo of a sedate MacMillan wearing a stiff collar and tie. "I'll bet Mac and I do some tall yelling and snake dancing when we hit the [Crocker Land] coast," he concluded. "We were practicing the other night going up Fifth Avenue."

American Geographical Society vice president Walter James complained that the frivolous piece would repel "the serious minded part of the public." AMNH president H. F. Osborn shared his outrage. Hovey urged his superiors "to take into consideration that the rising generation of college men, no matter how serious their aims in life, is frightful in its use of slang."

Hoping to restore the expedition's credibility, MacMillan sat for a sober interview with the *Boston Sunday Herald*. "This expedition of ours is to be no journey of conquest, but one in the interest of science," he said. It "will be of genuine benefit to the world's supply of knowledge."

Most features about the upcoming trip followed Borup's line, downplaying the expedition's scientific potential in favor of breathless speculation about "the last considerable mass of unknown land on our planet . . . the last great geographical problem." "MAY DEFINE AMERICA," the *New York Tribune*'s provocative headline blared. This was literally true, as Crocker Land was "the only part of this continent not geographically defined," But it also carried symbolic weight. Two young men, trained by a master, striking off on their own, exploring new lands—what could be more American?

By mid-March the team raised enough money to ensure a summertime departure so long as they got their supply and transportation affairs in order. MacMillan, Borup, and Colonel Borup interrogated sales representatives about rifles, photography gear, and construction materials. Hovey, with input from Peary, worked on chartering a vessel.

Borup and MacMillan dreamed of taking the *Roosevelt* north. Unfortunately, the Peary Arctic Club no longer owned the vessel. A Brooklyn-based merchant had purchased it and converted it into a wrecker. Hovey instead booked the *Diana*, a sealer that had been plying northern waters since 1870. At $3,500 a month, the price was high, but no better ship was available.

A balmy New York evening embraced the 1,000 invited guests who arrived at the American Museum of Natural History on April 5, 1912, for a celebration honoring both the third anniversary of Peary's North Pole triumph and Roald Amundsen's recent attainment of the South Pole. Distinguished visitors admired Peary's meteorites, Morris Jesup's marble image, and a Polar Inuit exhibit on their way to the museum's auditorium, where the stars of the exploring world were doffing hats and gladhanding donors, old friends, and professional rivals. American and Norwegian flags bearing the dates of Peary and Amundsen's achievements hung from the walls. Representatives from the American Geographical Society, the New York Academy of Sciences, Yale University, Worcester Academy, and Bowdoin College exchanged pleasantries with the night's featured attractions: Peary, Borup, and MacMillan.

Hovey organized this gathering not only to honor Peary and Amundsen, but also as a way to associate the Crocker Land mission with the world's greatest explorers. Board president Osborn, who presided over the affair, asked Peary to highlight his protégés' trip as "a continuation of your own work."

Peary obliged. After accepting a five-pointed medal carved from a shard of the Ahnighito meteorite, the commander praised both his junior colleagues and himself in a brief speech. When thinking about Crocker Land, he informed the crowd, "I can hardly restrain my enthusiasm, and long for just enough of that fabled fountain of youth to wash away some twenty years, so that I might be with my two boys, Borup and MacMillan, in their hour of victory." Recalling their role in his own victory, he declared that "no two men could be better fitted for the work by physique, temperament, experience and inclination."

Osborn took up the thread. "We believe in the great objects of their journey to the north polar sea," he said. "We have the utmost faith in them, in their courage, their high purpose and their intelligence, and we shall do our best to supply them with the sinews of exploration—namely, funds sufficient to care for them, their Eskimos and their dogs, as well as to enable them to make scientific observations, records and collections."

Borup and MacMillan offered brief thank-yous before taking their seats again. Borup disliked public speaking, especially when audiences expected proper English rather than slang. Osborn had told MacMillan to keep it short.

It was a brilliant send-off. Yet with only two months before departure, the co-leaders faced a myriad of loose ends. Essential supplies remained unpurchased, and their party remained incomplete. Borup rejected an application from former Peary assistant Matt Henson, accusing him of "disloyalty" bordering on "treachery" for giving lectures without Peary's permission. MacMillan signed up an old friend from Provincetown named Jonathan "Jot" Small as the party's cook, carpenter, mechanic, boat-builder, and all-around go-to guy. Finding a surgeon proved a more daunting task. In keeping with the expedition's red, white, and blue overtones, MacMillan wanted an American doctor, preferably one who was "strong, energetic, willing to get out and hustle." No such figure emerged from the candidate pool.

A thornier personnel issue cropped up when Colonel Borup filed what he called "a formal application" for a spot as Osborn's "personal representative" on the trip, a position that existed only in the colonel's head. His action placed the museum in an awkward position. His dominating presence might undermine his son's authority. Denying his petition, however, would cost the museum his prodigious capacity for fundraising.

Osborn asked Hovey to discourage the colonel, but gently. Apparently without George's knowledge, the curator convinced the colonel that his son would be better off without him. "It is useless for me to attempt to express myself as to how deeply I feel in the success of the Expedition," the colonel wrote. But, because success depended on George's "power of command," he admitted that "it would not do to take any action . . . which would in any way keen his responsibility."

"Gadzooks I never knew I could be so busy," Borup complained. As much as Hovey shielded him from the mundane tasks at which MacMillan excelled, the strain from what Borup called "this d——expedition" was grinding him down. He vented his frustration in odd ways. One evening he enlisted his sister for a good-luck ceremony. Yvette placed a candle on the mantel over their fireplace while George improvised a shrine from a horseshoe and a photo of Marie. He grabbed his revolver, made sure the chambers were empty, and began shooting imaginary bullets at the *torngarsuit*, or evil spirits, surrounding him. Yvette muttered "mysterious incantations" while they sacrificed a few of her hairs in the flame. Their ritual complete, they went outside and bowed three times to the new moon.

"I've been working my head off on a subject with the euphemistic title 'Optical Properties of Minerals,'" Borup told Marie Peary. "It's the stiffest and most uncomprehensible [*sic*] and intangible stuff I've ever tried to do." Science drained the joy from exploring, and as the *Diana's* departure date neared, he grew less certain that he wanted any part of it. "I need you, I need your love, I want you more than I ever have or will want anything or anybody ever again," he moaned. Chafing at their one-meeting-per-month arrangement, he exploited any means of gaining a few precious hours together. "Would that count as a monthly visit?" he inquired before ducking into Washington to give a talk and possibly get a peek at Marie. His love life, like his exploration career, had become a series of negotiations.

"I was and am very much of a tenderfoot and a duffer at the game," Borup confessed. A novice at romance, he did not see he was smothering the teenager. His plaintive requests for her to write every day overwhelmed her. So did his melodramatic anguish when she did not. Their relationship grew strained. Marie pondered the realities of attaching herself to an older man who was preparing to spend two years beyond her reach. Perhaps the situation reminded her of her father's on-again-off-again presence throughout her childhood.

A careworn expression shadowed Borup's face. His frustration mounted when a proposed late April meeting with Marie fell through. Feeling restless, he set up a boating trip with a friend from college named Winthrop Case.

Borup and Case possessed an easy camaraderie rooted in their outgoing personalities, sunny dispositions, and similar backgrounds. Case had arrived at Yale in 1908, just as Borup was leaving for the Arctic. He actually outperformed his predecessor, winning plaudits for his undergraduate work in geology and mining engineering and earning a varsity letter for track, an achievement Borup never managed during his time on the squad.

In 1911 Case began graduate studies at Yale's Sheffield Scientific School. He fell in with his fellow student, Borup, who became a regular guest at the Case home in Norwich, Connecticut. At one point, Borup asked Case to join the Crocker Land party. Case demurred, preferring to continue his formal education.

Borup tidied up some last-second expedition details before joining Case on Saturday, April 27, aboard an evening train bound for the coast. Political talk bounced around the car. President William Howard Taft and his former patron, Theodore Roosevelt, were crisscrossing Connecticut in advance of the state's Republican primary. Other riders spoke in hushed tones about the latest news of the *Titanic* disaster. Rumor had it that ships would soon start delivering the bodies of the dead to Halifax, Nova Scotia.

Borup and Case stepped from the train into a crisp New England night. Ominous clouds suggested that a wet April was about to get wetter. The pair hoped the weather would cooperate with their plans to canoe in Long Island Sound the following morning.

They awoke to fair skies and a stiff northwesterly breeze. The thermometer registered 40 degrees. Choppy waves rippled across the sound. It wasn't ideal weather for boating, but conditions were hardly treacherous enough to keep an Arctic veteran and his boon companion indoors. Borup helped slide Case's canoe into the water and cranked its outboard motor to life. Keeping Long Island to starboard, they putt-putted into the rising sun, meandering east for a spell before turning north into Niantic Bay.

A storm rolled in, strengthening the wind and waves. Borup and Case fought their small craft as it rolled on the swells.

At around 5 p.m., a quarry owner on shore named Harry Gardiner caught a glimpse of a boat floundering in the heavy seas. He watched in horror as the canoe overturned. Borup clung to the capsized boat. Case disappeared from view.

Gardiner rushed to his powerboat. It looked to be about a half-hour run to the accident site.

Coaxing maximum speed from his engine, Gardiner watched the desperate scene unfold from afar. Borup located Case, who had lost consciousness when he knocked his head against the boat. Borup swam through the chop and hauled his friend back to the overturned canoe. He struggled to hold Case afloat while maintaining a grip on the slippery craft. Neither of them was wearing a life jacket.

When Gardiner arrived, he found nothing but a cap and a coat floating on the water.

Gardiner reversed course to organize a search-and-rescue patrol. Both Borup and Case were strong swimmers. With some luck, they might have paddled to Two Tree or White Rock Island. A trio of motorboats scoured the area without success.

The next morning, April 29, brought overcast skies and rain showers. Case's father and brother arrived from Norwich to join the widening operation.

Searchers found the missing men's canoe, identifiable from the "S.W.C." printed on its side. A trawler dragging a quarter-mile offshore recovered Case's body that afternoon. George Borup's remains turned up a few hours later. Volunteers transferred the bodies to the Case cottage, where a medical examiner pronounced them dead.

Winthrop Case was twenty-one. George Borup was twenty-six.

5

A FINE FELLOW

MACMILLAN WAS IN BOSTON overseeing production of the expedition's pemmican when word came of Borup's death. Bittersweet memories of spending long days and sunlit nights in the Arctic with George washed over him. He could almost see the trails from their sledge runners etching parallel paths across an apparently endless stretch of ice. Fragments of old conversations rang in his ears—giddy talk of Crocker Land, or Antarctica, or wherever else fortune might lead them. Above all, he fought disbelief that such a vital spirit, "a friend who can never be replaced," was gone. MacMillan kept a newspaper clipping about the accident with him for the rest of his life.

On May 1, 1912, MacMillan boarded a train for New York, where he would join Peary and other dignitaries on the quick journey up to Ossining for Borup's funeral.

"My God, what a terrible thing," Peary exclaimed when he learned about the accident. "I cannot believe it or realize it." The commander looked shattered when MacMillan met him at Grand Central Terminal.

Peary's wife and children were not with him. Marie was in no shape to make the trip. "It's too awful for him to go out of the world like that, without warning," she wailed. "Oh it's horrible!" Marie felt guilty because she had been thinking about breaking

off her engagement. Now her fiancé was gone forever. The prospect of seeing him in a coffin overwhelmed her. "George was my
oldest and best friend, and I loved him dearly, tho not in the way
he wished," she wrote in her diary. "It's hard to picture the future
without George's smiling face, and jolly ways." Josephine Peary
remained at Eagle Island to comfort her daughter.

MacMillan and Peary boarded the train for Ossining. Yale University president Arthur Hadley, Borup's former geography professor Herbert Gregory, and AMNH president H. F. Osborn found
them in their car.

An earlier train had carried Borup's remains from New London, Connecticut, through his beloved New Haven, and on to the
home of his uncle, Francis Parkins, who hosted the funeral. Mac-
Millan watched in stunned silence while attendants draped the
Yale colors and an American flag over his friend's casket. Peary sat
nearby, gazing into the indeterminate distance, certain he would
break down if he spoke. Eight of Borup's classmates served as pall-
bearers. Members of Zeta Psi fraternity displayed the banner that
MacMillan and Borup had intended to plant on Crocker Land.

After the ceremony, a fleet of cars ferried MacMillan and the
other mourners to Dale Cemetery, where George Borup was lowered into a hole carved out beside his mother's grave.*

MacMillan returned to Boston. Peary and the rest decamped
for New York. MacMillan was alone, bearing not only the weight
of Borup's passing, but also the burden of an expedition thrown
into limbo. Despite their brothers-in-arms attitude, George had
been the face of the Crocker Land team. He was the star, the cho-
sen one, the next Peary. MacMillan was the behind-the-scenes
man, the one who freed Borup from such tedious minutiae as purchasing the right amount of hardtack or determining the optimal
thickness of ropes.

---

* Peary later donated the bell from the *Roosevelt* to be incorporated into
Borup's headstone.

Everlasting fame and scientific glory were still waiting out past
Cape Thomas Hubbard. Even as MacMillan grieved, he renewed
his determination that his mission—*their* mission—would happen.
And yet he wasn't sure whether he believed in himself. Sole leadership had never been his goal. Yes, he had guided boys at summer camp and at Worcester Academy. Guiding men on a multiyear
Arctic expedition was an altogether different matter. Much as he
wanted to go, he wasn't sure he could do it without Borup.

"Of course you will never find a man who, in temperament,
physique, enthusiasm and experience can equal George," Peary
advised E. O. Hovey. No one trusted MacMillan's leadership capabilities. Hovey, whose opinion meant the difference between
going and not going, could never quite articulate the reasons for
his lack of faith in MacMillan, who had as much Arctic experience
as Borup and had internalized Peary's methods just as thoroughly,
if not more so. MacMillan had a better grasp of the Inughuit's language and culture than Borup. His studies at Harvard gave him
ample grounding in the sciences. He was level-headed and depend-
able. On some unspoken level, Hovey simply could not embrace
the man. Perhaps he had grown too close to Borup to transfer his
affections. Borup was magnetic; MacMillan was reliable.

MacMillan "is a fine fellow," AMNH president H. F. Osborn told
Hovey, but "the breaking up of the cooperation between the two
men, the loss of the special training for the expedition which Mr.
Borup had received in the Museum and at Yale University, and the
difficulty in securing an experienced man to replace Mr. Borup . . .
all conspire to place the expedition in a new light." To Osborn's
thinking, Borup's death was "practically fatal to the carrying out
of the project." It would be "wise to abandon it."

Although not a sentimental man, Osborn dug through his files
until he found a recent letter from Borup. Grabbing a pair of scissors, he snipped the signature from the page. Like the mutilated
sheet of paper, the expedition had a gaping hole that could never

be filled. "The staff of the Museum has never sustained so sudden and so sorrowful a blow," he mourned.

"I confess that my interest in the subject has received a severe blow in the death of Borup," Peary sighed. Crocker Land's backers at Yale also lost heart. "I cannot think of anybody of the Borup type who could be placed in charge of the expedition," said Professor Herbert Gregory. Peary confirmed that MacMillan "could not do what Borup was expected to do." Peary thought Hovey should redirect the expedition's money toward a new Borup Fund for geological studies at the museum.

Although he never heard these conversations, MacMillan sensed the skepticism swirling around him. It seemed the Crocker Land expedition had really been an investment in Borup, with him as a kind of barnacle along for the ride.

A combination of financial and institutional pressures saved the mission. Hovey decided the project was so far along that the costs of canceling it exceeded the risks of continuing it. The museum would owe at least $8,000 in unpaid bills even if it cancelled every order it could. It would be cheaper to place nonperishable items in storage and formulate a new plan. There was also the museum's reputation to consider. Abandoning Crocker Land, warned Peary Arctic Club Secretary Herbert L. Bridgman, would "invite unfavorable remark and occupation of the field by others; compromise the prestige of the Museum . . . and unfavorably affect American influence in the scientific councils of the world."

The AMNH's board of trustees wavered for several weeks before agreeing to postpone the Crocker Land expedition's departure until the summer of 1913. It further resolved "that the Expedition be constituted a memorial of the young explorer who was so keenly interested in it and who was the mainspring of its present undertaking." MacMillan would remain as leader, or at least a leader—the museum deferred personnel decisions until the fall. MacMillan never complained about the museum's misgivings. He needed the AMNH more than it needed him.

"I miss George," he wrote to Peary. "We had planned to be together and to work together so much in the years to come that I am feeling very much alone. George was one of the best and no one will ever quite take his place with me." Feeling lost, MacMillan motored out of Boston in a 21-foot boat with his old friend Jot Small, who had been slated to go on the Crocker Land trip. Their destination was Labrador, a cruise of some 1,500 miles. MacMillan had no agenda other than to clear his head.

Before leaving, he composed a docile letter to Hovey. "Am making no plans that cannot be changed at your suggestion," it read. "As soon as I get back will get in touch with you. As I have told you repeatedly, I want to do whatever you decide is the best for me to carry out that expedition successfully. . . . Keep me informed, won't you?"

Four months in Labrador restored MacMillan's battered spirits. Indulging his interest in ethnography, he convinced over 100 Labrador Inuit to let him record their height, weight, and head size, along with the distance between pretty much any two parts of the body. Labrador also offered opportunities for ornithology. A lifelong bird enthusiast, MacMillan scampered up granite cliffs in search of rare eggs, on one occasion getting stuck on a sheer wall 50 feet above the surf, unable to either advance or retreat. A sharp-eyed harbormaster spotted him, scaled the cliff from the opposite direction, and lowered a rope. MacMillan and Small fought the elements at every turn. Howling autumn gales shoved their small craft toward jagged rocks. Small said he would never again visit this "God damn country." MacMillan, who rarely said anything stronger than "Great heavens!", teased his storm-tossed companion all the way home. This was exactly what he wanted from life: science spiced with excitement.

MacMillan's return aroused little interest in New York. Hovey had maintained a studious silence throughout his absence. The curator was committed to Crocker Land, not MacMillan, and he searched for a way to cut Borup's former partner out of the picture.

Hovey flirted with naming Vilhjalmur Stefansson, an iconoclastic Canadian who had recently returned from four years in the Alaskan Arctic, as the expedition's leader. Persistent rumors suggested that Stefansson, whose impulsive methods gave him a mixed reputation within the exploration community, was targeting Crocker Land as his next goal. Bringing him on board would therefore coopt a potential rival.

Hovey even considered fifty-eight-year-old Colonel H. D. Borup as a possible replacement. Following George's death the colonel retreated to Quebec's Notre Dame du Lac, where he idled away mournful days paddling across its pristine lakes. "The expedition is . . . too important, too costly to be confided solely to [MacMillan]," the colonel cautioned. MacMillan would need a Peary-type leader when trouble came, as it inevitably would. Borup denied any desire for personal fame or riches. Rather, he was desperate to complete his son's work. While conceding his age, he claimed outstanding health, and forwarded testimonials from doctors. He had lived an outdoor life, had survived multiple Canadian winters, and understood the expedition's inner workings as well as anyone.

"Your military training, your natural capacity for organization and for command and your personal characteristics are all exactly what are required and desired for the undertaking," Hovey said. Nevertheless, he concluded, "I am obliged to say frankly, as man to man, that it seems to me that you are not physically able to undertake such a severe trip."

In late October of 1912, with time getting short and no better option in sight, Hovey mailed a matter-of-fact invitation to MacMillan's apartment in Cambridge: "The Committee representing the organizing institutions of the Crocker Land Expedition has unanimously agreed to appoint you as the general leader of the Expedition." Hovey asked MacMillan to keep the offer secret, as if unsure whether he had done the right thing.

Ignoring Hovey's chilly tone, MacMillan rushed out a chipper reply. "I can simply promise this," he said. "I will do my utmost to carry out faithfully and well the outline of work as decided upon by [the] committee in charge." Even though MacMillan was no one's first choice, he was, in the end, the only choice.

At 9 a.m. on Monday, November 11, 1912, less than two weeks after accepting the museum's halfhearted offer, MacMillan passed under the AMNH's great arch and started climbing the stairs to Hovey's office. While MacMillan was in Labrador, the curator had signed up a pair of strangers, Dr. Elmer Ekblaw and Ensign Fitzhugh Green, for two-year commitments with the Crocker Land expedition. Today they would meet their leader.

Hovey's actions were cheeky, if not misguided. A geologist had no business judging candidates for a major Arctic expedition. Peary would never have tolerated such an insult. But Hovey held the purse strings and could cut MacMillan loose at any moment. MacMillan therefore exhibited no annoyance as he walked down the fifth-floor hallway. It wasn't his style.

On entering the curator's office, he did his best to perform a Peary-like appraisal of the two strangers standing before him. Ekblaw cut an unimpressive figure. The geology professor looked tired, and he was, having finished grading a batch of exams at the University of Illinois right before hopping a train from Champaign to New York. Balding, with a round, almost pudgy face, he looked a bit heavy for Arctic duty. In fact, he stood five feet ten inches tall and weighed a solid 180 pounds, or 2.57 pounds per inch, a shade above Peary's limit.

Fitzhugh Green cut a much sharper figure. Trim and handsome, he could easily become the new face of the expedition. Brown hair swept from right to left over a well-proportioned forehead. Piercing, maudlin eyes suggested an intelligent and inquisitive soul. If MacMillan squinted just right, the ramrod-straight twenty-five-year-old navy man looked a bit like Borup, only more classically handsome.

Green came from an illustrious family tree. Isabelle, his mother, was a bright, beautiful, and cynical woman who traced her lineage back to Henry Fitzhugh, who in 1321 received the title of Baron of Ravensworth from King Edward II of England. Ravensworth's descendants migrated to Virginia in the 1600s and promptly inter-married with the great clans of the tobacco-rich Tidewater region. One of Isabelle's ancestors had married the daughter of Robert "King" Carter, who was among the wealthiest men in colonial America. Others served as aides to General Washington during the Revolution. Isabelle's great-great-grandfather William Fitzhugh, husband of Thomas Jefferson's cousin Ann Randolph, had repre-sented Virginia in the Continental Congress. Robert E. Lee's wife, Mary Custis, was also related to the Fitzhughs.

Although Isabelle found her husband's family less impressive than her own, it too had eminent roots. Charles Green, her son Fitzhugh's father, was the grandson of a wealthy cotton merchant. Today, visitors to Savannah can visit the lavish, Gothic Revival-style Green–Meldrim house that was once part of the family estate.

The Civil War demolished both the Fitzhughs' and the Greens' finances. Scrambling to maintain at least middle-class status, Charles Green relocated with his Baltimore-born wife to St. Joseph, Mis-souri, where he opened a cotton brokerage office. When cotton profits dried up in the late nineteenth century, he slid into a mid-dling career as a produce broker.

Isabelle, raised on stories of great heroes and magnificent plan-tations, chafed at her confinement in a frontier city best known as the place where the coward Robert Ford shot Jesse James. She vented her thwarted ambitions on her son, pushing Fitzhugh to achieve greatness at all costs. Under her tutelage, Fitzhugh Green's life became a mad dash for glory. His ambition always lay just beyond his fingertips. Good looks, hard work, intellectual bril-liance, and a sycophantic attitude toward potential patrons vaulted him out of St. Joseph. In 1905 he earned a spot at the United States Naval Academy, where he trained as an ordnance and gunnery expert. Rotations aboard three battleships, the *Idaho*, the *Michigan*, and the *Iowa*, hinted at the possibility of future promotions. With a lucky break here or there, one day ensigns would be saluting Admiral Green.

Successful as he was, Green secretly loathed life in the navy. Peacetime offered few opportunities for the advancement he craved, and his paycheck couldn't support the kind of life he desired. Eager to supplement his income, he dabbled in writing and enrolled in an industrial management course, hoping it would put him in contact with prominent businessmen.

Green learned about the Crocker Land trip in July 1912, soon after Borup's death, from a former academy classmate named Ned Brandt, whose father was acquainted with Hovey through a tenuous chain of mutual friends. Brandt was considering applying for the expedition. When he backed out, Green convinced him to arrange a meeting with Hovey.

Green followed up with a personal appeal to the curator. "I understand to a large degree the hardship and work to be met on such a trip," he wrote. Mixed military–civilian Arctic expeditions often went awry when the military men imposed stringent discipline on civilians. The ensign, however, expected "no authority or other advantages on account of my position in the Navy or my experience at sea."

Green's personal credentials looked impeccable. In every way he seemed another Borup—maybe even better, if Hovey was being honest. Green rarely drank and did not smoke. He had been a member of the academy football and track squads; he was an avid golfer and tennis player. He had spent his youth hunting and camping on the Platte River in northern Missouri (where, he said, temperatures sometimes touched –30 degrees). He had taken long hikes through the Rocky Mountains, had a penchant for mapmaking and a love of machinery, navigation, geology, and meteorology. And he was willing to do anything asked of him. "I believe that I can recommend my cooking," he added.

Hovey granted him an audience. Steely-eyed, taut and lean, the ensign certainly looked the part of an Arctic explorer. Green also impressed Hovey as a lively, intelligent young man with a passion for scientific exploration. Hovey promised to hold his application until the museum made its final decisions on personnel.

Green kept himself in Hovey's line of sight, hanging around the museum whenever the *Iowa* was in port and issuing a steady stream of correspondence. His letters wavered between pleasant flattery and pushy insistence that he was the right man for the job. Green even convinced the navy to enroll him in graduate classes at George Washington University in Washington DC, a short train ride from the museum. Advanced education would increase his value to the navy, he told his superiors. In truth, graduate school was "a means to the end."

Considering what was at stake, Green can be forgiven for some gentle retrofitting of his record. For example, he cited his outstanding constitution as a key qualification for Arctic duty, yet for much of the previous year he had lived in hospitals. One day in August 1911, with the *Michigan* docked in Boston, not far from MacMillan's quarters in Cambridge, Green had clutched his right side in pain. Waves of nausea and fever washed over him. He rushed to Boston Naval Hospital, where surgeons performed an appendectomy. A postoperative infection left him bedridden for six weeks. As that was clearing up, typhoid struck, leaving the ensign weak and achy. Doctors discharged him in late November. A relapse the next day forced him into a civilian hospital. There he remained, too sick to be moved, until the end of the year. Still dragging, in the spring of 1912 he entered Castle Hot Springs sanitarium, a lavish resort in central Arizona where the well-to-do enjoyed restorative waters surrounded by palm trees and the impressive peaks of the Hieroglyphic Mountains. Navy doctors cleared his return to service a few days before he approached Ned Brandt about joining the Crocker Land expedition. Hovey was ignorant of all of this.

The curator penciled Green onto his roster in the fall of 1912. Green was overjoyed. Crocker Land got him away from the navy while opening a path toward fame, fortune, and glory—all the things he deserved, according to his mother. He began ingratiating himself with the expedition's moneymen. "To have gotten such institutions as the ones backing the trip behind oneself is an accomplishment worth years of work," he believed. "They have already shown that their word is an open sesame to everything that I ask for."

Fitzhugh Green dominated the conversation in Hovey's office. Speaking fast, without wasting a word, he described navy life and his program at George Washington University. Ekblaw, six years older than the ensign, sat back in awe. Green kept one eye on MacMillan throughout the proceedings. He knew what the prospective leader had accomplished with Peary, but wasn't yet sure whether this stranger had what it took to direct men through a crisis.

Green' performance floored MacMillan, who saw tremendous initiative and a gift for organization in the ensign. Against all odds, Hovey had turned up another Borup, another photogenic athlete with a radiant personality and a taste for adventure. There could be no better right-hand man than this Arctic superstar in the making. What MacMillan was to Peary, Green would be to MacMillan.

Green shared MacMillan's enthusiasm. "I have worked enough with men on shipboard and in the field to know how much difference it makes whether the leading spirit is all that it should be to promise success," he told Hovey the following day. "I feel now that I want to work under Mr. MacMillan and be with him."

Neither Hovey nor MacMillan saw the other Green, the one behind the go-getter façade, the troubled young man whose spirits rose and fell like the tides. And knowing more about him probably wouldn't have changed their assessment one bit. Even the great Peary endured periods of blackness.

Green's private notebooks exposed the brooding soul lurking within the hyperefficient ensign. "Oh why was brute born to be eaten, / Or the ant to be crushed by a tread?" he asked in "Written in a Bitter Moment," which he composed while the *Michigan* lay at anchor off Long Island sometime in 1911. "Oh why was I born to be beaten, / To see nearest friends among the dead? . . . 'Tis fate that is crushing and maiming, / Is sucking the blood from my heart, / Thy acid point arrows art aiming / At Dread, but in death he depart."

Another poem from the same period, "Murder in Rage," viewed a knifing from the victim's perspective: "Just a word / Overheard— / Passion stirred— / Vision Blurred! / One moment's stress, / Of steel agleam. / The crimsoned flesh— / A choking scream! / Ah—God!"

Green was bright, eager, and talented. He was also ambitious, insecure, and fatalistic. A fractured, flawed man, he combined elements of George Borup, Robert Peary, and Lord Byron. Borup had his unhappy moments, but he could never have created the grim world of "My Conscience," a dialogue between Green's public and private selves.

"Don't you see the coming drizzle?" Green asked himself. "Can't you see the fog is rolling?"

6

THE BOYS

DONALD MACMILLAN, FITZHUGH GREEN, and Elmer Ekblaw
left their November 1912 get-acquainted meeting with an extensive to-do list. Arctic expeditions departed New York in early summer to beat the autumn ice pack. MacMillan's team therefore had
only six months to acquire the supplies, survival gear, and scientific equipment needed for a two-year stay at the edge of the earth.
Any mistakes or oversights could cripple the expedition before it
even started.

The three explorers-to-be went their separate ways. Ekblaw
resumed his duties at Illinois, and Green continued his studies
at George Washington University. MacMillan went back to Harvard. He remained something of a mystery to his new crewmates.
Ekblaw and Green maintained a lively correspondence through the
winter of 1912–13 but rarely communicated with MacMillan. Mac-
Millan's silence deepened concerns about his leadership qualities.

Green emerged as the most active member of the party. "I think
that you have gotten a thoroughly valuable assistant in him," Hovey
informed MacMillan. The ensign's first priority was securing leave
from the navy. In a two-pronged offensive, he mobilized the museum's influential trustees to work their Washington contacts while
he launched a frontal assault on the fleet's byzantine bureaucracy.

Their combined efforts produced total victory when Secretary of the Navy George von L. Meyer placed Green on detached service with the Crocker Land expedition rather than giving him leave. The decision involved more than semantics; the navy paid the salaries of personnel on detached duty, but not those on leave. "This is a clean $1,500 to us," Hovey exclaimed.

Green's enthusiasm was boundless. Between classes he reread all of Peary's writings, in chronological order, and studied zoology in case other expedition members needed an assistant. Daily 15-mile hikes prepared his body for the rigors of sledging. Green cancelled a ten-day vacation so he could instead learn how to operate a seismograph and design a portable building to house the device. He conferred with professors of topography, repaired meteorological instruments at the Weather Bureau, and perfected his surveying skills in the offices of the Government Hydrographic Bureau. In his spare time, he dabbled in geology and paleontology at the Smithsonian Institution, and in magnetism at the Naval Observatory.

With minimal prodding from Hovey and MacMillan, Green turned his considerable charms on anyone who might save the expedition some money. He coaxed a $2,000 field magnetic set out of the Carnegie Institute and nearly $3,000 worth of equipment from the Naval Observatory. Among other items, the navy donated a chronometer, a magnetometer, reading glasses, India ink (in five colors), pencils, drawing paper, crowbars, and axes. Green convinced the service to pack and ship these goods at its own expense.

"If I am overstepping my authority down here let me know at once," he asked MacMillan. No one offered any objections.

Green reveled in his new prominence. An inveterate club-joiner, he bolstered his contacts with memberships in Phi Sigma Kappa and the National Geographic Society (a much greater honor than it is today). He rubbed elbows with senators, congressmen, and ambassadors. In the biggest prize of all, he met President and Mrs.

Taft at a White House reception. Green's tireless activity attracted so much attention that he hired a clipping service so he could follow the growing sheaf of newspaper stories about him. It was all for the expedition, he said, because "the more publicity it gets the more chance we have of getting influential people to back us up."

Green put himself in charge of the expedition's most exciting technological innovation. Arctic explorers spent months or even years operating beyond the reach of civilization, oblivious to what was happening with their families and in the wider world. A recent invention, wireless broadcasting, might liberate them from dangerous and demoralizing isolation. Any party with a powerful enough radio could maintain contact with friends, families, and supporting institutions no matter how remote its location. On a more practical level, newspaper editors would pay top dollar for regular updates from remote corners of the planet.

Walter Wellman, an American journalist who launched a quixotic campaign to pilot an airship to the North Pole, dispatched the first wireless communication from the Arctic in 1906. Wellman transmitted his message from Danes Island, 500 miles above Norway's northern coast in the Svalbard archipelago. It sped across the Barents Sea to Hammerfest in northern Norway, then to a receiving station at Tromsø that relayed it across the Atlantic to Washington DC, where operators forwarded it to Theodore Roosevelt's summer home in Oyster Bay. Delighted by all things new, the president savored the note: "Greetings, best wishes by first wireless message ever sent from Arctic regions. Wellman."

Rather than send a single transmission, the Crocker Land expedition planned on maintaining wireless contact throughout its time in the north. MacMillan's men would link a broadcasting station erected at their headquarters on Ellesmere Island with the Canadian government's Wolstenholme Island relay station, some 1,100 miles away. Operators there would forward the expedition's messages to New York for distribution. There were even plans afoot to load portable radio units onto sledges, enabling MacMillan to transmit live from Crocker Land. "The idea of being in direct frequent communication with an exploring party north of the 79° latitude is one to stir the blood and fire the imagination," Hovey crowed.

Green charmed the Canadian Government Radio Service into agreeing to transmit scientific messages ("such as the word of any discoveries") for free, while charging only ten cents a word for nonscientific messages. Museum officials had expected to pay ten times that amount. In another coup, he talked German radio manufacturer Telefunken into lending the expedition a wireless set worth around $2,000. "I am beginning to believe that you can get most anything," MacMillan marveled.

Once they had a wireless, the expedition needed an operator. Green convinced the navy to give them one. He interviewed several candidates before selecting twenty-two-year-old Jerome Allen, an electrician and radioman aboard the battleship *New Hampshire*, as the fourth member of the team. The Georgia native was a whiz with machines but had little relevant outdoor experience. Beyond being bored with "the mediocre routine of every-day service work," he couldn't really explain why he was interested in such a dangerous proposal. His restless spirit of adventure nevertheless impressed Green. In another sign of the ensign's rising authority, Green did not tell MacMillan about Allen until he had made the hire.

Green dispatched Allen to a General Electric plant in Erie, Pennsylvania, where technicians were building a special generator designed for extreme weather conditions. A three-kilowatt engine, operating in conjunction with a transformer and 3,000 pounds of storage batteries, would not only power the wireless radio, but also electrify the party's living quarters. With no repair shops in the north, Allen had to know the generator inside and out. A mistake now could not be fixed later.

As spring arrived, Allen began questioning whether the wireless was as powerful as Green predicted. By his calculations, if the expedition erected a pair of 150-foot aerials, a difficult and awkward prospect, it could push a signal about 1,000 miles, a touch short of Wolstenholme. If Allen was right, the Crocker Landers might invest a tremendous amount of effort in a pointless venture. Allen shared his concerns with Green, who disregarded them. Lest he overstep his leeway with a superior officer, the radioman didn't press his case.

For all his exterior confidence, Green harbored inner doubts about the trip. Part of his problem was sheer exhaustion. His professors at George Washington approved his master's thesis in May 1913, and he passed his final exams with flying colors. But graduation offered no reprieve from the multitude of expedition-related tasks awaiting him. Stressed out and feeling combative, he picked a fight with General Electric when the company's mechanics could not coax as much power from the generator as he wanted. A fiery response from a company executive prompted a hasty retreat. "I must ask you to bear all ill-will against me and not against the Expedition," he apologized. "I am quite sure that the men who are going north . . . can never forget that their lives for the next two years will have been made infinitely more livable solely through the efforts of yourself and the others who have been interested in our electrical equipment."

Dark thoughts clouded the ensign's mind. Green carried around a newspaper article about the recent deaths of Captain Robert Falcon Scott's entire Antarctic expedition. The ensign checked into the possibility of acquiring additional life insurance. His overbearing mother asked him to abandon the Crocker Land trip. An old friend from St. Joseph seconded her plea. "Just think of the worry and anxiety which you will cause while you are away," he said, "and if you never return . . . just think of the remaining years your Mother will have to spend on this Earth."

———

MacMillan scored straight As in his final semester at Harvard before moving to New York in spring 1913. He rented a comfortable apartment on Central Park West but spent most of his time at the museum, a short walk away, where he raised money, finalized provisions, and tackled a thousand other behind-the-scenes tasks. Chomping on gum while he worked, he immersed himself in the dull details of what promised to be an amazing journey. Let Green be the man of action. MacMillan saw himself as an overseer whose primary responsibility was keeping the overall expedition on track.

MacMillan felt good about the progress so far, and about his growing team. At his urging, Hovey signed up his longtime friend and traveling partner Jot Small as the expedition's cook and handyman. Small had reconsidered his disdain for that "God damn country" since the duo's return from Labrador. A sixth member came on board when the University of Illinois demanded the right to name an expedition zoologist in exchange for a $10,000 contribution which Ekblaw negotiated. Ekblaw selected his good friend Maurice (Tank) Tanquary, a fellow Illinois graduate teaching entomology at Kansas State. It was a curious selection made more for companionship than practicality, as the team would not find many insects on Crocker Land. With MacMillan, Allen, Ekblaw, Green, Small, and Tanquary on the roster, the group was complete, except for a surgeon.

MacMillan opened the May 11, 1913, *New York Sunday Tribune* with great expectancy. Leafing past a full-page, first-person narrative about Theodore Roosevelt's youthful experiences in the boxing ring, he found what he was looking for: an equally large feature entitled "Hope to Solve the Earth's Final Puzzle—Icy Crocker Land."

A *Tribune* reporter had visited MacMillan's apartment the previous day. Their tête-à-tête, and the resulting profile, marked his best opportunity to define his upcoming trip for the public. In 1909 newspapers painted Mac as the levelheaded contrast to the more passionate Borup. With George gone, the older partner shifted his message to match the sensibilities of adventure-hungry readers raised on sensationalist journalism. The *Tribune* was happy to play along. A cavalcade of catchy images peppered its spread, which was dominated by a full-length portrait of MacMillan clad in Arctic furs. Borup had submitted a similar photo for his February 1912 "slanguage" feature in the *New York Times*, the one that had relegated a stiff-looking MacMillan to the margins. Headshots of Green, Ekblaw, and Tanquary, along with scenes of Inughuit and icebergs, supplemented the central photograph. A map featuring a large black blob representing Crocker Land filled the upper right corner.

MacMillan's interview produced a rush of text that favored drama over science. "Will the spirit of adventure ever die?" the paper asked. "Will there ever be a time when men will fear to go forth to face unknown perils to snatch the laurel of fame? . . . No! . . . Brave men still live. Fame calls not in vain." Its manly spirit rising, the *Tribune* deemed MacMillan a latter-day Norseman, another Columbus, or Vespucci, or Magellan. Like them, he accepted the dangers that came with charging into the darkness. His hearty band would court death to crack "the sole riddle of the Earth which is still unanswered."

The Polar Inuit figured prominently in the article. MacMillan, whom the *Tribune* depicted as an expert ethnographer who spoke Inuktun "perfectly," promised to control the natives without using force. He described the Inughuit as "simple and peaceable" people, "with the minds and faith of children." They "will undoubtedly be filled with genuine Esquimau delight by the thought of working once more for their white friends, in whom they have an almost sacred faith," the *Tribune* agreed. MacMillan looked forward to teaching the natives to play baseball.

"Everything that modern science can devise will be taken along," the paper observed. High-tech gadgets would advance humanity's understanding of the planet. Sewing machines would domesticate the Inughuit women, electric lights would illuminate winter nights, and enameled kitchen utensils would preserve refined table manners. And through the miracle of radio, ordinary Americans could follow civilization's advance without ever donning a fur or hitching up a dog.

MacMillan's performance for the *Tribune* was an undeniable triumph. Valuable publicity rained down on the expedition and the museum. It did not, however, solve all of the explorer's problems, the most immediate being his inability to find a surgeon. With typical, methodical tenacity, Mac trolled hospitals, medical schools, and navy yards for a physician who was both in excellent shape and willing to put his domestic life on hold for two years.

Following innumerable dead ends and several cases of last-second cold feet, he received an application from a thirty-five-year-old bear of a man named Harrison Hunt, who had learned about the opening from a newspaper want ad calling for a physician willing to go north on short notice. Hunt had been planning to do postgraduate work in London, an ambitious step for a country doctor with a practice in remote Island Falls, Maine, but one befitting the son of a respected surgeon at Bangor's Eastern Maine General Hospital. Something in the notice struck a chord. Hunt asked his former mentor at Bowdoin College for a recommendation (MacMillan had overlapped with Hunt there but had not met him).

Hunt's inquiry reached MacMillan at the perfect moment. "I am up against it and must find my man at once," MacMillan wrote. Further inquiries confirmed that Hal Hunt was exactly what the expedition needed—with a Bowdoin pedigree. At six-foot-three and a solid 190 pounds, with blue eyes and a thick mop of dirty blond hair, he was Paul Bunyan with a scalpel, the kind of man who stomped into the woods with a rolled-up pancake in his pocket and a burning desire to see what lay over the farthest rise. "He just had to go adventuring," his granddaughter recalled. Hunt was also resourceful; during wintertime the doctor visited isolated patients using a primitive snowmobile he built from a motorcycle and a pair of cross-country skis.

"See that Hunt is appointed at once before we lose him," MacMillan urged Hovey. The museum, however, was less certain about MacMillan's find. Hovey and museum president Osborn worried about the doctor's family situation. Hunt had a wife, Marion, and a four-year-old daughter, Ruth. A man might crack during such a long separation from his loved ones.

Although he maintained a stoic exterior, Hunt shared their unease. His love for his family clashed with his love of the out-doors. A man of few words, he bared his dilemma in conversations with Marion. The Polar Inuit fascinated him. He wanted to take their measurements, investigate their diet, and examine their survival techniques. Hunt yearned for the kind of experience he couldn't find even in the vast woods of Maine. An untrammeled wilderness was enticing him with promises of freedom and an escape from the mundane responsibilities of house calls and housekeeping.

Marion's resistance crumbled beneath her husband's unshakeable conviction that the trip would broaden him as a physician and as a person. In late May, two weeks after he made his initial contact with MacMillan, the doctor accepted the museum's offer of $75 per month for the duration. "Hunt is certainly a crackajack, and we are very fortunate in adding him to the personnel of the Expedition," MacMillan enthused.

Hunt's commitment rounded out the seven-man team. Donald MacMillan was the leader, although everyone saw Fitzhugh Green as at least a close second. Elmer Ekblaw and Maurice Tanquary comprised the scientific core of the group. Jerome Allen and Jot

Small were the general laborers. Hal Hunt would keep everyone in fighting trim.

Far to the north, in the realm of the Inughuit, the ice off the Greenland coast was melting. A narrow window of opportunity opened for the brave few who dared to pass through to the realm beyond. It was time for farewells.

GOODBYE

SIX OF THE CROCKER LANDERS—Jot Small was waiting at Labrador's Battle Harbor—gathered at the Brooklyn Navy Yard early on the morning of July 1, 1913, to make final preparations for departure. Today was the Americans' last day in a real city for at least two years. All of them had imagined the weeks and months ahead. There was a good chance that some of them would not return from their Arctic journey. They barely knew one another, and of them only MacMillan had been in the far north for even a single day.

They located the forty-three-year-old *Diana* moored among the flotilla bobbing in the East River. It wasn't a beautiful ship, but it should get them where they were going. A single smokestack, dwarfed by three masts, poked from the stern of the 151-foot-long, oak-clad sealer. MacMillan's black Bowdoin flag flapped in the rigging alongside the banners of Yale University, the University of Illinois, and Ekblaw's Theta Nu Epsilon fraternity.

The accumulated stench of decades of slaughtered seals assaulted their noses. Green cast his sailor's eye over what everyone agreed was an unattractive ship, certainly a far cry from the crisp navy vessels anchored nearby. The *Diana*'s crow's nest, high up on the forward mast, reminded Green of the deadly ice floes ahead. He hoped the two small engines in the stern would provide sufficient power to grind through the obstructions between New York and the team's proposed winter quarters on Ellesmere Island.

Fog had delayed the *Diana's* arrival from St. John's, Newfoundland, by nearly a week. Its crew used more precious time clearing the holds and removing the extra bunks needed for the spring hunting season. Every day wasted in New York increased the chances of getting trapped in the ice. As the crew finished its work, MacMillan contemplated the mountain of crates piled on the dock. Most major expeditions, including Peary's, took days to load their ship. But MacMillan put out the word—the *Diana* was leaving tomorrow.

The morning sun hung low in the sky when a team of hastily hired stevedores started heaving boxes onto the deck. The Crocker Landers rolled up their sleeves and joined in.

It was only now, on the eve of departure, that the other men understood what MacMillan had been doing for the past several months. A precise calculus underlay the entire operation. Boxes marked with red crescents contained geology gear. Grey triangles marked clothing. Grey diamonds marked trade goods for the Inughuit. Green had done a spectacular job of gathering equipment, but MacMillan wrote the shopping list, and MacMillan checked off every item on it. He had internalized Peary's mantra: Successful expeditions are well-planned expeditions.

Sweating laborers hoisted aboard everything necessary for establishing a community in the Arctic. Five thousand pounds of whole-wheat hardtack. Sixteen thousand rounds of ammunition. Two thousand pounds of sugar. Ten thousand gallons of kerosene. Two thousand gallons of gasoline. One hundred pounds of maple sugar. Shovels, files, drills. Lumber, nails, sledge runners. Grape juice, chocolate, ground peanuts. Eight crates containing atmospheric kites. Thirty cases of storage batteries. The 1,500-pound wireless set. Two hundred pounds of explosives. A canary (a gift for a missionary's wife in Labrador). A dentist's kit. Books, sheet music, and magazines. Seven phonographs and more than three hundred records ("the Eskimos are very fond of music," Ekblaw told a reporter, "not opera or classical music, of course, but ragtime or a good march, with plenty of rhythm and melody to it").

The *Diana's* hold filled. Its decks vanished beneath stacks of crates. Tons of pemmican, dog biscuit, and coal still awaited them in Boston, as did even more supplies in Sydney, Nova Scotia.

Twelve hours of backbreaking work finished the job. Sweaty and exhausted, the expedition members showered, changed into formal clothes, and trooped into Manhattan for their farewell dinner.

Another departure occurred around the same time MacMillan led his men off the *Diana's* deck. Three thousand miles away in Seattle, the spiky-haired, narrow-eyed explorer Vilhjalmur Stefansson was boarding a ship for Nome, where he would join the 247-ton whaler *Karluk* on a voyage above Canada's northern fringe. It was no coincidence that his projected course would carry him close to Crocker Land.

Alert to the danger, Hovey made Stefansson promise to avoid the unexplored zone until 1915, giving MacMillan the first shot at the new land. Suspicions lingered despite this deal. Ekblaw had reported seeing Stefansson's psychiatrist snooping around Champaign. Green had eavesdropped on the explorer's associates in Washington DC in hopes of uncovering his true intentions. "There has never been any doubt in my mind about his trying to beat us to Crocker Land," the ensign warned.

Before Stefansson left Seattle, a reporter asked him what he hoped to find. "If there be land," he replied with an impish smile, "it is almost certain to be inhabited by human beings."

It was still sticky and nearly 90 degrees outside when the freshly scrubbed Crocker Landers passed between the ornate columns of the University Club's Fifty-fourth Street entrance for a party thrown in their honor. MacMillan may have felt a momentary pang of regret; George Borup's old apartment was a few blocks up Fifth Avenue. Mac was familiar with this place, as was Green, a club member. Allen, Ekblaw, Hunt, and Tanquary took in the rich wood paneling and ornate ceilings, modeled on Vatican murals, for the first time.

Each man nursed private worries. Like soldiers heading to war, some crew members had formalized their romantic relationships before shipping out. Ekblaw had announced his engagement to schoolteacher Augusta Krieger in May. Maurice Tanquary proposed to University of Illinois student Josephine Perry the following month. Jerome Allen had married Victoria Clark, a junior at the University of Iowa, on Friday, June 13. "We thought we would be happier if we parted married [rather] than merely engaged," Mrs. Allen told reporters. The other men turned inward. Green harbored his inner demons. Hunt wrestled with the pain of separating from his family. MacMillan scoured his mind for any overlooked details.

They all kept their problems to themselves while enjoying a feast of kingfish *sauté meunière*, roast spring lamb with mint jelly, cold Virginia ham, chicken gumbo, new peas, potatoes persillade, and pear salad. Green's eyes lit up when a server placed a bowl of fresh strawberry ice cream before him; he was an absolute fanatic for ice cream.

Osborn rose. The crowd quieted. Raising his glass for a toast, he praised George Borup, described the hard work of raising money, and reminded the deep-pocketed audience that the expedition was $10,000 short of what was now a $60,000 goal. Then he read a letter of support from H. D. Borup, who was still in Quebec mourning his son. A representative from Telefunken extolled the expedition's wireless set, which would broadcast exclusive messages to the *New York Tribune*. Hovey gave a brief speech, as did Dr. Walter James of the American Geographical Society. Each expedition member rose in turn to mumble a few words.

Then, to great applause, Admiral Peary conferred his blessing.

"MacMillan, I wish I were in your shoes," he said. "You are going to find Crocker Land, you and your men. The greatest reward you can have is the satisfaction of knowing you have set foot where no man has ever set his before. I recall tonight the yelping of the dogs, the crunching ice and the motion of the ship. But, as I felt when I saw the shores of Crocker Land, the work is not for me, but for a younger man, and you are that man, MacMillan. You are fitted in every way to make this achievement."

Everyone offered the commander hearty thanks, except for Hunt, who was stinging from his tense meeting with the explorer a few days earlier. Peary had taken offense when the doctor asked whether he was certain that Crocker Land existed. Peary struck Hunt as haughty and arrogant, exactly the kind of posturing that rubbed the stoic Mainer the wrong way.

Hunt clapped, for appearance's sake, but he didn't mean it.

Green awoke at 4:45 on the morning of July 2. His muscles aching, he rolled from his berth on the USS *Hancock*, the navy receiving ship where he had bunked for the past several weeks, and put on his clothes. His eyes were gritty following a restless night of agonizing over last-second details. He picked at his suit, which was already clinging to his sweaty skin. Taking a last look around, he walked down the *Hancock's* gangplank and made his way to the *Diana*. Now he belonged to the expedition, not the navy. It was liberating.

A crowd gathered as the sun rose. Friends, family, and curiosity seekers wearing linen collars and straw hats wandered the *Diana* with official visitor cards signed by MacMillan. Hovey and Osborn dropped by to wish everyone well. At their insistence, the team donned straw boaters and suit jackets for some photos. Hunt remained in shirtsleeves with his tie tucked between two buttons. He was fuming at the contract Hovey had shoved under his nose two days earlier. According to the document, party members assumed "all personal risks pertaining to the expedition" and renounced "any and all claims for damages for loss of life or for limb or for illness." The museum would stop paying their salaries if they died or were disabled. Hunt signed, but he wasn't happy about any agreement that left his wife and daughter adrift should disaster befall him. He stood stone-faced as the cameras clicked.

Temperatures climbed into the mid-nineties, a few degrees below the record high but brutal enough that five New Yorkers died of heatstroke that day. "Crocker Land expedition started for the Arctic at just the right time," a *New York World* columnist suggested. MacMillan contemplated the storm clouds building in the northwest. Alas, they loosed only a few drops on the ship without affecting afternoon temperatures. Green ducked out twice to take a shower.

MacMillan and Hovey went over final details. Although the two remained on decent terms, they had bickered several times in recent days. Hovey pestered MacMillan about collecting valuable walrus hides that would defray some unpaid expenses. They tangled over whether the profits from selling the expedition's story to the mass media would go to the museum or the explorer. MacMillan was also angry that Hovey had permitted the *Diana*'s owner, W & S Job and Company, to hire non-American sailors. The *Diana*'s crew of Newfoundlanders looked shady to Mac. Americans worked harder and drank less than Newfoundlanders, he said. Hovey laughed off his concerns.

Green called for a yard tug at 4:58 p.m. As the *Diana* built up steam, a courier arrived with a letter for MacMillan. He examined the sealed envelope, which bore the logo of the State Mutual Life Assurance Company of Worcester, Massachusetts. There was no return address, and no indication as to who sent it. "For You," someone had written across the front. Then, in smaller letters underneath, "To be opened when every thing's gone dead wrong. Hope you'll never have to open it!" MacMillan knew Worcester from his teaching days, but did not recognize the handwriting. Enjoying the mystery, he stashed the envelope among his things.

The tug made fast to the *Diana*. Ropes splashed into the water. A gong sounded on deck. With pennants fluttering from its halyards, the ship offered a celebratory blast of its horn. Cameras snapped and onlookers waved as it puffed up the East River, following the same course the *Roosevelt* had plied on a similarly hot day nearly five years earlier. A band aboard the USS *Hancock* played "Hail the Conquering Hero," "Auld Lang Syne," "The Girl I Left Behind," and, with a twinkle of collective mischief in their eyes, "In the Good Old Summertime." "May we return as happily," Green thought as the Bronx slid by to port, and Brooklyn to starboard.

The *Diana* anchored off City Island that evening. Its crew rolled from their hammocks at five the next morning to cast off for Boston, where they spent two days taking on more supplies. Captain Wayte delayed his departure from the Hub City when half of his crew disappeared into the warren of waterfront saloons. More lost time. Wayte rounded up as many of his men as he could find and weighed anchor. The pier receded into the distance, along with the expedition's wives, families, friends, and everything else familiar to them.

Privately, the near-strangers who held one another's lives in their hands mulled their chances of becoming the last humans to discover a new continent. An awesome prize, an awesome hope.

"Goodluck and Bon Voyage to you and your men," Peary cabled MacMillan.

Fitzhugh Green sat alone in his cramped cabin, rereading a one-word telegram from his mother in St. Joseph.

"Goodbye."

8

A TRUE LEADER

It took MacMillan years of dreaming, planning, learning, begging, and mourning to get a team heading toward Crocker Land. With the *Diana* on its way north, the expedition leader began whipping his party of strangers into shape. He had experienced only limited success by July 9, when he wired updates of his progress from the port of Sydney, on the eastern edge of Nova Scotia's Cape Breton Island. Their hasty departure from New York left the ship a mess. Heaps of crates turned staterooms into storerooms. MacMillan had to shovel through a mountain of salted peanuts to unearth his bunk. A white-frosted "Crocker Land" cake moldered on a table in the main saloon. Scientific instruments cluttered the men's quarters. Wet laundry flapped in the breeze as the golden canary chirped in its cage. MacMillan kept those tidbits out of his telegrams.

The *Diana* rolled so badly on the waves that MacMillan dug out his typewriter because he could not write legibly by hand. Green threw out his back while organizing pemmican boxes in the lazarette. His hands were blistered and bloody. Ekblaw and Tanquary vomited over the rail, then vomited again. Everyone able to eat agreed that the food was terrible. The ship's cook displayed a knack for disappearing at mealtimes. MacMillan cheered up his "boys" with a round of sit-ups.

The farther they got from civilization, the more they pondered their own mortality. Ekblaw, his stomach in revolt, committed his final requests to paper. "Should I lose my life in the North," he wrote, "I wish that my body be left there." Green composed his own "in the event of my death" letter. "Make burial as is most convenient at the time, making no attempt at transportation," he declared. "Burial at sea is preferred in case of choice."

MacMillan studied his men for clues about how they would perform in the field. Green and Hunt worked hard, never complained, and were good at everything. Tanquary and Ekblaw, on the other hand, were "helpless . . . too scientific to be at all practical." Their quarters were even messier than the rest of the ship. MacMillan considered their untidiness evidence of disordered minds. Ek was the more pathetic of the two, having already lost both his field glasses and his compass.

I have "done about all I can now to insure success in the way of good men and equipment and now fate will do the rest," MacMillan decided. Outwardly confident, he struggled under the weight of responsibility. He had to assess the strengths and weaknesses of his personnel. He had to temper the crew's tendency toward drunkenness. He had to figure out how to stuff the supplies waiting on the Sydney docks into an overloaded ship. And he had to evaluate his own performance. Peary provided a useful model, but MacMillan could not yet say whether he possessed the commander's gift for leadership.

So he walked the pitching deck, grinding through possibilities, searching for neglected details. He opened crates in his mind, asking whether anything was missing. An oversight could be corrected in Sydney, or even up at Battle Harbor, but not later. There were no stores in the far north.

For all his burdens, he was confident about the expedition. The *Diana* was creeping toward Sydney at a pedestrian eight knots per hour. Not fast, but fast enough to reach Ellesmere Island before the ice closed in for the winter. Soon the men would find their sea legs.

Yet something Peary had often said nagged at him: "When things are going well, look out! The Devil is only sleeping."

Sydney marked the jumping-off place for Arctic expeditions. Its growth from a handful of residents to 17,000 within a few years amazed MacMillan. Unfamiliar hotels and restaurants were everywhere. The reason for the recent expansion, the Dominion Iron and Steel Company's massive new mill, belched black smoke over neighborhoods of squat, working-class homes clumped in the town's southeast quarter. Brand-new railroad lines transported the coal that fed the plant's voracious furnaces.

While the crew emptied the hold of ballast to clear space for some of that coal, MacMillan and Green checked into the Hotel Sydney, a lovely, four-story Victorian building with a wraparound porch and distinctive corner tower. The clerk installed them in the same room Peary had rented on his way to the North Pole—a positive omen if ever there was one.

The Crocker Landers savored their final taste of civilization. They gorged themselves in restaurants, laughed at vaudeville shows and funny movies, wrote dozens of letters, and lobbed sarcastic comments when the Diana's crew headed for the saloons. Ek and Green hiked through the woods above town, savoring their last views of real trees. Mac purchased six pairs of woolen underwear for each man.

Crewmen filled the hold with 335 tons of coal and dumped 40 additional tons of it on deck. They stacked 13,000 linear feet of lumber around the coal pile, then shoved 35,000 pounds of dog biscuit belowdecks. Their deliberate pace frustrated MacMillan's men, who pitched in to speed things along. Green promptly tripped over a crate, splitting his chin and spraining his ankle. Dr. Hunt taped up the ensign's foot and sent him back into action. On went the expedition's icebox, which had been forwarded to Sydney after arriving at the Brooklyn Navy Yard right as the Diana hit midstream. On went two cases of thermometers, some dental cement, and, perhaps most precious, five pounds of candy.

Groaning under 1,000 tons of supplies, the *Diana* rode danger-ously close to the waterline. Its scuppers, the openings that drained water from the deck, skimmed the surface of the ocean. Sailors muttered that any decent wind would capsize the overburdened ship. Then they tottered off to the saloons.

Captain Wayte summoned his squad with a whistle at 9:30 p.m. on Saturday, July 12. No one responded. "As usual our crew are all drunk and good for nothing," MacMillan complained. Green spot-ted some of the stragglers lollygagging on the beach with bottles in hand. No amount of persuasion could distract them from their reveries. Norse, Hal Hunt's Airedale, prowled the unmanned deck before retiring to his owner's cabin. The Crocker Landers unrolled their sleeping bags atop biscuit cases and fell asleep.

Hungover crewmen dragged themselves on board at 11:30 the next morning. MacMillan dashed into town for the last round of mail. It was 5 p.m. before the *Diana* left the dock.

Captain Wayte hugged the Newfoundland coast in case he needed cover against a storm. Allen rested his back, having tweaked it lifting a box of dog biscuits. Tanquary stopped vomiting long enough to join Green for an impromptu concert on mandolin and guitar.

Tank's stomach betrayed him when a northeasterly blow hit the next day. Tons of water sloshed around the deck. None of the Crocker Landers save Green reported for breakfast.

The wind quieted by the time the *Diana* entered the Strait of Belle Isle, which separates Labrador from the island of Newfound-land. Tanquary rediscovered his singing voice as the seas, and his stomach, settled. Wet sheets and sodden sailors dried in the sunshine.

Dr. Hunt gave a shout of "Iceberg!" from his perch in the crow's nest. It was a big one, trailed by a host of growlers, or small bergs, caravanning toward their death in warmer waters to the south. The Americans rushed for their cameras.

"It looks now like perfect weather and a fine evening," MacMillan declared on July 15. Battle Harbor lay several hours over the horizon. A light mist, enough to give a touch of atmosphere, oozed in while the men readied their bedrolls.

A loud crash jerked everyone awake around 1 a.m. Vibrations shook the *Diana*. Then came a terrifying ripping sound, as if some creature were tearing the ship in half. The vessel lurched to port. "She went well up and out for'ard and laid down on her side like an old horse who has decided to quit," MacMillan later wrote. A "deathlike stillness" gave way to a babble of confused shouts. "Is that the bottom?" "Her back is busted!" "Where's the captain?" "Back her!" "If you do, she'll sink!" Panicked crew members prepared to abandon ship.

The *Diana* jolted to a halt atop a gravelly ridge 100 yards off a treeless, rocky cove called Barge Point. The overburdened ship was so heavy that it could not back off the rise, and anyway, incoming water had extinguished the boilers. An enormous iceberg loomed through the deepening fog off the port bow. Images of the *Titanic* flashed across some of the men's minds.

Captain Wayte staggered to the bridge, half dressed and reeking of Jamaican rum. "It'sh a bit o' lisht she has, ain't it?" he slurred. Wayte had committed a series of terrible errors before retiring for the evening. Determined to stay close to safety in case a sudden storm arose, he set a course that hugged the Labrador coast. The captain either was not aware or did not care that the prevailing tide would push him even closer to shore. Then, with icebergs proliferating in the foggy gloom, he turned over the helm to his half blind, half deaf mate and descended belowdecks to resume his drinking. The Americans had expressed doubts about the mate's capabilities. Wayte assured them that his man's "knowledge of arctic waters had become a sense in itself which rose above the assistance of common eyes or ears." The unfortunate mate couldn't hear the breakers when the ship approached the shoals.

"The crew lost their heads completely," Green reported. Panicked sailors rushed around with lanterns in hand and bundles over their shoulders. Wayte argued with his second mate over whether they had crashed into Labrador or Newfoundland. Green grabbed the third mate.

"What in hell are you doing?" he shouted.

"We're sinkin', sir. We're a-goin' down."

Green laughed. "We're already down as far as we can go," he said.

"No, no sir," the man replied, gaping at an iceberg.

"Float her off!" someone cried. Grabbing shovels, they started scooping coal into the sea. Their only hope was to lighten the *Diana* enough to lift it off the rocks. It was really their only choice. Rough seas would dash the ship to pieces. If they simply waited for assistance from some passing vessel, the ebbing tide would slowly increase the weight pressing on the seabed until rocks pierced the hull.

MacMillan feared the expedition was over. This was his first moment of crisis, the first test of whether he was a leader or a mere organizer. He opted for a symbolic yet decisive action: he and Hunt piloted a motorboat filled with dog biscuits to the shore. "I realized how pitifully feeble were our efforts, and how infinitesimally small the weight we had removed in comparison with the tons and tons which must be landed on the beach," he sighed. But they returned for another load, and another. Racing the tide, Wayte's crew flung coal, crates, barrels, and bags off the deck. They needed help, and fast.

MacMillan dispatched a messenger to Red Bay, about eight miles to the southwest, with telegrams beseeching the museum, Battle Harbor, and Job Brothers for relief ships, and a replacement for the *Diana*. There was no time to wait for a response; he must act on his own initiative. Rallying his men, he urged more speed to save their gear. MacMillan kept scanning the horizon for a ship. Finally, three fishing schooners appeared from the south, and hasty negotiations convinced the captains to haul whatever they could carry to Red Bay for $200 apiece. Of course, MacMillan didn't have $600 on him, so someone scribbled out a one-page promise of payment "within a reasonable time."

News of the wreck attracted local fishermen willing to help, for a price. MacMillan recognized many of them from his previous visits. He hired a few dozen with assurances that the museum would pay them back. They trusted him because of his reputation for honesty.

This improvised relief fleet distributed most of the expedition's remaining supplies across a mile of beach. Mac sent Green and Ekblaw ashore to guard their equipment against salvagers. The weary pair threw down a floor of boards, erected a tent, and surveyed the dismal scene. "All that we had so carefully planned and packed now strewn as by a storm," Green sighed. A mountain of dog biscuit. Precious crates in heaps. Coal everywhere. The sun set, and fog swallowed the ice-filled cove. Having no wood for a fire, Green and Ekblaw dined on nine cookies and a can of cold soup. A nearly full moon cut deep shadows in the rocks as it illuminated their joyless camp.

Morning brought new hope in the form of the Canadian revenue cutter *Stella Maris*. Its captain had spent a stormy night anchored at Cape Charles, 15 miles to the north, and expected to find the *Diana* pulverized on the rocks. Amazingly, the previous day's blow had bypassed Barge Point.

The *Stella Maris* tried winching the *Diana* off the rocks. No luck. The wounded vessel was still too heavy. Wayte's crew carried their bags ashore. No ship had ever been freed from Barge Point, they said. Undaunted, MacMillan's men piled more gear onto the *Stella Maris*. The *Diana*'s smokestack groaned and creaked with every shake from the ocean. One more ebb tide would finish the ship.

At six o'clock that evening, with the tide flowing out, the *Stella Maris* tied up to the *Diana* for a final effort. The *Diana*'s engineer stoked his boilers, half convinced they would explode. The ship reversed its screw while the *Stella Maris* heaved. With a hideous scraping sound, the *Diana* dragged free. A joyous cry arose as the crippled sealer dropped anchor in deep water about 300 yards from shore, wounded but still seaworthy.

MacMillan, his body dragging and his mind clouded from lack of sleep, began reloading his beached supplies onto the vulnerable *Diana*. At this crucial moment his hired locals demanded a dollar an hour for their further assistance. He waded into the group, "impatient to examine this new species of Labrador fisherman who valued his services so highly." Making liberal use of what he called "non-dictionary words," he talked them down to fifty cents.

Twilight descended on the modest flotilla as it resumed its round trips between the shore and the *Diana*. MacMillan kept a close eye on his crates. "I didn't even get a board for me barn door!" one old salt complained. At 2:40 a.m., with the work well in hand, Mac asked Green to take over. Forty-two straight hours of stress, physical toil, and snap decisions had left him so tired that he barely made it to his bunk.

"I frankly believe that the backers of the Expedition owe the value of our whole cargo to the remarkable faith in [MacMillan's] honesty that lives on the Labrador coast," Green wrote to Osborn. "Nor can it be overlooked that only a true leader could drive such labor thru day and night without rest." MacMillan left New York as an unknown quantity, a poor substitute for the martyred Borup. Barge Point proved his mettle. His calmness, resolve, and physical endurance saved the Crocker Land expedition. Any doubts his men might have had about him disappeared. Although weary, the Americans limped away from Barge Point as a cohesive unit committed to the expedition's success, and to one another.

On July 17, 1913, AMNH president Henry Fairfield Osborn was relaxing amid the luxury of Castle Rock, the magnificent estate his father had built in upstate New York in 1881 with some of his immense profits from the railroad industry. Osborn had escaped noisy, sweltering New York City for this retreat soon after the

Diana sailed. Since then he had received a few fragmentary reports of the *Diana*'s progress, the most recent one coming from Sydney. Assuming all went well, Osborn expected silence until the *Diana* reached Battle Harbor.

Nobody stumbled on Castle Rock accidentally. A winding dirt road marked its only access point. Nestled atop a lushly forested hill overlooking the Hudson River, the mansion's looming spire and red-slate roofs gave it a fairyland appearance that vaguely echoed the museum's own intricate silhouette. Visitors even passed under a low, stone arch as they approached the building.

One of Osborn's servants handed him a telephone. A voice from Manhattan had traveled 50 miles north to disturb his peace. Worse, it was a reporter, from the *New York Tribune*.

Are you aware that the *Diana* has wrecked? the speaker asked.

He was not. Director Frederic Lucas hadn't known either when the *Tribune* called him a few minutes earlier. Lucas rejected the story as the result of a false identification or a garbled communication.

Osborn asked for details. The reporter read a telegram from MacMillan to Job Brothers, the *Diana*'s owner, stating that the ship had run aground off Barge Point, a lonely cape some 40 miles downshore of Battle Harbor.

The *Diana* wasn't supposed to be anywhere near Barge Point, Osborn interjected. Was there bad weather or heavy fog in the area? The reporter did not know.

"Well," Osborn replied, "I want you to say that we all had and have the greatest faith in the officers of the ship. They know those coasts and they know Arctic work, and I'm sure that it was through no fault of theirs that the accident occurred." When the reporter asked, he acknowledged that the museum had not insured the $60,000 worth of gear on board.

"If the cargo of the *Diana* can be saved another ship will carry out the work," he continued. The more he thought about the situation, however, the worse it sounded. "This is a terrible blow for our hopes," he admitted. "Never did an expedition go north better equipped for the work which lay ahead of it than this Crocker Land expedition. . . . A setback such as this is almost irretrievable. I can only hope that some wealthy man will come forward and offer to aid us in starting another expedition if it should be that this one has to turn back."

Osborn hung up the phone believing that MacMillan's journey had ended before it even began.

Captain Wayte picked his way to Red Bay for the rest of the expedition's supplies, then swung the *Diana* back north so that he could assess the damage in Battle Harbor. These were tense days for MacMillan. Besides saving his gear, his top priority was convincing New York to allow the mission to continue.

Several days after receiving the call from the *Tribune*, Osborn, Hovey, and other officers at the museum still had only the vaguest idea of what was happening. No one in New York knew where the expedition was, what ship they were on, or where they were going. Fragmentary telegrams and newspaper reports suggested a total loss, or at least a severe setback.

With his expedition hanging in the balance, MacMillan sent the museum a stream of positive reports. "Conditions for northern work extremely favorable," he noted in one telegram. Ice conditions are "perfect," he observed in a follow-up, and "the boys [are] crazy to get north."

MacMillan "must think that the Expedition is hoodooed," Hovey exclaimed. With no solid information available, the curator had to trust the explorer's judgment. Hovey contacted Job Brothers, who offered another sealer, the *Erik*, for $4,250 a month, with a two-month minimum charter. MacMillan knew the ship, which had carried supplies for Peary in 1908. The AMNH's lawyers advised Hovey that the museum's contract for the *Diana* required it to pay another $3,800 monthly installment despite the wreck. All told, the unanticipated chartering, transfer, and salary expenses would put the expedition $16,250 in the red.

MacMillan's plight was worse than Hovey imagined. Job Brothers refused to lease the *Erik* until the expedition delivered the *Diana* to its headquarters at St. John's, Newfoundland, 400 miles from the ship's current berth in Battle Harbor. MacMillan objected. The *Diana* was taking on three inches of water an hour. Its keel was twisted, and its stack wobbled with every wave. Even a mild storm could swamp it.

A look at the calendar forced a change of heart. "It was now late in the year," MacMillan reasoned, "and only for a few days during the year are the doors of the Arctic open, and if one does not get inside when they are open, it means wait for another year." Crocker Land had consumed him for four years. He could not bear another delay. "If they won't bring the *Erik* here to me," he resolved, "I must go to her."

A vicious northwest gale hit the *Diana* on its way to St. John's. Water sloshed across the deck, and crewmen braced for the worst. Defying everyone's expectations, the ship survived the squall. MacMillan leapt from the *Diana* the moment it tied up at St. John's. He saw the *Erik* moored at the coal pier. Checking the time on the great clock in the cathedral overlooking the docks, he rushed to Will and Samuel Job's office and convinced the brothers to give him the *Erik* in exchange for his promise that the AMNH would pay for everything.

MacMillan hoped he was doing the right thing. Communication between New York and the north was slow and spotty. Both sides were acting on old information. MacMillan had received no official word that the museum would finance a second charter. Hovey thought the Crocker Landers were still in Battle Harbor. But Mac was determined to press on, and he liked what he saw in the *Erik*. Larger and stronger than the *Diana*, it was better suited for Arctic work. Green was less confident. "She was more roomy than our first craft," he agreed, "but old as the Ark and of motive power nearly as obscure." The weary ensign ambled into town for some ice cream while Mac hashed out the details.

Crocker Landers and crewmen spent two days transferring supplies onto the *Erik*, then lingered for an extra evening because the sailors were too drunk to sail. Stevedores scooped $2,000 worth of coal—bought on credit—onto the ship. On August 1, nearly a month after the expedition left New York, the *Erik* slipped out of St. John's bottle-shaped port with a new skipper, Captain Kehoe, at the helm. Although Kehoe gave evasive answers when asked about his Arctic experience, MacMillan took comfort when he saw officers and seamen who had worked on Peary's *Roosevelt* among the crew.

"Clean grit right through," Mac declared of his men. "We have had our hard luck," he decided. "From now on everything should go all right."

9

BLOCKED

THE *ERIK* CREPT NORTHWEST through Melville Bay, the broad concavity created by Greenland's sudden thrust to the west, at four miles per hour, half its maximum speed. Heavy fog shrouded the spectacular icebergs around it. Even with all the expedition's troubles, they had been fortunate so far. Sailors called Melville Bay "the Bergy Hole" or "the breaking-up yard." Conditions here depended on the summer winds, as fickle a savior as there was. Northerly breezes pushed the ice pack south, clearing Melville Bay of hazards. Prevailing southerly winds, however, drove obstacles into the bay, turning it into a deathtrap of jagged corners and cathedrals of ice.

The seabed beneath Melville Bay was a graveyard of ravaged sealers and whalers. Elisha Kane, MacMillan's hero, had almost joined those wrecks when shards falling from a crumbling berg nearly smashed the *Advance*. Crushing ice sank more than 200 ships between 1819 and 1852. Twenty vessels perished in 1830 alone, none more spectacularly than the *Racehorse*. When ice forced its way up through the keel and deck and shoved its three masts over the sides, the vessel literally turned inside out. Nearly 1,000 survivors from the *Racehorse* and other doomed ships milled about on floes during that horrible season. Legally bound to no captain, they indulged in a weeks-long drunken reverie, setting broken hulks aflame while waiting for the current to carry them to safety.

Fortunately for the Crocker Landers, 1913 was no 1830. Their trip from Battle Harbor had gone well, and the same northwest gales that sent MacMillan's crew scurrying to their bunks with seasickness also cleared most of the ice from Melville Bay. Except for the fog, conditions were ideal. When physically able, the men filled 100-pound bags of coal and posed for photographs with their new beards. They gaped when a walrus poked its ahead above the surface and admired the clouds of tiny auks gamboling overhead. Other than Jot Small falling through a coal hole and spraining his ankle, the expedition seemed back on track.

A glorious red sun, "like a fevered eye," penetrated the haze at 10 p.m. on August 15, ten days and 1,400 nautical miles out of Battle Harbor. Vibrant purples, scarlets, and greens pierced the grey gloom, illuminating an amazing sight 25 miles off the starboard bow. It was Greenland, the next major landmark on the expedition's path to winter quarters. A wall of deep sienna cliffs formed a protective barricade separating the narrow beach from the little-known interior. The Devil's Thumb, an 1,800-foot-tall shaft of black basalt, soared above the horizon. "This is a land of vastness," Ekblaw gasped. "Vast glaciers, colossal icefields, great mountains, illimitable distances, vast silences and vast loneliness; yet awful and inspiring."

MacMillan breathed a sigh of relief as he watched the midnight sun slide across the horizon. "I firmly believe that no one ever came north with so little trouble with ice," he said. The setbacks of the past six weeks, or indeed the past few years, no longer mattered. His adroit handling of the *Diana* fiasco earned him the confidence of his men. It was time to gather Peary's native helpers, enjoy the ride to Ellesmere Island, set up winter quarters, and finalize preparations for invading Crocker Land.

———

"Ah-gei-teq, ah-gei-teq, o-meak-suaq-mut!" MacMillan shouted in awkward Inuktun toward the *tupeq,* or skin tent, nestled beneath the black cliffs of Cape York. "Come out aboard the ship!" Captain Kehoe sounded the ship's whistle. Cape York marked the northern terminus of Melville Bay and the southern limit of the Polar Inuit's range. Whoever was living there would have seen the *Erik* coming hours before.

Four kayaks slipped into the water. Mac squinted, searching for familiar faces. As the rowers drew close he recognized Qajuuttaq, who had traveled with him in 1909. Mac chuckled, remembering the time Peary's cook fed the man a spoonful of Tabasco sauce when he was expecting maple syrup.

"His oleaginous coat of dirt cracked in diverse directions upon our mutual recognition," MacMillan wrote. Qajuuttaq clambered over the *Erik*'s rail "like a monkey" and shook everyone's hand, "white-man fashion." The curious Americans watched the reunion, forming their first opinions of the people who would surround them for the next two years. "I have never seen happier mortals," Green decided. Much to the ensign's surprise, Qajuuttaq and his companions did "not smell at all offensively, merely a slightly musty smell from the skin clothes they wear."

MacMillan quizzed Qajuuttaq. The strange language, a linguistic river of soft tones and long syllables, tickled the other Americans, who assumed MacMillan's Inuktun was better than it really was. Mac and Qajuuttaq's expressive intonation imparted significance even though the Crocker Landers had no idea what their leader was saying. Whatever the conversation was about, it possessed a pleasant, singsong quality alien to their ears. They picked up clues here and there, catching words repeated for emphasis and familiar syllables smashed together into lengthy phrases of uncertain meaning.

"Among themselves the Eskimos have an intimate way of conveying things, a method of expression and meaning which an outsider never grasps," Frederick Cook, Peary's bête noire, observed. "At most, white men can understand only a selected and more simple language with which the Eskimos convey their thoughts." MacMillan relayed the gist of his conversation while Qajuuttaq smuggled stray nails and bits of wood into his hood. Most of the tribe, around 220 people, was scattered throughout their northern grounds. Before visiting them, MacMillan wanted to recruit from among the handful that were off hunting about 20 miles to the south.

Captain Kehoe steered a southeasterly course until ice blocked their way. MacMillan called a retreat. They would get the southern families later. Over the next few days the *Erik* welcomed "desirable men," their families, and their dogs from Uummannaq,* Illuluarsuit, Neqi, and other settlements. A "settlement" meant any place where a few families gathered from time to time. Depending on hunting conditions, a "village" might remain unoccupied for three or four years. There was no sense of permanence and no infrastructure other than the remnants of temporary stone dwellings from years past.

Chaos reigned as some fifty Inughuit joined the expedition in groups of three or four, with their dogs in tow. MacMillan located Ulloriaq, Taliilannguaq, and Aqqioq. On came Tautsiannguaq and Nukappiannguaq. Aapilak, who knew Ellesmere Island as well as anyone, was a welcome passenger. So was Panippak, the grandson of Qillaq, the great *angakkoq*, or shaman. Panippak's son, the mighty Ittukusuk, a gifted hunter and one of Dr. Cook's traveling companions, also came aboard.

The *Erik* assumed the appearance of a floating rummage sale. Kayaks and *tupeqs* hung from the rigging and littered the deck. Sledges, harpoons, and furs—the accumulated wealth of the Polar

---

* The Inughuit hunting village of Uummannaq should not be confused with the larger community of the same name several hundred miles to the south, where in 1909 George Borup read of Yale's loss to Harvard.

Inuit—lay everywhere. MacMillan identified blankets, broken oars, and sails salvaged from Peary's expeditions. Children hung over the stern to watch the rudder and went below to admire the wheezing engine. Hunting parties clambered into whaleboats whenever a walrus came into view. Seventy dogs and thirty puppies mounted an incredible din. The Americans fenced off a pen amidships in hopes of containing the snarling pack but ended up surrendering most of the deck to a whirling mass of fur and teeth.

The crew warned Hunt that the wolf-dogs would kill his Airedale. While in his berth one evening, the doctor heard the din of canine combat. Rushing onto the deck, he found Norse battling a team of snarling sledge dogs. Norse held his own, much to Hunt's surprise. Having proven his toughness, the Airedale earned free passage among his northern cousins. Besides the cold, his only problem came when he strayed too close to a bitch with puppies. Infuriated by the intrusion, the larger dog clamped onto his nose. Norse squealed with pain, backpedaling until his antagonist released him. Lesson learned, he slunk off to fight another day.

Joint hunting trips with the Inughuit provided introductory courses in Arctic survival. On one such adventure, Green, Jot Small, and Carroll Sprigg, a judge from Ohio who had paid $1,000 for the privilege of riding up to Ellesmere, accompanied Ittukusuk and Aapilak on a walrus hunt. Setting out in the expedition's small motorboat, the *George Borup*, they sighted a 1,000-pound female cavorting with her calf. Sprigg shot the mother. Ittukusuk flung a harpoon into her. An inflated sealskin float on the harpoon prevented her from sinking. As the men celebrated their kill, the calf rammed the boat. It circled the craft, barking, then attacked the float.

Green suggested capturing the calf. Small took the rudder. Sprigg and the ensign worked a lasso over the animal's head. Shaking with laughter, they almost capsized a half dozen times before getting the rawhide line cinched tight. Another melee ensued as they hauled the beast, "bawling lustily," aboard. Ittukusuk and Aapilak sat on the walrus while Small motored everyone back to the *Erik*.

The prisoner flopped around the deck. Sprigg wanted to take it home with him, but the other Americans doubted they could procure enough mollusks and other invertebrates to feed a walrus. The calf's fate was sealed when a group of dogs attacked it. A well-placed bullet ended its misery. Hungry dogs made quick work of the body.

The *Erik* pushed up the Greenland coast to the Polar Inuit's northernmost outpost, Etah, the place where MacMillan and Borup had encountered Cook's associate Rudolph Franke in 1909. Etah sat more than 800 miles north of the Arctic Circle, at 78° 19' of latitude. A few natives joined the party there. Captain Kehoe then began probing for a promising lead across ice-choked Smith Sound so he could deposit his passengers on Ellesmere Island. No path emerged, so he returned to Etah.

Weather conditions deteriorated. The wind swung from the north to the southwest, jamming floes together until the narrow channel between Greenland and Ellesmere became a solid sheet of ice 12 feet thick in places. MacMillan, so confident a few days earlier, was nervous. It was imperative that he reach the other side of the channel. He planned on spending the winter spreading caches across Ellesmere toward Cape Thomas Hubbard, copying Peary's system of leapfrogging his way as close to his ultimate destination as possible. If he wintered on Greenland instead of Ellesmere, his cache parties would have to steer their heavy, supply-laden sledges across Smith Sound, a dangerous and time-consuming proposition.

Two more tries followed, both unsuccessful. Captain Kehoe treated the 30-mile-wide Smith Sound like a gaping chasm. Inexperience made him ice-shy. He refused to barrel into promising leads or challenge weak points in the pack. "Over timid in the extreme," Green complained. MacMillan urged Kehoe to take a chance, however small, to get them to their destination. Bob Bartlett would have got them through, he fumed.

Kehoe was terrified. The Barge Point debacle had put the Crocker Landers far behind schedule. Summer was ending, and the ice was closing in. Kehoe had left port with only two months of provisions on board. Should the ice trap his ship, his crew might starve long before the spring thaw released them. Food supplies were running low. MacMillan kept his team's stores under guard lest the sailors loot them.

MacMillan sent his men out hunting for walruses and Arctic hares. Kehoe dithered, afraid to push above Etah. Fearing their captain was about to surrender, the Americans started scouting potential sites for a headquarters on the Greenland side of the sound. There was still hope of reaching Ellesmere. Alone or in pairs, they climbed 1,100-foot-high Cape Ohlsen to inspect the ice and gaze at their destination. Each promising view sent them scurrying aboard the *Erik* for another futile attempt at a crossing.

August slipped away, and the Americans' frustration mounted. Sheets of new ice thickened with every frigid night. Flocks of auks passed overhead, bound for their winter grounds along the Labrador, Newfoundland, and New England coasts. Winter was approaching.

On the afternoon of August 25, Captain Kehoe steamed out of Etah's inlet for a fourth and final stab at getting over to Ellesmere. It proved a short trip, because the ice clogging Smith Sound was even denser than on previous attempts. Defeated, he steered the *Erik* back to Etah, having never gotten more than half way across. "To remain here, turned back, because a disinterested Newfoundland captain has the timidity of years, rankles a little," Green bristled. "Another great disappointment," MacMillan lamented.

George Borup had worried about this exact situation. "On no condition, if we can help it, do we want to make our winter quarters in Greenland," he had told the *New York Times* a few months before his death, "as we would not be able to push our fall campaign of advance supplies to Cape [Thomas] Hubbard the way we plan."

MacMillan had to rewrite the agenda. Etah, not Ellesmere, would be their winter home. At least it was familiar ground, the site of many rambles with Borup in 1908. It was an imperfect location, often exposed to heavy winds, but not without its merits. A fringe of looming cliffs provided a modicum of shelter and a potential location for wireless aerials. A freshwater stream trickled from the hills. Etah was also a good hunting spot, with abundant walruses lurking a few miles down the coast.

Kehoe anchored the *Erik* alongside a limestone ledge the men dubbed Provision Point. With help from the Inughuit, the crew began conveying the Americans' crates down a hastily constructed wooden gangway. Off came their radio, tools, and books. Green's precious candy. Thousands of board feet of lumber, more wood than existed in all of northern Greenland. Forty tons of coal. Somewhere in that man-made mountain was the envelope MacMillan should not open unless everything went "dead wrong."

Everyone moved at top speed. The Crocker Landers wanted a weatherproof camp before winter took hold. Captain Kehoe wanted his passengers gone before the ice captured his ship.

Mac's men spent their few resting moments writing long letters home, cognizant that those were the last words anyone would receive from them for at least eight months. Maybe more, depending on whether they were able to sledge their mail south at some point, and whether a Danish steamer reached southern Greenland next year. Maybe never.

They kept their messages positive, glossing over past difficulties in anticipation of future victories. Green praised MacMillan's "buoyant optimism and human insight." Ekblaw assured the museum that "we are all optimistic and determined," and promised that "the scientific projects of your Crocker Land Expedition will not be seriously affected by the change of plans." MacMillan composed cheerful missives for his family, an article for the *New York*

Tribune, and a salutary message intended for public consumption. "After we bid [the crew] goodbye, and they and the *Erik* are gone," he wrote, "we shall again turn our faces to the work and problems before us, alone except for the gentle, patient, little brown people, the Inuits, who will help us. We greet you all who have helped us, all who are interested in our welfare and think of us, and then the North claims us."

Hunt felt the pain of separation most of all. In many ways the surgeon was the stereotypical Mainer, a rugged man who did his job and buried his troubles deep inside. He had proven himself a top-notch field doctor who nursed his patients through the dings and ailments imposed by the strenuous life. Everyone admired his work ethic.

Now he was scared and lonely, two unfamiliar emotions for that great bear of a man. He was afraid of the cold, but no one needed to know that. The emotional strain was worse. Hunt loved adventure. He also loved the family he would not see for two years. He had never fully understood how important they were until he left them. Ruth, his young daughter, would be a different person by the time he came home—if he came home. He was even separating from Norse. The Airedale's coat was insufficient for Arctic temperatures, so the doctor sent him back with the *Erik*.

In this moment of parting, the stoic man revealed his tender heart. "My Own True Love," he began a letter to his wife, Marion. "This may be the last chance I will have to write you." Hunt's tidy, wide-spaced writing filled the page. "I am more than homesick to see you, dear, and just to think of two years ahead yet. . . . Will it ever come, sweetheart, when we shall be together again?"

He spoke with the finality of a long separation. "I love you more than everything else in this world," he said. "I always shall be true to you whether you are dead or alive, and if we do not meet again in this life, please don't forget me, as I shall not you.

"Take care of yourself and Ruth."

———

Captain Kehoe maneuvered the *Erik* out of Etah harbor on the afternoon of August 30. He was in such a hurry that he did not bother taking on ballast. Unlike the overloaded *Diana*, his ship bobbed like a cork on the waves. The *Erik* ran fine until a northeast gale picked up five days out of port. Then the underweighted ship pitched and rolled, nearly capsizing on more than one occasion. Kehoe steered dead into the wind, ran the engines at full power, and hoped for the best. By the time the storm died down thirty-six hours later, the ship had been pushed backwards 25 miles.

The *Erik* crawled into St. John's with its freshwater reserves running almost as low as its crew's faith in their captain. Kehoe managed a few huffy words to a *Tribune* reporter waiting on the dock. "I'm mighty glad to be clear of it all!" he said. "I never seen th' ice like it wuz up thar." Some sailors, speaking anonymously, insisted the captain had never been north of Battle Harbor, and had never before commanded a steamer. No one in St. John's remembered how he got the *Erik* assignment. When pressed, the Job brothers admitted that there were no other captains available at the time. They refused to discuss his prior experience. Kehoe denied the rumors without elaborating on his past. He was through with Crocker Land.

10

HOME

THE EXPEDITION CAST THE *ERIK* from their minds. "We are done with her dirty hulk," Green wrote in his diary. Hard work lay ahead. The Americans and their Inughuit allies stood on a beach, surrounded by hundreds of tons of food, equipment, and supplies. There was no hope of communicating with the outside world, no way of summoning reinforcements or getting assistance. Etah was not the home they wanted, but it was home nevertheless, or it would be once they transformed their lumber pile into the grandest dwelling ever built in the far north. Falling temperatures and thickening ice spurred them on. Shelter was their first priority. With that secured, they could turn their attention to mastering the ways of the amiable barbarians who populated this region, before invading—peacefully, in the name of civilization—a mysterious geographical foe.

But first, rest. Fatigued from their recent trials, some of the Crocker Landers crawled into tents. Others unrolled sleeping bags on the beach and squeezed their eyes tight against the late-night sun rolling across the horizon. Soon their snores—Jerome Allen's by far the loudest—harmonized with the rhythmic beat of the Arctic Ocean lapping at the thickening ice.

———

A few weeks later, MacMillan enjoyed a quiet moment atop the roof of his new headquarters, Borup Lodge. He had always loved climbing, whether the object in question was a cliff in Labrador, the belfry of Freeport's Congregational church, or the 120-foot-tall chapel at Bowdoin, which he had famously scaled while in college.

He had no such grand ambitions on this warm September afternoon. Steady sunshine pushed the thermometer near the 50-degree mark. Calm winds made it a perfect moment for surveying his little kingdom. Moreover, he had an audience. A clump of natives and sweater-clad Americans awaited his next move with eager eyes and expectant grins. Although a modest man, Mac loved performing, whether for Worcester Academy students or Arctic children.

Taking a deep breath, he crouched, tensed his thigh muscles, and flung himself off the roof.

He stuck the landing. A perfect backflip. Cheers all around. MacMillan scurried back to the top of the building. The applause subsided. Time for work.

Three interconnected yet conflicting worlds were visible from his perch. The most familiar, yet the most out of place, stood beneath his feet, where Borup Lodge, a low, hulking, 34-foot-square structure half buried in a hill, was taking shape. Inside, beneath the roof-cum-launching pad, most of MacMillan's men had gone back to framing its various rooms. Untidy heaps of barrels and crates surrounded the building. It looked like a general store had exploded. Even in its half-completed state, the lodge marked an obvious imposition on the rocky, treeless landscape.

A second world lay within a literal stone's throw. MacMillan could see five rock-and-sod hovels squatting around him, two to his left and three to his right. They were winter homes for Inughuit, and had been for many years. Borup Lodge symbolized the intrusion of American corporatism, materialism, and ingenuity into the natives' environment. Companies had donated many of the lodge's constituent parts, or had sold those parts for profit. Books, store-bought games, and ceramic dinner plates sat unpacked in crates, as did an electrical generator and a radio.

Capitalism and mass-produced goods were foreign to the natives, who practiced no business except the business of feeding one's family. Peary's exchanges of guns and other desirables for furs brought a kind of proto-capitalism to the far north, but to an Inughuit, being rich meant having plenty of meat and a team of strong dogs. Private property was irrelevant in a society where one survived by sharing food and shelter. "When a man has enough up here his work is over," Green observed. "He spends no feverish hours plotting for his neighbor's wealth. He does not debase himself by gloating over less fortunate Eskimos." Even the stone houses, their most permanent structures, belonged to whoever occupied them at the time.

MacMillan viewed the Polar Inuit as friends. Like Peary, he could not succeed without exploiting their hunting, navigational, and survival skills. Mac admired the Inughuit, and his fascination with their culture far outstripped his mentor's relative indifference. He acknowledged that he and his companions were marginal figures in their tight-knit community. Northwest Greenland was the Inughuit's home, not the Americans'. They had their own agenda, and their own lives. MacMillan could not simply tell them what to do.

But the relationship went both ways. For the moment the Inughuit seemed happy toiling for MacMillan. Besides appreciating his inherent kindness, association with the explorer and his party meant steady access to a seemingly limitless supply of goodies. Westerners romanticized the natives' proficiency for constructing sledges from bits of driftwood and lamps that burned animal fat. In reality, they preferred using long boards and alcohol fuel. Iron tools, knives, needles, and guns made their lives easier. They would be workhorses so long as the material rewards outweighed the physical and emotional burdens of the alliance.

Beyond Borup Lodge, and beyond the native dwellings, loomed

the third great factor in MacMillan's world: nature. At 78°19' of latitude, less than 400 miles from the Pole, Etah was the northernmost settlement on earth. Its harbor sat at the inside end of Foulke Fiord, a four-mile-long west-east inlet of Smith Sound. Reddish-brown sandstone cliffs, some of them 1,200 feet high, overlooked its pebbly beaches. Brother John's Glacier,* a ponderous ice mountain that had been oozing toward the sea since time immemorial, dominated the fiord's eastern terminus.

MacMillan saw enough life from atop his roof to quash the belief, popular among his countrymen, that the upper latitudes were a barren wasteland. Fields of purple saxifrage, yellow arctic poppies, and orange-lichened boulders blanketed the slopes surrounding Etah. To MacMillan, the scene resembled an exquisite Turkish rug. A freshwater stream, which would be the Americans' main source of drinking water until it froze over, burbled between the glacier and the inlet. The black and white specks dotting the cliffs were nesting auks. On Littleton Island, out beyond Foulke Fiord, countless eider ducks waddled across springy ground moss and rugged granite knobs. A resourceful hunter could find food even in winter, when the birds had migrated and the wind blew almost without end. Had there been no walruses, Arctic hares, and caribou around Etah, the Inughuit would not have lingered there.

History stretched out in every direction. Mac looked across Smith Sound to Cape Sabine, the site of Greely's starvation camp. From nearby Cape Ohlsen he could trace Peary's path toward the Pole. The *Roosevelt* had sat in this harbor five years ago, its decks reeking from whale meat and walrus carcasses. MacMillan had bent Borup's ear with tales of Greely and Kane during long walks over those hills. The tenderfeet had found checkers, nails, and broken bottles from Charles Francis Hall's 1872 expedition littering Polaris Beach. Borup had shot a puffin at Sunrise Point, the rocky outcrop overlooking Foulke Fiord's northern exit.

---

* Elisha Kent Kane named the glacier after, not surprisingly, his brother.

Nature was a wild card in this delicate interplay between cultures. Not even a hyperorganized planner like MacMillan could control the wind. Nor could he bend blizzards, sinkholes, polar bears, enraged walruses, or rogue ice floes to his will. Like Peary, MacMillan personified the natural world as either benevolent or malevolent according to the situation—and nature needed to be on his side if he dared hope for success.

Three entities—the Americans, the Inughuit, and nature—must align if MacMillan was to achieve his goal. So where did MacMillan fit in this Venn diagram of overlapping actors? As he stood atop Borup Lodge, it is easy to imagine him as a well-intentioned sovereign sizing up his domain. Mac was *naalagapaluk*, the little boss, the intermediary between the Americans, the Inughuit, and nature. He stood at the center of the chart and at the intersection of worlds. Under his command, his men would employ both modern tools and traditional wisdom to conquer the wilderness, transforming Arctic dreams into newsmaking reality.

MacMillan was too modest to view himself in such lofty terms. Nevertheless, his rooftop survey offered an invigorating moment pregnant with possibilities. He believed in his crew, and they in him. He had employed the most competent natives in the tribe. Nature had blessed him with a beautiful September day. Except for Borup's absence, everything was perfect.

Then he slipped. Spinning down the roof, he tumbled off the edge and landed in a heap on the rocks below. The fall could easily have killed him. Mac clutched his ankle in pain. Green waved his arms until he attracted Hunt and Allen's attention. They located a pair of crutches from their supplies and rushed to their leader's aid. Hunt examined Mac's leg for possible breaks. Luckily, the doctor detected only a serious sprain.

Ten minutes had passed since Mac executed his textbook backflip. Things changed quickly in the Arctic.

———

Early expeditions to the far north lived in tents, their ships, or rude huts. Greely's men assembled a prefabricated bunkhouse at Fort Conger. Peary lodged in some warm, dry cabins during his career (for his 1906 and 1908 trips he headquartered on the *Roosevelt*). None of them matched the splendors of Borup Lodge. With justifiable pride, MacMillan called his new home "the most palatial residence ever put up in the Arctic."

Construction began two days after the *Erik* left, when the Americans and their Inughuit helpers found their pickaxes, climbed a steep hill rising from the beach, and started hacking a level foundation from the rocky slope. This approach proved futile, so they broke out the dynamite. Each explosion sent the natives scrambling for cover. Some recoiled from the noise, some enjoyed the fireworks, and some worried that showers of falling debris would demolish their stone-and-sod shelters.

Hal Hunt grabbed his rifle and went after Arctic hares. The others, fueled by the doctor's kills, transformed a mountain of lumber into a snug base of operations under the direction of general contractor Jot Small. First they placed the floorboards, then raised double walls of spruce separated by a four-inch gap that accepted a layer of Cabot quilt, a springy mattress of eelgrass sandwiched between sheets of tough paper. Eelgrass's high silicon content made it a natural flame retardant. Rubberoid roofing material covered the external walls. Its black coloring gave Borup Lodge an unfinished appearance, like a modern home waiting for siding.

Shingling the roof became a contest, of course, with Ekblaw and Green speeding up one side and Tank and Allen racing up the other. Ek and Green claimed a small triumph by reaching the ridge board first.

A steep flight of wooden treads conveyed visitors from the beach to the front door. Guests entered an 18-by-20-foot living room centered around a large table and a warm stove. A pantry occupied the back right corner. Four doors, two on each side, led from the main room. Green and Small occupied the 8-by-10-foot bedroom in the front left corner. Hunt and Allen shared the back left room. MacMillan took the front right bedroom for himself, leaving the Illinoisans, Tanquary and Ekblaw, in the back right corner. Each bedroom had two windows.

A gap in the main room's left rear corner provided access to the lodge's practical core. Three rooms, open to each other, ran along the back of the house. First came the carpentry shop, where the Americans would build sledges and other gear. Then came the engine room, where Jerome Allen would monitor and service the electrical equipment. Last in the row was MacMillan's photographic darkroom. A large storage attic capped the house.

The seven Crocker Landers utilized every one of the lodge's 1,156 square feet. Wooden bookcases accommodated a library of hardbound Arctic travel narratives and volumes about meteorology, geology, and philosophy. Civic organizations had donated long runs of *Atlantic Monthly*, *Harper's*, and *The Century* magazines. Some of the men, especially Green the bookworm, had brought copies of Joseph Conrad, Charles Dickens, Bret Harte, O. Henry, Victor Hugo, Jack London, and Henry David Thoreau.

Shelves in the main room held mugs, plates, and pots. Rows of glass bottles occupied corner nooks. Metal spoons dangled from nails. A few mirrors, none of them quite level, hung on the walls. The men tacked up tasteful magazine cutouts of attractive women. Photos of loved ones and an assortment of college and American flags personalized various niches. MacMillan stashed his mysterious, not-to-be-opened letter among his possessions.

On September 10, the group celebrated their first breakfast in the new house. Their timing was perfect, as a heavy snow the previous night had forced them to dig out of their tents that morning.

Borup Lodge was weatherproof and livable. Allen and Green made it exceptional. Under their direction the natives lugged crates containing storage batteries and the disassembled generator up from Provision Point. On inspection, the men discovered that

Robert Peary at his
cairn atop Cape
Thomas Hubbard, 1906.

Peary's ship, the
Roosevelt, carried
Borup and MacMillan
north in 1908.

George Borup (left) and Donald MacMillan.

Donald MacMillan poses in Arctic furs, 1912.

Curator Edmund Otis Hovey pushed the American Museum of Natural History to support the Crocker Land expedition.

Ensign Fitzhugh Green in his
Navy uniform, circa 1911.

Maurice Tanquary in 1913.

The S.S. *Diana*, ready to take the Crocker Landers north.

Supplies for the Crocker Land expedition. Symbols on the crates correspond to their contents.

Nukappiannguaq hitches a ride north on the *Erik*.

Borup Lodge.

The view from Borup Lodge.

Elmer Ekblaw in his room in Borup Lodge.

Green, Tanquary, and Hunt atop Borup Lodge.

Dinner at Borup Lodge. From left to right are Tanquary, Small, Hunt,
MacMillan, Green, Ekblaw, and Allen.

Dr. Hal Hunt showing the effects of the weather.

MacMillan with Ittukusuk, his companion on the journey to Crocker Land.

The view from a *qamutit*, with dogs on individual traces.

rough handling during the various loadings and unloadings had banged up some of the batteries. Many showed signs of leakage.

Snow fell as the duo spread machinery around the electrical room. An occasional Inuk dropped by to watch the magnificent generator take shape. All the parts seemed operable, and nothing appeared to be missing, much to their relief. If a careless stevedore had left just one of their boxes in New York, or at the *Diana* shipwreck site, or at St. John's, the engine would be useless.

It took ten days of labor to complete the assembly. Green inserted a crank into the flywheel and gave it a whirl. Nothing. He tried again. Nothing. Allen stepped in for a try. Then MacMillan took a turn. It looked like it was going to be a dark winter.

Green and Allen dismantled the engine until they located the problem. Someone had filled the tank with kerosene rather than gasoline. The engine ran on either fuel, but it could not get started with the heavier oil gumming up its cylinders. The situation demanded improvisation. One of them pinched a bottle of ether from Hunt's medical supplies. Priming the engine with this super-combustible liquid, they revved it to life.

Allen charged the storage batteries and strung wires for twenty-seven incandescent lights. Each man had a reading lamp over his bed, a remarkable luxury during the perpetual darkness of an Arctic winter. As a capper, Allen ran a power line for a small searchlight mounted over the front door.

"How do you imagine such a thing is possible?" they asked one elderly Inughuit.

"The little cords must be hollow," he replied, "and carry oil which becomes very hot in the glass bladders."

Like rambunctious boys, the Americans delighted in using electricity against the natives. One favorite prank was to wire the door latch and wait for some unfortunate to shock himself when he entered. The victim's surprised yells produced howls of delight.

Homesteading work continued through the fall. Tank and Ek erected an eight-foot-deep shed along the front and left sides of the house. This addition offered extra storage space, a buffer against the prevailing winds, and living quarters for some of the natives wintering at Etah. Three families occupied canvas-lined areas in the shed, each furnished with a small oil stove and a pile of caribou, musk ox, and bear skins for bedding. Emulating the Americans, the women cut out pictures from magazines to use as decorations, something unknown before the arrival of Westerners.

A pile of empty crates along the lodge's north and east walls acted as an additional windbreak. A tunnel made from dog biscuit boxes stifled the blast of cold air that rushed in whenever someone opened the door. Borup Lodge was so snug that the Americans cracked open the door when outside temperatures hit –30 degrees.

Allen ran telephone lines between the house and two of the stone huts. The Inughuit embraced this new wonder, picking up the phone whenever they wanted something from the big house. "Thus far I have had requests for dog biscuits (not for dogs but for themselves), candles, traps, dog harnesses and traces," Mac reported. "I am very much in doubt as to whether or not the installation will pay for itself."

Nothing came easy in the Arctic. Allen fought an ongoing battle with his temperamental engine. He circled the machine, listening for signs of inefficiency or wear. A miniature rainforest formed whenever steam rising from the 300-gallon hot water tank melted the ice accumulated on the ceiling. Water dripped onto the unfortunate mechanic, then refroze when he shut down the equipment.

Allen got headaches so severe that Hunt dosed him with morphine. Suspecting a gas leak, the engineer spent weeks searching for the hole or loose joint responsible for his misery. The culprit, he eventually realized, was the house, not the engine. Borup Lodge was so tight that it trapped fumes inside, the same problem Mac-Millan encountered in 1909, when he almost suffocated Uisaakassak and Tautsiannguaq. Allen became the team's biggest proponent of an open-door policy.

Borup Lodge became a home. The central area displayed the lightly organized bedlam one would expect from seven men living together. A sturdy table dominated the space, surrounded by the random detritus of an Arctic expedition. Piles of clothes spilled from the tiny bedrooms into the common area. Dog harnesses and deerskin sleeping bags lay here and there. Depending on the success of recent hunts, hunks of frozen walrus meat might be sitting on the floor. A large stove provided heat, dried clothes hanging from racks above it, and received whatever Jot Small, whose culinary ineptitude earned him the ironic nickname Cook-soah (the great cook), decided to make for meals. "I suppose by this time we have eaten a number of socks and mittens in the ordinary course of events since they are always dropping off into the stew pot," Green speculated.

The wireless radio set was the crown jewel of the Crocker Landers' attempt to introduce modern conveniences to the Arctic. It was also their lowest priority, less important than building a house or assembling their generator. Allen and Green began working on it in October. The navy men identified a 900-foot cliff a mile from the house as the best location for an aerial. Everyone pitched in for a frustrating, twilit day of unspooling heavy cable over rocky terrain. Falling temperatures hinted at winter's impending arrival; Green's right foot was frostbitten by quitting time. He reversed the damage by wrapping a puppy around his unbooted foot until he regained feeling in his toes.

Allen and Green spent the next day clearing boulders and other obstructions from around the wire, then winching it tight. The cable snapped, undoing all their work. Allen's shoulders slumped with disappointment.

In the teeth of near-hurricane-force winds, they lugged another wire up the cliff and raised an aerial. Upon further reflection, Allen and Green decided it would work better on a different ridge. Relocating the tower took a few exhausting days. With the external equipment in place, the two men tested the system's components.

Everything was in working order. Excited, Allen clamped on his headphones and powered up the radio.

Silence.

He tried again. Nothing. Allen twisted knobs and rechecked every piece of the apparatus. Nothing but static. It didn't work the next day, either, or the one after that.

Perhaps the aerial wasn't high enough, Allen said, or maybe the equipment wasn't as powerful as Green had assumed. He had no idea that the Canadian government had reneged on its promise to build a receiving station at Cape Wolstenholme, 1,100 miles away on Quebec's northern tip. Without it, the closest station was at Belle Isle, some 1,400 miles from Etah. Although no one at Etah knew it, an operator at Belle Isle was monitoring the airwaves every Tuesday from 10 to 11 p.m. in case Allen sent a signal. Not even a stronger transmitter, broadcasting through a better-located aerial, could bridge such a gap with any consistency.

Allen fiddled with the set during spare moments. He postponed the project in December when encroaching ice severed the ground wires. Next summer, he said, he would attach cables to box kites, boosting the signal high above the cliffs. "You may hear from us yet," Mac wrote in a January 1914 letter that wouldn't reach its destination for many months, if ever.

Plans kept going awry. A drunken captain. An Arctic skipper who was afraid of ice. A headquarters on the wrong island. A useless radio. MacMillan's expedition should have been entertaining newspaper readers with live updates from Ellesmere Island. Instead, it was sitting in Greenland, operating in the dark.

Mac was determined to keep moving forward. Marooned at Etah, cut off from the world, and facing the round-the-clock darkness of winter, it was time for the Crocker Landers to receive a crash course in Arctic living. Before February, when the first sledges were scheduled to leave for Crocker Land, all three forces—American, Inughuit, and natural—must be working in harmony.

11

ARCTIC LIVING

On October 24, 1913, Fitzhugh Green took a break from fighting the radio aerial so he and Elmer Ekblaw could hike to the expedition's temperature gauge at Sunrise Point. Recording weather conditions was a mundane if essential task. The Crocker Land expedition was a scientific venture, and scientists wanted data. There was little romance in compiling charts.

Today was different. Both men climbed the small outcropping expecting to see something new, at least for them. After logging the numbers from the gauge, they hung around until the sun faded beneath the southern horizon.

"It is snowing hard tonight," Green wrote a few hours later. "We saw the sun for the last time in four months."

Modern life revolves around the clock. It tells us, to the exact minute, when to get up, where to go, when to eat, and when to sleep. And yet, time-conscious as we are, something primal within us still aligns our behavior with natural cues. We venture out into the lingering evenings of summer and hunker inside during long winter nights. The green shoots of spring inspire thoughts of fresh starts, or of love, or of cleaning. No matter how grim our circumstances, we take solace in the simple assurance that the sun will rise in the east tomorrow. The cosmic pulse of sunrise and sunset confirms our link with the greater universe and gives us a daily sense of rebirth.

That heartening solar cycle disintegrates at high latitudes, warping our very conception of normality. Summers at Etah are an endless blur of bright hours. The sun rolls along an elliptical, almost horizontal course around the sky, bobbing low without ever disappearing. Winters are even more disorienting. "Daytime" loses meaning when sunrise is a thin streak of light hugging the southern horizon and sunset the disappearance of that smudge.

Darkness, or twilight, depending on the phase of the moon, defines the environment. Starlight reflecting off ice and snow creates an eerie jigsaw pattern of blacks, greys, and deep blues. Elisha Kane compared the winter to something that "Milton or Dante might imagine—inorganic, desolate, mysterious." It made him feel like "a man who has looked upon a world unfinished by the hand of its Creator." Peary observed that "when the stars are hidden, the darkness is so thick that it seems as if it could almost be grasped with the hand."

Arctic travelers who prepared themselves for the cold often ended up fixating on the shadows. "The darkness is sometimes too much of a strain on the nerves," Danish explorer Peter Freuchen wrote, because "when a man is left utterly alone for four months of darkness without a glimpse of the sun, any event that interrupts his familiar routine may present a situation he cannot master." Tales of insomnia, lethargy, and irritability suffuse Arctic literature. Winter even demoralized the Polar Inuit. "A gloom descends heavily upon their spirits," Frederick Cook claimed. "A subtle sadness tinctures their life, and they are possessed by an impulse to weep."

Expedition leaders invented time-wasters for the sake of preserving sanity. Crewmen played unending card games, attended lectures, and mounted burlesque shows. When Kane overwintered in 1853–54, he staged a fancy-dress ball, organized foot races, and started a newspaper called *The Ice-Blink*. The paper's motto, *In Tenebrius Servare Fidem* ("In Darkness, Keep the Faith"), conveyed either optimism or a plea for optimism, depending on one's perspective. "In the darkness and consequent inaction, it was almost in vain that we sought to create topics of thought, and by a forced excitement to ward off the encroachments of disease," Kane reported.

Peary broke with his predecessors' practice of hibernating through the dark months. Observing that the Inughuit visited friends and relations across northwest Greenland during the winter, Peary saw no reason why his men shouldn't make good use of the time by laying caches along his intended route to the Pole. The commander operated on a lunar cycle, sending out a cache party as soon as the waxing moon provided adequate visibility for lengthy sledging trips.

MacMillan was the rare southerner who enjoyed the Arctic darkness. "A night like tonight . . . gets its grip on me and pulls with a clutch too hard to break," he mused in January 1914. "It is a full moon and the hills and harbor ice a-glittering."

None of the first-timers could predict how winter would affect them. Green, the secret poet, had ruminated on it more than the others. During a quiet moment in the Michigan's 1911 cruise from Cuba to Hampton Roads, he wrote "A Tropic Moonlight":

How infinitely pitiful I thought
To look upon the twilight Sea with unglad eyes.
For as my chair was placed upon the deck
That sky and sea seemed met. I missed the sighs
That speak in springtime's Night upon the land.

"This black monster is at our door," Green wrote in mock horror in November 1913. "He cannot enter, cannot harm. We defy him laughingly. . . . The horrors of the Arctic night are all rot."

Like Peary, MacMillan planned to keep his men so busy that they forgot that sunrise, sunset no longer applied. There were photographs to take and meteorological data to collect. More important, everyone must learn some basic Arctic survival techniques if they were to have any hope of achieving their goal. Once the men were comfortable with Arctic living, sledging teams could begin caching the supplies needed for next spring's run at Crocker Land. In between these activities, the Americans faced the everyday challenge of filling the hours.

"It is strange how busy we all are these days although there is really nothing to do," Green joked. Life at Borup Lodge settled into a quiet normality. Oatmeal, hash, and coffee for breakfast, then weather readings or other data-collecting, then a hike—except for Jot Small, who declared he was "not going out until next spring." At four o'clock a dinner of roast seal, roast caribou, or roast ptarmigan served with canned tomato soup, canned beans, canned potatoes, or whatever other preserved foods tickled their fancy.

Visitors came and went. Tanquary showed Qillugtooq and Nukappiannguaq how to operate the Victrola. Ekblaw, who had played football at Illinois, shuffled groups of natives onto an improvised gridiron in the hilly area out front. "My quarterback could not see over the center's head, and all my men were built close to the ground," he reported with a coach's eye for detail. "They had a fine disdain for the rules, and used to pile up promiscuously, but they had a good working knowledge of the object of the game." Green added that "our rules were rather anomalous and the result was a combination between football, basketball, and association ball [soccer], with a good deal of roughness thrown in."

When indoors, the men played poker and whist, at least until their disagreements about the rules grew too contentious. With anything besides solitaire a potential source of conflict, they ditched their cards for a chessboard. Dr. Hunt unpacked the set he used for matches against his father. He offered a pair of thick stockings to anyone who beat him.

Inspired by his challenge, the men became round-the-clock chess fiends. The Inughuit also picked up the game. Matches assumed the gravity of grandmaster duels. Players spent hours hunched over the board, mulling the consequences of every possible move.

Except when Small took a turn. Cook-soah wasn't a good player, but his strategy of moving his pieces as fast as possible while distracting his opponent with an avalanche of profane, Cape Cod-inflected chatter produced some victories. "I laughed so hard that my head feels funny," Green said after one contest.

So they worked, talked, laughed, and got to know one another. Small, as passionate as he was ignorant, bragged about his plan to catch seals with a trawling net, a feat he never accomplished. Allen told stories from his days as an electrician with a circus. Tanquary fed a white arctic fox that he trained to sit in his lap. They posed for photographs after shaving half their beards. "It is a happy life," they agreed.

"Bowdoin! MacMillan! MacMillan! MacMillan!"

MacMillan jerked awake. His mates were smiling down on him. It took a moment to figure out why they were shouting. It wasn't terror, it wasn't anger, and it wasn't danger.

It was November 10, his thirty-ninth birthday.

Happy though they were, the Crocker Landers' days assumed a frightening sameness. There were no Monday-to-Friday workweeks, Saturday matinees, or Sunday newspapers at Etah. With the sun below the horizon, the men couldn't even think in terms of day and night. Celebrations dispelled the monotony. It made perfect sense to transform MacMillan's special day into everyone's special day.

The birthday dinner was a raucous if proper affair. Mac opened postdated letters from home, one of them addressed to "Mr. Donald B. MacMillan, Hon. Mayor of Crocker Land." Small produced a green cake of indeterminate flavor, festooned with red candles someone found in a box. Hunt read a poem he composed for the occasion. Green shared some of his candy supply. MacMillan claimed in his diary that "liquor of all and any kind was tabooed by general agreement"—a white lie. Hunt admitted that they "put the spigot in the whisky cask." Green also confessed to having "a bit of grog."

Two weeks later, on Thanksgiving, the men cracked open a bottle of champagne in honor of both the Pilgrims and Tanquary, who had turned thirty-two the previous day. Clad in turtlenecks and button-down sweaters, they devoured a banquet served by a native boy dressed in collar and tie. With "unbelievable quantities of caribou, pie, and other dainties" jostling for space in their stomachs, the Americans gave the leftovers to the thirty-seven Inughuit residing at Etah. Upbeat music from the Victrola enlivened a conflict-free game of cards.

These celebrations brightened a dark Arctic night that was dragging the Americans toward what is now called seasonal affective disorder. Sleep schedules had gone haywire. Some of the men rose early in the morning. Others roamed Borup Lodge until the wee hours. Everyone suffered bouts of lethargy and days when they couldn't escape their bunks. Small, usually a ray of sunshine, slid into full-fledged depression. He looked haggard, and he rarely left the house. He remarked that they would all die come spring. I will be the first to go, he said, probably in March.

The approach of Christmas perked them up. December 25 meant new, postdated letters from home. It meant presents, music, and the prepackaged feast H. F. Osborn had sent north with them. Native girls strung popcorn around the lodge. Green rooted through crates until he found a stash of candy. Other boxes yielded an artificial tree and yards of ribbon. Ekblaw selected records for a holiday concert. Dozens of incoming visitors swelled Etah's population to an amazing seventy-three people—nearly one-third of the tribe. MacMillan had invited them especially for the occasion "in order to draw the men we expected to make up our sledge caravan."

All the Americans bathed on Christmas Eve. Ekblaw volunteered for Yuletide cooking duties. At 6 p.m. the group sat down for mock turtle soup, canned roast turkey, corn, cranberry sauce, plum pudding, and mince pie. A fresh tablecloth, their first since arriving at Etah, lent an air of informality.

Their bottles of wine had exploded from the cold, but the brandy survived. Christmas cards and cigars raised everyone's spirits. "Joy to the World," "Stille Nacht, Heilige Nacht," and "Holy, Holy, Holy" played on the Victrola. The men distributed dolls to the girls, toys to the boys, and various baubles to the adults. MacMillan portioned out a 17-pound fruitcake. Everyone retreated to their rooms at 1 a.m. to read their hoarded letters. It was a "glorious" day.

The chess matches, the grog-soaked parties, and the recorded music reverberating off Borup Lodge's insulated walls reflected the Crocker Landers' belief that decent living meant transplanting as many Western creations as possible. Understandably, they sought familiar touchstones in an alien environment. Playing cards, canned food, and cast-iron cookstoves were little pieces of home.

American consumer goods, however, would not get them to Crocker Land. MacMillan had begun the party's transition into a new material world before the *Diana* set sail. While in New York, he gave the men a choice: either purchase the best cold-weather clothing available in the city, or wear what the Inughuit wore. A quick consensus emerged: the men would wear native gear. Their decision pleased MacMillan, who considered a good suit of furs "absolutely essential and indeed indispensable" for Arctic work. Probably he would have forbidden New York woolens no matter how the men voted. Those garments would not have withstood an Arctic winter, to say nothing of the journey across the polar ice.

Early British explorers, most of them naval officers bent on preserving discipline, sent their men onto the ice in dress uniforms. Later visitors such as civilians Charles Francis Hall and Fridtjof Nansen adopted native dress. Resistance to furs continued nevertheless. Some expeditions aimed for a civilized middle ground, by wearing deerskins or other North American pelts. These tended to be of poor design—including coats with button-up fronts that allowed cold winds to rip through the gaps—and were stiffer and heavier than Greenlanders' garb.

"Clothing made from the fur of Arctic animals is the only kind suitable for serious work in these regions," said Peary, who recruited native women to transform seal, rabbit, fox, and polar bear pelts into incomparable exploration gear. MacMillan followed his mentor's example, employing a combination of charm and bribery to convince women to work for him. The arrangement benefited both parties. In exchange for the finest in survival wear, the Crocker Landers housed, fed, and traded with their new employees. Working for MacMillan doubled the women's burden, as they retained responsibility for clothing their own families.

Inughuit girls learned tailoring at their mothers' sides. By their teenage years, they had mastered the *ulu*, a semicircular blade used for scraping and cutting skins, and could sew watertight seams with sinew from a caribou or narwhal. In idle moments they chewed skins to render them more pliable. Older women often performed this duty because their ground-down teeth didn't tear through the pelts. They gave up the job when their teeth became too damaged.

Clothing in the North focused on functionality rather than individuality. Making clothes took long enough without adding beads or other useless adornments. Outsiders therefore saw little difference between one outfit and another. A trained eye, however, could identify an item's tailor from the stitching and the pattern of furs used. Each piece was a unique work of art.

By December each of the Americans faced the elements like a true Inughuit. Next to their skin they wore woolen underwear rather than auk-skin shirts, which were difficult to clean. Over that they pulled on caribou-skin *qulittaqs*, or coats—no buttons to fiddle with. Women's *qulittaqs* included elongated hoods for stashing infants. The men's had smaller hoods ringed with fox fur that protected cheeks and chins from frostbite. Drawstrings sealed the garment against the wind. In an emergency, a man created an effective sleeping bag by tightening the cords, pulling in his arms, and hitching a sleeve over his face.

Sheepskin or bearskin leggings came next. Polar bear was warmer than sheepskin, but sheepskin was more durable. If well-maintained, a pair of leggings might last a winter. When leggings got wet with snow, Inughuit women hung them up until they were dry, then chewed them until the stiff skin regained pliability.

Soft socks of Arctic hare kept feet warm no matter the temperature, but no Arctic explorer would last long without a good set of sealskin boots, or *kamiks* (Allen clung to his green cowhide boots until he got tired of thawing them over the stove every morning). Women made the light, flexible, and watertight footwear from the skin of a ringed or bearded seal scraped down to the thickness of paper. A drawstring at the knee kept heat in and snow out. When traveling, the Inughuit packed fistfuls of grass they had harvested during the summer between their boots and socks to absorb moisture. Wet feet soon became frostbitten feet, and that meant disaster. A daily change of grass could be the difference between life and death.

Sealskin mittens completed the Americans' new outfits. These took some getting used to because, unlike mittens in Maine or Iowa, they barely reached the men's wrists. As with everything the Inughuit did, this design had a purpose. Short mittens maximized hand function and were easy to put on and take off, something dog drivers did often. The long sleeves of a *qulittaq* covered the wrists and hands, providing protection from the elements when the mittens were off.

When complete, the Crocker Landers' new uniforms weighed a tad more than 10 pounds, much less than the men had expected. To their surprise, they stayed warm in −30-degree temperatures, although high winds still pierced their bodies. MacMillan insisted that "it would be absolutely impossible for a man clothed as we were to freeze to death."

Dr. Hunt winced when Sissu raised the stone. A growling pup lay pinned beneath the Inuk. Sissu brought down the stone in an expert arc, smashing the dog's carnissal molars. It was a cruel but essential ritual designed to prevent the animal from biting through its sealskin harness. Hunt recoiled from the scene. "Eskimos control their dogs by brutality, which is not necessary," he observed.

Sissu, an expert driver whose life depended on his mastery of dogs, disagreed. For him, dogs were neither pets nor companions, but rather a type of currency in a world without stores or mail-order catalogs. In normal times he traded them for goods. In times of need the weakest became food for himself and his stronger dogs. Dogs were also his primary mode of transportation. Without them he could not follow seals, walruses, and polar bears through their annual wanderings. A poor team meant a poor hunting season.

So he studied them with a gimlet eye, deciding at around four months which ones he would train and which he would kill. Once he had removed a pup's teeth, he harnessed it, taught it the whip, and measured its physical endurance. If it lagged behind or did not cooperate with the team, he killed it. Survivors went into permanent service at around seven months. Around half of his dogs lived that long.

Nineteenth-century Europeans tried to improve on native methods of travel. Overzealous commanders saw pulling an 800-pound load through waist-deep snow as a test of manliness. Sir George Nares told his crew what to expect during their 1875 human-powered assault on the Pole. "If they could ever imagine the hardest work they had ever been called upon to perform in their lives intensified to the utmost degree," he cautioned, "it would only be as child's play in comparison with the work they would have to perform whilst sledging." Peary brought eight burros from Santa

Fe on his 1893 Arctic trip. They proved useless as pack animals but provided hearty meals for his dogs.

"The Eskimo polar dog is absolutely the only motor for polar work, and will remain so until superseded by the aeroplane," Peary concluded years later, "and when he is no longer of use as a motor, he can be utilized as fuel for the other motors or the men of the party."

MacMillan never considered using human-drawn sleds, or burros, or ponies (which a 1900 British Antarctic expedition tried, with predictably disastrous results). He had sledges manufactured in Maine and brought them in pieces to the north. Assembly began as soon as his men completed the carpentry shop. MacMillan emulated Peary's modifications of traditional Inughuit designs. His qamutits were about 12 feet in length, longer than native sledges and therefore able to carry more. Wooden planks hewn from the tall forests of Maine made this adjustment possible. Steel runners replaced ones made of walrus ivory. Flexible rocker runners increased maneuverability.

With the Inughuit taking the lead in construction, the shop produced eighteen qamutits by New Year's Day. Each was a thing of beauty, with oak sides and soft pine crossbeams held fast with thongs. Strong teeth were the most commonly used tools, supplemented by long knives and the occasional bow drill. On cold days, the craftsman shot holes through the wood with a rifle rather than bother with a drill.

Inughuit boys learned driving from a young age. The Americans had only a few months to do the same. MacMillan sped up the process by assigning each of them to a small group of teachers. When not stringing lights, coaxing the engine, or playing chess, the men took hands-on courses in basic survival. This was rudimentary stuff for the natives, the polar equivalent of learning one's ABCs.

Captaining a qamutit required patience, physical strength, and an almost intuitive connection with the dogs. A typical team consisted of ten animals attached to individual, 15-foot-long leads splayed out in a fan shape. This hitching method freed each dog to pick its own path over pressure ridges while minimizing the chance of the entire pack plunging into a lead. It also exposed shirkers; a slack trace invited a nip from the driver's 20-foot whip. The system did produce inefficiencies and frustrations. Outer dogs pulled at angles rather than straight ahead. Dogs often took divergent paths around an obstacle, sending the sled crashing into it. Righting and reloading capsized sledges was a regular part of sledge travel. Dogs snarled their traces about once an hour, requiring the driver to disentangle the lines with his teeth and unmittened hands while shoving the angry animals away with his feet and fists.

A shout went up from the natives: *qamutits* in the distance.

The Inughuit were not a sentimental people. They came and went at a moment's notice, often with few farewells and no hint of their destination. Their transitory ways puzzled the Americans, who struggled to accept that a family living in their shed when they went to sleep might be gone when they woke up.

Detached as they might seem, the natives got excited when new faces showed up. This arrival inspired particular interest. As the *qamutits* neared, Mac identified one of the drivers as Uutaaq, a legend among the Polar Inuit. Even the Arctic greenhorns had heard of him. A five-foot-eight-inch, round-faced hunter in his late thirties with a stern expression and an aquiline nose, Uutaaq had been an integral part of Peary's 1906 farthest north trip and his 1909 North Pole run. Peary called him "one of the sturdiest of the tribe," a high compliment considering the toughness of the average Inuk.

Uutaaq had not seen any Americans since Peary left, so he and his companion, Minik, a twenty-two- or twenty-three-year-old man with a square face and a strong jaw, hitched up their dogs for Etah when they learned that *naalagapaluk*, the little boss, had returned. Minik stood silently, betraying no awareness that the white men were watching him intently, while Uutaaq began speaking.

MacMillan translated for the other Crocker Landers. Uutaaq

was in a touchy mood, interspersing cheery anecdotes about Peary with complaints that the commander had never delivered all the goods he had promised his helpers. But the men kept their eyes on his partner. Once the older man exhausted himself, MacMillan turned to Minik.

Have you forgotten your English? he ventured.

"I guess not," Minik replied in a confident voice.

The Crocker Landers had never met anyone like Minik. At some level he had achieved what they were striving toward. Famous in two worlds, he was respected among the Inughuit yet familiar with American ways.

In 1897, when Minik was seven, Peary had loaded him and five of his tribesmen, including his father, Qisuk, aboard the *Hope*. Once back in New York, the commander presented the six bewildered people, along with five barrels of human remains, to the AMNH.

The museum accepted Peary's donation but had no idea what to do with this living exhibit, even though it had asked the commander to bring home an Inughuit for its anthropologists, most notably Franz Boas, to study. Officials stashed the Greenlanders in the basement. Newspapermen gawked at them and street urchins stared at them through the window well. Matt Henson hung around for a while to interpret for the frightened northerners. Peary never visited.

Minik struggled in his strange environment. He and the others battled illness from the moment they landed. Reporters jeered when they tried to heal themselves with traditional songs and rituals. Tuberculosis killed four of the six transplants, including Qisuk. The museum staged a fake funeral for the boy's benefit, then rendered Qisuk's remains so his bones could be added to its collection. Minik discovered the deception years later but never recovered his father's body.

An AMNH employee named William Wallace adopted Minik, whose presence had become a nuisance to the museum. The boy learned English, attended school, and lived an outdoorsy existence while continuing to battle an array of Western diseases. Always moody, he enjoyed life in New York City but never shook his mistrust of Americans.

Minik was a melancholy seventeen-year-old when a string of financial misdealings ruined the Wallace family. He quit school, checked into a cheap boardinghouse, and worked a series of menial jobs. Peary's 1908 announcement of another Pole run roused him to action. "If you expect to find the Pole this time there will be no need of a future trip," he wrote. "You found room enough to bring me [here]. . . . Why can't you take me back?" Peary refused him an audience. My ship is full, he replied through an intermediary.

In 1909 Minik snagged a spot on Peary's relief schooner, the *Jeanie*. As the ship neared Melville Bay he debated whether this voyage represented a homecoming or an exile. Raised in two irreconcilable civilizations, he felt close to neither.

Minik walked onto Greenland's soil for the first time in twelve years with nothing beyond a set of clothes and a basic medical kit. Curious Polar Inuit circled the foreigner who looked like them. The tribe was small enough that there was no such thing as a stranger. This man is Qisuk's son, translators explained. Their revelation broke the proverbial ice. Minik could rejoin the tribe.

Minik devoted himself to regaining his lost identity. An elderly relative named Soqqaq retaught him the language. He honed his hunting skills until he was among the best in the tribe. Yet he never fully embraced his Inughuit roots. His marriage to Arnannguaq proved disastrous. Disgruntled, he began taking longer hunting trips. On occasion he told stories about a place where trees touched the sky and sledges moved without dogs. Behind the bravado, he wondered whether he belonged in the north.

The Crocker Landers' arrival caught him between two worlds. Minik's conversation with MacMillan—in English—rambled from Melville Bay to Coney Island. MacMillan's men deemed him "a fine fellow" yet resisted the concept of an Americanized Eskimo. "It seems very funny to us to suddenly have this man, in appearance no different from the ordinary Eskimo, suddenly come to us and talk to us in our own language, and with us about our own land," Allen said.

MacMillan hired Minik as an interpreter. Although some of the Americans spoke "broken Eskimo," few of the natives were interested in learning English, which would serve no purpose after their visitors left. Mac saw many uses for this bicultural man. Minik could decipher the inscrutable Polar Inuit's inner thoughts, gather recruits for "anthropological and ethnological" experiments, and help sign up the best Inughuit for the expedition.

Fitzhugh Green saw Byronic glamour in the young man's angst. Minik's biography encompassed the kind of drama the ensign craved for himself. "He wants the south," Green concluded, "and at the same time admits that he could not live without the ice and snow that gives him life today." Minik was a "savage boy snatched from his home in the Arctic desert, planted in the blaze of New York life." Happiness would always elude him. "It is always so with the wanderer," Green sighed. "I believe I know the feeling myself and will never outgrow it."

With his headquarters established and his party acclimating to their environment, MacMillan laid the foundations for his next move. He rounded up his visitors on December 3, two days after Minik's arrival, to discuss his springtime agenda. Apparently, the Inughuit did not know exactly why *naalagapaluk* had come.

MacMillan described his program: a long sledge to Cape Thomas Hubbard, a journey over the ice, a new continent. His speech garnered a mixed response. The natives were eager to hunt in the rich game regions of Ellesmere Island. Crocker Land was a different matter. Some doubted it existed. Others wondered why they should travel so far for uncertain results. A few grumbled about poorly made sledges and one-sided bartering.

MacMillan tried to rebut their skepticism, with little success.

Then Uutaaq started talking. He recalled seeing rabbit tracks 250 miles out on the polar sea, a sure indication of nearby land. Heads nodded in agreement. MacMillan believed he had sold the mission. Unwilling to push the topic, he changed subjects and told the story of the *Titanic*, a boat larger than any man-made object his audience had ever seen, and the mighty iceberg that condemned it to the ocean floor.

12

REACHING OUT

"OUR ATTACK ON CROCKER LAND really began this morning," MacMillan wrote in his diary on December 6, 1913. At 7 a.m., in a flurry of barking dogs and stern "Huk! Huk!"s, five sledges lurched from the halo of the front porch light into an icy realm illuminated by a half moon and an ocean of stars. Elmer Ekblaw and Fitzhugh Green snuggled down atop two of those *qamutits*. MacMillan deemed them too raw to handle their own teams, so they traveled as passengers rather than drivers. Avikinnguaq and Taitsiaq accompanied Ekblaw, while Aapilak, Piugaattoq, and Sissu chaperoned Green. Their destination was Anoritooq, an abandoned Inughuit settlement 30 miles north of Etah, where they would establish the first of a series of caches in support of the upcoming Crocker Land trip. Hard work today saved trouble later; the expedition could leave Etah with lighter sledges if food, fuel oil, and other supplies awaited them along the way.

Captain Kehoe's ineptitude had left the Americans on the wrong side of Smith Sound and a few hundred miles farther from MacMillan's destination than he had intended. Rather than following Peary's path across the north coast of Ellesmere from Cape Sheridan to Cape Thomas Hubbard, then jumping onto the polar sea and heading for Crocker Land, the expedition would first have to cross the sound, then traverse Ellesmere Island's interior until it reached the polar sea. Not even the Inughuit knew much about some parts of Ellesmere, so MacMillan could not be sure of finding passable terrain or enough game to sustain his party. Of course, no one could say whether any animals lived on Crocker Land. If hunting there was poor, the expedition might well run out of food hundreds of miles from home. So their best chance of success lay in depositing supplies along their proposed route.

The cache party returned to Etah two days later, having dumped 400 pounds of biscuit, pemmican, powdered milk, and oil at Anoritooq despite temperatures of around –39 degrees, twenty degrees colder than Etah. Besides fulfilling their mission, the men also brought the welcome news that the 30-mile-wide Smith Sound was frozen solid, making the upcoming crossing to Ellesmere "comparatively easy." This was cause for celebration. Strong tides and heavy currents in the sound discouraged ice formation. In some years the party would have had to veer far to the north before finding good ice. No ice meant no dogsleds, which meant no Crocker Land.

MacMillan ordered Ekblaw and Green to cross the sound again and create another depot at Cape Sabine. They must hurry lest a southern wind bust up the pack. Early on the morning of the 11th, with 1,738 pounds of provisions on their *qamutits*, they skittered through a blur of dim sunlight onto Foulke Fiord.

Green held on tight, wobbly from a case of the flu that had limited his diet to a few spoonfuls of mush per day. He tested his belly on *nikku*, a piece of dried narwhal meat that looked and tasted like a plug of tobacco. He kept it down, and kept on going.

As luck would have it, more appealing fare happened across the group's path. A shout of *"Nanorsuaq!"* rang out—polar bear. Sensing fresh meat, the yelping dogs strained against their traces. Ekblaw and Green fumbled for their rifles. Piugaattoq got the first one, a big mother bear. Taitsiaq bagged one of her cubs. Green shot a second cub as it was diving into a lead. Sissu harpooned the runaway, which dragged him into the water, a dangerous development given an air temperature of −40 degrees. "These men seem made of iron," Green gasped when Sissu shrugged off the incident.

At these temperatures, the pelts stiffened before the hunters finished disemboweling their prey. Angry red splotches covered Ek's right hand where his skin had frozen to his rifle. That night they cooked bear steaks on alcohol stoves. Following custom, Ek and Green ate the hearts of the prey they'd killed. The Inughuit sang a low, thrumming bear song. "It sounds like the devil and is enough to scare anyone into hysterics," the Americans decided. The thermometer fell to −48 degrees, then fell off a rock and broke.

Everyone awoke the next morning in the two snow houses the natives had built. They feasted some more, then headed west onto Smith Sound. Ek and Green trotted alongside the dogs, stopping often to shove their sledges over, through, or around the snowdrifts covering the ice. Greenland receded into the mist as Ellesmere's jagged coast emerged.

The drivers set a course for the distant cleft marking Cape Sabine's location. After seven hours of hand-to-snow combat came another cry of "*Nanorsuaq!*" Piugaattoq had sighted a large male. Reenergized by the prospect of food, the dogs lurched toward the bear, nearly toppling their passengers in the process. The cornered animal summited a small iceberg, then came crashing toward the men. A blast from Taitsiaq's .44 knocked it down. Roaring in pain, *nanorsuaq* found itself surrounded by seventy-six snarling wolf-dogs, shrieking as the enraged bear smashed them with its huge paws. The men dispatched the 1,000-pound beast with rifle butts and killing irons while restraining their dogs from consuming the entire bear themselves.

Ekblaw, the Midwestern scientist, gnawed on a polar bear rib amid a crowd of "greasy barbarians." With the wind howling outside and 50 tough miles in their legs, the Americans planned on spending the rest of the day feasting and napping. But at 4 p.m., the

natives told them to mount up. For whatever reason—the Polar
Inuit rarely explained themselves—they were pressing on to Cape
Sabine, some 25 miles away, to lay their cache. A thirteen-hour
round trip returned the party to the killing grounds. The Americans could not believe what they had done, or rather what the
Inughuit had made them do. Green, his eyesight blurred from
the stinging snow, shuddered that "a white man would have been
forced to stop and probably would have frozen to death."

Their mission complete, the next day the natives steered their
teams toward Etah. Even a novice sledger could sense the dogs'
exhaustion. The animals drooped in their harnesses as they dragged
empty *qamutits* eastward across the sound. Green insisted on taking
the reins from Sissu. Three dogs' hearts failed during his 15 miles
in command. The Inughuit started sniping at the ensign. When
he ignored their complaints, they took out their frustration on the
dogs, several of whom became food for the others. "The return trip
was devoid of interest," Green later wrote.

MacMillan was on night watch when he heard shouting in the
distance. Switching on the front light, he informed the drivers'
wives that their men were back. Party members piled into the
lodge with stories of bear hunts and deep snow. The two supply
runs brought the Americans a little closer to Crocker Land and
gave MacMillan some insight into how his people performed under
harsh conditions. Like Peary, he studied his men's capacity for suffering and their ability to work together. Soon he would have to
distribute roles for the long trip.

Dr. Hunt hadn't expected to do much doctoring other than treating minor aches, sprains, and muscle pulls. Museum curator
E. O. Hovey, who had never been north, said that "the climate of
the Arctic regions is so healthful for white men that there is not
likely to be much for the doctor to do." MacMillan had advertised
for a "strong, fearless and enthusiastic" surgeon, not a gifted one.
Hunt's letters of recommendation therefore focused more on his

"moral character . . . courage and love of adventure" than on his medical skills.

Hunt conducted weekly weigh-ins, monitored blood pressures, and checked hemoglobin numbers whenever the men consented to a pinprick. He patched up the ankle MacMillan sprained when he fell off the roof and splinted Tanquary's arm when the scientist broke it goofing around on a sled. In truth, he spent far more time hunting than seeing patients. A lifetime of tracking moose and deer through the woods of Maine had left him as handy with a rifle as with a scalpel.

In early December, around the time that Green and Ekblaw made their supply runs, Hunt learned about a sick child 150 miles to the south, near North Star Bay. MacMillan gave him permission to make the trip. Besides creating a positive impression of the expedition among the natives, it would also give the doctor valuable experience in the field.

Within forty-eight hours, Hunt was following two Inughuit onto the sea ice, the fastest road south, under the gauzy light of a new moon. Along the way he treated a man who had become partially paralyzed two years before, perhaps from a stroke.

Four days of sledging brought the trio to North Star Bay. Hunt's dogs, not yet in top form, licked their bloody feet. The doctor diagnosed a case of rheumatism before moving on to his intended patient, a twelve-year-old girl with diarrhea, a high fever, and a painful abdomen. It was typhoid, a disease unknown in these parts before the arrival of Westerners.

Word of the doctor's presence spread. A man with two damaged fingers showed up. A rifle cartridge had exploded in his hand nearly a year before. Hunt amputated the digits by the faint light of a soapstone lamp. A native assistant dosed out the ether.

"Hunt is a fearful worker and is willing to do too much," Mac-Millan said. The doctor's appointment book filled up as word of his prowess spread. Asiajuk sledged into Etah two days after Christmas complaining about difficult, painful urination. It was an easy diagnosis; his wife had contracted gonorrhea from a sailor on a whaling ship about four years previously. Hunt had already treated two other cases.

Hunt considered the elderly Asiajuk to be "one of the most gentlemanly and trustworthy men I have ever met." An examination revealed that the Inuk's bladder was full to the point of rupturing. The doctor cleared the center table in the lodge for an emergency operation. "Brought to them by our Christian civilization," Hunt grumbled of Asiajuk's affliction. The patient was back on his feet within a few days.

More Inughuit arrived, complaining of the flu, the mumps, or coughs. Hunt performed another dining-table operation on New Year's Eve, this one to remove Atusunnguaq's infected toe. Someone threw out the specimen with their breakfast scraps. "I would like to know which dog had the morsel," Green laughed.

For the Inughuit, survival depended on reading clues embedded throughout their environment. The shape and movement of clouds, the halo around the moon, the brightness of stars, the path of an animal track, and the direction of a bird's flight all offered clues for solving these puzzles. By analyzing these indicators, Inughuit could predict with a fair amount of accuracy what the weather would be like the next day, where seals and walruses would be next week, and where they could find snow for temporary igloos.

Natural selection had fine-tuned their bodies for northwest Greenland. Humans are ill-suited for frigid climates. Our long limbs, thin and furless skin, and high profile all speed heat loss. But the Polar Inuit's rapid basal metabolisms generate enough body heat to maintain a high core temperature even in subzero conditions. They recover more quickly from chillings, and have an exceptional rate of blood flow to their extremities. They also tend to be more compact than Westerners.

As the rash of illnesses indicated, the tribe had no defenses against Western microbes. A single epidemic could wipe out the entire 250-person group, although their wide geographic dispersal made such a catastrophe unlikely. "They did not ask for us to come; we literally invaded their territory," Hunt worried. "We will disrupt the equilibrium of their society, and I wonder if we can in any way help them to hold onto their great qualities of self-reliance, originality, and kindliness, as our way of life encroaches on theirs."

Crocker Land was losing relevance for the doctor, who committed himself to improving the natives' well being and preserving their traditions. His respect for their way of life marked him as an unusually tolerant man in an era defined by social Darwinistic hierarchies of humanity and scientific racists' assertions that whites were biologically or perhaps even divinely destined to dominate dark-skinned races.

Hunt saw not superior and inferior people, but rather humans in need of medical attention, and he was the only person within hundreds of miles able to provide it. "While I am here I shall be their *nakorsaq*, or doctor," he decided. "This is not in my contract, so the requirements of the expedition must always come first, but when I can, I shall go wherever I am called." Hunt's sense of duty had sustained him through countless rural house calls in Maine. Now it pushed him to minister to one of the world's most isolated peoples.

Hal Hunt had found a new sense of purpose in the Arctic, but he could not escape the pull of home. The doctor fastened pictures of his wife and daughter on the ceiling over his bunk so their faces would be the first things he saw when he woke up. "Oftentimes I wonder whatever I could have been thinking of when I left them for such a long time," he wrote.

At times his homesickness translated into prickliness. He squabbled with the other men, especially MacMillan, whom he saw as too stubborn to take advice about maintaining healthy conditions in the lodge. Hunt did his job, and he did it well, even when regret overwhelmed him. "I would a thousand times rather be home today," he wrote on New Year's Day.

―――――

"I am of Scandinavian parentage," Elmer Ekblaw bragged when Hovey had asked him whether he could thrive in the Arctic, but soon the Illinois farm kid who became a geology professor at the state's flagship university began wondering exactly what he had gotten himself into. Ekblaw was a rah-rah guy and a campus mainstay who in 1910 helped organize the school's first homecoming festivities. He hadn't the slightest idea of how to be an explorer. "Will we take books of any kind with us?" he asked MacMillan. "What preparations do we make to keep ourselves amused profitably during the nights of storm, of no moonlight?"

Much to MacMillan's surprise, Ekblaw blossomed into a steady contributor who, unlike the increasingly miserable doctor, was having the time of his life. "I wish I might stay here five years," he sighed. Ekblaw enjoyed playing the Victrola for the natives and coaching their ad-hoc football games. As a scientist, he found the region fascinating. The geologist developed into a scientific polyglot, adding botany and zoology to his professional portfolio. Happy days of studying erosion patterns, preserving plant specimens, and studying the nesting habits of local bird species sustained him through the challenging first months at Etah.

MacMillan gave Ekblaw a present. Qillugtooq, who had clowned around in an old army uniform during Mac's visit to Fort Conger four years earlier, had arrived at Etah with an interesting piece of information, perhaps worthy of some gift or special favor from the Americans. I have discovered a meteorite as large as your cookstove, he said.

MacMillan wanted Ekblaw to see what Qillugtooq had found. Meteorites were big prizes sure to attract favorable press at home. MacMillan also saw the three-week trip as a means of ridding himself of some of his houseguests; the Inughuit's dogs were consuming pemmican at a frightful pace. Moreover, Qillugtooq said he had told a Danish trader named Knud Rasmussen about the find, and that Rasmussen had claimed the meteorite for the King of

Denmark. MacMillan could trump his claim by putting Ekblaw on the scene.

Qillugtooq, Arnannguaq, Aqqioq, Ivalu, and Tautsiannguaq left Etah on January 3 with Ekblaw in tow. The scientist made the 300-mile journey with his jaw agape. Majestic geological formations rose in every direction, representing several lifetimes' worth of potential research topics.

Ekblaw's outbound leg ended at the modest North Star Bay home of Knud Rasmussen, a self-described "civilized savage Eskimo." Born in Greenland to a Danish father and a Danish-Greenlandic mother, Rasmussen had tried his hand at exploration, ethnology, and the European lecture circuit before opening a small trading station in 1910 with a friend and fellow Dane, Peter Freuchen. They called their store Thule, after the Greeks' *ultima thule*, or farthest north.

Rasmussen had just returned from a 1,000-mile trip to northern Greenland when Ekblaw's party showed up at his door. There was little food in the house except for a year-old quarter of walrus. In something between generosity and a test, he offered his guest a taste. Ekblaw choked down the rancid meat. The two quickly bonded. Rasmussen was "a gentleman, every inch a man . . . a boon companion," Ekblaw said. Together they went searching for the meteorite. Even though neither of them had seen the rock, Rasmussen bluffed Ekblaw into believing that he had purchased it from Qillugtooq. When they located it, Rasmussen allowed the American to chip off a sliver of "his" property.*

Rasmussen and Freuchen had been pondering a Crocker Land expedition of their own but vacated the field when the museum announced its intentions. Whether from genuine concern or to discourage his competitors, he filled Ekblaw's head with dire warnings about what lay ahead. The weather will be foul for the next few

---

* The three-ton Savik I meteorite is now at the Natural History Museum of Denmark, in Copenhagen.

months, he said, so MacMillan should postpone his departure for Crocker Land until March. Otherwise, he would not find enough musk oxen to keep his party going. If truthful, the "civilized savage" had outlined an interesting paradox. To survive, the Americans must remain at Etah until spring neared, but leaving so late increased the likelihood of crashing through thin ice on the polar sea, or of getting stranded due to ice melt. Quite a lot for a Midwestern geologist to consider.

Ekblaw arrived back in Etah on January 21 nursing both these concerns and another. Inughuit traveling north from Upernavik had carried influenza and mumps to North Star Bay. Sure enough, the crew at Borup Lodge developed symptoms within a few days. Ekblaw's face swelled. Green started vomiting.

MacMillan insisted that "minor plagues" would not derail their mission. He either did not realize, or more likely did not want to admit, that a mysterious illness in Etah might discourage the natives from returning in early February, when he planned on launching his campaign. No Inughuit, no Crocker Land.

MacMillan faced another mounting problem from a most unlikely source. Fitzhugh Green had been his rock. The ensign had located supplies, cut red tape, and lifted the organizational burden from his leader's shoulders. No task, whether scientific or physical, seemed beyond the young ensign's capabilities. MacMillan saw him as a worthy successor should disaster strike.

Within this sturdy exterior, the two halves of Green's erratic character—the scientist and the poet—were at war. Although he spent the winter of 1913–14 dutifully reading up on ornithology and terrestrial magnetism, his Romantic side was coming to the fore. Green wandered off on 30-mile hikes through the Arctic night, reimagining the geological formations around him as monkeys, chickens, and other animals. He searched for the ghosts of previous travelers but never found them. These harmless practices stood somewhere between the poetic and the literal. While not expecting to encounter actual fur-clad spirits or polar bears made of ice, he nevertheless invested nature with spiritual significance, much like Thoreau, Emerson, and other Transcendentalists.

Green also fell in love. He had first glimpsed the woman on the *Erik*, skinning auks with her hands and teeth. "The wonderful expressiveness of her face attracted me to her," he confided to his diary. She was older than him, somewhere in her mid-thirties, and was four feet nine inches tall. The ensign watched from afar throughout the voyage north, then snatched occasional glances at her whenever she visited Etah. When she showed up for the Thanksgiving feast, he mustered the nerve to ask MacMillan for her name. "Ah-we-ung-on-ah," he wrote—his phonetic rendering of Avianngorneq.

They flirted a bit, with Green speaking in halting Inuktun. He sensed the need for caution, reminding himself "that her husband, Torngi is the largest man in the tribe." Torngi was in fact five feet eight inches and 177 pounds, a veritable giant by Inughuit standards. As a sign of good intentions, Green allowed Torngi to share his bunk in the lodge. Green also fell for "the prettiest woman in the tribe": Tautsiannguaq's wife, Ivalu, who was around twenty years old. "Her eyes and mouth would grace the handsomest white woman in the south," he gushed, "and her coloring is matchless."

Green was hardly the first Westerner to lust after an Inughuit woman. Jot Small was "quite enamored" with Aqatannguaq. Peary, who placed Inughuit women at the bottom of his social hierarchy, distributed them among his party regardless of their marital status. Matt Henson's loving relationship with an Inuk woman produced a son, Anaakkaq. Peary himself had two sons, Anaakkaq and Kaali, by "the belle of the tribe," Piugaattoq's wife Aleqasinnguaq.

Many early-twentieth-century Americans disparaged nonwhites as amoral primitives with no conception of proper, monogamous marriage. In fact, the Polar Inuit had strict conventions regarding marriage, just not the same ones embraced in warmer latitudes.

For example, they observed taboos against inbreeding even though they had no scientific understanding of genetics. Standards varied over the years, sometimes forbidding marriages between distant cousins, a restriction that would have prevented the future First Family, Franklin and Eleanor Roosevelt, from marrying in 1905.

Demographics dictated other marriage "laws." Wife-swapping, with the woman's consent, increased when population numbers dipped, although this practice was more about sharing available labor than producing offspring. Hunters often "loaned" their wives to other men before leaving on long trips. Abhorrent to most Americans, these customs were a matter of survival for the Inughuit. Fridtjof Nansen noted, "after all is said and done, it is possible that the most essential difference between our morality and that of the Eskimos is that with us the worst things take place behind the scenes . . . while among the Eskimos everything happens on the open stage."

MacMillan never betrayed any concern about Green's reveries, if he was even aware of them. Nor did he react when the ensign started arguing about what to bring on the Crocker Land trip, and how to pack their gear. Green pitched a fit when Mac told him that he would ride on a sledge rather than drive one. This decision made sense, as Green hadn't displayed much skill during test runs, but it galled him nevertheless. It seemed unmanly to discover a new land as a passenger. Peary would have agreed—hence his strenuous (and false) denials to critics who accused him of riding most of the way to the Pole.

"I am crazy to get out again and hate this staying at home," Green complained. Routine duties such as gathering weather data bored him. His moodiness pervaded Borup Lodge. Small considered building a partition in their tiny room because the ensign's nighttime wanderings kept him awake. Green moved into a nearby snow house, grumbling that the lodge was too stuffy.

Green started ignoring his responsibilities, and what he did do, he did sloppily. "They are not very great," he said of his daily tasks, yet completing them seemed an unbearable burden. It wasn't until January, four months into their stay, that he unpacked the seismograph. He spent more time complaining about the cranky tide gauge than he did observing it. Minor complications—buildups of humidity, cracks in the ice—overwhelmed him. "I find a new ailment almost every day," he moaned.

People change under extreme circumstances. Hunt discovered a passion for new people and a deep love for those he had left behind. Ekblaw located the adventurer-scientist within the stolid professor. Green's response ran in a different direction. The man who had simultaneously attended graduate school, purchased supplies, recruited personnel, petitioned navy brass, and mastered scientific disciplines vanished somewhere north of Melville Bay. In his place stood a gloomy Romantic who was good in the field but disruptive in camp. Science had lost its appeal. Poetry had won the day.

"Never in my life will I have anything so delicious as these walks in the brilliant moonlight," he mused following a long ramble. Green struggled to congeal the fragmented images jostling in his brain into something cohesive. "The keen difference between dreaming the day dreams of today and the dreams of no day at all, of no country, gain, nor man ——— the sordid blank that separates the best hopes of true ambition from the smallest pictured fancy of youth and health and love ——— this is the wall that separates the garden of my moonlight walks from the potato patch of my hopes and fears for the work to come," he typed during one disjointed moment.

"Can one of us restrain a smile?" he asked in the most private of his several journals.

MacMillan was an excellent organizer and a forceful leader, but he exhibited a curious indifference to the evolutions occurring among his personnel. His writings display a single-minded focus on the mission combined with a serene conviction that the boys would turn out all right. Mac had fallen in love with the Arctic, and so would they.

"Our gang is coming," Allen commented in early February. The Inughuit MacMillan had enlisted in the fall began pouring in from the southern settlements. A pale halo of reddish light heralded the imminent demise of the long winter night. Sunrise would soon impose the vivid colors of spring onto the blue-grey world. On first sighting the new sun, an Inuk would hold one bare hand in the air so that its warm rays could dance on their fingers.

MacMillan had tested and retested his equipment, scoured Arctic narratives, and pored over maps. Drawing from scanty reports of Ellesmere Island's interior, he had ferreted out every fiord and hill that might push his team off course. Every day mattered. The longer the exploration party was away, the more likely it was that melting ice would strand them far from home. MacMillan figured they could survive a summer on Ellesmere but was less certain about finding sufficient game on Crocker Land.

On February 11, MacMillan hefted his big Remington typewriter onto the table so that he could write out his final instructions. Jot Small and Jerome Allen would take care of the lodge while the others were gone. Like a nervous parent leaving a teenager home alone, Mac warned Small and Allen to beware of fire, watch for drips in the attic, and prevent the natives from pilfering oil. "Make our home just as pleasant as you can for everybody," he advised. Provide visitors with tea, sugar, biscuit, and meat, if you have enough. Tell the women—most of whom would have husbands on the trip—to keep the place tidy. Expect instructions about how to treat anyone we send back early. Like Peary, MacMillan planned to weed out the weakest drivers and dogs as he went along until only the sharp point of the spear remained. Loyal soldiers deserved food and shelter at Etah. Cowards deserved only enough to get them to their spring hunting grounds.

MacMillan had another piece of unfinished business. Inserting a clean sheet of Crocker Land expedition letterhead into the machine, he updated his will. If I don't return, please deliver the large bearskin in the attic to Bowdoin, he typed. Send the fox skins to Freeport, but save one for Ekblaw. Give the big bolt-action rifle to whichever Eskimo is judged most worthy. Distribute the Victrolas and rifles among our drivers.

The Crocker Landers had become experts at farewells, having already said their goodbyes in New York, Boston, Battle Harbor, and St. John's. But this one had a finality none of the others could match. MacMillan, Ekblaw, Green, Hunt, and Tanquary were going to the edge of the Earth. Should someone fall, his body would probably be lost forever, another vanished victim of humanity's relentless exploration of the unknown.

MacMillan had accounted for countless scenarios and trained his men to his satisfaction. Many of Peary's top guides were traveling at his side. Like his mentor, however, he agonized over the likelihood of some unforeseen disaster. "I am looking for trouble and guarding against it in every possible way," he informed Hovey in a letter. "The evil spirit of the Arctic is always watching and can change success into misfortune and failure within a few hours."

13

THE EVIL SPIRIT

In October 1913, as the Crocker Land team was settling into Borup Lodge, two Russian icebreakers eased into the tiny Alaskan trading post of St. Michael to take on coal. The *Taimyr* and the *Vaigach* were top-of-the-line vessels built for places other ships dared not go. For three years they had probed the frozen polar sea above Siberia for a lane of ice-free water that would enable year-round passage between Russia's northern ports, such as Murmansk, and warmer seas. Their search for a Northeast Passage continued a quest that extended back to the days of Peter the Great.

The squadron's leader, a St. Petersburg Naval Academy graduate and Russo-Japanese War veteran named Boris Vilkitsky, brought remarkable news to St. Michael. Lieutenant Vilkitsky's tiny fleet had been steaming across a patch of open water when his crew sighted high peaks in a place where his charts showed no land. Vilkitsky redirected the icebreakers toward the unexpected sight. The land grew from a few isolated mountaintops into a mass extending beyond the horizon. An excursion party rowed ashore so it could plant the Russian flag on what the lieutenant dubbed Nicholas II Land in honor of the reigning tsar.

Eager to determine the magnitude of his find, Vilkitsky followed the coast northwest for nearly 200 miles before the ice pack prevented him from going further. His road ended at 81° north, but the land kept going without any apparent end. The ships were 600 miles from the Pole, and 150 miles north of Etah—on the other side of the world.

Vilkitsky's brief telegram from St. Michael rocketed through the exploration community. According to the report, Nicholas II Land had little vegetation but abundant birds, reindeer, and polar bears. Early indications suggested that it covered half a million square miles, an area roughly equal to Greenland. Its size and location suggested that Vilkitsky had stumbled on the western edge of Crocker Land. American newspapers declared vindication for Dr. Rollin Harris, the tidal expert from the United States Geodetical and Coastal Survey whose predictions in the early 1900s had ignited speculations about an Arctic continent. "Existence of land in the unexplored portion of the Arctic Ocean should surprise no one," Peary told reporters asking about Vilkitsky's discovery.

The Russians might have found Crocker Land, and they weren't even looking for it. The Canadians were looking for it, but at that moment no one could find their expedition. Vilhjalmur Stefansson had not been heard from since his ship, the *Karluk*, had left Nome with Peary's former captain, Bob Bartlett, at the helm. Bartlett had reservations about the voyage. "She will never come back," he told Peary after inspecting the decrepit vessel. Bartlett's thirst for notoriety trumped his seafaring instincts. "I would love to land on Crocker Land," he said. "Hope to God [the *Karluk*] stays afloat long enough to get near it. . . . I hope with all my heart that things will come out better than I anticipate."

A handful of letters from Stefansson's crew reached the United States not long after Vilkitsky visited St. Michael. Although frustratingly vague, they suggested that the Canadian and some of his companions had lost contact with the *Karluk* while on a hunting trip across the Arctic ice. None of the men knew where either Stefansson or the *Karluk* was. One, or the other, or both, could be on Crocker Land. Or they could be dead.

Further investigation would reveal that Vilkitsky had stumbled across what is today called Severnaya Zemlya, a cluster of around seventy-five islands encompassing around 14,000 square miles of territory. This was not Crocker Land. Nevertheless, his discovery, along with the mystery of Stefansson's whereabouts, focused public attention on the Arctic. "Popular interest in polar research has never been at so high a pitch as it is today," meteorologist Charles Fitzhugh Talman opined in the *American Review of Reviews*. Because "the era of pole-hunting is now happily over," he continued, "the really important problems of the circumpolar regions can henceforth be attacked with a single mind." Like many other scientists, Talman viewed the quests for ninety north and south as "athletic feats" of little interest to researchers. "From a scientific standpoint," he concluded, "enough work remains to be done in these regions to last for several generations."

An amateur wordsmith named George B. Morewood offered a different perspective. In "Crocker Land," a poem published in the *New York Times*, he asked why "Vikings' sons" risked their lives "to find a land in the frozen north . . . where never the foot of man has trod."

"Are they forced on by their lust for gold," he wondered, "To brave the dangers this land must hold?"

> Nay, they are seeking the Arctic shore
> That the world may know just one thing more.
> For man may live, or man may die,
> But the tide of knowledge, rising high,
> Must ever flow on, from age to age—
> And this is his greatest heritage!

Adventure captivated Americans, not science.

Donald MacMillan was nearly 2,000 miles away from the latest edition of the *New York Times*, the *Review of Reviews*, or any other English-language publication. He had never heard of Vilkitsky and had no idea where Stefansson was. He didn't even know that Theodore Roosevelt, everyone's favorite adventurer, had run off to Brazil to explore an unmapped tributary of the Amazon called, ominously, the River of Doubt.

Mac had more important things on his mind as 1914 began. As a student of Arctic history, he was certainly familiar with Frederick George Jackson, a British explorer from the 1890s who liked to tell the story of a "distinguished Arctic discoverer" packing his *qamutit* for a long trip. While his dogs howled outside, the would-be explorer sat in his cabin, weighing a handkerchief in his hand, paralyzed with indecision over whether he should bring it or save weight by leaving it behind. "It is only by careful attention to weights that good results can be attained," Jackson concluded.

MacMillan was weighing hundreds of metaphorical handkerchiefs, winnowing out every extraneous item and every unnecessary mile of travel. Other than wintering in Greenland rather than on Ellesmere Island, the grand overview he had fashioned in New York remained intact. Eighteen sledges, divided into three teams, would leave Etah with 9,000 pounds of food and gear, enough for roughly eighty days. Four sledges would turn back at Beitstad Fiord, about 30 miles into the Ellesmere interior. The fourteen remaining teams would continue west, hunting whenever possible, until they reached Cape Thomas Hubbard, Axel Heiberg Island's northernmost point and the spot where Peary saw Crocker Land for the second time.

Cape Thomas Hubbard represented the failsafe point. From there Hunt and Tanquary's squadrons would split off to map unexplored portions of Axel Heiberg, leaving Ekblaw, Green, MacMillan, and their Inughuit companions to cross the polar sea to Crocker Land. Mac's party would survey as much of the continent as they could before hustling back over the pack ice in the spring. Should the breakup beat them, they would live off whatever game could be found on Crocker Land, assuming there was game there.

MacMillan gave Green the honor of commanding the first

team. According to Mac's precise instructions, the ensign would lead seven sledges to Cape Thomas Hubbard, picking up supplies cached the previous year and killing fresh meat at every opportunity. Upon reaching the cape, Green and his Inughuit should hole up and wait for the others. Ekblaw, Tank, and Hunt would follow. MacMillan preferred to dispatch his troops on successive days rather than going all together. Smaller units meant less rushing around and more attention to detail. Staged rollouts also saved time and labor, because the initial sledger broke a trail for the others and left behind snowhouses for shelter.

MacMillan's plan came straight from Peary's playbook. Green's effort would maximize the expedition's available food and oil while minimizing the strain on the leader. In essence, Green was playing the role that MacMillan and Borup had handled on the North Pole trip.

Green contemplated his equipment. What did one need when exploring a new continent? An extra set of clothes, three pairs of *kamiks*, and a sack of grass to keep his feet dry. Notebooks, pencils, laxatives. A hat, goggles, a bottle of diluted cocaine to combat snow blindness. Scissors, needles, and thread. Camera, film, binoculars, thermometers, watches, and a compass. Matches. A rifle and ammunition. An oil stove and a can opener. Snowshoes. Hair clippers. One roll of toilet paper.

No amount of strategizing could guarantee a smooth trip. "The evil spirit of the Arctic is always watching," MacMillan said, "and can change success into misfortune and failure within a few hours." Every step introduced uncontrollable variables. Pressure ridges and leads of open water awaited them. A vicious gale could halt travel for days. An ill-placed rock might twist an ankle. A hunting accident or an angry polar bear might do worse.

Another enemy—disease—had infiltrated Borup Lodge. Iggiannguaq, a talented driver, lay in Jot Small's room with the mumps. The aged Panippak swooned with the flu. Qillugtooq also begged off due to illness ("and cold feet," MacMillan grumbled). Green was recovering from a spate of coughing and vomiting. Ekblaw's mumps swelled his face. MacMillan determined to get out before his entire crew took ill.

MacMillan was mulling these difficulties on February 6, the day before Green's scheduled departure, when Tautsiannguaq ambled into the lodge to get some kerosene for his stove. MacMillan waved toward the wall of cans. Grabbing a five-gallon tin, Tautsiannguaq left *naalagapaluk* to his thoughts.

A loud boom a few minutes later sent MacMillan sprinting out the door. Smoke billowed from Tautsiannguaq's igloo. MacMillan rushed inside. The Inuk held his head in agony. Unable to read the writing on the tins, he had grabbed a can of gasoline instead of kerosene. MacMillan had forgotten that the man was illiterate. Tautsiannguaq had axed open the tin and filled the already-lit stove. The resulting explosion burned most of the hair from his head. "All of the skin which once covered Tau-ching-wa's face was gone," MacMillan dutifully recorded. "Too quick," the Inughuit moaned in Inuktun, "too quick." It was a miracle he was still alive; it was his second close call with MacMillan around, the first being his near-suffocation in 1909.

"We fully expect to be hungry and cold as we have never been before," Green wrote in a going-away letter to his mother. Despite such gloom, February 7, 1914, offered benevolent conditions, at least in Arctic terms. Green's thermometer read –20 degrees, not at all bad for the time of year. More important, the twilit sky was clear and the wind calm. Perfect traveling weather. His head was calm, his illness gone. Completing his final check, he shook hands with his mates, nodded at the seven native drivers, and put Etah behind him.

Maurice Tanquary readied his squadron the next day. Again, fortune shone bright, delivering –17-degree temperatures with almost no wind. The Americans repeated yesterday's goodbye ritual. Allen took a break from untangling two miles of depth-sounding wire—"something which Green should have attended to weeks ago," Mac complained—to shake the zoologist's mittened hand.

Ekblaw's turn came the next morning. MacMillan examined the geologist's swollen face, worried about sending him before his mumps fully subsided. But there was no other option. Off went the professor, with a stiff breeze at his back.

Hunt went fourth, riding out on February 10. To everyone's surprise, Tautsiannguaq drove his own team. With his scorched face swaddled in white gauze and throbbing in pain, he had no business exposing himself to the elements. He looked "like the Devil himself," Mac decided. But he put on a good show of toughness. Grunting a sharp "Huk! Huk!" at his dogs, he led the doctor away from the lodge with a snap of his whip.

MacMillan, Allen, and Small were the only Americans left at Etah, and Mac was leaving as soon as possible. The lodge remained lively nevertheless. Three Inughuit moved into the photographic darkroom. Four more took up residence in a crawl space under the floor. Others occupied Ek, Green, Hunt, and Tank's empty bunks.

Things got even more crowded when Knud Rasmussen piloted his dogs into Etah. News traveled slowly in northwest Greenland, but the constant movement of small groups of people eventually got everyone caught up on major events. The Dane had heard MacMillan was leaving in February, so he drove 150 miles up from North Star Bay to see him off. As was typical of the region's culture, he made himself right at home, taking late-night bread-baking lessons from Jot Small and commandeering the Victrola for a series of impromptu concerts.

MacMillan welcomed the distraction. While Rasmussen fiddled with the oven and flipped through phonograph records, sixteen of his men were fighting the elements somewhere between his bunk and Cape Thomas Hubbard, 483 miles away in a straight line. Not that anyone could ride a straight line in that hummocky, glacier-filled terrain. Those men were there because he had put them there, and they were beyond his power to help them.

Disaster could strike at any moment. Mac's most recent trip, a routine 45-mile run to Neqi, had nearly turned fatal when he drove his dogs within inches of a 40-foot cliff rendered invisible by the chromatic homogeneity of the Arctic night. A sheet of ice looked like empty space to anyone not paying close attention. MacMillan had been enjoying the rushing breeze on his face, "blissfully ignorant" of his surroundings, when he almost killed himself, his team, and Nukappiannguaq and Viivi, the couple in the sledge behind him.

MacMillan, Minik, and Piugaattoq planned on striking out twenty-four hours behind Hunt. Mac awoke bleary-eyed on the morning of February 11—the sun had almost reached the point where "morning" assumed celestial significance—following a sleepless night of worrying about whether he had everything he needed for the next three or more months. Mac left his "To be opened when every thing's gone dead wrong" letter in his room. He didn't expect everything to go dead wrong. If it did, nothing in that envelope was going to help him.

A familiar howling noise touched his ears. Padding to the door, he peeked outside. A gale-force wind sent him cringing back. Crocker Land would have to wait.

The next day was more promising. Mac ate a leisurely breakfast before loading his sledge. Crisp morning air caressed his fur-rimmed face. The thermometer registered a comfortable −22 degrees, and the wind blew at a manageable 20 miles per hour. Not ideal, but doable.

Rasmussen, Allen, and Small walked onto the ice to see off the party. Removing their mittens, they fumbled with their cameras, hoping for some dramatic shots of the first steps of their leader's historic journey. MacMillan joked that either their fingers or their shutters would freeze if they weren't careful.

With a crack of the whip, three teams of dogs sprang into action. Off they went, yowling and snapping into the distance.

Allen, Small, and Rasmussen watched until the sledges faded to an indistinct smudge. Rasmussen declared that he would be leaving soon. Small went back to his baking. Allen fired up his cantankerous engine so he could top off the batteries.

Allen was deep in mechanical bliss when he heard an unexpected sound. Stepping into the common room, he watched in amazement as Mac, Minik, and Piugaattoq walked through the door. Their assault on Crocker Land had lasted 120 minutes, the time it took to sledge to the mouth of Etah harbor and back. High water had turned the ice foot, the semi-permanent band of ice along the shore created by the tide's rise and fall, into a slushy mess. The uneven surface would wreak havoc with the dogs' feet. With hundreds of tough miles between them and Crocker Land, MacMillan decided to abort than court disaster.

So the Victrola again played late into the night.

"Friday the 13th!" MacMillan observed in his field diary. An inauspicious date for his third attempt at escaping Etah, but with the others out there somewhere, it was important to get moving. Following an early breakfast, he reloaded his sledge by electric light and the faint "dawn." Allen moped around; today was his one-year wedding anniversary. Rasmussen was packing too, having decided to head south for home.

At 9 a.m., MacMillan, Minik, and Piugaattoq ventured out again. The wind was calm and the ice foot frozen. MacMillan admired the familiar landmarks shushing by. What stories would he have the next time he passed Sunrise Point, or Polaris Beach, or Cape Ohlsen? Or the hills he had tramped with Borup? George would have loved this—a long excursion, thrills ahead, virgin land waiting.

Up the Greenland shore they went, free from any vestige of civilization. Almost. Minik attracted MacMillan's attention about an hour into their run. He had forgotten his tobacco box. "Can't discover new land without tobacco!" MacMillan laughed. Feeling indulgent, Mac slowed his team so the Inuk could loop back to Etah, grab his precious stash, and catch up before the end of the day. "I am glad that, as yet, I am not a slave to the habit," MacMillan wrote.

Following a restful night, a six-hour pull carried the three men across Smith Sound to Peary's old Payer Harbor shack at Cape Sabine. MacMillan found a cache of dog pemmican and other supplies waiting for them. His advance parties were doing their job. The house, nestled in a small depression and covered with snow, was a mess. Windows gone, no floors, "gloomy and dirty . . . filthy beyond description," MacMillan noted. "If Peary remained in this hut two years he deserves the North Pole." It would suffice for an overnight shelter. Good thing, because Piugaattoq was in no condition to build a snow house. The native felt woozy, and was complaining about a headache and swollen testicles. Mumps.

No time to nurse the ailing. MacMillan must keep pushing west. His companions would be wondering why their leader hadn't caught up. His team maneuvered their sledges onto the smooth ice of Buchanan Bay, a frozen highway splitting the two imposing ice caps that dominated Ellesmere's eastern reaches. Every hitching hole, empty pemmican tin, and patch of yellow-stained ice they passed was another sign that they were on the trail.

After a 30-mile march, much of it on foot, and taking on hundreds of pounds of food from caches, the trio yearned for a restful sleep. It was not to be. The snow was too dry to carve into blocks for a house, and they had not brought a tent. So, with temperatures dipping to –50 degrees, they prepared for a night in "Tramp's Hotel." MacMillan, Minik, and Piugaattoq tipped their vehicles on edge to break the wind. Mac's underclothes were damp with perspiration. Without a shelter, he had no choice but to keep them on. His caribou-skin sleeping bag was so stiff with ice crystals that he might tear it if he tried to get inside.

Minik and Piugaattoq settled in for the night. MacMillan sat on the ice, leaned against his sledge, and closed his eyes. His teeth chattered as he squirmed on the ice, fighting to quiet his mind. "Never again if I can possibly avoid it," he decreed.

Dark hills of cold, volcanic rock loomed over the scene. To all appearances, the only animals within that bowl-shaped vastness were one American, two Inughuit, and a few dozen dogs. The blowing wind rustled neither grass nor flower nor shrub. The nearest tree was hundreds of miles away. No birds interrupted the silence with song. A visitor from the southern latitudes might conclude that the living had no business in this realm of dead things, of rocks, and snow, and ice.

MacMillan closed his eyes. Sleep overtook him.

"The song of the sea ice is a very peculiar one," remarked Second Lieutenant Joseph Powell following his 1882 cruise in the Bering Sea. "It is not loud, yet it can be heard to a great distance. It is neither a surge, nor a wash, but a kind of slow, crashing, groaning, shrieking sound, in which sharp silvery tinklings mingle with the low, thunderous undertone of a rushing tempest. . . . The effect is strangely weird and almost solemn—as if it were the distant hum of an active living world breaking across the boundaries of silence, solitude and death."

Contrary to what most temperate-zone dwellers supposed, the ice beneath MacMillan's sleeping body was, in both a literal and figurative sense, alive. When grafted to the shore rather than adrift at sea, polar ice appears as permanent as a slab of limestone. Mac-Millan had no fear of it dissolving beneath him; temperatures that night were so low that water tossed into the air would crystallize before hitting the ground. MacMillan also knew there was no such thing as a stable ice field. Like plants and animals, the solid surface was engaged in a never-ending dance with larger environmental forces. It contracted when temperatures fell, opening cracks that filled with new ice. Warming temperatures made it swell until it pushed against the shore with tremendous force. Unearthly moans, bangs, and screeches issued from its heaving surface. Fissures emerged with shotgun-like cracks.

Conditions were even wilder out on Smith Sound. There, on

the open sea, currents and winds tugged at the pack, ripping open leads and piling up loose floes. Waves eroded the ice from underneath, shaking it with a semi-regular pulse sometimes detectable on the surface.

Just as MacMillan had many words for describing "earth"—sandy, loamy, muddy, grassy, rocky, pebbly—Arctic natives employed a wide vocabulary when describing ice. It was as vital that they know whether ice was thick, young, slushy, punctured with seal blowholes, or smeared with walrus feces as it was for an American farmer to know whether a piece of land was arid, fertile, or marshy. Ice conditions dictated the timing of hunting trips and the direction of sledging trips. Survival demanded a precise understanding of its present and future status. Experienced observers, such as MacMillan's native companions, could distinguish greenish first-year ice from bluish multiyear ice.

Ice played an important role in the Polar Inuit's cosmology. Once, while listening to floes grind as a tidal crack closed, MacMillan told Iggiannguaq that he found the noise eerie.

"That is too bad," Iggiannguaq said.

"Why?" MacMillan asked.

"They can't get out," Iggiannguaq responded. "They are the souls of those who have been drowned. They are doomed to remain there forever crying out for release and entrance into that happy world beyond."

MacMillan had a decent understanding of ice's figurative "life," and of its spiritual importance. Less apparent was the fact that an entire ecosystem was thriving beneath his chilly posterior. More than 200 species of single-celled algae called diatoms were breaking down organic matter excreted on the pack's underside by bacteria and other algae. Nanoflagellates ranging in length from 2 to 20 micrometers (a micrometer is one one-thousandth of a millimeter) grazed on the diatoms. Dinoflagellates, some of them 40 micrometers long and able to move three feet per hour, snacked on anything smaller than them.

Tiny brine channels and water bubbles within floes housed vast concentrations of life. These microscopic animals gravitated toward the bottom of the pack, where they received little sunlight but found temperatures and salinity levels resembling what could be found in the ocean proper. Several species of tiny crustaceans called copepods, along with their relatives, shrimp-like amphipods, joined the parade of organisms inhabiting the porous ice. Safe from cod and other predators, they replicated on a minuscule scale the same struggle of kill or be killed occurring in the visible worlds above and below them.

MacMillan, focused on finding something enormous, ignored the zoological cornucopia lying inches away from him. He slept his unsettled sleep, ignorant of the billions of creatures thriving in the noisy, rambunctious ice.

Warm. MacMillan's improvised bed on the ice felt warm. Unusually warm. Hot, really.

Fire!

MacMillan jerked awake, adrenaline surging and instinct seizing control of his body. He spun around. Flames rose from the short sleeping bag he used as a pillow.

He had told the men again and again—be careful of fire. A misplaced spark could ignite their house, leaving them without shelter for the duration of their stay.

An instant passed before he realized his sheepskin shirt was also on fire.

A few terrified moments of rolling and patting extinguished the flames. MacMillan sat on the ice, coughing smoke.

"A bit too close," he wrote in his diary, his words encompassing both his proximity to the fire and the narrowness of his escape. He shouldn't have fallen asleep so close to that cozy blaze built from empty biscuit boxes.

———

Mac, Minik, and Piugaattoq hitched up their dogs as soon as the singed American regained his composure. The others were out ahead of them, and things were not going well. They passed two dead dogs on the trail. Dogs died on long trips, but not so soon. Mac found a message from Dr. Hunt, who he assumed was far up the trail, informing him that Ittukusuk, one of his best men, had the mumps. Unable to travel, the Inuk spent three agonizing days alone with the doctor. According to Hunt's note, they had left not long before MacMillan arrived. Ittukusuk still could not walk, so they must be close.

Two hours later, they saw Hunt pushing his sledge over a pressure ridge. Ittukusuk was riding atop the load. Hunt explained the situation. His team had caught up with Ekblaw at Peary's Payer Harbor hut, where the geologist was waiting out a blizzard, then continued on together. Ek's inexperience nearly killed him. Even with the temperature at –50 degrees, the thickset scientist (2.57 pounds per inch) was sweating on the trail. The doctor advised him to change from his half-length *qulittaq* into thinner clothes, to no avail.

Sweat was the enemy of the Arctic traveler. With every drop he perspired, Ek made it easier for the wind to wick away body heat. He was trembling by the time they bunked down for the night. Ek lay atop his wet *qulittaq*, back to back with Hunt behind a windbreak made from boxes. Hunt awoke several times throughout the night. "I could feel Ek shivering," he later remembered. "Just as long as he shivered I knew he was alive."

The next morning, the same day Mac left Etah, brought more trouble. Ek's *qulittaq* had frozen overnight. It took an eternity for him to wedge his arms into the flat, furry iceblock. His fingers showed signs of frostbite.

Hours later, Ittukusuk took ill. Hunt volunteered to stay behind with him. The doctor was in a foul mood. Ekblaw's *qulittaq* mishap convinced him that Mac had outfitted himself better than his companions. Loneliness bothered him even more than his physical discomforts. Ittukusuk tried to stay chipper. Hunt, "with nothing to do and lots of spare time to think," grumped around camp. He missed his family.

With MacMillan brought up to date—although Hunt kept his personal problems to himself—it was time to get moving. Ittukusuk adjusted his position on the sledge before the combined parties launched themselves westward.

To MacMillan's dismay, they encountered Ekblaw, Green, Tanquary, and their guides one hour later. Their presence baffled Mac. These were his advance units. They should be well on the way to Cape Thomas Hubbard, yet here they were at Hayes Fiord, a mere 100 miles from Etah.

What is happening? MacMillan asked. Green spoke for everyone. He was in no mood for a fight. The ensign had not expected such extreme cold. He was bone-tired. For the past several nights he had not fallen asleep so much as lost consciousness. His feet were wet. Every part of his body hurt.

Green's misery extended to the rest of the group. A few days earlier, the venerated Uutaaq had told the Americans his tribesmen could go no farther. Sissu, Aqqioq, and some of the other Inughuit were vomiting. The dogs were vomiting too, bringing up a sickly yellow liquid. Diarrhea brought the pack even lower. The Inughuit blamed the dog pemmican: too salty. Our dogs will all die, Uutaaq told Green. No doubt my wife is dead too. He wished he were dead. We will hunt rabbits and seals until *naalagapaluk* arrives, Uutaaq decreed. Then we will go home.

MacMillan sent Minik to confirm Green's story while he took stock of the situation. Hacking coughs punctured the silence. Swollen faces evinced little interest in Crocker Land. Men lurched around in drug-induced hazes—Green had eased their pain with narcotics. Ulloriaq had shot his best dog after deeming it too weak to make it home. Minik's report reinforced MacMillan's assessment. They must retreat, and fast.

Mac put a happy spin on their failure, advising everyone that they had left early enough in the season to allow ample time for another shot at Crocker Land. Inside, he was raging. "I have come to the conclusion that there are several 'quitters' among the number, and much dead timber which I must get rid of," he fumed in his diary. Cowardice, not illness, had sidetracked his mission. The dogs looked fine to him. It was 1909 all over again, except this time he, not Peary, faced a revolt from the Inughuit.

"The hirelings refused to advance," Green sneered, ignoring his own rattled state. MacMillan blamed their intransigence on "chicken-hearted" elders like Uutaaq. A younger, leaner expedition was the answer. "Young Eskimos . . . are fond of adventure and willing to take a chance, while the older men wish to make certain of getting home," he said.

Seventeen coughing, spitting, road-weary explorers began their retreat to Etah on February 18. MacMillan ordered Green and Ekblaw to leave their nonessential gear; they could pick it up on their next time by. Hunt and Tanquary received no such command; their quest for Crocker Land was over.

His personnel decisions appeared to be driven by seniority as much as by competency. Neither Hunt nor Tanquary had blundered on this trip. If anything, Green and Ekblaw had performed worse. The ensign and the geologist, however, were the museum's first two recruits, and between them they could handle most of the basic science required on Crocker Land, so long as Green maintained his equilibrium and Ekblaw quit making silly mistakes. With fewer people to supervise, MacMillan figured he could solve any problems before they became too acute.

MacMillan was eager to rid himself of mutineers and curious about whether the dogs were as sick as the Inughuit claimed. His team, the freshest of the lot, set a blistering pace. Everyone else's dogs looked fine until one of Aapilannguaq's dropped in its traces. Only then did Mac admit that the pemmican was far saltier than it should have been. It must have been an embarrassment for him;

Peary had stressed the importance of personally supervising the production of pemmican.

The return crossing of Smith Sound became one more slap in the face. A blizzard shoved the dogs and the lightened sledges around the ice. The men, their heads buried in the furs atop their loads, fought to hold a steady course. A westerly gale screamed with such ferocity that the *qamutits* kept blowing out in front of the dogs.

The storm scattered the fragile armada. Trusting the others to find their way, Mac urged his dogs toward Etah. Eleven of his seventeen sledges were missing. Ek and Tank were nowhere to be seen.

Jerome Allen and Jot Small geared down operations at Borup Lodge as soon as the expedition left Etah. Allen tinkered with his engine. Small kept closing the outside door despite Allen's grumbling that the fumes would sicken them. Jot preferred sick to cold. He promptly wound up bedridden with violent headaches which he treated with morphine.

A mood of dull regularity permeated the cabin. With only a skeleton crew on hand and the springtime dawn on its way, Allen powered down the lights. Reading and writing became difficult. The women complained that it was too dark to sew. Allen's (married) eye lit on Tautsiannguaq's wife Ivalu, looking pretty in the red flannel shirt MacMillan had given her. "It would not be going too far to say that she is really beautiful," Allen wrote, his word choice suggesting either modesty or disbelief. Fitzhugh Green had recorded similar sentiments about Ivalu six weeks earlier.

Jot was sleeping when MacMillan and Minik's *qamutits* hove into view at 5 p.m. on February 19. Sledges blew this way and that in the fierce wind. Allen stared at them in confusion. A parade of natives marched outside as a welcome brigade. "They thought that one of the white men must have died," MacMillan decided. Allen roused Small, who bustled into the pantry for something to put on the stove.

Windblown stragglers arrived throughout the night. Ekblaw dragged in twenty hours behind MacMillan. The scientist's frost-bitten cheek and hand confirmed his declaration that he had never been colder. Tank came in an hour later with frozen cheeks and a nose that "looked like it might have been scrapping with a hot soldering iron."

Clumps of natives gathered out of earshot, talking and gesturing animatedly. The Americans figured they were debating whether the material rewards from working with MacMillan again out-weighed the dangers of a second journey. *Naalagapaluk*'s first try for Crocker Land had inspired little confidence.

Aapilannguaq, Green, Hunt, and Sissu rolled in several days later, having waited out a three-day blizzard in the cabin at Payer Harbor. Green may have had that delay in mind a short time later, when he wrote "Storm":

Into the bitter, battering gale
Bury your noses white,
Blinded and crouching and hugging the trail.
Hell has gone loose tonight. . . .
Madness is near men cry for naught
In the blizzard's rage.
'Tis war of power: small man's forgot
Where Polar Fields engage.

"It is pretty flat to be home again so soon," Green wrote. Hunt disagreed. With his guide incapacitated, he had fought the dogs all the way back. "They were ugly," he said. "It takes all there is in a man to keep up with one of these Eskimo dog teams, and I have done it enough to dislike it very much." Walking presented an equal challenge. Two "whopping big blisters" on his aching feet left him limping down the trail. His bearskin pants forced him into an uncomfortable gait and made his legs drip with sweat.

Sickness, loneliness, and overexposure had sapped the expedition's enthusiasm. Green alone was anxious to renew the battle. MacMillan had lost faith in the Inughuit, except for Minik, Aqqioq, and a few other stalwarts. He sent some away and dispatched others to hunt walruses. The expedition party would need a large stockpile to compensate for the oversalted dog pemmican.

MacMillan never questioned whether he should try again. Every day at Etah meant one less day in the field. Each delay raised the chances of thin ice or open water. Time was his greatest enemy.

14

SLAUGHTER GROUND

ON FEBRUARY 3, 1851, Robert McClure, an Irishman sailing under the flag of Great Britain, stood on the deck of HMS *Investigator*, a converted merchant ship clad in sturdy oak and equipped with both sails and a 10-horsepower engine. McClure's mission was twofold: determine the whereabouts of Sir John Franklin, whose crew had disappeared somewhere north of Canada a few years earlier, and discover a navigable Northwest Passage between the Arctic Ocean and warmer waters.

McClure had been at sea for eleven months. From its starting point in Woolrich, England, the *Investigator* split the Strait of Magellan before tracing the coastline of the Americas north to the Bering Strait, where it entered the Arctic Ocean. Local Inuit offered no information on Franklin's location. The ship plowed east, above Canada's northern coast, until the ice captured his vessel.

This February morning marked a new beginning. McClure watched in rapture as the sun peeped above the horizon for the first time in months. "Few but the dweller in those high latitudes can understand the joy with which the return of that bright luminary was hailed," he said, "and the congratulations exchanged upon having been spared to rejoice again in the blessed sunlight, were mingled with heartfelt aspirations for the future."

Over sixty years later, on February 24, 1914, another sunrise found an Arctic team in a less celebratory mood. Jerome Allen first saw the sun while lying in his bunk with a 103° fever and his face swollen with mumps. He read a few pages by sunlight, something he hadn't done for months, then collapsed in a sweaty heap when the light dimmed an hour later.

Fitzhugh Green stalked around Borup Lodge. He ignored his ailing comrade; everyone had been sick recently. Instead, he focused his mind, and his eyes, outdoors. Sunlight brought disappointment. Spring represented failure because melting ice meant the end of sledging season. "It is so late now that we must not delay or it will be impossible to do the work on the Polar Sea," he worried.

MacMillan circled March 2 as the new departure date. A ten-day break between outings should give his hunters ample time to stockpile enough walrus meat to build up the weakened dogs for the opening leg of the journey. Any further delay, even a day or two, could prove disastrous.

MacMillan ended up waiting nineteen excruciating days before everything fell into place. Storms delayed the Inughuit's departure for the walrus grounds. Then they couldn't find any walrus. Illness, foul weather, starving dogs, and the advancing season soured the mood around camp. Summoning his past career as a physical education teacher, MacMillan proposed a series of morale-building athletic contests. No one was interested.

A sense of torpor engulfed Borup Lodge. Warm weather settled in and the sun rose higher every day. Pools of open water dotted the harbor. The men relished lazy hours stalking Arctic hares and guillemots, among the first birds to migrate north for the summer.

The walrus party returned on March 7 with great hunks of frozen meat atop their *qamutits*. Their dogs had full bellies and improved dispositions.

MacMillan tarried for two days longer to wrap up final details. An advance party of four Inughuit made a caching run to Ellesmere

Island. Ekblaw practiced driving the team Mac had purchased for him from Iggiannguaq. Green, a marginally better driver, tried out his pack, which was cobbled together from three different teams and was not accustomed to working together. Mac's dogs had been together for months.

MacMillan placed Hunt in charge of headquarters, with strict instructions regarding provisions. A select list of Inughuit, most of them related to the expedition's guides, deserved regular food and shelter. Ulloriaq, who had traded six of his dogs to Green, should "be treated as one of the family and is to be given whatever he may ask for in reason." Hunt was free to share tea, sugar, and biscuit with visitors, but should be sparing with their uncertain supply of meat and must not lend rifles. A basic level of hospitality made good sense because the Americans might need the natives' assistance later. Make sure the Inughuit don't steal anything, especially oil, MacMillan added.

"Again we are started toward Crocker Land," MacMillan exulted on March 11. Fears of an imminent thaw seemed ridiculous. A stiff northern wind whipped snow into their eyes. The thermometer held steady at –31 degrees. "Rather a rough day," MacMillan wrote, with understatement. Under normal circumstances the men would have stayed indoors. But they could wait no longer.

This time the party packed by sunlight rather than electric light. It didn't take long, as each traveler carried only some clothes and four tins of dog pemmican—48 pounds, enough to get them to their caches.

Eight years of speculation and dreaming culminated in this moment. Years of planning, fundraising, and personal loss. Allen set up the movie camera on a pressure ridge to capture the moment. He cranked through a few feet of celluloid before the camera froze up. There would be no footage of the Crocker Landers' departure.

With a stern "Huk! Huk!" and a flash of traces, the race for Crocker Land was on. Again.

Ellesmere Island has been described as "the most extreme place in North America." It is hard to quibble with this characterization. The island, the tenth largest in the world, lays bare the brute forces shaping our planet. Volcanic rocks echo the violent creation of the Earth's crust. Massive glaciers as much as 4,000 feet thick gouge deep channels in the surface. Gravelly flats provide evidence of ancient rivers. Jagged mountains up to 7,000 feet high offer stunning panoramas of spectacular grey-brown cliffs, snowcapped hills, and crystal-clear lakes.

Ellesmere lies 2,000 miles from a tree and 2,500 miles from a road. In 1914, when MacMillan's team invaded, no one lived on the island.* For MacMillan, Ekblaw, and Green, the silence was almost unearthly. Ears that instinctively filtered out multiple layers of man-made noise—conversations, streetcars, whirring engines—strained for anything besides the roaring wind and snow grains scratching across the surface. It was a kind of loneliness none of them had experienced in the United States.

Ellesmere was filled with so many alien things that their minds registered it as a blank slate. They could not attune themselves to the slow grind of geological forces, or to the titanic power of glaciers capable of shoving multiton boulders one tortuous millimeter at a time. It was easy for them to see emptiness, a blank or somehow unfinished landscape, rather than a rugged environment housing a delicate yet flourishing ecosystem. Hares, wolves, and musk oxen (the Polar Inuit called Ellesmere *Umingmak Nuna*, or "Musk Ox Land") scratched out an existence by eating either each other or plants equipped through eons of evolution to survive where most flora cannot. If ever there was a place where the strong survived, it was here.

MacMillan considered himself a scientific polyglot with interests ranging from ethnography to geology to meteorology to paleontol-

---

* Today Ellesmere has a population of fewer than 150 people.

ogy. Ellesmere offered rich possibilities for all of those disciplines. Mysterious tribes had lived on the island hundreds and even a few thousand years before. Fossilized dinosaurs, crocodiles, and tortoises lay enmeshed in the forbidding rocks, as did traces of the lush forests and swampy lowlands that covered the island tens of millions of years ago.

Mac's primary interest, however, was in getting off Ellesmere and onto the polar sea as soon as possible. Peary's 1906 trip to Cape Thomas Hubbard began at Cape Sheridan and ran west across Ellesmere's northern coast. MacMillan, from his base at Etah, would have had to travel far up Ellesmere's coast just to reach Cape Sheridan, so he plotted a more direct, and more dangerous, route. Once across Smith Sound, he would pass Peary's hut at Payer Harbor on the way to his cache at Hayes Sound. From there, he would traverse Beitstad Glacier, the colossal hunk of ice straddling the island's spine. His path grew murkier from there. Of his party, only Piugaattoq had ever been beyond Beitstad. Somehow they would descend the glacier and hook up with Bay Fiord, an inlet that connected with Eureka Sound, the six-mile-wide band of ice linking Ellesmere with Axel Heiberg Island. With Axel Heiberg on his left and Ellesmere on his right, Mac would follow the ice highway north until it merged with Nansen Sound, the road to Cape Thomas Hubbard, at the northern tip of Axel Heiberg. From there he would venture onto the polar sea until he hit Crocker Land.

"Impossible," MacMillan declared.

He stared in disbelief at the 55-foot-high face of Beitstad Glacier. His men had traveled 160 miles west from Etah only to bump up against a two-mile-wide barricade with sheer cliffs on either side. It was the Arctic equivalent of a brick wall.

MacMillan had to get eleven men, about 100 dogs, and three tons of equipment to the top of the equivalent of a six-story building. At –50 degrees. From there, the men had to make the steep climb toward the glacier's cap, which by his reckoning topped 4,700 feet in altitude.

There was no other path. They could not go around, and retreat meant defeat. Yet there seemed to be no way of overcoming the obstruction.

Impossible.

It had been a brutal week for the group. Nothing special, considering their location, but brutal nevertheless. The trip had started well. Mac's party crossed Smith Sound in six hours—a record time. One of the natives bagged a polar bear. Not only was the kill a positive omen, it also stretched their provisions and kept the dogs eating meat rather than oversalted pemmican. As planned, the team met their advance party of four Inughuit at Peary's Payer Harbor hut, loaded the walrus meat cached there, and proceeded into a biting wind to the supply dump at Hayes Sound.

Much to their relief, no bears or wolves had disrupted their cache of pemmican, meat, and oil. MacMillan retrieved important equipment left behind on their previous visit, including binoculars, a sextant, an artificial horizon used for navigation, and sounding wire, essential for determining the polar sea's depth. He also loaded a can of chocolate, a high-calorie, high-energy snack that had the added benefit of heartening the sweet-toothed Green.

With heavy sledges, they plunged down the valley leading toward Beitstad Glacier. Red granite cliffs pressing from both sides testified to the breathtaking power of erosion. "The geology of it all is an open book," an awestruck Green remarked, "fluctuation of climate; recession of ice-cap; submergence of glacier-cut U-valleys to fiords; and finally the proof of biological mutation in shell deposits and Devonian fossils—until all sense of human time fades away."

They followed the valley for 30 winding miles in −50-degree temperatures. Smooth ice transitioned into a choppy mix of hard-packed snow, gravel, and stones. Dogs strained at their traces as the

men heaved their *qamutits* over the uneven surface. The rocky terrain indicated that the glacier was near. A mile of pushing brought
them to the looming wall that MacMillan was contemplating. Six
days had passed since they left Etah.

MacMillan had no idea what to do next. Making matters worse,
one of his companions was in distress. "I have considered him to
be practically indestructible," he said of Elmer Ekblaw, "and am
puzzled to know his trouble." Pain covered the geologist's face. His
walk was unsteady. MacMillan swathed him in furs, fed him some
malted milk, and returned his attention to the obstacle.

Piugaattoq, the only one who had been here before, and Qajuuttaq, who joined the group at Payer Harbor, were doing the same
thing. The two Inughuit paced before the glacier, smiling and joking, giving an impression of nonchalance in the face of an imposing obstacle. This combination of indifference and determination
typified their culture. Modesty was the best policy in a society
built on mutual interdependence. Any fool could recognize men of
extraordinary talent. The truly great did not advertise their abilities lest they appear arrogant. Braggarts could find themselves on
the literal and figurative outside when they needed help in a storm
or during a food shortage.

Piugaattoq grabbed an ice ax. Qajuuttaq fetched a pick. Aqqioq
soon joined them. Piugaattoq hacked a small platform into the glacier. The three men worked at a phenomenal pace, making parallel gashes in an object that usually inflicted rather than absorbed
damage, until two flights of steps emerged. The Americans looked
on with wonder. Not only had the natives terraced a mountain in
a few hours, they had done so with incredible precision. Each step
ended with a raised lip for a handhold.

Aqqioq was soon standing atop MacMillan's "impossible" bar-
rier. From here the slope decreased to around 60 degrees, too
steep to walk unaided. Knotting a rope around his waist, Aqqioq
started widening the distance between his stair treads, carrying

the handholds up the hill. "I can walk without steps," he shouted to Piugaattoq. Delighted, Piugaattoq slapped his thighs and grinned at Green.

"Make it fast," Piugaattoq yelled.

Aqqioq chipped two small holes in the ice, looped a rope through them, tested his improvised ringbolt, and descended the glacier. Sweaty from their effort, the Inughuit ate an early supper before burrowing out a shelter in a snowbank at the glacier's foot.

"Who will ever believe this!" MacMillan laughed.

It took most of a day to haul their gear up the slope. Ittukusuk, whose furs covered a dense mass of chest, back, and neck muscles, fastened his 125-pound *qamutit* to a tumpline and bulled it to the top. Up went the meat, the oil cans, and the pemmican tins. Up went 100 howling dogs, one at a time, by a rope cinched around their bellies.

The Inughuit stood off on their own and began bombarding Piugaattoq with questions about the road ahead. Contrary to what MacMillan believed, Crocker Land meant little to them. It was far from their families and familiar hunting grounds. None of them would ever travel there again, no matter what they found. Their peers at Etah doubted whether this mysterious continent existed. Even if it did, it was uncertain whether they would make it back to Etah before the ice pack broke up.

Minik spent the night deep in thought. In the morning he pulled MacMillan aside and told him he was going home. MacMillan protested, but Minik insisted the expedition would be fine without him. Just like that, the Americans lost their best intermediary with the natives.

MacMillan gave Minik enough food to get him back and a note ordering Dr. Hunt to provide generous allotments of sugar, tea, and tobacco. Mac's benevolence concealed his true feelings. "I feel that we are well rid of a worthless and useless thing," the American vented in his diary. "[Minik] decided that hard work didn't agree with him so [he] left." It was a baseless accusation. Minik's peers considered him a hard worker. More likely, the Inuk doubted the rationality of the expedition. MacMillan appeared to be as obsessed as the hated Peary. From Minik's perspective, he had better get out before he crossed the point of no return.

MacMillan was giving his gear a final check when Ekblaw called him over. "Did you know that Tautsiannguaq had gone too?" he asked. Scoffing, Mac looked around for his guide. Ekblaw pointed up the fiord, where they saw two sledges heading east. Tautsiann-guaq's departure mystified the Americans, who remained baffled by the unsentimentality of the Inughuit. An American would have explained why he was leaving, or held his tongue and done his duty. Tautsiannguaq saw no need for either approach. When he was ready to leave, he left.

Minus its "two deserters," the crew dumped all the pemmican and biscuits they could not haul with their diminishing fleet at the base of the glacier and muscled their overloaded *qamutits* up the slope. Exhausted dogs struggled for every foot of progress while their drivers walked beside them or pushed from behind, screaming at them to take another step.

MacMillan listened closely that night when the remaining Inu-ghuit chatted about the day's events around a fire. Much of their talk escaped him, but he picked up the gist of their conversation. Apparently, when Minik left, someone began talking about Taut-siannguaq's pretty wife, Ivalu—who had captured both Green and Allen's hearts. Rumor had it that Minik also desired Ivalu's com-pany. As Green rather fancifully reported, Aqqioq said that "[Taut-siannguaq's] wife, is as the sunlight before his eyes, and Minik is a wolf." Tautsiannguaq was shadowing the would-be Lothario. "His wife was at stake, and off he went," MacMillan observed.

MacMillan kept a sharp eye on his remaining guides. Everyone seemed happy enough, but so had Minik and Tautsiannguaq. Addi-tional desertions would end his campaign. "If they will only stay by us until we strike musk-ox I believe we have a good chance for Crocker Land," he said.

He also watched his own men. Green was doing an adequate job with his dogs, but Ekblaw's poor sledging skills were obvious. Worse, as Green informed MacMillan, Ekblaw's feet were frozen. It was every Arctic explorer's nightmare. "Frozen cheeks, nose, or ears are of little concern," MacMillan said, "but when a man's feet are frozen he is through."

Mac summoned Ek, who removed his boots. Everyone leaned in for a look at the swollen, blistered feet. Worse than Peary's, the Inughuit muttered. Their opinion shocked the geologist, who had read about the crude operation to remove the commander's toes. "It is only superficial," Mac insisted, perhaps remembering his own disappointment when Peary had sent him home with frostbitten feet. Mac knew Ekblaw was finished but hoped for a miracle that would keep him on the trail a while longer.

From atop Beitstad Glacier's western terminus the men saw Bay Fiord spread out before them. Eureka Sound, their highway to Cape Thomas Hubbard, peeked from between snow-capped hills in the distance. Piugaattoq picked out a treacherous if manageable route down the ice wall and through the valleys. Ekblaw was suffering. So were the others. Deep snow slowed their progress. Dogs constantly slipped into narrow fissures in the ice.

Piugaattoq called a halt when he saw musk ox tracks. Ekblaw limped off with Piugaattoq and Aqqioq to bag a specimen for the University of Illinois. The hunters returned triumphant a few hours later. Seven kills—plenty for everyone. "Living high on heart, tongue, liver, and sirloin steak," MacMillan reported. A light mood pervaded the camp for the first time in days. Their bellies full, everyone slept easy through the –54° night.

Ekblaw could go no farther. MacMillan dissolved their union during a lazy moment of skinning, butchering, and eating. "He is clean grit and will be a great loss to me," Mac declared, but the geologist's bad feet and subpar driving made him a liability. Qajuuttaq would escort him back to Etah. At nearly sixty years of age, the Inuk was by far the expedition's oldest member, and he was complaining about MacMillan's stinginess with gifts. Better to part before one or both of the men become real problems.

Checking their supplies, MacMillan counted just eleven gallons of oil, not enough to fuel their stoves to Crocker Land and back. "Green," he said, "the oil is pretty well down. I expect that I shall have to send you back over."

The ensign slumped at the idea of going back up, across, and down Beitstad Glacier so he could grab more oil from the cache, then retracing his steps to overtake MacMillan. But this was his job. He was the bowstring, and MacMillan was the arrow.

MacMillan assigned Aqqioq and Nukappiannguaq to accompany the ensign. They carried only a few days' supplies and a load of musk ox skins that they were to deposit at the cache. Green and Ekblaw's teams would ride together to the far side of Beitstad Glacier, at which point Green would load up supplies and turn around while Ekblaw continued on to Etah. Meanwhile, MacMillan's team would head north, hunting along the way and stashing their kills so that Green and his Inughuit wouldn't have to waste time searching for food. In nine days, MacMillan, Ittukusuk, and Piugaattoq would meet Green, Aqqioq, and Nukappiannguaq at Cape Thomas Hubbard.

On March 23 the Americans said their goodbyes. Glorious weather tempered the sorrow of parting. Although the thermometer read –50 degrees, so cold that urine steamed in the air and froze before hitting the ground, the sun shone bright and the air was still. Five sledges headed east. Three went north.

"Am lonesome tonight," MacMillan wrote in his journal. Ittukusuk and Piugaattoq built a fine snow house. A lamp constructed from an old pemmican tin, a bit of musk ox tallow, and a wick of cotton cloth lit the room. Despite the chill outside, it was so warm inside that water dripped down the curved walls.

Yet MacMillan was uneasy. The defections of Minik and Tautsiannguaq rattled him more than he let on. He hoped Ittukusuk and Piugaattoq—"fine, faithful fellows"— would stay with him. Isolation magnified his discomfort. Being the only white man within 30 or 40 miles troubled him.

As the sputtering flame cast flickering shadows against the wall, he composed his final thoughts for the evening. With a steady hand, he put pencil to paper: "I am anxious to be on the march again toward Cape Thomas Hubbard, where I can look out on the Polar ice toward that land which I am after."

Ekblaw wanted to see musk oxen, perhaps the most enigmatic land animals in the high Arctic, before leaving Ellesmere Island. Westerners could fit the region's other terrestrial creatures into familiar paradigms, whether bear or bird or wolf. Musk oxen, on the other hand were . . . well, it wasn't exactly clear. Early explorers considered them relatives of buffalo, or maybe oxen, or possibly cows. The musk ox's scientific name, *Ovibos moschatus*, which translates roughly as "sheeplike cow with a musky smell," reflects their confusion. The Inughuit, who paid less attention to taxonomy than Westerners did, nevertheless gave musk oxen an equally descriptive name: *umimmat*, "animal with skin like a beard."

The Inughuit had the better side of the argument. Compounds in the musk ox's urine produce a strong, musk-like odor during the summer rutting season, but the animals have no proper musk glands and are remote relatives of both cows and sheep. Their only close living relative is the takin, a moose-like resident of the Himalayas whose rich pelt may have inspired the legend of Jason and the Golden Fleece.

Full-grown males can stand five feet tall and top 700 pounds. Shaggy blankets of fur make them look even bigger. Musk oxen dress in layers, like children leaving the house on a winter day. A two-inch-thick undercoat covers every inch of their body except for their hooves, horns, and philtrim (the area between the nose and upper lip). This underfur, or *qiviut*, is miraculous stuff, softer than cashmere and eight times warmer than sheep's wool. A layer of long, coarse fur hanging from the animal's belly, rump, and flanks supplements the *qiviut*, and a sturdy mane protects its shoulders. Two-foot-long hairs on its throat inspired the natives' "skin-like-a-beard" moniker.

Musk oxen emerged in Asia around one million years ago. Migrating east over many millennia, they traversed the land bridge to North America between 200,000 and 90,000 years ago. During the Wisconsonian glaciation, an ice age lasting from roughly 85,000 to 11,000 years ago, they roamed as far south as Virginia and the American Midwest. When the climate warmed they followed the retreating glaciers north, finding new homes in Greenland, Ellesmere, and other Arctic islands.

Musk oxen are perfectly adapted for their environment. In the summer they amass huge fat reserves by consuming swaths of plants growing in areas blown clear of snow. This fuel enables them to maintain an internal temperature of 101 degrees. Inner fires and outer protections shield them against conditions even polar bears can't handle. Their fur traps heat so well that snow accumulates on their shoulders and backs rather than melting. They conserve energy by remaining as still as possible. Mac's men often mistook a herd of musk oxen for a spray of grey-brown boulders. On the rare occasions when musk oxen do move in winter, they lumber along in single file, placing their feet in their leader's tracks rather than wasting energy by cutting a separate path through the snow.

Slow-moving herbivores seem like easy pickings for aggressive carnivores such as the Arctic wolf. Again, evolution has provided defenses. A musk ox's eye is a thing of wonder, able to perceive predators from a great distance. It protrudes from the skull, standing clear of the fur while widening the animal's field of vision. Horizontal pupils create a broad panorama. Musk oxen can narrow or even close their pupils to prevent snow blindness. A double retina intensifies the low-light images received during the Arctic winter.

When a wolf pack approaches, the herd deploys its forces with Napoleonic precision, shaping itself into either a line, with the strongest bull at the center and younger members at the flanks, or a circle, with the weakest members inside. These echelons of fur sometimes intimidate wolves into leaving. If not, the bulls launch quick, head-down sallies at the enemy, overwhelming them with flashing horns and sheer bulk. Wolves think long and hard before tangling with a herd of fifty or more musk oxen.

Musk oxen's stationary defense schemes made them easy prey for human predators, who picked them off one at a time while the rest of the herd held stock-still. "I hunted them on a large scale and in a systematic way," Peary wrote in *Secrets of Polar Travel*. Shoot them "back of the fore shoulder or in the neck, at the base of the skull," he advised. "Frontal or head shots are a waste of ammunition." The commander had heard stories of hunters pouring 300 bullets into a musk ox without killing it.

Henry Ford would have admired Peary's disassembly line. Natives removed the skins, rolled them so they would fit on sledges, and delivered them to women who scraped and prepared them for use or sale. Hearts, livers, and kidneys were cached under rocks. Dogs ate the remaining viscera. The men sucked the marrow from large bones before vacating the kill site. "In this way," Peary said, "nothing was wasted."

Peary's expeditions shot somewhere around 1,000 musk oxen, nearly all of them on Ellesmere. MacMillan would further deplete the herd. With few other sources of game, he had little choice. Every step west took him farther from the seal and walrus grounds. Ellesmere hosted enormous Arctic hares, but even a 12-pound giant provided scant nourishment for 100 dogs. Mac could not carry enough meat to feed his team throughout the trip. His dogs suffered on the oversalted pemmican. So it was musk ox or nothing—an easy choice for the Arctic traveler.

Green stood atop one of the steps hacked into the eastern face of Beitstad Glacier, "filled with the beauty" of the fiord stretching before him.

The gorgeous scene eased the tension of three hard marches

through a relentless wind. Ekblaw rode whenever possible, increasing the burden on the sagging dogs, who ate pemmican one day and nothing the other two. Soft snow prevented the Inughuit from building shelters, so at night the men hunkered inside their furs, letting hot tea carry them into an unsettled slumber.

With gravity on their side, getting down the glacier face was easier than getting up. Aqqioq and Nukappiannguaq began lowering sledges and supplies. Green admired the parallel cliffs running on either side of him, the cool smoothness of the ice, and the gravelly expanse of the awaiting path.

Some instinct made him look up. A blur of wood and fur blazed toward him. Green jumped to one side, pinwheeling his arms for balance as a sledge loaded with musk ox furs smashed into the rocks below. He regained his equilibrium, peered into the 20-foot void, and shuddered at the fate he had so narrowly avoided.

Twenty-four hours later the men reached the "big cache" at Hayes Sound, the separation point for Ek and Green. An unexpected wave of homesickness washed over Green when Qajuuttaq led Ekblaw away. The ensign missed the snug home nestled at the back of Etah fiord, especially the big can of molasses in the pantry. With his sweet tooth throbbing, Green steered his heavy sledge back to the west.

Green considered himself to be one of the Three Musketeers, with Aqqioq and Nukappiannguaq as his boon companions. All of them were around twenty-five years old, although only Green was certain of his age. Green, the hopelessly Romantic sailor; Aqqioq, chubby-cheeked with shoulder-length black hair; and Nukappiannguaq, soulful eyes peering from his long face, made an interesting trio. Battling implacable nature, discovering new lands—it was Green's fantasy come true.

This triumvirate could never truly be all for one and one for all. Green wanted adventure and glory. The natives wanted to deliver their employer to his destination and get paid. "Their life was a sublimely simple fight for food and clothing," Green reflected. "Mine was a cruel struggle of such labyrinthine intricacy that only genius could be rich and none be truly contented save the shrewdest philosophers." Green imagined his traveling companions as noble savages at one with their environment and content with whatever gifts nature yielded, whereas he, "the cultured, pampered ascendant of ages, knew not the contentful joy of indifference." He simultaneously envied and demeaned his companions, using them to critique his own society while reducing their existence to a grubby search for subsistence.

At night the men huddled "like three giant dirt-brown caterpillars suddenly cast together." Lice frustrated Green's attempts at sleep. Legend held that lice had arrived in Greenland in tiny kayaks. One day, a louse and a worm, also paddling a kayak, decided to race ashore and climb on a person. The louse got there first, and settled into a man's armpit. The worm, humiliated in defeat, hid in the earth. Green wouldn't have believed the myth. He blamed the infestation on Nukappiannguaq.

Each day seemed harder than the one before it. Green, Aqqioq, and Nukappiannguaq wrestled their *qamutits* over obstacles, screamed at their teams, and froze their fingers while untangling snarled traces. Pain radiated from a mysterious boil on Green's right arm—his whip arm—whenever he raised it. A cut on his index finger from a tin can got infected.

Green's Romantic side cherished these tests of manliness. Something deeper in his psyche rejected the drudgery of the trail. A strange rhythm bounced through his head as he trotted alongside his sledge. "One-two-three, four-five-six, seven-eight-nine," he repeated. Periodically he jerked back to consciousness, aware that he had been counting his dogs over and over and over again. "I cannot explain the psychology of this queer conceit," he said.

Green invested his dogs with personalities and backstories. According to his narrative, his king dog, the white one with brown ears and a deep chest, was courting "the Red Queen." ("Take a bone from a dog: what remains?" the Red Queen asks Alice in

Through the Looking Glass. "The dog's temper would remain," says the Queen, answering her own question.) The king had a romantic rival in "the Grand Duke." Green imagined three others as siblings, including a sister named Yvonne, a name worthy of her courtly demeanor. "Two forlorn and extremely uninteresting individuals" became "the Geologist" and "the Botanist." Ekblaw and Tanquary would have disapproved.

Then there was the giant black dog with an aloof attitude and "philosophical stoicism" in his black eyes. Green could not grasp this one's essence, so he never named it. "I always thought that he must have been disappointed in love, or had some other great sorrow in his life," the ensign said, revealing as much about himself as the animal. "Powerfully built, intelligent, and hard working as he was he never had the slightest association with his team mates. He could easily have become king had he so wished; in fact he paid none of the usual homage to the ruling power and ignored the king dog at all times." This was a canine Romantic hero, a noble, wounded soul worthy of greatness but ill-equipped to seize it.

On they went. One-two-three, four-five-six, seven-eight-nine. Surviving on a diet of pemmican. No hunting, Mac had said. Hunting will slow you down. For mile after mile they chased MacMillan, cheering whenever they found one of his team's old snow houses, which inevitably contained a cheerful note and, sometimes, a bit of frozen musk ox. Fresh meat was more sustaining, but frozen was better than nothing.

On April 2, ten days after the relief party split from MacMillan, a snowstorm wiped away the trail. Aqqioq, Green, and Nukappiannguaq set a course and hoped for the best. MacMillan's course remained elusive. The dogs scented bear tracks several times over the next few days, but Green ignored them, bent on following orders. Aqqioq grew frustrated with the lost opportunities to feed himself and his team. Fed up with Green's bewildering refusal to hunt, he halted his sledge. Aqqioq gazed into the distance, pointing at a herd of musk oxen. Green shook his head. They must ride, not hunt.

Aqqioq and Nukappiannguaq sat down and started talking, punctuating their conversation with occasional glances at the musk oxen.

"I think we had better stop," Aqqioq said, depositing an exhausted dog atop his load.

No, Green replied. If his guides hunted, they would want to build an igloo so they could enjoy a lazy day of eating. We must move.

Aqqioq saw no reason to starve when game was near. The Inuk stalked off, snatched his camp ax from his *qamutit*, and brained the dog.

Huk! Huk! They rode until midnight. Nukappiannguaq's dogs ate their walrus-skin traces while he slept.

Green's men were nearing mutiny. Their dogs were too weak for long marches. The ensign doubled over with persistent stomach cramps. He kept his illness quiet for fear the natives would use it as an excuse for retreat. "My teeth chattered so that the few fillings I had not already pried out on frozen meat were vibrated from their holes by the constant rattling of my jaws," Green wrote. "I couldn't keep warm. It was mortifying."

A few days later, following a ten-hour pull through gale-force winds and drifting snow, the Botanist died. Soon after, Aqqioq started jumping and shouting. He had located one of MacMillan's old igloos. That meant meat.

They searched the camp for an hour before uncovering a scrap of Mac's note. "Slaughter ground," it read. That sounded disturbing but was quite the opposite. MacMillan's team had killed many musk oxen here. But where were they? MacMillan's directions to the cache were gone. A wolf or a fox had carried it off.

Nukappiannguaq interrogated Green. How far ahead is *naalagapaluk*? Where is the cache? Green could not say. Those words on the paper must mean something, Nukappiannguaq retorted. "He became almost insolent," the ensign gasped. Green berated the Inuk, in English. "The meat is out there," he said, waving his arms at the expanse. "If you want it go and hunt for it." His companions stormed off, returning empty-handed a few hours later.

Foul weather greeted them the next morning. Green pushed forward anyway. The dogs were so exhausted that the team cached half of their suplies to lighten their sledges. "I explained the situation as well as I could to my men," Green later wrote. "They did as I told them without comment. At such times the native is glad to have a white man to think for him."

Aqqioq and Nukappiannguaq led the way. Fifteen minutes later, the sun broke through the clouds, revealing a snow house. A note, dated three days earlier, directed them to a mountain of musk oxen meat. A "slaughter ground," to be sure.

Green's team dove into the cache. To their delight, some of it had not yet frozen. The dogs ate their fill. The men ate their fill, rested for a while, and ate their fill again. "A great day!" Green exclaimed. No more sledging, only eating and sleeping.

They remained at the slaughter ground for two full days, storing up energy for the final push to Cape Thomas Hubbard. Green figured on locating MacMillan within forty-eight hours. In fact it took twice that long, with more hard times along the route. Fierce winds drove snow into their eyes and obscured MacMillan's tracks. Green worried about passing his leader without seeing him. Starvation was too close for him to lose time doubling back.

"My team is pretty well done up," Green noted on April 10, three days out from the slaughter ground. They had returned to a salty pemmican diet with a little meat mixed in. Three of Green's dogs were dead. Aqqioq and Nukappiannguaq were driving teams of just six dogs apiece. Two more died the next day, leaving ten survivors between the two Inughuit. Green had Aqqioq and Nukappiannguaq combine their teams and began a desultory march into the wind. Seventeen weak dogs, three hungry men, two sledges, and one blizzard.

Relief, or at least reunion, came at 11:30 that night, when the trail-weary trio bumped into MacMillan's group crowded in a dugout at the base of a cliff, having arrived only eight hours earlier. "Thank heavens," Green wrote. "Thank God!" MacMillan wrote. After a 400-mile chase, the ensign had delivered enough oil and pemmican to get them onto the polar ice. Mac proclaimed it "grand, good work."

MacMillan described his travels with Ittukusuk and Piugaattoq. Conditions at first had been ideal, with perfect weather and smooth ice. "The Lord has been good to us," MacMillan noted in his journal. Unlike Green's battered unit, his men enjoyed calm winds and temperatures in the –20s. Abundant foxes, hares, and musk oxen kept them in fine trim. "We are certainly in a land of plenty," Mac enthused.

Their good fortune peaked on March 31. While an obsessive Green was counting his dogs far to the east, Ittukusuk and Piugaattoq were obliterating dozens of musk oxen at the "slaughter ground" camp. "Like savages they had slaughtered the whole herd for the pure love of killing, although they knew that we could not possibly use so many," MacMillan later related. The two hunters accumulated so much fresh meat that their dogs refused to eat any more. Ittukusuk seized great hunks of raw meat with his teeth and sawed through them with his knife until, stuffed, he tossed his knife against the wall, pitched a slab of meat back into a pan, and collapsed. Morning found him complaining of a painful leg and swollen jaw. His ailments may have been real, or they may have been a ploy to remain an extra day, which is exactly what MacMillan did. Ittukusuk and Piugaattoq had built an unusually large and comfortable snow house, one better suited for an extended stay than an overnight camp. Following their lead, MacMillan grabbed another piece of musk ox.

With *kamiks* dried, *qamutits* mended, and bellies bursting, MacMillan got the Inughuit mushing again. Their luck turned sour on Nansen Sound, the frozen strait separating Ellesmere from Axel

Heiberg Island. Strong winds and blowing snow left them groping through a whiteout. When they lost sight of land they maintained a general northerly course by keeping the wind in their faces.

Bad weather pounded them until even MacMillan, a relentless optimist, wavered. "This is one of the days when I have thought of my home in Freeport and the comfort of my sister's big sitting room," he admitted on April 8, the day Green left the slaughter camp. The advancing calendar worried him. Peary had celebrated the Pole five years and two days earlier. MacMillan had barely crossed 80° north.

On one particularly awful morning, Ittukusuk and Piugaattoq scouted ahead while MacMillan stayed behind to untangle frozen traces with his bare hands. Once he hitched his team, they tore off helter-skelter after a caribou. Mac corralled them and started untangling all over again. The wind picked up the moment he hit the trail. Blowing snow covered Ittukusuk's and Piugaattoq's tracks. His dogs pulled the *qamutit* onto bare ground, a terrible surface for sledging. Dreams of hot tea were floating through Mac's head by the time he found the men carving out a shelter. He crawled in to help finish the job. The dogs climbed atop the structure, which collapsed on Ittukusuk. Mac gritted his teeth. "Nothing to do but swear, then grin and go at it again," he said. "The day is over, thank God!" he wrote from inside their reconstructed shelter. Then Ittukusuk's team broke loose. Another day on the trail.

Persistent storms prevented them from getting their bearings. Cape Thomas Hubbard was close, but they elected to wait out the weather before finding it. So they sat in their snow cave, listening to the wind rage. "Again we get it hard," MacMillan wrote on April 10. "The worst day we have had."

Green's appearance lifted their spirits. By happy coincidence, the storm abated. The two Americans tramped through the hills in search of Peary's Cape Thomas Hubbard cairn. The rockpile should have stood out, but neither of them saw anything. Frustrated, they resolved to bypass the landmark and head northwest onto the ice. Crocker Land was too big to miss no matter their precise starting point.

All four of the Polar Inuit had done tremendous jobs of hunting, navigating, breaking trail, and building shelters during the past month. The expedition would never have survived without them. Nevertheless, Mac needed to pare down his party. Aqqioq and Nukappiannguaq had destroyed themselves getting Green this far. Mac sent them home. Their dogs were exhausted, and the expedition had to stretch its remaining food. Musk oxen did not live on the polar sea. Starting from a pool of a hundred Inughuit men and a bevy of American applicants, the Crocker Land expedition was down to Donald MacMillan, Fitzhugh Green, Ittukusuk, Piugaattoq, four sledges, and 1,400 pounds of supplies.

"We plan to leave tomorrow no matter what the weather is as it is getting so late," Green penciled in his field journal.

All was quiet at Borup Lodge. The calendar on the wall read May 5, 1914. Jot Small was asleep. Jerome Allen was puttering around the house. Most of the Inughuit had left for their southern settlements. Tanquary and Ekblaw went with them. The geologist's frost-bitten foot was much improved. A few days earlier Hunt had heard about a sick woman 50 miles to the south and set off behind the worst-looking and least cooperative team of mismatched mutts anyone had ever seen to attend her. Allen told him his mongrels would never survive the trip. "Then I'll walk," Hunt snarled.

Allen was bored. Minik and Tautsiannguaq had passed through on March 22 with an update from MacMillan. Minik had visited a few times since then, most recently in mid-April on his way north to hunt bear. He spoke well of MacMillan and urged his tribemates to keep supporting the expedition.

Two distant dots promised a distraction. They turned out to be Aqqioq and Nukappiannguaq, who had endured a gruesome three weeks since leaving Green and MacMillan at the northern tip of Axel Heiberg Island, somewhere near Cape Thomas Hubbard. Sixteen of their twenty dogs were dead. The Inughuit would have starved too had they not found a herd of musk oxen at a critical moment.

Weary and hungry, the men handed Allen a letter dated April 14, the day before they left the Americans. "We are here all ready for the Polar Sea, dogs in good shape and plenty of food," MacMillan had written. Treat Aqqioq and Nukappiannguaq "in the best possible manner," he continued. Let them stay in the house. Give them tea, biscuit, and sugar. Let them use our rifles. "Favor them as much as possible."

Aqqioq and Nukappiannguaq were special cases. "We <u>cannot</u> feed visitors," Mac continued. "Give them nothing. We have our boys now who will stay by us and do not require any more." Make sure the Eskimos don't steal our oil.

We will be home in early June, should all go well.

Allen did a quick mental calculation. Three weeks had passed since MacMillan penciled these words. His party could be on Crocker Land. They could be on their way back. They could be at the bottom of the polar sea, or trapped on an ice floe. Wherever they were, it was hundreds of miles from the nearest human habitation. The arrow had flown. Time would tell whether it hit its target.

15

ON THE ICE

"ALL KINDS OF A DAY," an exhausted MacMillan wrote on April 16. He and Green looked like men who had not bathed or changed clothes for over a month, which was exactly what they were. Extreme Arctic sunlight had burned their faces black. Shabby beards sprouted from their faces. Lice nested in their various nooks and crannies.

The Crocker Land party never found Cape Thomas Hubbard, which looked prominent on a map but proved elusive among the twists and turns of the coastline of Axel Heiberg Island. Abandoning the search, the two Americans and two Inughuit piled onto four *qamutits* and mushed onto the frozen Arctic Ocean at around ten o'clock in the morning. It seemed an auspicious moment to start a great journey. Calm winds, bright sunshine, and excellent sledging raised their spirits. The dogs mushed over level ice interspersed with a few lumpy hillocks. Eight miles out they spotted the cape's broad, snow-covered dome off to the west. No point heading back.

"Many are under the impression that the ice of the polar sea is smooth as glass and that explorers simply ride to their destination on dog sledges," Peary chided. MacMillan knew better. Sledging across the polar sea was like driving a streetcar across a field of boulders. Peary called it "indescribable chaos."

The first pressure ridges came about 10 miles out, some of

228

them lifting 30 feet above the surface. MacMillan, Ittukusuk, and Piugaattoq climbed a tall ridge for a look around. Long minutes passed without conversation while the natives scanned the jumble ahead. MacMillan didn't like their body language. The Inughuit started muttering in low tones between themselves. Mac caught enough of their talk to get worried. "Much water," they mumbled in Inuktun. MacMillan peered northwest. The Inughuit saw evidence of open water, mist perhaps, but he could not locate the source of their concern. "Will not freeze," they whispered. "The ice is moving. . . . The sun is high."

MacMillan jollied them along, slapping Ittukusuk on the back and teasing Piugaattoq. The ice is much better than last time, he said. We shall feed our dogs two cans of pemmican rather than one tonight. I will give you rifles and ammunition. The Inughuit looked skeptical but returned to their teams.

"Almost impossible," Green sighed as he plunged his *qamutit* into the ripped-up field of ridges and rubble ice. Gusts blew them around as they pushed, pulled, and dragged themselves forward. Icicles dangled from their beards and eyebrows. This was sledging only in the sense that they had sledges. In reality, it was conquering a miniature mountain chain while towing hundreds of pounds of supplies. The *qamutits* tipped again and again. Green smashed his right knee on the ice. The men fell so many times that it is a wonder no one broke a rib. They tripped over dogs and impaled themselves on the upstanders of their sledges. "Good God!" Mac shouted. "I feel like an ant in an ice cream freezer!"

The four adventurers muscled through two brutal miles of ridges before bunking down for the night. MacMillan's customary optimism was draining away. His men were demoralized and the dogs weak. Green's big black loner, the one with philosophical stoicism in his eyes, crawled off to die alone. "I hate to see these friends of ours leave us one by one," MacMillan said. Lightening Green's load, he transferred more supplies onto his own sledge. Even his dogs, the best of the four teams, were depleted. There was no fresh meat, and oversalted pemmican would not keep them going for much longer.

Piugaattoq looked nervous when he hitched up his team the next morning. Fortunately, the men soon broke into a section of smooth ice. They "wondered what the Arctic devil had in store" for them. Sure enough, a few hours later they encountered their first major lead. Stretching a quarter-mile across and extending "apparently around the world," it presented an insurmountable obstacle to further progress. MacMillan sent Ittukusuk and Piugaattoq searching for its end. When they failed, there was nothing to do but set up camp and hope the water froze soon. A similar lead rebuffed Peary in 1906. MacMillan prayed for better luck.

MacMillan wasn't going anywhere for a while, so he used this opportunity to take some soundings. He had brought a spool of 2,000 fathoms of piano wire for this exact purpose. Researchers were hungry for information on the polar sea, the least understood of the world's oceans. Depth charts helped them to better understand how tides and currents operated. They also provided clues as to the whereabouts of land. Shallow water suggested a nearby landmass. Deep water marked the open ocean beyond the continental shelf.

Mac fastened the spool to the back of a sledge, tied one of the expedition's two heavy picks to the loose end, and unreeled it into the lead. Down went the pick, sinking 25, 50, 100 fathoms.* Mac and Green took turns at the crank. The Americans squirmed as the pick reached 200, then 300 fathoms. There should be a bottom. Either they were standing over a deep hole in the ocean or, much more likely, a strong current was pushing the sounding apparatus along a horizontal plane rather than allowing it to sink. Whichever the case, and they hoped it was the latter, the experiment proved worthless.

They cranked up the wire in fifteen-minute shifts. Shoulder and

---

* A fathom is 6 feet, or 1.8 meters.

back muscles ached in the –25-degree temperatures. It was a miserable experience, made worse by its futility. The wind strengthened as the day dragged on.

West Greenland Inuit blamed the wind on man. A story tells of how, many years ago, a hunter encountered a polar bear carrying a large sack.

"What is inside?" the man inquired.

"Just a big load of shit, that's all," the bear replied.

"Why are you carrying it?" the hunter asked.

"I might get hungry during my journey," the animal answered.

The man laughed. Gifted with a beautiful voice, he sang the beast to sleep with a lullaby, then grabbed the bag and peeked inside. All the wind in the world rushed out, free to haunt humanity forever. "Oh, Great Bear," the hunter begged. "You can have my wife for a month, only get rid of this wind." It was too late. Nothing could undo the curious man's evil deed.

MacMillan's sounding party fought the badly kinked line fathom by fathom. Piugaattoq took the handle for the final rotations. A few minutes later he stuck his head into the Americans' igloo. Our pick is gone, he said. It broke loose at some point. Not only had they wasted the day, they had also lost a vital piece of equipment. "I had carried that heavy reel of wire for 400 miles in the hopes of making a contribution to science," MacMillan moaned, "and now without us sounding at all I am obliged to throw it away." The other pick was too valuable to risk, and he could not think of anything else to use as a weight. Mac carried the 40-pound reel to a high spot and walked away, feeling like "a pallbearer at a funeral."

Ittukusuk woke them the next morning. The lead has frozen over, he said. Hitching their dogs, the four men rode parallel to the new stretch of ice, looking for the best place to cross. Gray ice was too thin; the coloration came from the water slurping beneath it. Ittukusuk tapped a promising-looking patch of white ice with his whipstock. It was acceptable. Wanting to be sure, he sent his dogs over first. Piugaattoq followed, then Green. The ice bowed and flexed like a rubber band. "He will never get there," MacMillan gasped. But he did. Mac brought up the rear. Two of his dogs crashed through the surface. Mac yanked the leads lest the whole sledge go under, then bodily hauled out the waterlogged pair. The dogs shook the water from their fur, gnawed ice from between their toes, and continued on their way.

The party hit another lead a few hours later. It soon froze over, allowing for another precarious crossing. Then came a field of intimidating pressure ridges. Sweat covered the men as they wrestled their sledges over the barriers. Mac's *qamutit* rolled on top of him, nearly breaking his leg, an injury that might have proven fatal so far from land. Piugaattoq suffered a severe ankle sprain. Green picked up bruises all over his body.

Ittukusuk and Piugaattoq kept stealing away for private conversations. On encountering yet another lead, they sat down, watched the water, and listened to the ice grind. Many leads this year, Piugaattoq said. Ittukusuk suggested, in his roundabout way, that they should perhaps head back. When the lead froze, they let the Americans cross first, a sure sign of their diminishing enthusiasm.

MacMillan answered the challenge, putting his team up front to break trail for the others. "For a white man this task is almost too difficult to be undertaken," Green worried. The Inughuit followed listlessly. If they left, MacMillan and Green would have no choice but to go with them.

"Most of the time Eskimos are acting; rarely are their masks off," French anthropologist Jean Malaurie once remarked. One of the great tragedies of Arctic history is that so little is known about the Inughuit who facilitated Westerners' discoveries and scientific advancements. Folklore, oral histories, and explorers' journals give some sense of their characters, beliefs, and social structures, but it is impossible to say much about any individual Inuk, except for a rare case such as Minik, who had lived in the United States and crossed paths with numerous Westerners.

"They are people of peculiar temperament, very much like children, and should be handled like children," Peary said of the Inughuit. MacMillan felt a deeper attachment to the tribe yet portrayed them in similar terms. They are "real children of nature," he believed, "almost as wild as the animals which they hunt." Both men admired the Polar Inuit's adaptability while deeming them "not qualified to lead." This was an odd assertion, as members of the tribe led Peary to the upper latitudes and MacMillan 40 miles onto the polar sea. Neither man could have survived without their guides, yet neither admitted that the natives were calling the shots.

"In general," Malaurie argued, "the Eskimo is utterly indifferent to anything that does not directly concern his own people." Other places and other cultures meant little to people engaged in a perpetual fight for survival. The world beyond northwest Greenland was as incomprehensible to them as the ocean is to a goldfish. Native legends said the Polar Inuit had been the only humans until a young, attractive woman rejected all the eligible men her father offered for marriage and instead married a dog. Their offspring initiated the other races of the earth.

Not much can be said about individual members of this indifferent, mask-wearing group. Most available evidence comes from explorers' diaries and books, and most explorers put themselves, not the Inughuit, at the center of their story. Sometimes the natives are unnamed, sometimes they are only names, and sometimes they have many names. Ittukusuk, for example, appears in various sources as Etookeshuk, E-took-e-shoo, Etukeshoo, Etookeshoe, E-took-e-shue, and Itookuechuk. The Inughuit's tradition of naming children after the recently deceased meant there were at least two Ittukusuks in the tribe in 1914 and have been more since. There are also multiple Piugaattoqs in the historical record.

Ittukusuk was a handsome man with dark eyes framed by shoulder-length black hair and an expressive smile. At times he sported a thin mustache, shaving it off in summer. Powerful quadriceps, a deep chest, and a compact frame gave him a body like a gymnast.

MacMillan photographed Ittukusuk several times and, as part of his anthropological studies, measured him from head to toe, shoulder to fingertip, and hip to knee. Mac even recorded the length, width, and depth of the Inuk's kayak. But neither he nor the other Crocker Landers composed a detailed biography or an extensive character study of the man MacMillan called "the best Eskimo I have ever employed." Ittukusuk is for the most part a mere name on the page, an image frozen in time.

"Our best man . . . clean grit," MacMillan said of Ittukusuk. Elmer Ekblaw called him "loyal, capable, and energetic." About twenty-six years old and, at just under five feet two inches, a touch short for an Inughuit, Ittukusuk was regarded as one of the tribe's top hunters and drivers. No one was better at drilling Arctic hares with a slingshot. He made an ideal partner for MacMillan, who shared his energy and, on occasion, his impatience.

Ittukusuk was as close to royalty as existed among the Polar Inuit. Panippak, his father, was a powerful seer and a great hunter. Ittukusuk was named for his grandfather, Panippak's father, which meant the former Ittukusuk's spirit inhabited the young man's body. Therefore, he called Panippak "my son," while Panippak called Ittukusuk "my father."

For all his gifts, Ittukusuk had endured a bad run. In 1908, as an eager twenty-year-old, he leapt at the opportunity to join Dr. Cook's quixotic bid for the North Pole. Ittukusuk was the doctor's constant companion. Later, when Mac quizzed him about the hated Cook's movements, he said they had never ventured more than three sleeps from land in all their time away.

If the sometimes unreliable Peter Freuchen, Knud Rasmussen's assistant at the Thule trading station, can be believed, Ittukusuk's post-Cook years were a mess. His dogs all died. Cook's promises of great riches never materialized. And Peary, who arrived in Greenland while Ittukusuk was off with the doctor, ostracized the traitors who had backed his rival. Ittukusuk's wife Arnaluk joined Peary's army of seamstresses and performed odd jobs around camp. One of Peary's favorites, Kridtluqtoq, wanted her for himself, so Peary dissolved Arnaluk's marriage to Ittukusuk and gave her to the loyal Inuk.

Freuchen's story has some holes. MacMillan's censuses of the Inughuit, although sketchy, show no "Arnaluk" or "Arnaluq." Neither Cook, Peary, nor Borup mentioned anyone by that name in their books, although Western writers rendered native names so differently as to render them unrecognizable. Perhaps Freuchen was having a bit of a joke—one English–Inukitut dictionary defines *arnaluk* as "bitch," in the sense of a female dog, or "prostitute." As for the lecherous Kridtluqtoq, Freuchen may have been speaking of Qillugtooq, or, as the Crocker Landers called him, Koodlooktoo. If so, MacMillan's censuses have him married to a woman named Al-nay-doo-ah.

Whatever happened during Peary's stay, by 1913 Ittukusuk had wed twenty-seven-year-old Alneah (who may appear elsewhere as "Alningwah" or "Arnannguaq"—the record isn't definitive). Despite his upbeat personality, theirs was a rocky marriage punctuated by violent outbursts. Fitzhugh Green stumbled into one of their brawls. "She was struggling, swearing and spitting," he reported. "She grabbed a pot and would have thrown it had not [Ittukusuk] shot his arm under her elbow and deflected her aim." Alneah's fits were legendary among the Americans. At one point she became convinced she was a walrus.

Alneah probably had a miscarriage sometime around 1909, and the couple's lack of children was another source of marital discord. Although it is impossible to know whether she became pregnant again, or why the couple never had kids, they both loved children. Ittukusuk became a kind of universal uncle. Alneah's desire for motherhood grew into an obsession; she carried other women's babies in her *qulittaq* whenever the opportunity presented itself.

Ittukusuk's adventurous spirit may have stemmed from a desire to escape his wife. Maybe Crocker Land presented an opportunity for redemption, or riches. Perhaps his friendship with MacMillan— and their mutual admiration was genuine—reflected a yearning for levelheaded companionship. MacMillan in some ways resembled Cook more than Peary, although he would have disputed that comparison. Both led more by charm and reason than by coercion and intimidation. Ittukusuk had got on well with Cook. Possibly he saw Mac in a similar vein.

Piugaattoq's lifelines are even fainter than Ittukusuk's. Knud Rasmussen called him "a calm and extraordinarily sober-minded man, who could not cause dispute or quarrel of any sort." By coincidence, the Inuk's name echoes Rasmussen's analysis; *piugaattoq* means "the peaceful one."

MacMillan never measured Piugaattoq, so nothing is known of his stature. The few photographs of him add little information. Either MacMillan or Green (probably MacMillan) snapped two pictures of him cradling a live caribou near Cape Thomas Hubbard. Piugaattoq sits in profile with his hood obscuring his features. Peary included a small picture of him, the only clear view of his round face, in *Nearest the Pole*. It is not a flattering image. In it, the Inuk squints and scowls as if staring into the sun. Long, matted hair sticks out at crazy angles. His demeanor suggests a child waking up for the first day of school after summer vacation.

Piugaattoq was in his mid-thirties. An accomplished traveler, he was a veteran of many Peary expeditions and was familiar with eastern Ellesmere Island. He and Panippak, Ittukusuk's father, were Matt Henson's companions on the 1906 Pole run that ended at the "Big Lead." Despite advancing age, he possessed sharp eyes and was a brilliant shot with a rifle, perhaps even better than Ittukusuk. MacMillan trusted him implicitly, bringing him along whenever he left Etah.

Piugaattoq must have been a charming man, because he won the beautiful Aleqasinnguaq's hand in marriage. Aleqasinnguaq (MacMillan rendered her name as Aw-duck-ah-hing-wah, Peary called her Allakasingwah, and others called her Aleqasina) was in her early thirties, four feet ten inches and 110 pounds. We know exactly what she looked like because Peary published a nude photo of her sprawled across some rocks—for anthropological purposes, of course—in his book *Northward over the Great Ice*. Peary described her as "the belle of the tribe" in an 1896 diary entry. In 1899, when Aleqasinnguaq was around nineteen, the commander fathered her first child, a boy named Anaakkaq. (MacMillan called him "Annowkah" in his census, and the Inuk also answered to "Saamik" or "Sammie") They had another son, Kaali ("Kardah," in the census), in 1906.

Piugaattoq married Aleqasinnguaq sometime between those two births. The couple had two children of their own, daughters Aviakulluk and Suakannguaq. As the birth of Kaali suggests, Piugaattoq shared Aleqasinnguaq with Peary during the commander's trips north. Wife-sharing was common among the Inughuit, and the arrangement ensured the Inuk a larger bounty of Peary's gifts.

Aleqasinnguaq and the kids stayed at Borup Lodge when Piugaattoq left, as did Ittukusuk's wife Alneah. Although Inughuit customs discouraged jealousy, Alneah may have cast covetous glances at Aleqasinnguaq, who was pregnant with her fifth child. Dr. Hunt guessed she would deliver about a month after her husband returned.

MacMillan and Green must have been aware of at least the broad outlines of their companions' lives. But, except for a brushstroke here and there, they never painted an accurate portrait of them for the outside world. The Americans' journals were for recording scientific data, tracking everyday activities, and, on occasion, offering generalized statements about the people keeping them alive, priorities reflecting their conviction that readers were more interested in them than in their hosts.

———

"We hope to make a landfall in the next few days," Green wrote on April 19, after his fourth day on the ice. MacMillan figured they were around 52 miles out from shore. A persistent mist obscured their view to the northwest, preventing them from getting a bead on Crocker Land. Nor could MacMillan get a clear fix on the sun to plot their exact coordinates. Cape Thomas Hubbard was visible in the distance behind them, as if beckoning them home.

Days passed in a blur of leads and light snow. The party made steady progress, marching about 17 miles in a few eight-hour stretches. Cape Thomas Hubbard faded over the horizon. A dark blob in the distance, presumably Cape Colgate, offered the only hint of solid ground. The men looked northwest, trying to will away the mist blocking their view.

Arctic fog is a dense, soggy creature whose chill greyness can linger for days or even weeks at a time, rendering navigation all but impossible. Smothering the landscape in its gloomy embrace, it dampens sound so thoroughly that sailors who got lost in it often could not hear nearby mates firing guns to signal their way back. It is so thick that two people standing together might not see each other.

Green and MacMillan conserved their dogs' strength by walking most of the way, tiptoeing through the fog step by careful step. Ittukusuk and Piugaattoq conserved their own strength by riding. Dogs dropped every day despite generous feedings of pemmican. Patches of yellow oil and brown liquid marked their trail. "Four days more and we are through," MacMillan decided.

Ask anyone from the temperate latitudes for a description of Arctic life, and within ten seconds they will use the word "igloo." The domed snow house, or, in Inuktun, an *igluvigaq*, is as important to popular images of the far north as are polar bears and dogsleds. It conjures images of rosy-cheeked Eskimos living in vast expanses of pure white. Perhaps the igloo's fame stems from its relative familiarity. Of all the items in the Arctic survival toolkit, it is the only one that can be replicated at home. American children do not sew seal-skin boots or repurpose narwhal tusks into sled runners. They do, however, have an almost instinctual desire to hollow out mounds of snow. The igloo's vaguely insouciant nature—using snow to stay warm and protect oneself from snow—enhances its appeal.

The Polar Inuit used snow houses as temporary dwellings. In summer they lived in skin tents called *tupeqs*. In winter they built or refurbished stone houses lined with sod. *Igluvigait* (the plural of *igluvigaq*) were employed only when traveling, and when conditions were right.

Inughuit parents instructed their children in building snow houses, but igloos were by no means child's play. Great expertise went into finding the ideal materials and construction site. A master builder such as Ittukusuk or Piugaattoq paid close attention when walking over snow. Good snow barely showed a footprint. A clear imprint meant that the snow was too soft for an igloo; the building would crumble. If there was no imprint, the snow was too hard, too much work to cut, too heavy to carry, and too difficult to shape.

Upon finding a promising spot for a shelter, an Inuk dropped to his knees and probed the snow with a whipstock or caribou antler. Did it penetrate evenly, or were there alternating layers of easy and hard? If so, the snow would split into layers when they cut it.

Erecting an igloo required precise craftsmanship—this was no heap-and-hollow venture. Using a long knife, the builder sliced a rectangle in the snow, then kicked out the block. A decent igloo required about sixty blocks. Working in a right-to-left spiral, he laid a block, beveled the edges, and banged it into place with his hand. Higher and higher the spiral wound, each layer tilting more horizontally than the one below. The last few tiers hung over empty space, awaiting a capstone that locked them in place. When complete, an igloo was so strong that a polar bear could stand on top of it. A short entrance tunnel kept wind from entering the house. A plug of snow blocked the tunnel at night. The edifice was so tight it required a vent hole, as MacMillan learned back in 1909 when he almost suffocated Tautsiannguaq and Uisaakassak. Two experienced men could erect a comfortable igloo in about an hour.

Entering a snow house was like entering another world, a "fairy-land," according to MacMillan. Blue light filtering in from outside cast a mystical glow over the interior. Unearthly silence pervaded the dome. Only the strongest gale could be heard. A single soapstone lamp with a bit of moss for a wick and a glob of fat for fuel could illuminate and heat the entire room. A few skins on the floor added warmth. Because warm air rises and cold air sinks, igloos included raised sleeping platforms made of snow. Temperatures inside could top 50 degrees even in −50-degree weather.

Out on the ice, igloos were the only decent option for shelter. Mac had no interest in sleeping against a tipped-over *qamutit*, as he had out on Smith Sound when he lit himself on fire. "Night" had lost its meaning, as the sun never dipped below the horizon, so Ittukusuk and Piugaattoq built a snow house whenever they were tired.

Days assumed a harsh routine. More leads. Wait for a freeze, then cross over rubbery ice, then wait for another freeze. Another snow house. Another restless sleep. Double rations of oversalted pemmican both sustained and enervated the dogs, who were weakening by the hour. Mac lightened everyone's *qamutits* by caching a heap of oil, biscuit, and pemmican on the ice; if they got lucky they would find the supplies on the way back.

Green tried making a navigational sighting through the fog but managed only to frost his fingers. Dead reckoning put them about 78 miles out from shore. Food was running low, the dogs were dying, and the Inughuit were thinking about home. As they floundered across the ice, far from the relative safety of Ellesmere Island, there was one more thing to worry about.

Spring was coming, and with it the thaw.

16

PUJOQ

"We've got it!"

Green was the first one out of the igloo on the morning of April 21. The mist had finally dissipated, affording a clear view to the northwest.

"We have it!" Green shouted, sprinting back to the entrance tunnel. "We have it!"

MacMillan spilled through the hole. He and Green scaled a nearby swell. "There it was as plain as day," Mac exclaimed. "Hills, valleys, and ice cap—a tremendous land extending through 150 degrees of the horizon." Crocker Land matched Peary's description. As Dr. Rollin A. Harris had predicted, it looked vast, even continental. Mac and Green could barely begin exploring it before the thaw set in. They would have to return next year to map just a portion of it. New plant and animal species might be waiting for them. Fossils of strange creatures might be impressed on the rocks. There might, dare they even think it, be people there.

Green and MacMillan considered their next step. Of course they would traverse the gap, but there were so many promising inlets and excellent landmarks that it was hard to decide where to make landfall.

The Americans were still debating when Piugaattoq and Ittuku-suk crawled from the igloo and mounted the ridge. Mac asked

Piugaattoq to recommend a course of action. The natives scrutinized Crocker Land. Mac gave them their peace. A minute passed, then another. The waiting grew unbearable.

"*Pujoq*," Piugaattoq said.

Pujoq. Inuktun for "mist."

MacMillan turned to Ittukusuk. It is land, he insisted.

Perhaps, Ittukusuk shrugged. Perhaps.

Green had seen all kinds of optical illusions during his years at sea. That was no *pujoq*, he insisted. The men withdrew to the igloo to continue the argument over hot tea and an eight-ounce ration of pemmican. "Could Peary with all his experience have been mistaken?" MacMillan wondered.

Before going anywhere, they needed to determine where they were. Green unpacked the sextant and chronometer. Mac, meanwhile, gazed at Crocker Land. It flickered and waved in the sunlight. Green calculated that they were standing at 81° 52′ north latitude, 103° 32′ west longitude. This jibed with their dead reckoning. If that thing out there was anything, it was Crocker Land.

Green remained adamant—Crocker Land was right there. MacMillan wasn't sure. But they agreed on their next step. They could not go back without being certain. Spring thaw or no, their only choice was to press on until the image, whether new land or *pujoq*, clarified itself.

The next morning dawned "clear as a bell." Crocker Land blazed on the northwest horizon. MacMillan sent his subordinates forward while he made a second set of sightings. Confirming Green's reading, he chased down his advance party. He found them drying their *kamiks* in the sun, far short of their assigned mileage. Green explained that the Inughuit had decided to set up camp before reaching their goal. MacMillan confronted the natives. Piugaattoq announced he was going home. Leads were opening, and they were pursuing a phantom. MacMillan shouted that Piugaattoq "was not going back but was going on just as far as I was and the sooner he covered our distance the sooner we would start back."

For all his bluster, MacMillan was running out of time.

April 23 was a brilliant, cloudless day. MacMillan, Green, Ittuku-suk, and Piugaattoq set out with light sledges, caching most of their supplies for the return trip. They were making more of a recon-naissance probe than an actual assault on Crocker Land.

MacMillan deemed it "the worst sledging" he had ever seen. Great piles of ice flipped their *qamutits* again and again. Crocker Land hovered on the horizon, beckoning them forward yet never getting closer.

MacMillan surrendered. The party had slogged about three miles in four and a half punishing hours. His calculations put them 150 miles from Cape Thomas Hubbard, well beyond Peary's esti-mate of where Crocker Land's shoreline should be. "We were on the brown spot on the map and had covered our distance," Mac-Millan said.

With Green at his side, he climbed a pressure ridge for a look around. From their perch they could see 75 miles in each direction. "It was absolutely clear, not a cloud in the sky but we saw nothing," Green observed. The ice ahead presented "a crushed up chaotic mass" that Green compared to "a great meadow-land divided into small pastures by high hedges." Crocker Land had vanished.

The empty horizon awoke MacMillan from a four-and-a-half-year-long dream. He had committed countless hours to this expe-dition. He had been overshadowed by his closest friend, and had buried that same friend. He had fought worthless ship captains, imposing glaciers, and fearsome ice. He had risked his life for an illusion.

There was no Crocker Land, only a mere "will-o'-the-wisp, ever receding, ever changing, ever beckoning." Their destination had evaporated with the mist, and there was no reason to keep going. Ahead there was only ice and more ice. Taking a last look, they turned their teams south. With a "Huk! Huk!" they set out across the rubble.

Mac wanted one final proof. Returning to the team's northernmost camp, camp eight, he fastened his last ax to a roll of Barbour's linen thread, a strong line used for sewing leather. Unspooling it into a small lead, he counted the fathoms ticking by. No bottom at 150 fathoms, the end of the reel. Mac was beyond the continental shelf, and far from any major landmass. Again came the stark reality: there was no Crocker Land.

"I have done as well as I could and must be content," he sighed. Mac spent the sunlit evening documenting his experience. He draped an American flag—the one he was going to plant on Crocker Land—over the front of their snow house. A clumpy pressure ridge looming behind it reminded him of the day's travails. Jamming a Bowdoin College flag on top, he gathered the men for a group photo. Green placed a U.S. Navy banner. Mac pulled the string that triggered the shutter.

MacMillan, Green, Ittukusuk, and Piugaattoq's outward journey ended at 82° 30′ north, 150 miles from Cape Thomas Hubbard, about 500 miles from the North Pole, and nearly 800 miles from the nearest humans. At that moment, they were the most isolated people in the world.

Green was depressed. "Disappointment is a hard lot after real effort," he said. Ittukusuk and Piugaattoq were excited at going home and worried about conditions along the way. MacMillan was in a contemplative mood. "A great feeling of relief tonight," he wrote in his journal. "My dream of 5 years is off."

A strange choice of words, and one which he never retreated from or elaborated upon. Relief—not resentment, outrage, or disillusionment. At this pivotal point in the expedition, and in his life, MacMillan kept his words to a bland minimum. Perhaps he did not want to write anything offensive to Peary or his sponsors at the museum. Perhaps, notwithstanding his pre-trip enthusiasm, he had viewed the Crocker Land expedition as the mere testing of a hypothesis. Any answer was better than no answer. "We have done what we came to do—prove or disprove the existence of Crocker Land," he explained. Maybe Crocker Land had been nothing more than a fundraising tool, a means for getting him back to his beloved far north, rather than an actual obsession.

None of these explanations make sense. Certainly Peary and the museum would have excused him for voicing frustration in his journal. And MacMillan was such a straight arrow that massive deception seems beyond him. Years' worth of letters to Borup, Peary, Hovey, and others prove he wanted Crocker Land.

There are more charitable, and probably more accurate, reasons for MacMillan's muted response. The explorer had internalized his role as leader to the point where it was not a title so much as a way of life. He saw himself as a teacher, as he had been for most of his adult life, and as a role model. Losing one's temper could be fatal in the Arctic. It impeded one's judgment and prompted rash decisions. MacMillan was always a calming influence. His cool rationality had moderated Borup's impetuous heat. If Borup was a young Theodore Roosevelt, MacMillan was more a William Howard Taft, warm and methodical but, lacking his peer's charisma, condemned to second-rate status. Borup penned over-the-top pieces about hunting walruses. MacMillan filled notebooks with Inuktun words. He took whatever came with aplomb, savoring the good times while maintaining hope through the bad. It was a very Inughuit way of looking at life.

"We should get home in 1915 or 1916, if we find Crocker Land," MacMillan had insisted in a pre-departure interview. "If we do not, well, we'll stay there until we do." They did not, and the time for good-natured bravado had passed. The museum had sent him north to explore Crocker Land. Because it did not exist, he had completed his mission. Expanding human knowledge, even in an addition-by-subtraction sort of way, brought a sense of resolution. He was free to pursue new dreams. Perhaps this insight prompted his feeling of relief.

Besides, this was no time to fly off the handle. The lives of four men depended on outrunning the breakup of the ice. They had crossed thirty-four leads on the way out. No one could predict what the return route might bring. Shifting pans might have obscured their trail and relocated their old shelters. The pack ice could separate without refreezing. MacMillan saw himself as the glue holding the group together. Green in particular took his cues from him. Neither fury nor despair would do any good. Their mission accomplished, they were headed home. That was the correct attitude, and MacMillan embraced it.

His plan was simple: get to Cape Thomas Hubbard as fast as possible. With good weather they could double-march all the way, reusing their old igloos and living on supplies cached along the route. Above all else, they must not lose their trail. "It might mean our life," Mac warned.

The next day, they lost it.

A strong southwesterly wind slapped their faces and blew snow over the faint etchings of their runners. They held course as best they could, shifting direction whenever someone glimpsed a sign of their previous passage. Mac put Ittukusuk in the lead, trusting the native's eyes and field sense more than his own. Green yo-yoed off the back of the line. A sudden squall or an accident might snap the cord, leaving the ensign on his own, something he was ill-prepared for.

A small lead halted their progress and allowed them to regroup. It also brought some disturbing news. MacMillan asked Ittukusuk to point out their runner marks. I haven't seen them for several miles, the Inuk replied. Neither had Piugaattoq. "In their characteristic, happy-go-lucky way, they had headed across country," MacMillan rationalized.

"The trail must be found and found at once," he insisted. The longer they tarried, the farther the pack would drift, taking their tracks, their snow houses, and their cached supplies along with it. Mac sent the two natives in opposite directions along the lead's

Fitzhugh Green on the polar sea.

One of the few surviving photographs of Piugaattoq, holding a caribou.

Ittukusuk in 1914.

The Crocker Land expedition's eighth camp on the polar sea.

Fitzhugh Green using a sextant and an artificial horizon to determine the Crocker Land expedition's location on the polar sea.

Green at Peary's Cape Thomas Hubbard cairn.

Mac returning from the Crocker Land trip.

Green following his ordeal on Axel Heiberg Island.

Jerome Allen in the
summer of 1914.

E. O. Hovey at the wheel of the *George B. Cluett*.

Captain George Comer.

The *George B. Cluett* in Parker Snow Bay.

Peter Freuchen and Knud Rasmussen's house at Thule.

Explorer/businessman Knud Rasmussen's ships and supplies proved key for the Crocker Land expedition.

The *Neptune*
in the ice near Etah.

A *fata morgana*,
as seen from
Cape Colgate.

Donald MacMillan, at home in the Arctic.

edge. Ittukusuk and Piugaattoq returned thirty minutes later, having found nothing. Mac sent them out for another try. Nothing.

The men argued about which way the current had taken their trail. It is that way, Piugaattoq pointed. Ittukusuk "grinned and said he didn't know." Flustered, MacMillan ordered them to find the path. Piugaattoq tromped off to the east. Ittukusuk rode a hunk of young ice across the gap and headed southeast, as if making a beeline for the coast. "I thought he was crazy and that we would never see him again," MacMillan remarked. Paralyzed, Mac and Green kicked out a dimple in the ice and hunkered down.

For an hour the Americans sat, feeling alone. Then the dogs snapped to attention. Mac and Green followed their gaze southeast. A dot was approaching. It was Ittukusuk. The Inuk waved his arms, signaling them to come on. They collected Piugaattoq, jumped the lead, and reunited with Ittukusuk, who had not deserted them, but rather taken a fresh approach to the problem. His sharp eyes had caught the trail, patchy and faint, in a direction no one else had considered. Ittukusuk may well have saved the expedition, and their lives. "That day's work by those Eskimos . . . was nothing short of marvelous," a revitalized MacMillan declared.

Like bloodhounds on a weak scent, they lost the trail, then found it, then lost it again. A wave of relief washed over MacMillan when they sighted an igloo's black entrance hole against the white background of the ice. Green was nowhere to be seen, having again fallen behind the others. Mac, Ittukusuk, and Piugaattoq were drinking tea when he straggled in an hour later. The Red Queen, the center of his imagined love triangle with his king dog and the Grand Duke, had died in harness. His remaining dogs were in bad shape.

Still air and radiant sunshine greeted the team when they rolled out of bed at 3:15 the next morning. Bright light scorched their blackened faces and inflamed their swollen eyes. Mac winced from the pain of snow blindness. The sledgers followed their old runner grooves without difficulty. Cape Thomas Hubbard loomed far in the distance. The group stopped at camp six for tea and a snack before proceeding on to camp five rather than having a sleep. Another 35 miles in the books, another double-feed of salty pemmican to the dogs, who were "frightfully thin and needed every ounce of it." Dysentery left the animals almost too weak to pull.

The season was late, and their teams were in pathetic shape. A spate of foul weather might break up the ice and finish them. But fortune provided another quiet, sunny day. Cape Thomas Hubbard rose before them, Crocker Land behind them. "It was so much like land that I could make out mountains and valleys," Green remarked. "We are unable to get away from it," MacMillan added. "It seems to take a positive delight at having enticed us on for nothing." The sledges whizzed past camp four. By a stroke of luck, the leads that had disrupted their northbound leg were frozen solid. The party reached camp three at 9 p.m. Its dogs were on the verge of collapse.

Retracing their route to camps two and one would pull the sledges away from Cape Thomas Hubbard and toward the leads and pressure ridges that had disrupted their first few days on the ice. MacMillan wanted Peary's record from his cairn at the cape. Skeptics would demand proof that MacMillan had reached the polar sea. Perhaps more pressing, from Mac's perspective, critics might impugn Peary's reputation when the world learned the truth about Crocker Land. Recovering his cairn note would quiet anyone who doubted that he had even visited northern Axel Heiberg Island.

So MacMillan dashed for the high shoreline. His luck held, as the weather remained mild and the ice relatively smooth. Mac and Green hadn't been able to find Cape Thomas Hubbard on the way out. On the way back, they spotted Peary's cairn from far away. It had to be Peary's because no other person had reached this point.

"Land again!" Green enthused when their feet touched the shore. It had been a typical trip by polar sea standards, meaning it had been a remarkable, grueling journey. In thirteen days the group had tramped through 300 miles of vicious cold, hostile terrain, and life-threatening delays. Serious injuries might have befallen them at any one of dozens of moments. Only a handful of people had survived anything like it.

Ittukusuk and Piugaattoq set up camp while the Americans discussed their next move. With weak dog teams, dwindling food reserves, and uncertain hunting, they had no good options. Mac argued for climbing the 1,600-foot peak separating them from Peary's note without delay. "No one knows what the morrow will bring in the Arctic," he explained. A sudden storm might pin them down until their food ran out. Green agreed, without enthusiasm.

They drank some tea, ate dinner, and set out for the top. Mac-Millan had underestimated the challenge. The snow was deeper than expected, and its surface crust did not support their weight. Each step of the ascent became a muscle-searing ordeal of crunch, lift, crunch, lift. Cape Thomas Hubbard turned out to be an up-and-down climb with several distinct summits rather than a single peak. Mac and Green lost sight of the cairn when they reached the shore, so they were unable to chart a precise point of attack. It took them several tortuous hours to locate the correct peak.

There, "outlined against the blue sky," Mac and Green saw the snow-covered cairn rising shoulder-high from a flattened ridge. MacMillan now had proof that Peary, Iggiannguaq, and Ulloriaq had stood at this spot in 1906. The Crocker Land story had begun right here, when Peary again observed the mysterious vision he had first discerned from Cape Colgate. Like Peary, Mac and Green experienced a mixture of defeat and elation as they stood on the ridge. Peary had lost the Pole but gained a new continent. MacMillan had lost the continent but gained certainty.

The heavens were as crystal clear as they had been eight years earlier. MacMillan and Green looked northwest. Crocker Land extended out before them. Lifting their binoculars, they admired its ghostly hills, its shadowy valleys, and its snowcapped peaks. For a fleeting moment they believed again. Then the moment passed, even though the apparition remained.

MacMillan rooted around the cairn until he unearthed a rusting cocoa tin near its base. Inside was a piece of Peary's silk American flag and a note.

Mac followed explorers' etiquette to a T. Fishing out a pencil, he made an exact copy of Peary's record, which he placed in the cocoa tin. Evidence of the commander's victory would survive even if Mac and Green perished. Mac put the original note in his bag, then placed his own message in the cairn:

April 28, 1914
Arrived here today from point on Polar Sea 125 miles north west true from here. Leave tomorrow for Cape Colgate— there for Etah, Greenland.

D. B. MacMillan
Fitzhugh Green

It seemed an inadequate description of the past few weeks; brevity was the rule when writing barehanded in –30-degree temperatures.

Peary had left another marker somewhere nearby, but MacMillan and Green were done for the day. They posed for photographs in front of the cairn. Green grabbed some rocks for Ekblaw. Drained, the pair plodded down the hill. They had three days of food, their dogs were dying, and a storm could blow in at any moment. Etah was several hundred miles away. They needed to "move, and move at once."

CROCKER LAND

IT IS UNLIKELY THAT MACMILLAN, Green, or any of the other Crocker Landers had seen Georges Méliès's *Conquest of the Pole*, one of the oddest movies released in 1912. The picture recycled ideas from earlier Méliès films, particularly *The Impossible Voyage* (1904) and his revolutionary *A Trip to the Moon* (1902). *Conquest of the Pole* follows a succession of fame-hungry French scientists who employ a string of absurd ploys to reach ninety north. One tries a balloon, which explodes. Another drives a comical caravan of trucks. A third pilots a whimsical, griffin-headed airplane past flying fish, a literal big dipper, and angelic women bearing oversized snow-flakes, before landing on a ragged landscape of broad plateaus and spiky ice. His crew marches onto the Arctic surface wearing stylish coats better suited for strolling the Champs Élysées.

A menacing, pipe-smoking snow giant rises from a hole in the ice, ensnares the terrified explorers in its spindly arms, and pops a man into its mouth. The others appear doomed until one of them escapes the monster's clutches, wheels in a cannon, and blasts the beast, which spits out its catch and sinks back beneath the surface. In a comical twist, the adventurers get stuck to the magnetic North Pole, represented by a whirling spire of ice. Helpless, they spin until the Pole tips into the ocean, prompting a final rescue by the daring pilot. Seals and penguins applaud as the plane spirits them south.

"Strange is the power which this land exercises over the mind," Norwegian explorer Fridtjof Nansen observed. The remote Arctic has always defied assumptions about its true nature. No wonder sixteenth-century British explorer Martin Frobisher called the area west of Greenland *Meta Incognita*, or "limits unknown." Famed adventurer Henry Hudson said that the North Pole was marked with a black basalt boulder and surrounded by a warm, navigable sea. The myth of a temperate polar sea endured well into the nineteenth century. Before heading north in 1879, Captain George Washington DeLong of the *Jeannette* received letters warning him about sea monsters in the upper latitudes, and about the intense heat venting from the Earth's hollow center at the Pole.

In a way then, *Conquest of the Pole*'s fanciful representation rings with truth. Méliès fed audiences' expectations of the unexpected because that was what the Arctic had always given them. How could one explain the narwhal, a whale with an eight-foot tusk jutting from its lip? Or the presence of tribes with no awareness of the outside world? Or the disappearance of well-equipped exploration parties, such as that of Sir John Franklin? Where was S. A. Andrée, the Swedish balloonist last seen in 1897 floating toward the Pole with two companions? Just as MacMillan and Green were leaving Etah for Crocker Land, the *Pittsburgh Post* ran a piece suggesting that the missing Swede was "living in the beautiful region which is said to exist around the pole." Even the much-heralded race for the Pole ended in confusion. When Méliès's film appeared, it remained unclear whether the first man to reach ninety north was Frederick Cook, Robert Peary, or Matt Henson, or whether any of them had been there at all.

The four explorers camped near Cape Thomas Hubbard in April 1914 had witnessed the Arctic's most amazing trick. Not even Harry Houdini could make a half million square miles of land vanish. Peary, who understood the region better than any other Westerner, said that Crocker Land existed. It didn't. Government scientists, using the latest, most comprehensive data available, said that Crocker Land existed. It didn't.

How could so many people have been wrong? It is a deceptively simple question. Understanding what Crocker Land was, why so many people said it was there, and why MacMillan chased it requires a journey through science, history, and psychology.

What seems real is often not. Our brains fool us all the time. We see things from the corners of our eyes that aren't there. We misremember conversations. We labor under false memories. In most circumstances, however, our perception of what is real in the physical world is accurate. A tree is a tree. Grass is grass. The squirrel flitting across the sidewalk is in fact a squirrel. But such basic certainties as these dissipate in the high latitudes, where what you *see* is not necessarily what *is*. A pancake-flat expanse of white might camouflage a cliff. Faraway objects can appear close, and nearby objects far away, without reference points or a clear background to establish perspective. A herd of massive musk oxen might resemble an innocuous spray of pebbles. Distant polar bears morph into nearby rabbits. During Robert Falcon Scott's final Antarctic mission, his men mistook old biscuit boxes for huts and pony droppings for a herd of cattle.

These optical illusions do not explain Crocker Land. Peary did not mistake a pemmican tin for a continent. So what did he see in 1906, and what did MacMillan and Green see in 1914?

Enormous pans of ice do sometimes pass Ellesmere Island, the most famous of these being Fletcher's Ice Island. In 1952, U.S. Air Force colonel Joseph Fletcher established a research station on a nine-mile-long, kidney-shaped ice table floating 150 miles from the North Pole. Scientists occupied the base off and on for nearly thirty years as it gyred around the Beaufort Sea before breaking up in the North Atlantic. Maybe Peary saw a similar object that ocean currents had carried away by the time MacMillan arrived eight years later.

He did not. Ice islands are essentially two-dimensional objects, discounting the invisible crags riding beneath the ocean's surface. There is a remote possibility that Peary might have mistaken one for land, but not for the land of high hills and deep valleys he described. Nor does positing an ice island explain why MacMillan and Green chased an identical object in the same location.

Crocker Land was no ice island. It wasn't a tangible object at all. Arctic conditions produce all manner of mirages. Whiteouts occur when light ricocheting between snow-covered land and an overcast sky causes the horizon to vanish. Light refracting through clouds of ice crystals sometimes creates what is called a sun dog, a halo around the sun with bright spots on either side of the circle. "Arctic frost smoke" occurs when cold air glides over water so slowly that the surface remains undisturbed, causing a release of heat and moisture from the water that produces an illusion of steam. In 1597, explorer William Barents's men proclaimed a miracle when the spring sun appeared at Novaya Zemlya, off the north coast of Russia, twelve days earlier than expected. It was not a miracle; a layer of warm air atop a cool, dense layer caused light to bend, giving Barents a peek over the horizon. Astronomically, the sun had not yet risen. Meteorologically, it had. This same phenomenon can make boats appear to hover in the sky.

Crocker Land was in all likelihood a mirage known as a *fata morgana*. The name combines the Latin word for "fairy" with the Arthurian figure Morgan le Fay to convey the sense of a fairy castle or magical land. Common in the Arctic and a few other locations, such as the Strait of Messina, which separates Italy from Sicily, a *fata morgana* occurs when temperature inversions (warm air over cold) refract, stretch, and invert an image to the point where it becomes unrecognizable. These complex mirages stack several layers of images, some upside down and some right side up, to produce impressions of mountains or other vertical objects. Most sightings of the legendary Flying Dutchman were actually *fata morganas*.

"It becomes a nervous thing to report a discovery of land in these regions without actually landing on it," the explorer Sir Robert McClure cautioned in 1850. While watching pack ice during a thunderstorm, he saw "a continuous line of chalk cliffs, from forty to fifty feet in height," leap from the surface. The British explorer John Ross abandoned his 1818 search for the Northwest Passage when he spotted a line of mountains blocking the waterway between Baffin Island and Devon Island. The heights, which he called the Croker Mountains in honor of the first secretary of the Admiralty, John Croker, were not really there. They were a *fata morgana*.

"We were forced to the conclusion that it was a mirage of the sea ice," MacMillan wrote in his diary. "This phenomenon has fooled . . . many a good man and deceived Peary, I believe, in 1906 when he stood on the heights of Cape Thomas Hubbard." Few people have stood atop that lonely outpost since MacMillan. At least one of those who has, writer–photographer Jerry Kobalenko, recently observed the same mirage that Peary and MacMillan saw. In a way, then, Crocker Land still exists.

Peary likely saw a *fata morgana*, because others have seen the same illusion at that location. The more intriguing question is whether the commander *knew* he was being deceived yet reported the illusion as a reality. Dr. Cook, Peary's great rival, called him "one of the most ungracious and selfish characters in history." Cook, hardly an unbiased source, had his own uneasy relationship with the truth, but this time his assessment was accurate. Only Peary could say for sure, but numerous pieces of evidence indicate that he misled the world in order to advance his personal agenda.

It is difficult to imagine an experienced hand like Peary being hoodwinked by a mirage, even a convincing one. Although *fata morganas* can momentarily resemble land, their images flicker and warp over time. They narrow and broaden, giving whatever "land" they depict a funhouse-mirror appearance. Iggiannguaq and Ulloriaq, the two Inughuit who accompanied him to Cape Thomas Hubbard, dismissed Crocker Land as *pujoq*, or mist, the moment they saw it.

Even if we accept Peary at his word, his actions in 1906 and beyond do not suggest a man celebrating a major discovery. Peary's diary entry for June 24, 1906, the day he allegedly saw Crocker Land for the first time, is mute on the subject. "A day of comfort, of interest, of *accomplishment*," he wrote. The accomplishment in question was his summiting of Cape Colgate, which he calls "C[ape] ——" in his diary because he hadn't yet named it. He wrote about the nice weather, and about seeing deer tracks, a sandpiper, and two brants. He wondered whether he was on a small island rather than Axel Heiberg, which he refers to as "Jesup Land" in honor of his financial angel, Morris Jesup.

Then comes this description of the view from atop "Cape ——": "Here Jesup Land lay before me to the W; to the East C[ape] Fanshaw[e] Martin & to the S the channel ? between Grant Land [Peary's name for the northern part of Ellesmere Island] and Jesup Land." His diary never mentioned Crocker Land. In fact, he specifically noted that there was "no land visible west of Jesup," the precise location where he later placed the new continent.

Peary made no entries between June 24 and June 28, the day he reached Cape Thomas Hubbard. His June 28 entry devotes considerable attention to Iggiannguaq's hunting activities while recounting the three-man team's ascent of the cape in a few lines. "We went on up an easy ascent of loose rocks after dealing with banks of snow, reaching the summit (about 1600′) comfortably in an hour & a half from camp," Peary wrote. "With the completion of my work on the summit, & the building of the cairn, we came down." No Crocker Land. Not even a mention of seeing a *fata morgana*, if in fact he saw one that day.

Peary's cairn records do not mention any new land. The note

MacMillan and Green found inside a cocoa tin on Cape Thomas Hubbard read simply: "Peary, June 28, 1906," with the commander's signature on the other side. Green would soon find a record that Peary stashed in a saccharine bottle on the foreshore of Cape Thomas Hubbard. Dated June 30, 1906, it read:

> Arrived here noon June 27th from the Peary Arctic Club's steamship *Roosevelt*, which wintered off C[ape] Sheridan, Grant Land. Killed two deer within half an hour of landing and secured eleven in all. The 27th and 28th fine clear days giving good view of the northern horizon from the summit of the Cape. The 29th and 30th southwesterly gale with rain and snow. Have with me 2 Eskimos and 12 dogs. Expect to start back tonight. R. E. Peary, U.S.N.

In 1954, Geoffrey Hattersley Smith recovered a Peary note from a cairn on Cape Bourne, Ellesmere Island. Dated July 5, 1906, this third message is as unenlightening as the two others. "Have been west across the Channel to the next land to the west," it reads. That "next land" was Axel Heiberg Island.

There are more problems. We can be certain that the explorer brought his camera on the Cape Colgate and Cape Thomas Hubbard climbs because he included photographs of both in various publications. Strangely, however, he never published a picture of Crocker Land. Nor does the collection of his photographs housed in the National Archives contain any such image. Peary's audiences loved exciting scenes from the far north. Had he mistaken a *fata morgana* for real land, it seems astonishing that he would not have at least tried to capture an image of it for posterity.

Peary's actions on returning to the *Roosevelt* further undermine his later claim of having seen a new continent. His close associate Captain Bob Bartlett's diary entry for July 30, 1906, reads simply: "Commander reached ship 3:30 am. All well." Bartlett does not mention a vast island.

One small point in Peary's favor is expedition surgeon Dr. Louis Wolf's ambiguous diary notation from the same day. "Commander arrived this morning," Wolf wrote. "He has made a survey of the West Coast of Grant Land [the northern part of Ellesmere Island] and also discovered new lands." Here at last is evidence of Peary's truthfulness. But what did Wolf mean by "lands," plural? Did he mean Crocker Land? And if so, why use the plural? There is a remote chance that Peary spotted tiny Meighen Island, some 100 miles from Cape Thomas Hubbard, and failed to mention it in his diary and cache notes. From that vantage point, however, Meighen Island is below the horizon, becoming visible only when abnormal air conditions produce an unusual amount of refraction. This theory requires us to believe that Peary conflated an island less than 20 miles across, located to the southwest of Cape Thomas Hubbard, with a continent lying northwest of the cape. It fails to explain how he saw the same mirage from Cape Colgate, 30 miles to the northeast. Most likely, Wolf's "new lands" referred to the previously unexplored parts of Ellesmere Island that the commander crossed after passing Cape Aldrich. Peary himself refers to the area to the west of Cape Aldrich as "new land" in *Nearest the Pole*.

Peary said nothing about Crocker Land when he returned to New York. He never mentioned it to any of the reporters clamoring for interviews, or in any of the hundreds of letters he wrote. He did not mention it when he addressed the Peary Arctic Club on December 12, 1906—with George Crocker in attendance—or when he accepted the National Geographic Society's Hubbard Medal from President Theodore Roosevelt two days later, or at the annual New York Delta Kappa Epsilon Association dinner on January 17, 1907. His 1907 lecture tour included slides of Cape Colgate and Cape Thomas Hubbard, but none of Crocker Land, which he never mentioned.

Peary debuted Crocker Land in 1907's *Nearest the Pole*, and in an edited excerpt from the book that appeared in the March 1907 issue of *Harper's Magazine* under the title "Nearest the North Pole." Months after his return, he finally described the "snow-clad summits to the northwest" that caused him to "look longingly . . . and in fancy trod its shores." Peary does not yet name this place, but it is clearly Crocker Land.

Perhaps Peary played a long game, keeping mum about his expedition's greatest achievement in order to make the biggest possible publicity splash. Book royalties and magazine contracts generated from the excitement could raise considerable funds toward his next Pole run.

Peary's notes for *Nearest the Pole* prove that this wasn't the case. A typed rough draft—with his handwriting on the paper—matches the language he would use in the book as it follows Peary, Iggiannguaq, and Ulloriaq toward Cape Colgate. Both texts quote Peary's June 24 diary entry. But while the draft includes Peary's "no land visible" line, the book omits it. The published versions of *Nearest the Pole* and "Nearest the North Pole" insert a new reference to "faint white summits" in the northwest. This is a crucial point. Mountains that do not exist in Peary's journal, or in the draft of his book, have materialized in the final product.

Peary's draft version of the events of June 28, the date of his second Crocker Land sighting, opens with the exact words that appear in *Nearest the Pole*. In identical phrases, he describes a few foggy days, Iggiannguaq hunting hares, and the climb up Cape Thomas Hubbard. "We went on up an easy ascent of loose rocks alternating with banks of snow reaching the summit (about 1600′) comfortably in an hour and a half from camp," both versions read. Peary (or Peary's ghostwriter) was working straight from his diary.

Peary's typed draft continues: "With the completion of my work on the summit, and the building of the cairn, we came down to the sledge and dogs, from whence I returned to camp." *Nearest the Pole* uses these same words, but it also shoehorns in three new paragraphs. The two key paragraphs read:

The clear day greatly favored my work in taking a round of angles, and with the glasses I could make out apparently a little more distinctly, the snow-clad summits of the distant land in the northwest, above the ice horizon.

My heart leapt the intervening miles of ice as I looked longingly at the land, and in fancy I trod its shores and climbed its summits, even though I knew that that pleasure could be only for another in another season. While I was thus engaged my men made out three deer in a valley south of us.

Peary condensed these paragraphs for his *Harper's* article while retaining their point.

Peary had made false claims before. In 1892, for example, he announced that he had solved the riddle of whether Greenland was an island or a larger mass that stretched over and beyond the North Pole. Greenland must be an island, he said, because he had reached its northern extremity. From there he had seen another large island, which he named Peary Land, across a strait he called the Peary Channel. Greenland is in fact an island. Peary was wrong about everything else. "Peary Land" was more Greenland, and the "Peary Channel" merely a fiord. Years later, when Knud Rasmussen recovered Peary's cairn note, the Dane observed that Peary had referred to "Peary Channel" as "Independence Fiord" in his note. As Rasmussen explained, "it must therefore have been at a later date that the idea arose as to a channel between North Greenland and Peary Land." In other words, Peary lied about reaching Greenland's north shore.

Peary had clear motivations for inventing Crocker Land. His goal was the North Pole. He needed money, and his backers demanded results. His 1906 expedition had been a disaster by any measure. "Crocker Land" could save the trip by giving donors a tangible prize, along with the hope that their name might one day adorn a geographical monument. It was a useful fundraising hook.

Inventing a continent has fewer consequences than one might expect. Arctic explorers made mistakes all the time. Peary could always blame mists or mirages if someone called his bluff. And it was entirely possible that there really was land northwest of Ellesmere. Native folklore suggested it, as did the animal tracks that had been seen on the polar sea. Dr. Rollin A. Harris began publishing his findings in 1904, so Peary was aware of the emerging scientific consensus supporting an undiscovered Arctic territory. In any case, no one would get anywhere close to Crocker Land before he launched his final attempt at the Pole. With all the hoopla accompanying that achievement, who would fuss about a few paragraphs in one of his old books?

After publishing *Nearest the Pole*, Peary fell silent on the subject of Crocker Land. Once George Crocker rejected his appeals for money, the new continent served no further purpose.

Were Borup and MacMillan in on the secret? Did they use Crocker Land as a fundraising hook?

No one can prove that they did *not* know the truth about Crocker Land, but there is no evidence that the tenderfeet were in on Peary's fraud. In the hundreds of letters Borup and MacMillan wrote, neither suggests that Peary was lying—never to each other, never to friends, never to family. Nor do MacMillan's expedition diaries contain any indication that he suspected Crocker Land was a lie. The doubts of Iggiannguaq and Ulloriaq rattled him a bit, but his faith in Peary outstripped his faith in the Inughuit. When Crocker Land evaporated, he was convinced that the Arctic had deceived Peary, not that Peary had deceived him.

Less tangibly, neither MacMillan nor Borup were the kind of men to perpetrate such a fraud. They lacked Peary's overweening lust for fame and his ruthless disdain for anyone standing between him and his goal. Borup seemed almost indifferent to his celebrity. More than anything, he wanted adventure, and Marie Peary. MacMillan viewed himself as more of a scientist than a flag-planter, and would have been happy spending two years measuring Inughuit or collecting bird eggs. And both men were so morally upright that it is hard to imagine them misleading potential donors for their own aggrandizement.

Mac was not the sort of leader who endangered his subordinates. Although he sometimes risked his own health, such as when he backflipped off the roof of Borup Lodge, he took his men's well-being as a sacred charge and would never have sent them on a wild goose chase. Had he left Etah knowing that Crocker Land did not exist but needing to make a good show of proving it, he could have dismissed the mirage from atop Cape Thomas Hubbard rather than dragging Green, Ittukusuk, and Piugaattoq onto the polar sea.

So, the most likely scenario is also the most distasteful. Peary saw a *fata morgana* from either Cape Colgate or Cape Thomas Hubbard, or perhaps both. Nothing worth writing about in his cache notes or diary, but convincing enough to inspire a story about new land. Then he inserted the remarkable tale into his book in order to raise money. Peary did not inform George Crocker about the new continent until the explorer received the proofs for *Nearest the Pole*, which had the banker's name imprinted on one of its maps. Both men had spent considerable time in New York since Peary's return, so Crocker was hardly out of reach. Peary said he had not contacted him earlier because "[you] would not care to be troubled by matters that were not essentially vital." How could Crocker be "troubled" by learning that Peary had quite literally put his name on the map?

MacMillan, a ravenous consumer of Arctic literature, must have read about Crocker Land before joining Peary's 1908–09 expedition. Having fallen in love with the Arctic and embraced the commander as a father figure, it was only natural that he would want to advance his mentor's work by conquering Crocker Land. His new best friend, Borup, made an obvious travel partner. And Peary, who was battling Dr. Cook's allies over his North Pole claim, could not deny the continent's existence even had he wanted to. Admitting he had been wrong—admitting he had lied—would devastate his credibility at the most crucial moment in his career. So he let his boys go. Peary had such confidence in his teaching methods that he was sure Borup and MacMillan would survive the trip.

Crocker Land was an illusion that grew into a lie that took on a life of its own. Borup and MacMillan turned the lie into a dream fueled by their shared love of adventure and a mutual desire for scientific advancement and manly glory. In 1914, MacMillan and his companions exposed the illusion yet left the lie intact; they never challenged Peary's veracity, at least not publicly. MacMillan and Green were far too enamored of the commander to denounce him. Ittukusuk and Piugaattoq might have questioned Peary among their tribemates, but no one recorded their words.

Nor did the end of Crocker Land mark the end of the Crocker Land expedition. Ittukusuk and Piugaattoq were still hundreds of miles from their families. MacMillan and Green were a few thousand miles from home. None of them would reach their destination anytime soon.

BOOK
2

PANIC

"WE PLAN TO SEPARATE TOMORROW," Green noted from the Crocker Land party's camp in the shadow of Cape Thomas Hubbard.

MacMillan was in the same position Peary faced in 1906 when the commander turned back from 87° 6'. His primary mission was a bust. Peary, denied the North Pole, sledged west to explore new lands beyond Cape Aldrich, thus beginning the Crocker Land story. MacMillan, having erased Crocker Land from the map, had to figure out his next move.

His original plan had Ekblaw, Hunt, and Tanquary accompanying him to the cape before splitting up to map sections of Axel Heiberg Island. With that no longer an option, he proposed a scaled-down version of the same idea. He and Ittukusuk would travel northeast, across Nansen Sound, and head for Cape Colgate in order to recover Peary's cairn note. Meanwhile, Green and Piugaattoq would chart the virgin coastline between their current location and a cairn the Norwegian Otto Sverdrup had built in 1901, 25 miles to the southwest. No one had ever seen Sverdrup's marker, so MacMillan considered it an important target. Sverdrup's cairn note was supposed to have claimed Axel Heiberg for Norway, so it had tremendous geopolitical consequence. The two parties were to reunite at the old dugout, the one MacMillan's dogs had caved in on the hapless Ittukusuk, and where Green had rejoined him at the end of his resupply run, in three days.

"All the adventurous blood in my veins boiled up at the prospect," Green crowed. Bluster though he might, the weary ensign faced a difficult mission. The polar sea had delivered a thumping. The party's remaining dogs were exhausted, their sledges were rickety, and their spirits were low. They had only three days of food.

MacMillan awoke at around 3 a.m. on April 29. The air felt wrong, almost ominous. A "long-delayed storm was certainly coming," MacMillan believed. He wanted to get moving before the storm hit or else the natives would hunker down until the blow passed. They would eat through their supplies, leaving them in worse shape when the weather cleared.

Over breakfast, Piugaattoq suggested staying put. MacMillan ignored him. The wind gathered force as they loaded their *qamutits*. MacMillan and Green huddled to discuss last-minute issues. With everything settled, they checked their traces and whipped the dogs into action. Four sledges set off in two directions. MacMillan, his vision obscured by the blowing snow, looked over his shoulder at his departing companions.

"Good-bye, Piugaattoq!" he shouted.

The Inuk shouted something in reply. Furious winds carried the sound away from MacMillan's ears.

"Again we get it," MacMillan sighed. "Old Torngak, the Arctic devil, did not see us come in yesterday from out to sea but layed for us today." He and Ittukusuk drove into the teeth of a blizzard. Swirling snow stung their eyes and obscured their vision. Howling gusts sucked breath from their lungs. Their teams strained to make progress against the gale.

Seeking shelter, the pair searched for a nearby igloo they had built during their outbound trip. It was too soupy to see, so they groped along the cliffs with their faces buried in the furs atop their *qamutits*, hoping to get lucky. MacMillan said that they had passed the shelter. Ittukusuk disagreed, and pressed on until, with a gleeful yell, he found it. The roof had collapsed and the cavity was full of snow. With feet and hands they cleared out the debris. They stuffed bags of grass in the entryway, opened the ventilation hole, and lit the oil stove. Warm tea and pemmican filled their bellies.

Outside, the wind roared. MacMillan called it "the most uncomfortable night that we have had." Melting snow dampened their clothes. Both men suffered from intestinal distress. MacMillan could not sleep for fear that Green and Piugaattoq were even worse off.

Mac and Ittukusuk awoke in more of a tomb than a shelter. The ceiling pressed so low that the men bumped their heads when they sat up. Hours passed in silent coexistence. Every so often one of them crawled to the entrance to check the weather, which remained horrid. "Impossible!" Mac spat. The dogs, who had not been fed for two days, were mere bumps under a blanket of snow.

Claustrophobia gnawed at him. "We can't stand this any longer," he said. Desperate for movement, the American decided to light out for their old dugout. MacMillan's sense of duty pushed him from the igloo. He could have waited out the storm before heading for the rendezvous point, but he wanted to fetch Peary's cairn note, and the dugout was on the way to Cape Colgate. Leaving was dangerous. He and Ittukusuk could get lost or separated during the 10-mile trip, or they might miss the dugout and be forced to improvise a shelter in a blizzard. At best, the dugout was merely a different place to get snowed in.

MacMillan and Ittukusuk floundered into the storm, stopping often to untangle traces or catch their bearings. Eight brutal hours passed before Ittukusuk glimpsed the entrance hole of their old dugout. Battered and drained, the men crept inside to boil some tea and collect themselves.

MacMillan had exchanged one bad situation for another. He

hunkered down in the dugout, too stunned to act. Ittukusuk took charge of their survival. Hearing a lull in the weather, the Inuk downed some tea, grabbed a rifle, and strode into the hills, returning several hours later with two dead caribou. The men feasted on hearts, livers, and kidneys, and fed the dogs the rest. Although it was the middle of the afternoon, MacMillan and Ittukusuk fell asleep, "so full that we could hardly breathe."

Violent winds and blowing snow greeted them the next morning. With the dogs exhausted and the weather uncooperative, MacMillan abandoned his plan to reach Cape Colgate. Another failed mission. Fifty-two days in the field had broken him. He resolved to stay put, let Green and Piugaattoq find them, and head for Etah. "Will be glad to leave this cape," he wrote in his journal, "believe that it blows here all the time."

Ittukusuk repaired his battered *qamutit* and went after more caribou. "He certainly is energetic," marveled Mac, who was warming stockings, boots, and himself over the three stoves blazing in the dugout. The hunter returned four hours later with three carcasses on his sledge, another good feed for them and their dogs. MacMillan considered his performance evidence of "good luck and good pluck."

MacMillan kept checking the northern horizon for two sledges rounding the point. One imaginary deadline after another passed. Green and Piugaattoq will arrive by noon, he told himself. Then that evening. Then tomorrow morning. Green's three-day excursion stretched into its sixth day. Unless Piugaattoq had equaled Ittukusuk's success at hunting, the ensign's food was long gone. MacMillan watched the unchanging scene. The shore rising from broken ice, a high bluff, a white hill.

At 11 a.m. on May 4, he saw a single speck coming around the hill. It was either Green or Piugaattoq. He waited for a second dot. None appeared.

Something terrible must have happened to Green. Piugaattoq

was the expert, Mac reasoned. If anyone was going to survive a blizzard, it was the Inuk.

MacMillan sprinted toward the black spot, straining for any clue to the figure's identity. Slowly the shape resolved into a dog team. It was Piugaattoq's. The *qamutit* closed to 300 feet, 200 feet. Those were definitely Piugaattoq's dogs. But something was wrong. At 100 feet MacMillan noticed that the man did not sit or drive like Piugaattoq. Snow goggles obscured his identity.

The glasses came off, revealing Fitzhugh Green atop Piugaattoq's sledge. He looked like he had endured a terrible ordeal.

"Mac," he croaked, "this is what is left of your southern division."

A few days before finding MacMillan, Ensign Fitzhugh Green, United States Navy, scion of an illustrious Tidewater family, was sitting in a pitch-black hole reeking of his own vomit. His lungs burned for oxygen in the thick, heavy air. An Arctic blast screamed outside. Piugaattoq sat next to him. Green was certain the Inuk was out to get him, although he couldn't fathom why. The ensign was terrified. That day had without a doubt been his worst in the Arctic. He feared it might also be his last.

The mission sounded simple: head 25 miles down the coast, locate Sverdrup's cairn, and meet MacMillan at the dugout. But nothing was easy on this trip. Gale-force winds shoved him and Piugaattoq around Cape Thomas Hubbard. Piugaattoq recommended turning back. He saw no reason to risk his life for a piece of paper. They could not hunt in a blizzard and stood a decent chance of getting separated. Green, determined to complete his assignment, commanded him onward.

Swirling snow stung Green's eyes. Whiteout conditions reduced Piugaattoq's trail to an occasional scratch. Green was doomed without him. Piugaattoq had the oil, the stoves, and the savvy needed to outlast this weather. The ensign's dogs quit, refusing to budge no matter how much he whipped them. He staggered forward on foot until he stumbled into Piugaattoq lying facedown in the furs atop his *qamutit*, protecting himself from the tempest while waiting for the American to catch up. In his growing paranoia, Green accused the Inuk of straying off the trail in an attempt to elude him. In fact, Piugaattoq's sledge was *making* the trail.

Green watched Piugaattoq build a small igloo up against a snowdrift. Escaping the wind solved but one of their problems. Damp clothes chilled their bodies. Blowing snow plugged the shelter's air hole. The stove sputtered so badly that the men could not brew any warm, comforting tea. "We were a mess," Green said. A shadow on the wall marked the upward progress of the snow; the storm was consuming them.

The situation demanded calm, and Green was panicking. Piugaattoq ordered his terrified companion to hold still while he tunneled upward. Green sat helpess as the Inuk hollowed out a second igloo atop their first one. The American started losing consciousness. Piugaattoq scooped open the air shaft, bringing in a rush of fresh air. Green revived.

Writing had always been Green's release. Unable to silence his inner monologue, he jotted down random ideas, scraps of poems, and programs for focusing his hyperactive mind in every spare moment. Now his hurried script poured down the pages of his field journal. "Black as night in the hole," he scribbled. His entries during the storm have the feel of a man writing for posterity, as if he was imagining a later explorer removing the book from his frozen hand.

Green and Piugaattoq moldered in their hole for hours before sensing that the wind was subsiding. They ventured outside. Green dug around until he unearthed one of the upstanders of his sledge. Excavating further, he rescued his Kodak camera and some film.

Piugaattoq found his *qamutit* in a shallower drift and exhumed his shivering dogs from their snowy tombs. Green didn't bother, figuring his team had smothered under at least 15 feet of hard-packed snow—an improbable amount of accumulation for such a short period. He blamed Piugaattoq for the loss, accusing his companion of tying up his own animals in a safe place while allowing Green's to asphyxiate. The American inflated Piugaattoq's grumbling into a one-man campaign to sabotage the expedition. When the Inuk criticized MacMillan's overall strategy, Green charged him with treason.

Green and Piugaattoq had no food, and the storm was regaining momentum. Staying seemed as suicidal as leaving. They retreated inside the igloo. Several hours later, the wind quieted, opening a window for escape. A gentle snow dusted them as they packed their remaining gear on Piugaattoq's *qamutit*. We will head southwest, for the cairn, Green declared. Piugaattoq recoiled in shock. Green was a mental wreck yet wanted to press on despite their terrible circumstances. Piugaattoq tried to reason with him. Mac said we should go only one sleep down the coast before retreating, he explained. We must go back.

Green exploded in righteous fury. In *naalagapaluk*'s absence, he was in charge, he said. We will go southwest and find Sverdrup's cairn.

Heavy winds resumed while the men gestured and talked past each other. Thwarted again by nature, they reentered their hole to continue the fight inside. The weather settled down four hours later, but the men had not. Piugaattoq "absolutely refused to do anything but return." Green, with failing nerve and no dogs, was powerless to stop him.

Piugaattoq made ready for departure. He invited the American to ride on his *qamutit*. Green refused. My feet feel frostbitten, he said, so I must restore circulation by walking. This may have been true. His boots were in terrible shape, and in his panicked state he might have forgotten to line them with grass. Piugaattoq thought it far better to lose a foot than to lose one's life, which was exactly what Green seemed intent on doing.

The Inuk shrugged as he huk-hukked his sledge onto the smooth ice. Green lagged behind, growing more convinced with each step that Piugaattoq was intent on deserting him. Green asked him to slow down. Piugaattoq "sullenly refused." Piugaattoq again asked Green to ride rather than walk. Green declined. Piugaattoq whipped up his dogs. The American trailed, certain he was being left behind. Meanwhile, the blizzard began stirring again.

Piugaattoq had a flawless track record with both Peary and MacMillan. All available evidence suggests that he was a kind and generous man, hardly the type to abandon even the abusive ensign to a miserable death in the field. Bred in a culture that abhorred interpersonal conflict, he may have been maintaining a safe distance from an apparent madman, or setting a quick tempo to force blood into the American's chilled feet. If they got separated, Green could follow his runner tracks to their next camp.

Green detected malice in Piugaattoq's heart. All the emotions of the past few days roiled within him. He was cold, hungry, frightened, and mistrustful. His life was in the hands of a virtual stranger with whom he could barely communicate, much less understand on any meaningful, emotional level. There was no one else within miles, no one to save him from this nightmare. Green was special—his mother had always told him so. Hovey had said the same thing. And Ekblaw. And MacMillan. Was this a suitable ending for someone like him? Dying frozen and alone, discarded by—murdered by—a savage?

Shouting Piugaattoq to another halt, Green grabbed the Inuk's rifle from the sledge. He ordered Piugaattoq to get behind him so he could not escape.

According to Green's diary, a few minutes later he caught Piugaattoq whipping up his team and driving "away from me." What he meant isn't clear. They were on the coast, with cliffs to their right and the polar sea on their left. Piugaattoq had no reason to go in in either of those directions. "Away from me" implies movement in the opposite direction, toward their suffocation shelter and away from their rendezvous with MacMillan, the same foolhardy option Piugaattoq had rebelled against a few hours earlier. Perhaps the broken Green interpreted something innocent as a hostile move. Maybe he saw Piugaattoq lashing his dogs forward. Or maybe he invented a crisis to justify his subsequent actions.

Green recorded several versions of the story. All of them begin with him sprinting after Piugaattoq, then firing a warning shot over the Inuk's head. Piugaattoq kept going. Green fired again, this time hitting him in either the shoulder or the chest. If Green was telling the whole truth, it must have been a remarkable shot, fired at a dead run by an exhausted man with bad feet at a target receding at high speed.

What happened next is even murkier. In one version, Piugaattoq's dogs stopped pulling when their driver tumbled from his *qamutit*. Green "ran up and found the man unconscious." In another, more chilling version, Green put a second bullet in Piugaattoq's chest, then fired a third into his head. The divergent narratives then reconnect. Green lashed Piugaattoq to the sledge. Taking command of the team, Green arrived back at the suffocation igloo around eight hours later with no clear memory of how he had found the place.

No matter the details, the result was the same. Ensign Fitzhugh Green had murdered Piugaattoq, a well-respected Polar Inuit. For reasons he did not quite understand, Green propped up the dead man on the shelter's sleeping platform. He tossed a scrap of sealskin on the floor, pulled his arms inside his sleeves, and fell asleep.

Had Piugaattoq died among his own people, his tribemates would have laid him out on a skin, fully dressed, with extra clothes on top and a second skin covering the whole. Piugaattoq would be warm forever. His companions would cover his remains with a small cairn of rocks. Permafrost makes a poor medium for digging graves. Mourners would place a lamp and fuel nearby and leave behind his sledge, his kayak, his weapons, and his tools.

The Polar Inuit had a strong taboo against touching the dead, preferring to drag a corpse with a line than carry it. East Greenland Inuit told the story of Him-Whose-Penis-Stretches-Down-To-His-

Knees, who handled a body before sleeping with his wife. When the man emerged from his house the next morning, a huge raven swooped down and bit off part of his manhood. From then on, the tale goes, he became Him-Whose-Penis-Barely-Peeps-From-Its-Cave.

While he was alive, Piugaattoq harbored no thoughts of heaven, at least not in the Christian sense. "We do not believe in any God, as you do," one Inuk advised Knud Rasmussen. Rather than worship a single, omnipotent being, the natives perceived a world where numerous spirits interacted with the material realm. Powerful *angakkoqs*, or shamans, communicated with supernatural forces in times of illness, famine, or bad hunting. *Angakkoqs* were usually the tribe's best hunters, though on occasion the Inughuit recognized spiritual gifts in women. Hunting prowess demonstrated mastery over spirit animals. With drum songs and dances, the *angakkoq* used séances to persuade spirits to use their influence for the group's benefit.

Piugaattoq's soul directed his actions throughout his life. Like a shadow, it resembled him, resided outside his corporeal body, and was always close by. "The soul is what makes you beautiful, makes you a man," one Inuk explained. A potent *angakkoq* could see a person's soul and, if so inclined, steal it and bury it in the snow. If that happened, the victim would soon die unless another *angakkoq* rescued his soul from its prison.

Piugaattoq's corpse sat in Green's shelter. His soul remained restless. Taboos forbade anyone to mention his name lest they weaken its power. Newborns cried because they felt incomplete without a name. *Angakkoqs* or wise women bestowed names, for only they heard the spirits. One day Piugaattoq's soul would speak, and a child would receive his name. At that point the boy became a kind of reincarnation of the past Piugaattoq. The child was both himself and the deceased, whose spirit would assist him until he reached adolescence, just as the living man had protected MacMillan and Green over the past two months. Piugaattoq's soul would then disengage and pass into either the sea or the sky. Both were good places; the Inughuit did not have a heaven–hell duality.

Green had the same dream he had almost every night. He was walking through a lush, tree-filled valley capped by a brilliant blue sky. His journey delivered him to a cluster of dazzling white lilacs. Beyond them was a half-open door. A plump, elderly baker he remembered from his childhood in Missouri invited him into a room bursting with cakes and other goodies. His mouth watered at the sight. But before he could tuck in, the baker turned to an Inughuit. *"Sinnepah tima"* the man said in pidgin Inuktun. "Wake up."

Green opened his eyes. Piugaattoq stared at him with a cold, lifeless expression.

"The situation is an unhappy one," Green wrote. "Here I am in a howling blizzard with a dead Esquimo, a strange team and a few soaking or frozen garments." It took him a second to register what was happening. Startled into action, he kicked out the plug in the entry hole, dragged Piugaattoq outside by the shoulders, and hid the body behind an iceberg. Before leaving the corpse, Green removed Piugaattoq's boots, which were in far better shape than his own.

Green's eyes burned with snow blindness. He was alone.

His devotion to duty turned obsessive. He considered resuming his search for Sverdrup's cairn before deciding the weather was too foul. Then he climbed aboard Piugaattoq's sledge—his fears for his frozen feet apparently calmed—and started toward his rendezvous with MacMillan.

On the way he located Peary's second Cape Thomas Hubbard cairn, which contained the commander's note dated June 30, 1906. Green's toes must have been feeling better—if they had been frost-bitten in the first place—because he walked seven or eight miles before locating the record. His stashed his own message in a hard rubber matchbox and placed it inside the cairn. It contained a few lines about the polar sea trip and a blunt assesment of the previous day: "The Esquimo [he never uses Piugaattoq's name] refused to obey my orders to remain or to advance S W. He later attempted to desert me for the second time since leaving MacMillan. I ran after him and fired the rifle into the air. He did not stop. I then shot him."

"Providence has watched over us," Green exclaimed when his hungry team lurched past Cape Thomas Hubbard. Looking out to sea, he observed that the same gale that had driven the Crocker Landers underground had also blown apart the pack ice. Huge lanes of open water pocked the polar sea. Had MacMillan taken them one day farther out, they would not have made it back.

"Mac, this is what is left of your southern division."

"Good God, Green, is Piugaattoq dead?" MacMillan cried.

"Yes, Piugaattoq is dead," Green answered. "My dogs were buried alive; my sledge is under the snow 40 miles away."

Green related his version of Piugaattoq's treachery and described "splitting [the Inuk's] head open so that his brains fell out."

MacMillan probed for some rational explanation. Green admitted that Piugaattoq had invited him aboard his *qamutit*. "I would much rather freeze both feet than shoot one of the best Eskimos we have ever had," MacMillan groused. He judged Green's act "a deliberate murder."

Ittukusuk stood waiting for some explanation. Mac couldn't tell him the truth. The tribe would desert the expedition, and perhaps even take retaliatory action, if Ittukusuk spread word that Green was a murderer. In "halting Eskimo and in pantomime," Green concocted a story about an avalanche burying Piugaattoq yet somehow sparing him. Mac said nothing. Green gave Piugaattoq's *kamiks* to Ittukusuk, who showed little emotion at either the news or the gift.

Ittukusuk's muted reaction seems typical of Inughuit stoicism. It could also have been a sign of fear. Ittukusuk knew enough English that he might have pieced together the truth. Or he may have been playing dumb rather than confront a killer, especially when the Americans outnumbered him.

MacMillan brewed some tea for Green. They fed what were now his dogs, packed their gear, and headed south with the wind at their backs.

They were still a long way from Etah. Food was running low. Temperatures climbed into the forties. Puddles of water splotched the ice. Speed was essential if they were to get across Smith Sound.

Deep snowdrifts hindered their progress, an unusual problem considering the advanced season and Ellesmere Island's aridity. Hardly the vast snowpile of popular imagination, in most years it resembled a frigid desert. Green had the worst going because his snowshoes were buried with his *qamutit*. Each day was another torturous ordeal of crunching alone through the thin crust, dragging far behind the others, urging his exhausted dogs forward.

Ittukusuk saved the group again and again. It was Ittukusuk who brought down four caribou after MacMillan fired a few errant shots and gave up (he blamed his poor aim on atmospheric refraction). Ittukusuk repaired the old, damaged igloos along their trail. Ittukusuk fitted their sledges with sails so they could whiz down frozen Nansen Sound. Ittukusuk rigged a sealskin line to lower their equipment down the sheer face of Beitstad Glacier. And, when they were starving, Ittukusuk identified three sticks he spotted in the snow as directions to a cache deposited by a relief party.

One of MacMillan's team, Brindle, started delivering puppies. She ate the first one before the other dogs snapped it up for themselves. MacMillan grabbed her second pup, but it died thirty minutes later. He stuck the third squirming pup inside his *qulittaq*. It kept squeezing through a tear in the back. MacMillan sewed up the gap and slogged for thirteen hours in snowshoes with the wriggling dog pressed against him. At the end of the day he returned the pup to Brindle, who disregarded it. Ittukusuk put it out of its misery.

While camping atop Beitstad Glacier, Ittukusuk saw one of Green's best dogs convulsing on the ground.

"Look! The black dog chokes," he said.

A lump of pemmican had lodged in its throat. Ittukusuk tried to pry the chunk loose with his whipstock. Green leapt in with a knife for an emergency tracheotomy, slashing open the dog's throat. Ittukusuk held out its tongue while Green performed artificial respiration. Despite their heroic efforts, it died within minutes. Its passing capped an "unlucky day" in which Green lost his water bottle, tipped his *qamutit*, exhausted himself chasing down his runaway team, and cracked a sled runner.

Half dead, the surviving men and dogs staggered into Peary's Payer Harbor hut. Etah lay 30 miles across the sound. The ice looked solid. Inside the hut they found a note from Dr. Hunt and a small store of supplies, including some chocolate, much to Green's delight.

Ittukusuk gave a shout: two *qamutits* approaching. Ulloriaq and Agpalersuraassuk materialized with loads of food and supplies. The doctor, worried that warming temperatures might maroon the party on Ellesmere, had sent the two men and all the available dogs to find them. Ittukusuk repeated the story of Piugaattoq and the avalanche within earshot of MacMillan and Green. No one recorded the Inughuit's reaction. Agpalersuraassuk was the brother of Piuqaattoq's wife Aleqasinnguaq.

Reinvigorated, the group stepped onto Smith Sound at midnight on May 21 and reached the Greenland side six hours later. Approaching Etah from the north, they encountered Jot Small and Panippak heading out on a seal hunt. Ittukusuk greeted his father while Small shared the news from home. Jot had killed the first wolf seen around Etah in a long time. Ekblaw and Tanquary were with Peter Freuchen at North Star Bay. Knud Rasmussen was in Denmark. Qulatannguaq's daughter had died in a sledging accident. Piugaattoq's brother, Pualuna, had been carried away on an ice floe and was probably dead.

MacMillan sent Agpalersuraassuk ahead with word of their impending arrival. He arrived to find the lodge "deep in grief." Mac watched Ittukusuk as the Inughuit peppered the hunter with questions about Piugaattoq. He picked up enough words to convince himself that the avalanche story had stuck.

Green seemed oblivious to the commotion. His feet were apparently fine, and he marveled at how clean the lodge was. He had worn the same clothes for two months and had not bathed since mid-March. Intense sunlight had burned his face black. "Of course it was fun to be home again," he wrote. "Not an ache or a pain, not a bruise or blister did we suffer to mar the pleasure of our arrival. But we could not but feel a regret that . . . our whips must be laid aside."

MacMillan pulled Aleqasinnguaq into a side room to talk about her husband. Go back and dig him out, she said. *"Toquvoq,"* MacMillan replied. "He is dead." We will support you and your children so long as we are here, he assured her. He never told her the truth about Piugaattoq's death.

MacMillan let Doctor Hunt in on the secret several days later. Hunt barely contained his outrage. Green "did not consider it murder" because Piugaattoq "was just a savage," he seethed. He understood the need for secrecy, but the prospect of living with "a man who had killed my friend" galled him. Fuming, he discontinued his diary lest someone stumble across an indiscreet statement. Jerome Allen, the radio man, also stopped writing, although he did not say why.

On June 29, five weeks after her husband's murderer returned to Etah, Aleqasinnguaq went into labor in a *tupeq* a few yards from Borup Lodge. She named the healthy, seven-and-a-half-pound boy Peter.

A few days later, Ulloriaq's wife Aqatannguaq delivered the couple's fourth child, their first son. The boy received the name Piugaattoq. The slain man's soul would follow the newborn until he came of age. The peaceful one was reborn.

19

SUNDOWN

JULY 1914, SUMMER IN northwest Greenland. Two months had passed since MacMillan unpacked his *qamutit*, shed his grimy furs, shaved his scraggly beard, and scrubbed the accumulated grit of ten horrific weeks from his body.

Most Americans, if they remembered him at all, imagined Mac-Millan shivering in some barren, white wasteland. Nothing could have been farther from the truth. He was sitting in his home at Etah, writing letters in a sleeveless jersey. The lodge's doors and windows were open, and the thermometer on his desk read 53 degrees. His "To be opened when every thing's gone dead wrong" envelope sat a few feet from his elbow, and a million miles from his mind.

Borup Lodge was quiet. MacMillan had tied up his dogs on a grassy hill near the house. The men were either hunting or paddling their skin-sheathed kayaks in the ice-checkered harbor. Ekblaw and Tanquary were summering with Peter Freuchen, Knud Rasmussen's partner, at the Danish trading station 150 miles to the south. Jerome Allen was off with the expedition's movie camera. None of the Americans had any idea that thickheaded politicians and generals were a few weeks away from plunging Europe into the worst war in history.

MacMillan set down his pencil and limped outside for some

exercise. A few weeks earlier he had fallen from a 30-foot cliff onto the ice foot, dislocating two toes and bruising his ego. It was a miracle he was alive.

Mac stepped from the lodge into a glorious vista of natural splendors. Colorful floral carpets blanketed the surrounding slopes. Purple saxifrage speckled the crevasses between rocks. Arctic poppies lifted yellow petals toward the sky. Fields of white heather, the bell-shaped blooms hanging from rugged stems, popped from the brownish-grey soil. Mac counted eighteen different types of flowers within a minute. Arctic wasteland indeed, he laughed.

With Crocker Land off the map, MacMillan's main task was to ensure that his men survived until the museum sent a rescue ship the following year, in the summer of 1915. This was what they had signed on for—a two-year hitch at the edge of the world. MacMillan was the only one who wanted to stay longer. Each time he opened his journal, a sturdy hardback with "Crocker Land Expedition of the American Museum of Natural History and the American Geographical Society, 1913–1915" embossed on the front, he was reminded of the inevitable end of his mission.

Surprisingly for such a detail-oriented man, he had paid little attention to his party's food consumption. Ekblaw had attempted a detailed inventory a few months earlier but failed to locate many of their crates in the deep snow. Ek thought they were all right but worried that their supplies of pemmican, milk, flour, and butter might be low. Dr. Hunt wanted MacMillan to stop trading food for fox skins. Adventure tourists or big-game hunters sometimes chartered ships for the extreme north. When they did, sponsoring organizations such as the museum paid to send mail, extra food, or equipment with them. But no one came this year.

For a passionate ornithologist like MacMillan, the return of the birds marked a high point of the year. In his heart, he was still the young Mainer who looked up the Latin names of birds he saw while walking to class. He swooned at the powerful wings of the glaucous gull (*Larus hyperboreus*, he wrote in his ornithological field journal) and admired the swift, aggressive gyrfalcon (*Falco islandus*). Eider ducks (*Somateria mollissima borealis*) showed up in mid-May, not long before the brant (*Branta bernicla glaucogastra*) completed their annual eastward migration from Denmark and Ireland. Happy days of watching flocks bustle along rock faces and admiring the cacophony of birdsong awaited him.

Birds were useful as well as beautiful. Jot Small could roast them, or put them in stews or soups. Summertime birds also enabled winter survival. The Americans tended to avoid exotic Inughuit dishes. MacMillan, however, tolerated *kiviaq*, a delicacy made from either auks or black guillemots, foot-long fish eaters that frequented Smith Sound's jagged cliffs. The Polar Inuit sealed a few hundred birds inside a sealskin bag and secreted it in a shady spot, where it fermented for seven or more months. When done right, melting fat from the skin combined with decomposing flesh to produce a flavorful treat that smelled and tasted like a combination of licorice and overripe cheese. The Inughuit ate the entire contents except for beaks, feathers, and feet.

Eggs were a more familiar staple. The natives preserved them for winter by placing them under rocks until they froze hard. A three-day jaunt to Littleton Island, a short motorboat ride from Etah, gathered more than 3,000 eggs from multiple species. A follow-up party grabbed another 1,000 eggs. As a bonus, the expedition located a sixty-year-old record from a member of Elisha Kane's party. Birds plus Arctic history—Mac was in heaven.

"Playing little awks / Up among the rocks, / Chattering and whispering, / Shriek and whistle, how you sing! / Playing little awks," Fitzhugh Green wrote in a bit of playful doggerel. The tiny auk, or dovekie, played a special role in the Arctic's avian–man relationship. The birds nested by the millions in the craggy cliffs along the fiord. Green figured they outnumbered every other animal except lice. Their annual appearance inspired a carnvial atmosphere among the Inughuit, who grabbed long-handled nets and trooped into the coastal hills for the year's easiest hunt. Women sometimes snared a dozen birds with a single sweep of their 12-foot-long poles. Children plunked the strays with stones.

A quick squeeze with the thumbs stopped the dovekie's heart. Hunters ate them raw on the spot or cached them in a bag. Auk skins were a valuable commodity. Women chewed the pelts, removing the fat and making them pliable, then sewed hundreds together into birdskin shirts.

MacMillan saw Greenland as "a garden on top of the earth." There were enough birds to compensate for the poor walrus hunt. Dr. Hunt's brilliant shooting produced a steady stream of fresh game. As Mac surveyed the realm beyond his cramped writing desk on that lovely summer afternoon, he was confident that, even though his main objective had proven a phantasm, his expedition was going well.

Ekblaw and Tanquary had not accomplished much since being dropped off at Etah, and were upset about their leader's focus on Crocker Land rather than on research. The expedition's shortage of crucial equipment compounded their frustration. Ek and Tank had the wrong magnifying lenses, lacked essential chemicals, and needed precision scales and balances to conduct their work.

Ekblaw returned from the Crocker Land trip with downcast spirits and feet so frostbitten he could barely walk. A visit from Peter Freuchen lifted his mood. He and Tanquary accepted the impetuous Dane's invitation to summer at Thule, the trading station at North Star Bay. Ekblaw hoped to conduct a geological survey of Melville Bay. Tanquary was eager to do some zoological work. Freuchen assured them he had plenty of supplies. We will travel fast, he said, so pack light. Other than "a little fruit and some other tinned goods," they carried no food when they sledged out of Etah on April 26, three days after MacMillan and Green put the Crocker Land illusion at their backs.

On August 9, with winter approaching, MacMillan and Jot Small set out in the expedition's motorboat, the *George Borup*, to fetch the scientists. Small turned over the 12-horsepower Wolverine engine and began maneuvering through the loose ice. They traveled at a pedestrian pace, stopping for visits with Inughuit acquaintances along the way south.

MacMillan would have lifted his speed had he known what was happening with his scientists. Ekblaw and Tanquary endured some wrong turns and a nasty blizzard on their trip to North Star Bay— the typical tribulations of Arctic travel. Unfortunately, this was the high point of their summer. Hungry natives had eaten most of Freuchen's stores. Freuchen told the Americans they could live off the land and need not ration their canned goods. Hunting turned out to be far worse than the Dane expected. The larders were bare by June 1. "Peter apparently meant well, but he shed responsibility as a seal sheds water," Ekblaw complained. Like the Inughuit, Freuchen came and went without warning.

Ekblaw contracted a terrible case of snow blindness when he forgot to bring his snow goggles on a seal hunting excursion with Minik. "Never have I suffered such keen or intense agony," he said. Ek screamed in pain while Tanquary and Freuchen shot him with morphine and dripped cocaine in his eyes. The geologist's eyesight returned within a few days, and he never again went sledging without goggles. Several weeks later he almost drowned when his dogs and sledge crashed through a thin spot in the ice that a more experienced driver would have recognized with ease.

Conditions worsened as the summer dragged on. Minik delivered enough seal meat to keep the Americans alive, if barely. Ekblaw and Tanquary had no way of communicating with Etah. Starving and ragged, the scientists quarreled over trivialities. By August they were down to tea and four prunes per day. Through July and into August they waited for a ship—any ship, whether one of the expedition's small boats or Knud Rasmussen's steamer on its semi-annual run from Copenhagen. They accomplished little in the way of science.

Ekblaw was "botanizing" in the hills behind Thule when he

glimpsed a mast in the distance. Anticipating rescue, he tried to run but was too weak. He stumbled toward the ship. It was the *George Borup*. Tanquary was on board eating Jot's buckwheat pancakes. The refugees displayed the prune stones they had been cracking open and sucking clean. MacMillan grimaced at seeing his men "pretty well starved out." He and Jot distributed pancakes and canned pears until the scientists could eat no more.

"When are we going home?" they asked.

"Right now; just as soon as we can get out," MacMillan replied.

Twenty hours later they were back in Etah, "without one regret that the summer was over."

Actually, the entire expedition shared a single regret that summer: other than the postdated correspondence they brought with them, none of the men had received word from home in over a year. Girlfriends and wives hung in limbo, their images frozen in July 1913. Hunt's little girl was growing up. Elderly relatives might be ailing or dead. Friends might have gotten married, or had children, or switched jobs. The men reread well-creased letters and vented their frustrations on a punching bag hanging from the ceiling.

August 30 broke clear and cold following a week of storms. MacMillan paddled his new kayak into the harbor. It was eerily quiet. The birds had left, taking their songs with them. Mac heard the rumbling of an engine. Moments later, the *George Borup* emerged from behind one of the small islands dotting the harbor's mouth on its way back from a long walrus hunt. Dogs barked from the deck. Small, Ekblaw, and their Inughuit guides waved with unusual enthusiasm. We have mail, they shouted.

A blizzard had pinned them down near Cape Alexander, about 15 miles south of Etah. Jot and Ek decided to risk the trip home after sitting tight for six days. As they maneuvered through the chop, a launch appeared to the south. It was Freuchen.

The Dane explained his predicament. On board he had a load of mail that Knud Rasmussen's steamer, the *Kap York*, had brought from Copenhagen to North Star Bay, but there was not enough time to retrieve the Americans' outgoing mail from Etah before the *Kap York* headed south.

Ekblaw begged Freuchen for a few minutes. Borrowing a few sheets of the Dane's letterhead, he wrote two letters. The first went to his fiancé, Augusta Krieger. "We are all well," he assured her. "I have had a hard, strenuous year, but I am now safe, in good health, sound as ever. . . . We must have a ship next year, in 1915. Our work will be done and we expect to be back." Freuchen kept interrupting while the American penciled a second note, this one to the museum. Ekblaw felt rushed. Waves tossed the ship. The words wouldn't come. How to explain an entire year in two pages? Focus on the most important items. We're well. "Mac has said that we *must* get back next year." What else? Oh yes: "Green and Mac went out 125 miles in thrilling at"—no, cross out those last three words— "on Polar Sea and found no Crockerland, had thrilling escapes from disaster." Ekblaw apologized for his poor handwriting ("a wild sea is raging") and for writing such a short letter. He handed over the papers and said goodbye to Freuchen.

"A day of days! Our mail has come!" Green shouted when the *Borup* made port. The men scurried to their quarters like children with Christmas presents. MacMillan read sixty-two letters about family affairs, football games, a diplomatic standoff between the United States and Mexico, Theodore Roosevelt exploring a tributary of the Amazon, Captain Vilkitsky discovering Nicholas II Land, a pilot looping the loop, and the disappearance of the *Karluk*.

MacMillan cringed at the many congratulations for conquering Crocker Land. Another sting came when he opened E. O. Hovey's message. The curator interspersed bland pleasantries with criticisms of Mac's performance. "We should have liked longer letters ourselves, and an article from you for publication in *Harper's Magazine* would have been most *acceptable* to the Magazine and *most helpful* to the Crocker Land Expedition," he scolded.

Most of the Etah crew fell ill within days of receiving their mail.

Germs, whether American or Danish or both, were stronger than even the heartiest Arctic explorer.

If only their radio had worked. Jerome Allen spent the summer of 1914 trying to coax more power from the device. The navy electrician scoured the hills for a better location for the party's aerial. Nothing worked, and he took the failures personally. "Allen is not a strong man and needs to be watched or he will overwork," MacMillan wrote.

With MacMillan's permission, in August Allen and Green moved the radio, the electric motor, and themselves to Starr Island, a rocky speck at the south end of the fiord entrance. Named for a member of Isaac Israel Hayes's 1860–61 expedition, the island was far enough from any obstructions that a signal might reach a receiving station, though Allen doubted it. Green had nothing to do with operating the radio. Life in the lodge bored him, and he wanted a change of scenery.

Allen and Green roughed out a 10-by-15-foot shack at the foot of a rocky hill, a few feet above the high-water line. Wide, horizontal boards formed the walls and ceiling. Flattened cans and cases became shingles. The radio, switchboard, and electric plant dominated one corner. A three-shelf bookcase and small table occupied another. A few lights, a one-burner stove, and a sleeping area filled the room. External light came through a single, one-foot-square window overlooking the water.

With the hut completed—the navy boys dubbed it the "Joy Forever"—Allen renewed his radio experiments. On October 11, he tossed a large box kite with an aerial wire attached into a heavy breeze. Bucking and straining against its burden, the six-foot-tall kite lifted about 500 feet of cable. Allen clamped on his headphones. He toyed with the knobs, listening for any sign of the outside world. He heard nothing, not even static. The kite wasn't high enough.

A few days later he tried again. High winds shredded the kite.

Allen made repairs. The kite crashed into the roof. More flights followed. Kites dashed into the ground and floated onto the growing ice pack. Allen linked two kites together. "He put both kites up," Green reported, "and God immediately put them down." Five futile weeks later, in November, Allen released his last kite into the breeze. The wire snapped. The kite sailed north, never to be seen again.

"Our wireless is now dead," MacMillan declared.

"This summer has been a very happy one," Green said. The ensign exhibited no obvious ill effects from his traumatic trek onto the polar sea. He accompanied some Inughuit on hunting trips and took long walks when the weather was pleasant. Nobody mentioned the murder. It was as if Piugaattoq had never existed.

But something was wrong. Green's contributions to the expedition tailed off into nothingness. He fiddled with a busted chronometer, did "a moiety of magnetic observing," and poked around for a good place to set up the tidal gauge. At Starr Island, he went duck hunting rather than help Allen with his kites. No one called him on his inactivity. Self-segregated at the Joy Forever hut, the ensign hid his emotional collapse.

"Still sane but getting queer," Green wrote in his private journal. Deeply introspective, he sensed that something was wrong. "The black winter days are not the most chilling nor the wettest," he mused, "but the mental torture of them is at times insufferable." He wondered why he alone lost "all sense of proportion" during the winter night. Confident of his own superiority, he concluded that the difference between him and them was that "I am doomed to think," whereas the others, especially the Inughuit, "do not think."

"I have yet to decide whether . . . I have an artistic temperament or am just a plain simple damn fool," Green wrote. Confused by other people, he turned inward. He studied biology, taught himself shorthand, and dabbled in psychology. Books freed him from an "insufferable life of forced intimacy." Green hated his shack-mate Allen's habit of humming through his nose. He hated Allen's ignorance. He hated Allen's cooking. Strangely, he liked Allen as a person. He just didn't care about him. "As a rule we do not bother each other much with any kind of conversation," he said.

Green romanticized his misery, cackling that "I have my books and I have *not* the world." He quoted Byron in his journal ("There is a pleasure in the pathless woods, / There is a rapture on the lonely shore, / There is society where none intrudes / By the deep Sea, and music in its roar"). He observed with delight that "Thoreau's house at Walden was just the size of this one." Green's sincere, charming, delusional inner turmoil recalled a gifted yet troubled adolescent grasping at an uncertain future. But the ensign was no teenager, and the high Arctic was no place for unstable minds. Volatility, as Green had proven, could be lethal.

The ensign reversed his natural sleep schedule so that he could minimize contact with Allen. "It is very, very lonely," he lamented during one moonless night. He felt he was "in space, out of the world in the universe of worlds, moving like the moon with other dead bodies." Mac called the Arctic a garden. Green thought it was "not meant for man but as a kind of warehouse for the storage of all unpleasant things from which the Creator wished man to be free."

Green's unstable psyche manifested itself in obsessive activities reminiscent of the prior winter's compulsive dog counting. On one of his rambles around the island, he discovered a small cleft bisecting two granite lumps. He marched "back and forth" through the 40-foot-long gap, "flanked by black walls and alive only to the problems in my mind." Igloo-building provided another outlet. Familiarity with snow-house construction was a good survival tool, but for Green it became a fixation. He erected one snow house after another, often interrupting his sleep to go hack out some blocks.

It is tempting to view Green's compulsive igloo-building as a subconscious reliving of his nightmare in the collapsing snow house with Piugaattoq. Tangible reminders of the murder haunted the Joy Forever in the form of Piugaattoq's widow Aleqasinnguaq and her infant son Peter. Aleqasinnguaq was depressed, and she unloaded her angst on Green. Perhaps she saw him as sympathetic. Perhaps she knew more than she let on and was trying to prick his conscience. Whatever her intentions, her laments that her older children no longer loved her and that her younger ones over- whelmed her fell on stone ears. "Some people would find these tales of woe very boring," Green wrote, "but I get the keenest pleasure out of them." Unlike the dullards in the lodge, she "never repeats, never has the same sorrow two days in succession; and whatever the tragic circumstances may be she relates them with such wide-eyed pathos that I involuntarily sympathize . . . leaving me such a stock of human interest as can amuse me for days after- ward." Whether from heartlessness or cold bluff, Green treated her like a character in a novel, or as a case study for his own private treatise on human behavior.

A batch of letters from late 1914 reveals Green's descent into something approaching madness. The recipient was Anna C., a young woman who exercised a powerful hold over him, if she existed. The ensign's unsent correspondence to her shows a man clutching at psychological straws. "Dearest . . . I love you more than ever because I know better *why* and *how* I *love* you," he wrote. "A year from now I expect to be on my way to you."

"To you, Bill."

Bill. Green signed all his letters to her "Bill." More precisely, he signed them "Bill Jones." And she was not "Anna," but rather "Dan." To make things even stranger, Donald MacMillan's family and close friends called him "Dan." It is unclear what to make of this. Green was not being duplicitous or leading a double life; the contents of the letters show that Anna/Dan was aware of Green's true identity. Was Green transferring secret feelings for MacMillan onto a girlfriend? Possibly, but his voluminous papers offer no sup- porting evidence for this hypothesis.

Green's explanation of the pseudonyms deepens the mystery. "Do you wonder why I call you Dan?" he asked in one letter. "To your mother and father you are Anna—to the world A— C—. To me you are *my own*, and when I can't suppress the feeling, I say 'Dan' which is my own; and, to me means *you*."

Green's missives to Anna/Dan grew more incoherent with every passing week of wintertime darkness. A forum where passion and privacy mixed, these letters were opportunities for Green to bare his true self. His uncensored heart dispensed clouds of words that added up to nothing. "Of course I owe my life to you," he scrawled, "but . . . I must say it before you send me away . . . In there where I was before you sent for me they say things are not like they used to be. One Old Thought calls it a renaissance or something like that. All the common loafers say it's just lunacy— But the great crowd of nice, strong new ones, and the cheerful ones, like me Bill, just go about the business whistling & singing & nodding at one another . . . and anytime one of the old grumblers comes up to know what this nonsense all means The Singing Ones just point to their little badge—like mine, Bill, see it says 'WE LOVE ANNA' on it—and go ahead working harder & more happily than ever. Oh, it's great, Bill! . . . All right, I won't chatter anymore. . . . Don't you wish you were going too?"

Fitzhugh Green was cracking up. "We are like children groping in the dark for a window latch," he observed.

"A very happy season has just begun," MacMillan wrote when the sun disappeared in October 1914. "Moonlit nights, smooth ice, well rested dogs, and lots of company" awaited him and the men, who "do not dread in the least this long period of darkness." For all its dangers and disappointments, the Arctic had become his second home. Its rhythms excited him. Its exotic beauty entranced him. Its people enthralled him. Crocker Land's disappearance left his conscience unscarred. He planned to enjoy his last several months before a rescue ship arrived in the summer.

In his bliss, MacMillan either did not identify or did not admit the problems within his party. Walrus meat was scarce following a miserable autumn hunt. Ekblaw and Tanquary muttered about their leader's priorities. Small was again hibernating in the house, as he had the previous winter. Allen was chronically ill, and was still living on Starr Island even though Mac had ordered him back to Etah.

Dr. Hunt didn't want to be in Greenland any more. "I ask your forgiveness for going on this trip," he wrote his wife. "It was thoughtlessness. I want to get back now much more than I wanted to go then." The men depended on his rifle skills. MacMillan lauded him as "the Nimrod of our crowd" (speaking of the biblical hunter) without recognizing his disenchantment. The doctor loved the chase almost as much as he loved privacy. Hunting was his escape. "As everyone is free to enter the living room at any time," he complained, "we can never be sure of a moment's solitude while in the house." Although he liked Mac, he found him a weak leader, prone to inconsistency and careless with their supplies. He also suspected that MacMillan took all the best equipment for himself. The doctor didn't suffer fools lightly, but neither did he reveal his anger. For the expedition's sake, he held his tongue.

Some of the men were sleeping during the days and wandering the house at night. They bickered about trivial matters, complained about the natives emptying their cupboards, and sniped at one another for making a mess in the common room. They had exhausted all possible topics of conversation. "How easy is it to talk about the weather!" Green joked. "But what else is there to talk about?"

20

MAIL

Fitzhugh Green administered ether while Dr. Hunt contemplated his instruments. Jot Small lay unconscious on the big table. Inughuit observers gasped when Hunt jammed a scalpel into Small's gut. Children fled the house.

Hunt widened the incision. Sneering at his patient, he reached in and extracted a hunk of liver. The doctor set it aside, then removed a can of meat. Then a ball of twine and some rocks. With a flourish, he plunged his arm into the cavity and produced a baby. Hunt walked to the pantry for a bread knife, decapitated Small, and tossed his lifeless body into the audience.

It took a minute for everyone to figure out what had happened. Jot was alive, Hunt had operated on a dummy, and the whole charade was intended as amusement. It was December 19, 1914, and the Crocker Landers were celebrating Christmas with a variety show. Besides Hunt's macabre routine, the group—even the Joy Forever duo had returned for the occasion—sang and danced on a makeshift stage. A bedsheet curtain opened and closed between acts, much to the natives' delight. Mac performed some sleight-of-hand tricks. Tank and Jot did a blackface minstrel routine. The party marked one of the few times in many months that all the men had laughed together.

The men cut into a Christmas fruitcake and opened postdated

letters. "When you read this you will have penetrated some of the mysteries of Crocker Land and you will have had a long period of the enjoyment of the leadership of a great expedition," one of MacMillan's dear friends wrote.

Christmas came early that year because MacMillan and Tanquary, along with several guides, were heading south the next day with the mail. It was a 1,000-mile round trip to Upernavik, where the letters would sit until the first outbound ship left for Copenhagen in the spring. The men were frantic. Their loved ones had heard nothing from them beyond the hasty notes Ekblaw scrawled aboard Freuchen's boat, if in fact those messages had left Greenland. MacMillan needed to inform the museum about his spring 1915 plans and reaffirm the need for a ship to carry them home. Financial donors would want to learn what the expedition was up to. So would the press.

Mac wanted to go alone, with an Inughuit escort, but granted Tanquary's request to tag along. Tank was "a fine fellow," Mac reasoned, "and, of all the men he would be my choice of a companion for such a trip." The balding, bearded zoologist was the least physically fit of the bunch. He was a terrible sledge driver and had underperformed in the field. But he pushed for more opportunities to conduct scientific surveys, and MacMillan was willing to give him another chance. He hardened Tank with some training walks and trusted the Inughuit to nurse the scientist through the ordeal.

Bad weather delayed their departure for five days. On Christmas Eve the men transferred the supplies heaped in the common room onto six sledges, giving special attention to a 20-pound wooden case containing 300 letters sealed inside waterproof biscuit tins. The Inughuit saw this more as a fun trip to visit friends and relatives than as a hard slog. Torngi and his wife, Green's old love interest Avianngorneq, were bringing their little daughter. Ittukusuk brought his wife Alneah.

Green cheered hardest of all when the *qamutits* pulled away. "My plan was to celebrate the departure of the crowd so sincerely that they would not have the face to hang around any longer," he wrote in his diary. "I don't suppose my ruse was even noticed but at all events they left, and that was the best that could be desired."

The party stopped at North Star Bay, where, to Mac's great surprise, Minik came out to greet him. Peter Freuchen proved a gracious host. The presence of three native women from south Greenland offered extra incentive to tarry a few days. Freuchen's scratchy Victrola provided the soundtrack for a dance. Mac stomped through a few quadrilles. Far more entertaining was the sight of mighty Ittukusuk thumping from corner to corner, in his polar bear leggings, "absolutely helpless and plainly bewildered."

Ittukusuk looked more comfortable the next morning, when he huk-hukked his team out of North Star Bay under the pale glow of a full moon. Tanquary weaved behind him, struggling to get a feel for his team. MacMillan deemed the zoologist an acceptable musher, considering that he had never driven a sledge farther than five miles. Freuchen rode behind them, having agreed to guide the party across Melville Bay. Freuchen said the 170-mile trip would take three days. Mac held his tongue when the garrulous trader loaded one seal on each *qamutit*, enough to feed the dogs for two days. Freuchen was assuming perfect weather and traveling conditions, something no one should do in the Arctic.

The party celebrated the first day of 1915 in one of Iggiann-guaq's old stone houses. Freuchen held the floor, bragging about King Christian IX twice expelling him from Denmark for being a socialist. Or maybe for something else. Or maybe not at all—the tale evolved with the telling. MacMillan believed Freuchen could lead him across Melville Bay, a trip the Dane had made several times, but beyond that, he wasn't sure what to think about the chattering man with the wild hair, smiling eyes, and bushy beard.

Freuchen had been a misfit since birth. One of seven children, he had a love for travel stories and a gift for mischief. He was the kind of kid who put roosters in his teacher's desk and skipped school to go sailing. By the time he earned a philosophy degree from the University of Copenhagen, he was impatient to embark on a life of adventure. Screwing up his courage, he visited Ludvig Mylius-Erichsen, a famous Danish explorer who was seeking money for an expedition to chart Greenland's northeast coast.

Mylius-Erichsen's fundraising efforts came up short, but he did get Freuchen a job shoveling coal and firing furnaces on the steamer *Hans Egede*. "I felt I had never seen such beauty," Freuchen gasped when he first saw Greenland. It was home. He made the return voyage, paid his parents a brief visit, and signed on with Mylius-Erichsen, who by now had sufficient cash on hand.

Mylius-Erichsen's 1906 *Danmark* expedition redrew Peary's inaccurate maps and exposed the fiction of "Peary Land," the landmass that was supposed to lie across a strait from Greenland but was actually part of Greenland itself. Despite its achievements, the expedition was poorly outfitted and led. Mylius-Erichsen insisted on sleeping in drafty tents rather than igloos. Ultimately, he and two companions died of starvation while on a sledging trip. Freuchen wasn't with them. He spent the winter of 1906–07 making weather observations from a 9-by-15-foot shack.

Freuchen made his way back to Copenhagen, where he enjoyed huge crowds and an audience with King Frederick VIII. He considered returning to school before an encounter with Knud Rasmussen set him on a different path. Rasmussen, a famous explorer and writer, was establishing a trading station for the Polar Inuit, and he wanted Freuchen, Denmark's new Arctic hero, to be his partner. Freuchen jumped at the chance. The pair spent more than a year raising money. In 1910 they purchased a rickety ship and enough supplies to get them started. The Crocker Landers were the first party of Westerners to visit the Thule station.

"We have reached something but no one knows what," MacMillan recorded in his diary on January 9, 1915. Heavy mist coated Melville Bay, the bergy hole more than 200 miles southwest of Etah. A quick assessment of the situation revealed the depths of his predicament. Six men sleeping on the ice: two Americans, himself and Tanquary; Freuchen; and three Polar Inuit, the faithful Ittukusuk, another Ittukusuk (known by the Americans as Ittukusuk II), and one of Freuchen's associates, the West Greenlander Hendrik Olsen. No dog food. No meat. No food of any kind except for some crackers and a little tea. Wet clothes. A thermometer reading –40 degrees. And no idea where they were.

They had wandered around the bay for five days. Overcast conditions obscured the coastline. Icebergs looked like islands. Islands looked like the mainland. Freuchen hadn't brought a compass, so no one was sure which way to turn. Whenever possible MacMillan navigated by the stars, using either the Pleiades or the Great Square of Pegasus to point them in a southeasterly direction. Soft snow atop the pack ice made for poor sledging. MacMillan donned his snowshoes and broke trail one thigh-busting step at a time.

"With no food, and no knowledge of where we are, [this] could develop into a serious affair," MacMillan deadpanned. A bad situation got worse when Olsen, who was in trouble for losing a bag of biscuits and a can of fuel somewhere on the trail, fell ill following an eighteen-hour march. MacMillan stuffed him inside a sleeping bag and lashed him to his qamutit.

The downward spiral of Arctic survival began. Olsen coughed and wheezed atop the sledge. Freuchen suffered chronic nosebleeds. Before going to sleep the men hid their traces in their bags so the starving dogs wouldn't devour them. One night the ravenous pack, smelling the traces, attacked Freuchen. "Dey are eating my head!" he woke up screaming. MacMillan drove them off with his whip and went back to bed. The dogs mounted a counterattack. MacMillan paced the ice like a sentry, whip in hand.

Feeble dogs became food for the rest of the pack. Each man's daily ration consisted of four ounces of hardtack and a few sips of tea. Fatigue consumed them. No amount of persuasion could keep the dogs moving. Rather than build a shelter, the weary sledgers fell asleep in the snow.

MacMillan awoke at 5 a.m. on January 14, the tenth day of their ordeal, to discover that the fog had lifted. He saw land—clear, decisive land—10 miles away. Ittukusuk said he recognized the place. Grateful for their luck, the men drank some tea, swallowed the last of their biscuit (purloined from the mail crate—someone had sent a few pounds south for a relative), and hitched their dying dogs. MacMillan broke trail for his team, the only one with enough strength to lead.

Greenland drew into focus. There were two igloos in the distance. The party had almost reached land when MacMillan crashed through the ice. He threw out his hands, catching himself on the edges of the hole before his head submerged. Soaked to the chest in –30-degree temperatures, he decided to risk hypothermia rather than spend time drying his clothes. Everyone dumped their possessions on the snow and whipped their dogs to go faster. Empty *qamutits* made for light loads.

MacMillan, stiff and frozen, barreled into one of the igloos. "I have never beheld abject fear so fully depicted upon the countenance of man," he later laughed. His dramatic entrance roused a sleeping couple, who interpreted the "dirty-faced, full-whiskered object" as some horrible creature. MacMillan recognized the occupants and soon set things straight. Tanquary, Freuchen, Olsen, and the Ittukusuks devoured the hapless family's supply of raw bear, narwhal, caribou, and seal meat until their bellies were full. They were saved.

The travelers gorged themselves for eight luxurious days before MacMillan announced their next move. He would head north with Ittukusuk to get back to Etah for the spring work season. Tanquary, who had exceeded his leader's low expectations, would accompany

Freuchen and the two other Inughuit on to Upernavik. Tanquary was essentially luggage at this point, but MacMillan didn't trust Freuchen with the precious mail, the reason for all their agony.

On January 22, MacMillan handed Tanquary a letter for E. O. Hovey at the museum. "I expect a ship this year to come for the expedition," it read. "Its work at Etah is through." MacMillan requested additional supplies, thinking he might remain for another year of ethnographic and ornithological work. In case the museum refused, he sent a similar request to his friend Jerry Look.

MacMillan and Ittukusuk made Etah on February 7. A downbeat crew greeted them at Borup Lodge. Meat was in short supply, and influenza was rampant. Ekblaw had packed his specimens, nonessential scientific equipment, and a good portion of his personal possessions even though the relief ship wouldn't arrive for at least five months. Small and Hunt had declared war when Small started building *qamutits* in the common room. Allen and Green had rejoined the group but were physical wrecks. Allen was bedridden. Green was feverish, and his joints ached with rheumatism. Hunt thought the ensign was having a nervous breakdown. MacMillan blamed everyone's problems on "poor cooking and irregular habits."

Tanquary got the mail to Upernavik, although he had no idea when all those letters would reach their addressees. The trip marked one of the few times he had felt useful since heading north.

On the way back to Etah the scientist got sloppy and froze both big toes. True to his stoic nature, he completed the agonizing journey without complaining. "He is made of the stuff that heroes grow from," Ekblaw exclaimed. Hunt recommended immediate amputation. Tanquary stalled, hoping his feet would pink up with time. This delay compounded his misery. He held out until the toes withered to the point that the bones were exposed. In a scene reminiscent of the Christmas party follies, Hunt etherized the scientist on the dining room table. Tank, still semiconscious, held steady while the doctor leaned on the bone-cutters.

By then, the sun was above the horizon, signaling the imminent arrival of birds and flowers. The Crocker Landers had weathered their second sundown. The frat-house atmosphere of 1913–14 was gone. A weatherbeaten, battle-weary crew occupied Borup Lodge. MacMillan remained optimistic. Everyone else was fraying around the edges. But relief was on its way. The Americans needed to hold out until late summer, when a rescue ship would steam into Etah harbor.

THE WORLD BEYOND

OCTOBER 1914. AT ETAH, the seven Crocker Landers were preparing for their second Arctic winter and thinking of home. Two thousand miles to the south, in St. John's, Newfoundland, a most unusual event was occurring. The Americans had stopped there the previous year on their way north. Autumn was the off-season in that seafaring town. Docks fell quiet when cod season ended. October was a time for finding one's land legs, reconnecting with family, and swapping stories in rowdy saloons.

This year was different. A war declared an ocean away—optimistic people called it the war to end all wars—had touched one of the world's loneliest outposts. A motley collection of teachers, trappers, farmers, and fishermen, reminted as the Newfoundland Regiment, marched toward an awaiting troop transport, HMS *Florizel*, on their way to defend the British Empire from Kaiser Wilhelm's Huns. Cheering crowds doffed hats and waved handkerchiefs at soldiers swaggering past in blue puttees and caps. The regiment's insignia, a caribou head wreathed in gold, was pure Newfoundland. Civilians and combatants joined in a stirring rendition of "Auld Lang Syne."

Many of those warriors were marching to their deaths. After training in Great Britain, the Newfoundland Regiment went to the Middle East as part of the disastrous Gallipoli campaign. The survivors returned to Europe in time for the Battle of the Somme, where German machine guns inflicted casualties on 742 out of 810 men in the unit. "It was a magnificent display of trained and disciplined valor," a member of General Douglas Haig's staff informed Newfoundland's prime minister, "and its assault only failed of success because dead men can advance no further."

The Crocker Landers left New York during the last year of a uneasy peace that had lasted since 1871, when the Franco-Prussian War ended. They sailed away from a civilization that believed mankind was rational and good, and that heroic individuals could win laurels in the name of humanity. That world was dying. Mac-Millan's men were among the few Westerners with near-perfect ignorance of a conflict that would shape their expedition. Peter Freuchen passed along hazy rumors of a fight between France and Germany. He also claimed the United States was at war with Japan, Great Britain, and Russia, a prospect so ludicrous that MacMillan's crew dismissed everything the Dane said about current events. Blissfully unaware of the Marne, Ypres, trench warfare, and poison gas attacks, the seven men in voluntary exile in the far north still believed that their country cared about them.

H. D. Borup, George's grieving father, embraced the quiet life of a retired outdoorsman. Quebec's Hôtel Cloutier, a three-story, white-clapboarded retreat with a wraparound porch and a lovely view of Lake Temíscouata, became his home. Fishing and hunting dulled his pain, yet Crocker Land haunted him. It was not a place on the map so much as a continent-sized monument to George. "I am constantly finding myself pulling for Mac," he wrote to E. O. Hovey, one of his few links with the outside world. "I want him to succeed with all my heart." Hovey shared the colonel's determination. "One thing is sure," he replied, "Mac is going to carry out his program or die in the attempt."

Borup, living in an isolated village, and Hovey, in Manhattan's

Upper West Side, were equally in the dark about Mac's status. The museum considered the Crocker Land expedition the most important of its twenty-three ongoing field parties. Without a doubt it was the most expensive, and getting pricier all the time. But Hovey had heard nothing from them since the fall of 1913, when the *Erik* delivered their goodbye letters.

Silence invited speculation. One *New York Tribune* feature imagined the Americans civilizing the "little brown men of the Arctic" and recruiting them for a combined assault on the "vast continent." It described MacMillan's team as a "band of daring souls" anxious to "battle with cold and hunger and unknown dangers." The *Tribune* expected the group to return with "such a trophy as none has gathered since Columbus returned to Spain—the discovery of a new continent."

In May 1914, on the same day that Green performed a tracheotomy on his dog, Hovey received a cable from Knud Rasmussen in Copenhagen advising him that the Crocker Landers were well, and were preparing to leave for the polar sea, when he saw them in March. Rasmussen also forwarded a few letters from MacMillan, Green, and Ekblaw.

Writing with the public in mind, the Crocker Landers reflected the jaunty, devil-may-care attitude expected of brave white pioneers. "By the time you get this we shall be exploring new land. Of this we have no doubt," MacMillan reported. The men "are enthusiastic . . . and we are all optimistic." Hunt was saving lives, Allen was running the machines, Green was compiling meteorological data, Small was keeping everyone laughing, and Tank was pitching in wherever possible. Everyone is "just as happy as ever and singing most of the time." Ekblaw described his trip to see "Rasmussen's" meteorite as "fraught with much adventure, much interesting and novel experience and all the scientific observation I could make by moonlight." Green called Borup Lodge "a howling success" and dismissed "the horrors of the Arctic night" as "all rot."

Hovey relayed the most interesting bits to the newspapers, beginning with the *New York Tribune*, which milked them for several days' worth of material.

And then, nothing. A blanket of silence fell over the expedition. Rasmussen's delivery left everything hanging in the balance. Americans were on the cusp of invading Crocker Land, with no guarantees of safe return. Public interest faded as months passed without word from the north.

"Our lot is nothing compared with the poor mothers over in Europe," Ella Hunt, Hal's mother, told Hovey when Europe stumbled into the Great War. Stoic Mainer that she was, Mrs. Hunt refrained from burdening the curator with her fears for her son. Uncertainty about Hal's condition consumed her nevertheless.

Hovey became an unwilling confidant for anxious families from Maine to Iowa. His bland, vague answers to their fretful questions often elevated rather than eased their concerns. The curator rarely shared updates about the expedition without first being asked. To be fair, he had little information worth disseminating. No ships went into or out of Greenland during the long winter, so the dearth of news was in no way alarming.

Silence grated on the families. Victoria Allen, Jerome's new wife, begged for her husband's release. "It would be little less than a miracle should Mr. Allen be able to establish wireless connection with civilization," she wrote from Maquoketa, Iowa. "Since this is so, why should he spend two more years on a hopeless project!" Yes, Jerome had to run the engine, but, she observed, electricity was "far more of a luxury and curiosity than a necessity." Assuming some tourist or sealing ship visited Etah in 1914, couldn't the museum annul Jerome's contract and send him home? Hovey replied that someone had to watch the house and maintain meteorological records while the others were away.

As it turned out, no ship visited north Greenland in 1914. Hovey didn't tell the families that until long after he knew.

―――――

On November 23, 1914, Hovey found a well-traveled envelope on his desk when he arrived at work. The scribbled letter Elmer Ekblaw had given Peter Freuchen on August 29 rode to North Star Bay on Freuchen's boat, then to Copenhagen on Rasmussen's *Kap York*, then across the Atlantic to New York City, and the museum.

Hovey ripped open the envelope and scanned the two sheets inside. Wild seas, given up on a ship this year, must have a ship next year, no Crocker Land.

No Crocker Land.

Disbelief washed over him. Hovey considered the implications of this development. The expedition, and the museum, were at a critical moment. War news had driven the Crocker Land expedition and nearly everything else out of the newspapers. An unintentional media blackout, exacerbated by the absence of news from the north, hampered fundraising efforts for a venture running $20,000 in the red. This latest blow worsened the museum's financial dilemma. Crocker Land was a fiasco, and no one wanted to throw money behind a fiasco.

Hovey found a red pencil in his desk. Circling Ekblaw's "no Crocker Land" sentence, he wrote "omit" in the margin. "In justice to MacMillan we cannot make any references to his and Green's experiences on the Polar Sea," he explained in an interoffice memo to AMNH president H. F. Osborn. "Of course it is a disappointment that they found no Crocker Land, but apparently they went far enough to establish its existence or non-existence . . . and that is a result of some geographic importance."

Hovey considered burying the story, but elected instead to get out in front of it by putting the best possible spin on Crocker Land's disappearance. The next day he invited a *New York Tribune* reporter to his office. Hovey filled his guest with all the exciting Arctic details he could muster, describing terrible ice conditions, MacMillan and Green's courageous assault on the polar sea, and the team's crowded scientific agenda. Hovey didn't actually have any fresh information on these subjects, so he improvised the details. "Undoubtedly . . . they made soundings and other observations which will be a recompense for the expedition," he added.

His attempt at framing the story failed. Crocker Land "has either melted or moved," the *Tribune* joked. "Crocker Land has disappeared," the *New York Sun* noted in mock amazement. One tongue-in-cheek piece, first run in the *Kansas City Times* and then syndicated around the country, suggested that the government declare Crocker Land open to homesteaders. If it did, hardy Midwesterners would scour the Arctic until they found the missing acreage. "The fact that it has ice on it and won't grow fur will not deter them," the *Times* laughed.

The erasure of Crocker Land from the globe reignited the great North Pole controversy. "Crocker Land is not the only discovery of Mr. Peary's that has taken unto itself wings and vanished into the great unknown," a *Washington Times* correspondent observed. An intrepid *Philadelphia Public Ledger* reporter tracked down Frederick Cook in Cincinnati for a comment. The disgraced doctor grinned on hearing the news. "Five years ago I told folks there wasn't any such land," he exulted. "On my way to the North Pole"—he cleared his throat for emphasis—"I looked carefully for it. It wasn't there."

As with most things involving the good doctor, the truth is more complicated. In his 1911 book *My Attainment of the Pole*, Cook twice mentioned that Peary's Inughuit guides denied seeing Crocker Land. Yet, he continued, "I still prefer to believe that Crocker Land does deserve a place on the map." Cook also ignored the fact that MacMillan's revelation undercut his claim to have discovered a large island, which he called Bradley Land, north of Crocker Land's supposed location. Cook had posited that Bradley Land and Crocker Land might be different parts of the same continent.

Peary was in Washington DC when the *Tribune* reached him for a quote. "I believe I sighted Crocker Land in 1906," he huffed, "but I do not care to make any comment until I read the full report." He struck a more conciliatory tone the next day. "It is almost an axiom in Arctic exploration that one can never be entirely sure of what he sees until he has put his foot on it," he wrote in a statement. False sightings, optical illusions, and errant claims littered Arctic history. Confirmation of the expedition's safety trumped the trivial matter of whether Crocker Land was real.

Peary retreated into silence, leaving his defense in the hands of his supporters. American Geographical Society president Dr. William Lingelbach informed the *Public Ledger* that "there is no danger of Peary becoming a second Doctor Cook" because "any explorer, depending upon his eye, is likely to be mistaken." A *New York Sun* editorial insisted that Peary was "either deceived by a mirage or land was actually seen by him." Peary escaped the revelation with his reputation intact.

"Are you planning to send a ship North to bring the boys home this summer?" Victoria Allen asked Hovey in February 1915, as the sun was reappearing at Etah. "If so may I know when you plan to send it?" MacMillan's sister Jessie was asking similar questions. "About when will a ship go for them?" she inquired, "and what ship?" Ekblaw's fiancée Augusta Krieger wondered when she could send up some magazines containing news of "the present stirring events" in Europe.

None of these women suspected that Hovey wasn't reading their letters. The curator wasn't even in the United States when they arrived. His wife Esther had died on December 1 following a long illness. Hovey moped around New York for a few months, then left in early February for a Caribbean vacation. He told colleagues he was going to study volcanoes, but no one expected him to work much while cruising around Martinique, Barbados, Bermuda, and St. Lucia.

Hovey appointed George Sherwood, the museum's assistant secretary and curator of public education, as the Crocker Land committee's acting chair. Sherwood, with his graying, thinning hair and salt-and-pepper moustache, looked every bit the stiff scientist. A twinkle in his eye betrayed a sense of humor lacking in Hovey.

Sherwood entered the scene at a ticklish moment. To get his men home this summer—and with Hovey gone, they were "his" men—he must somehow charter a ship, and soon. The expedition had about $700 in the bank. It needed around $17,000 more to cover its existing debts and the coming year's expenses. Sherwood, a relative stranger to the Arctic exploration community, had no idea where to find the money.

"The terrible war now raging in Europe has affected the financial markets of the United States so unfavorably that we may not be able to raise money enough to charter a ship," Hovey had acknowledged before dumping the issue in Sherwood's lap. Governments snatched up every available vessel, fuel prices were climbing, and the Germans had imposed an unrestricted submarine warfare zone around Great Britain. Every ship, of whatever origin, was a target for U-boats.

Sherwood scared up a few possibilities, all of them either too expensive or too fragile. "I wish you were in my office for about five minutes in order that I could wring your neck or otherwise mutilate your anatomy for skipping off to the West Indies and leaving this Crocker Land proposition on my hands," Sherwood half joked in a letter to Hovey.

Sherwood's best option was the *George B. Cluett*. Its owner, the Grenfell Association, a charitable organization with stations strung along the Labrador coast, wanted $8,000 for the charter, an outrageous price but no worse than the museum's other possibilities. If nothing else, the three-masted schooner cut an impressive figure. Less than four years old, 135 feet long, and clad in steel plate, it looked every bit the Arctic warrior.

Sherwood knew nothing about ships, so he asked a friend of the museum, a burly, balding, mustachioed Connecticut whaler named George Comer, for advice. Comer thought the *Cluett's*

75-horsepower engine, intended as a supplement for sails rather than as primary power, was more appropriate for a coastal vessel than an icebreaker but believed the museum was unlikely to find anything better.

Sherwood placed Comer's report alongside another negative assessment. The Carnegie Institution had chartered the *Cluett* in the summer of 1914 (for $5,000) to survey the coast of Labrador, more than 1,000 miles south of Etah. "The fact that the vessel did not have the requisite power to work through . . . that ice caused us considerable delay," a Carnegie representative informed Sherwood. Carnegie's man questioned "whether this vessel has both the motive power and the structural strength necessary for a voyage to Etah." Moreover, the *Cluett* had leaked "quite seriously" by summer's end.

Sherwood could not afford to be choosy. He signed a contract with the Grenfell Association in early April 1915 after talking the charity down to $7,000 for a three-month charter. Comer signed up as the *Cluett*'s ice pilot, ready for action in case the ship's captain, H. C. Pickels, required assistance in the upper latitudes.

Sherwood also reserved a spot for Hovey, who was on his way back from the Caribbean. The curator had never been north, and Sherwood thought he might enjoy the experience. "There is plenty for me to do at the Museum," Hovey said, "but the opportunity to see a most interesting and out of the way country is too tempting for a geologist to decline." Besides, the round trip would take only six or eight weeks, "and thus I should not be away from New York much longer than my usual vacation."

The museum had the *Cluett*, but it couldn't pay for it. An expedition pitched at $20,000, then boosted to $50,000, had already cost $63,324. Sherwood ignored the problem.

We are "seriously in debt," Hovey gasped on returning to the office. Donors were not in a giving mood. The University of Illinois declined to contribute more money to bring home its faculty members. Yale University refused. Thomas Hubbard, a reliable giver, had recently passed away. Peary also rejected Hovey's appeal, citing "circumstances."

New Crocker Land expedition mail, the batch MacMillan and Tanquary had hauled around while starving on Melville Bay, arrived via Copenhagen in late May. Envelopes stamped "Opened By Censor" reinforced how much the world had changed since the Americans' departure.

New York at last learned some of what had happened the previous spring. "Our year's work is done," MacMillan wrote in an August 1914 letter. "In a way it is not at all satisfactory and very disappointing, but looking at it in another light we did all that man could do." Mac tiptoed around potential controversy. "How Pee-ah-wah-to lost his life I cannot tell you here for certain reasons," he hedged. Green was even less forthcoming. His narrative of the polar sea trip never mentioned either Piugaattoq's name or his death.

These reports are "extremely valuable," President Osborn argued, and the press must hear only positive news. Hovey red-penned MacMillan's discussion of diarrhea-inducing dog pemmican and his comment that Ulloriaq and Iggiannguaq had told him that they never believed in Crocker Land, although "they did see what Peary himself called land." The museum waited several weeks before sharing the material with the families.

The resulting burst of publicity goosed Hovey's fundraising efforts. A letter to past donors teased big announcements in the near future. "We have reason to believe that important geographic and other scientific results have been achieved through the work of [MacMillan] and his associates," it declared. Puffery like this helped the museum raise around $7,000 by late June—not enough to wipe out its debt, but enough to keep the expedition afloat, for a while.

For fifty-two-year-old Edmund Otis Hovey, geologist and volcano aficionado, a summer trip to Etah aboard the *Cluett* sounded like a good time. The curator's professional work had taken him around the world, with stops in the American Southwest, Latin America, and Europe. This voyage promised a mix of professional satisfaction and excitement that those other destinations could not match.

The curator insisted he was traveling north as the museum's official representative. Not even he could explain what this position entailed. He had no Arctic experience and only the faintest idea of what MacMillan's party was doing, so there was little for him to do other than extend greetings from New York and deliver the latest intelligence from home.

Hovey inspected the *Cluett* in June 1915, when the ship passed through New York to take on supplies for a run up to Labrador. "I think that she will meet our requirements very well," he informed Captain Pickels. July 1, the first day of the museum's charter, came and went with the *Cluett* nowhere in sight. The curator packed his winter hat and overcoat and waited. Days passed before Pickels sent a wire notifying Hovey that he was running behind schedule. "Greatly disturbed" by the delay, Hovey pleaded for more speed lest the Arctic window close on them.

Hovey caught a train for Sydney, Nova Scotia, to meet the tardy vessel. He asked the locals about MacMillan, and discovered to his surprise that he was a respected figure among area fishermen and merchants.

When the *Cluett* chugged into Sydney, two weeks late, Hovey and George Comer, who had joined the curator in Nova Scotia, were appalled by its condition. The ship was undermanned, and its engine needed overhauling. Repair teams tore apart the vessel. Hovey supplemented the skeleton crew with a new second mate, five seamen, and a cabin boy. "The days are slipping away," he worried, "and I wish more than ever that we had a good steamer." Pickels struck the Americans as a competent braggart, vague about his Arctic experience but brash enough to convince them of his skills.

By July 19, the *Cluett* was seaworthy. Comer said there was ample opportunity to retrieve the men before the ice closed in, so long as the weather cooperated. Strong southerly breezes would deliver the schooner to Etah with time to spare. Hovey had confidence in Comer's expertise, but not in his optimism. As he walked the deck, Hovey thought the wind was ominously calm.

One of the curator's assistants had sent a lighthearted message a few days earlier. "If this should be the last letter I write," it read, "I wish you the best of luck and a good trip; and please Dr. Hovey *don't* get caught in the ice."

22

DISINTEGRATION

"Boston? Why am I in Boston?" MacMillan asked himself as he wandered the familiar streets of the Hub City. His sisters had been with him a moment ago, but disappeared when he entered the theater. The show was over—he couldn't remember what it had been about—and he was walking alone toward his hotel. A flash of panic hit him. The boys were still at Etah. Why had he abandoned them? Rescue plans rushed into his mind. Who should he contact first, the museum or the *New York Tribune*? Someone had to send a relief ship before his men starved. He had failed the team.

MacMillan awoke with a start. His surroundings eased into focus. White. A snow house. Walrus hunt. March 1915. He was in the hunting grounds of Pitoraarfik, and so were the others. Subconscious paranoia aside, all was well.

MacMillan was a hard worker, an excellent organizer, and an upbeat personality whose self-centeredness prevented him from understanding what was going on inside his men's heads. He was not arrogant. Rather, his love for the Arctic was so intense that he could not imagine the men feeling any other way. And they, estranged from their leader, kept their feelings private.

Crocker Land had brought the seven Americans together. When that vanished, along with their dreams of fame and glory, the only things unifying the group were a mutual hostility and a shared desire for home. Arguments broke out around the table. Half of the team was inert. Green "is not at all himself," Mac observed, without realizing that the ensign had become a bottle of emotional poison. Green shut himself in his room, claiming he was too busy studying to do any work. The ensign's toxic attitude infected Allen, who emulated his antisocial existence. Tanquary remained bedridden for weeks following the gruesome amputation of his toes.

MacMillan steered clear of interpersonal disputes and disregarded the men's emotional difficulties. A more immediate problem occupied his attention. "Our meat supply is very low," he worried. The spring walrus hunt was the worst in memory. The Crocker Landers had enough food for themselves, at least for the moment, but their dogs, and the natives' dogs, were starving. Some people were killing their weakest ones for food. Blubber was also in short supply. Lacking fuel for their lamps, the Inughuit started burning their *qamutits.*

In most years, Pitoraarfik, the Polar Inuit's primary spring walrus grounds, was a festive place where families and old friends gathered to swap stories. Not so in 1915. That year's frigid temperatures kept the sea ice intact far beyond its normal extent. Walruses and seals typically basked on pans close to land and within easy range of hunters. With cold weather holding the pack together, hunters had to drive their hungry teams miles onto the ice for any shot at prey. Most returned empty-handed. The ice extended out so far that hunters risked leads opening behind them—a rogue floe might carry them away. Making things worse, disease ripped through the camp. In what was becoming an annual occurrence, the Greenlanders hacked and vomited even as their bellies grumbled with hunger.

MacMillan had sledged from Etah to Pitoraarfik hoping the rumors of starvation were exaggerations. They weren't; the Inughuit were suffering "one of the hardest years which they have had for a long time."

Their troubles impacted his plans. MacMillan was considering an ambitious geographical, geological, zoological, and botanical schedule designed in part as compensation for the Crocker Land bust. He and Green would retrace last year's route across Ellesmere Island before swinging southwest toward King Christian Island, a flat, desolate, 249-square-mile hunk of rock.* It interested MacMillan because it was there, and because it had some unexplored areas. In the meantime, Ekblaw would head northwest for Ellesmere Island's Lake Hazen district. Tanquary would approach Lake Hazen from a different direction, mapping and conducting scientific surveys along the way. Doctor Hunt would serve as a flying relief squadron, setting caches along the Ellesmere coast.

The Arctic devil MacMillan so often spoke of dismantled this agenda. Tanquary could hardly walk, much less sledge. Green was a ruined husk. Hunt was apathetic. And without walrus meat, it was difficult to assemble one passable dog team, much less four.

MacMillan again pared down his ambitions. For months Ekblaw had pestered him about the expedition's paltry scientific record. MacMillan suggested he ride along on the King Christian Island trip. Frustrated, Ekblaw explained that he could not conduct accurate surveys at a breakneck pace. Mac conceded the point. He prioritized Ekblaw's mission to Ellesmere, condemning himself to a summer of ornithology and ethnology around Etah.

MacMillan left the details of Ekblaw's 1,200-mile journey in the scientist's hands. Ekblaw, no great sledger, took his new team on some short practice runs in preparation for a late March departure. He hired MacMillan's traveling partner, Ittukusuk, and Asiajuk, a former companion of Peary, as his guides. The two Inughuit complemented each other well. Asiajuk was older and wiser than Ittukusuk, who was stronger and a more gifted hunter.

The men suffered a few few false starts before escaping Etah on March 26. MacMillan was happy to see them go, as their depar-

---

* King Christian Island is of great interest today because of its vast reserves of natural gas.

ture extended his food supplies. A single walrus flipper was costing him five gallons of oil, enough to purchase an entire walrus in previous years.

Ek cruised across Smith Sound on rock-hard ice. Last year's trip had left him broken and frostbitten. Today, with Asiajuk leading the way, he was healthy, able, and doing science. Bypassing Beitstad Fiord, they crossed Sverdrup Pass before traversing Bay Fiord and proceeding up Eureka Sound. Ekblaw collected Paleozoic fossils with childlike glee. Ittukusuk and Asiajuk kept him full of musk ox as they pushed into Ellesmere's unknown regions.

Ironically, the Midwestern scientist was compiling a more impressive record of geographical discovery than MacMillan, the Arctic veteran and putative conqueror of Crocker Land. Borup Fiord went onto the map, as did the Osborn Mountains, Mount Hovey, Cape James (in honor of University of Illinois president Edmund James), and Tanquary Fiord. "I could have hugged Asiajuk," Ekblaw exclaimed after making yet another find.

Following four days of exploring Tanquary Fiord, the trio circled back toward Lake Hazen, a 40-mile-long slash hidden in a deep valley in the northeast corner of Ellesmere. Ekblaw's emotions ping-ponged. Stunning glaciers, high mountains, and looming cliffs "as grand as any I saw in the North" brought him close to tears. Then, while camping near the head of Greely Fiord, a gloomy foreboding gripped him. This is "one of the dreariest, loneliest, coldest spots on this old globe of ours," he wrote.

Ekblaw had to get back to Greenland before the ice broke up or else the rescue ship would waste precious days searching for him on Ellesmere. Loneliness was creeping in. He figured that someone would meet him at Lake Hazen, then at Fort Conger, where he suffered a sudden attack of stomach cramps so severe that he wrote some "good-by messages" before recovering.

Ekblaw's party had been in the field for two and a half months when they met Ulloriaq, Aqqioq, and Fitzhugh Green near Greenland's Cape Independence. "I was glad to talk American again," the geologist sighed.

Green was making his first extended trip since the previous year's disaster. MacMillan expressed no reservations about dispatching the disgraced ensign on this important relief mission. With Tanquary incapacitated and Hunt splitting time between killing game and treating the infirm, his personnel options were in any case limited.

Green was more interested in escaping the "unsociable atmosphere at the headquarters table" than in following his leader's instructions. Mac wanted detailed maps of his course. Improving the existing vague, inaccurate charts would give the expedition another scientific achievement. Green did study the landscape. He admired majestic Humboldt Glacier and counted the polar bear tracks crisscrossing his path. He drew cartoons and sketched interesting-looking boulders. Deeming the old maps "adequate," he took a few desultory bearings and called it a day.

Green and Ekblaw's unified, six-sledge expedition reached Etah in half the time it had taken Green to make the outbound trip. The ensign was pleased with their speed, unaware that Ekblaw was setting a blistering pace because his preening, dreaming, chattering companion drove him crazy. When they pulled up outside the lodge on June 16, the nut-brown Ekblaw hopped from a *qamutit* loaded with musk ox skins and told MacMillan that he would never work with Green again. "Says he cannot get along with him," a puzzled MacMillan recorded. He granted Ekblaw's request, reasoning that the geologist "is easily my best man."

Ekblaw's trek provided an upbeat coda for an expedition that kept striking wrong notes. Nobody was taking magnetic or seismographic readings, and the party's meteorological records were spotty. Tanquary was preparing specimens but remained unfit for fieldwork. Allen and Small hunted and hung around the lodge.

While Ekblaw was away, Mac had indulged his passion for Inughuit life. Considering the time and effort expended in getting the Crocker Land expedition underway, he was unsure whether he'd ever come north again. He let his men come and go as they pleased, offering little direction or oversight.

MacMillan meandered wherever game animals led him, most of the time with Aqqioq at his side. He justified these wanderings as exercises in ethnography. He transcribed oral histories, to the extent that his limited language skills made possible, and measured Inuk subjects with no systemic research program in mind. Mostly he dallied with the Polar Inuit. "I wish I were one of them," he thought, while watching the natives going about their daily business.

Food remained in short supply. Many of the dogs were wobbling on their feet. Vicious intestinal disorders left their drivers in a similar state. Violent summer snowstorms depressed egg collection, which might have suffered anyway following the previous year's enormous haul. They gathered fewer than 2,000 eggs in 1915, compared with over 5,000 the previous summer. MacMillan was dismayed. Fewer eggs meant fewer ornithological specimens. Meanwhile, his men watched their flour and sugar reserves dwindle. On their own initiative, they stopped sharing these staples with houseguests. MacMillan assumed that the natives would "give us a part of all they get" should the Americans' food situation worsen.

Peter Freuchen, a potential lifeline, was also low on food. Unsure when the next ship would come, and unsure whether Denmark was an independent nation or a German conquest, he hoarded his remaining supplies. Persistent rumors suggested that Freuchen was unhappy with his American colleagues. If true, his frustration likely stemmed from MacMillan's willingness to pay higher prices for fox skins than he himself could afford. In the Dane's eyes, the Crocker Landers were squeezing him into bankruptcy.

None of this bothered MacMillan, who was considering a bold idea. His last batch of outgoing mail had included an order for enough supplies to last him another year. Assuming those letters got through, and assuming the rescue ship carried the requested

provisions, he was "strongly tempted" to land everything on Ellesmere's southern coast "and have another try at Crocker Land."
Despite the previous summer's disappointment on the polar sea, he
still believed in a lost Arctic continent. The data had not changed.
Scientists said there was land out there, and he was determined
to find it. MacMillan shared his plan with some of the men, who
wanted nothing to do his scheme. Exploration no longer interested
them. Home was calling.

Hunt stood outside Borup Lodge, staring down ice-pocked Foulke
Fiord toward Smith Sound. "By God! There she is, sure as hell!"
he roared. The doctor clamped his binoculars to his face. Masts,
rigging, a hull. The ship was coming. Was it the *Roosevelt*? It wasn't
the *Diana* or the *Erik*. Perhaps the three-masted *Neptune*? It didn't
matter. Whatever the vessel, the important thing was that rescuers
were on their way.

The shape loomed on the horizon for hours without getting
any closer. Hunt watched in dismay as the ebbing tide carried his
savior out of sight. An iceberg. It was only an iceberg. Too disappointed for words, he retreated into the lodge.

"Jerome [Allen] is counting the days now and checking them off
each night up to the arrival of the ship," MacMillan noted. Abandoning all pretense of conducting scientific research, the Crocker
Landers focused on getting away from Greenland as fast as possible. Ekblaw and Tanquary packed hundreds of wooden specimen
boxes. Crates of personal gear accumulated in the lodge, outside
the lodge, alongside Green and Allen's Joy Forever shack, and on
the beach. The men predicted a ship by August 1. MacMillan put
its arrival between August 15 and 20, selecting a later date to tamp
down anticipation.

Horrible ice conditions plagued northwest Greenland. Unsea-
sonal snow and ice storms dashed hopes of an early breakup. The
weather zigzagged, 55-degree days that puddled the fiord alternating with days of stiff gales and subfreezing temperatures. Linger-

ing ice accumulations might prevent rescuers from penetrating Melville Bay.

"We are expecting a ship every day," Green noted in early August. Jot Small, who hadn't taken a bath in two years, was talking about immersing himself the moment his deliverers arrived.

"As far as I am concerned it makes very little difference," MacMillan said of his team's obsession. The expedition leader was a man apart. He looked forward to a ship only because rescue would alleviate his party's desperation. In 1909, the last time he had left the Arctic, he and Borup were planning their assault on Crocker Land. Six years later, he wondered whether he would ever revisit the region that was becoming his home.

MacMillan enacted the sad rituals of separation. Two years earlier H. D. Borup had asked him to give George's field glasses to the Inuk "who stood by us and was faithful to the last." MacMillan decided that Aqqioq deserved that honor. He handed over the glasses, a .45 Smith and Wesson, and 100 cartridges when Aqqioq and Ulloriaq left for their hunting grounds at Anoritooq. "I have seen them for the last time," he grieved as their figures faded into the distance. He gave Ittukusuk his automatic rifle when the hunter departed a few days later.

Two months of summer storms finally passed. Calm winds stilled the waters in front of the lodge. Etah's flowered hills reflected off the rippling surface like dancing schools of multihued fish. Natives expecting a ship laden with goodies started filtering in. The Americans trained their eyes south, and waited.

23

IN A PICKEL

"*Umiak-suah!*" Jerome Allen shouted in his best impression of Inuktun. "*Umiak-suah!*" He rushed into the lodge, shouting, "A ship! A ship!" The radioman had never recovered from his winter in the Joy Forever shack on Starr Island. He tired easily and endured chronic stomach pain that he blamed on the expedition's whole-wheat hardtack. Moving faster than he had in a long time, he grabbed a pair of field glasses and dashed back outside. He brought the ship into focus.

It was an iceberg. Another illusion. Allen shuffled inside.

Only Allen and Hunt were still expecting relief on September 5, the day the iceberg passed Etah. The reality of a third year in the Arctic unleashed pent-up tensions within the group. A nasty confrontation occurred when Dr. Hunt accused Mac of endangering everyone by trading food for fox skins. MacMillan defended the practice. We need the Polar Inuit's good will, he said, and the skins will help ameliorate the expedition's egregious cost overruns.

Without permission from MacMillan, the Crocker Landers appointed a three-man committee to ration food and fuel, and to post monthly accountings of their reserves. They expelled most of the Inughuit from the house because they ate too much. Two women, Viivi and Piugaattoq's widow Aleqasinnguaq, stayed on to do the sewing and housework in exchange for tea, hardtack, and oil. MacMillan got to keep Qaarqutsiaq, whom he called "Jimmie," as his "general assistant." Jimmie worked for tea (without milk or sugar), dog biscuit, and a little tobacco.

MacMillan was unaware of how deep the men's discontent ran. Jot Small remained devoted to his longtime friend. Allen, Ekblaw, Green, and Tanquary, on the other hand, secretly named Hunt as their shadow leader, ready to assume command if MacMillan reneged on the agreement. "This was mutiny," Hunt acknowledged.

MacMillan cast his sleepy eyes around his tent, wondering why Aqqioq was shouting. Ten days had passed since Allen mistook the iceberg for a ship. Weary from the previous day's seal hunt, Mac had no interest in waking up at four in the morning. But the volume of Aqqioq's voice suggested something important, so he lurched into the brisk, dark day. Slowly his circumstances clicked into place. Mid-September. Neqi, a popular hunting site 45 miles south of Etah. Jot was around somewhere. Probably still sleeping. Aqqioq's constant companion Ulloriaq would be close by. Why was Aqqioq making that awful din?

MacMillan followed the Inuk's pointing finger. A shape in the water. The faint putt-putting of a motor. Too small for a steamer. It looked like Peter Freuchen's motorboat. Peter coming for a visit?

Ekblaw, Green, and Tanquary waved from the rail. Mac had left them at Etah a few days earlier. He didn't see Dr. Hunt.

Jerome Allen's voice rang out. "Dr. Hovey is here!"

Hovey stepped into view. "How is it for going home?" he yelled.

Jot and Mac rowed out to the boat to hear Hovey explain why he was floating off the coast of Neqi in Peter Freuchen's boat several weeks after the expedition had dismissed any chance of rescue.

The *George B. Cluett*'s departure from Sydney, tardy though it was, could not have been more auspicious. Sunlight dappled the water and sparkled on the roof of the town's giant coal plant. Hovey filmed the ship nosing away from the pier, then had it return to pick him up—movie studios were always buying footage of exotic locations. Captain Pickels boasted that he would have his new, inexperienced crew humming in unison before the *Cluett* reached Greenland. Chum, Pickels's purebred Newfoundland dog, capered around the deck.

The *Cluett* cruised along at five knots per hour, fast enough for a worry-free round trip. A buoyant spirit pervaded the ship. Pickels and Comer swapped outrageous sea stories. Between them they had a wealth of material. Pickels had run away from home at age thirteen and plied the waves for twenty years, the past four in Labrador and Newfoundland for the Grenfell Association. Comer boasted forty years' experience, at ports from Africa to Hudson's Bay. The captains were two sides of the same coin, stolidly built salts with piercing gazes and bushy moustaches. Reveling in the camaraderie, Hovey cranked up the Victrola that Admiral Peary had donated as a gift for Uutaaq, one of the Inughuit on his trip to the North Pole. Chum approached the machine with amazement, looking for all the world like a furrier version of Nipper, the dog in the famous "His Master's Voice" advertisements.

Then the *Cluett*'s engine broke. A cracked flywheel slipped off the crankshaft. Pickels and his engineer improvised some makeshift repairs in Battle Harbor but could not keep the propeller turning. The crew unfurled the sails and pushed on. Hovey had figured on finding MacMillan by August 15, leaving plenty of time to outrun the encroaching ice. Instead, mid-August found the *Cluett* stalled at Melville Bay's southern limit, some 300 miles from its goal.

Hovey took photographs, stroked a sealskin he planned to display in his office, and waited for something to happen. Pickels nibbled at the ice without challenging it. His crew displayed little discipline or drive. Comer wondered why he was there; the captain never asked his ice pilot for advice. Comer was shocked to discover that the *Cluett* lacked such basic Arctic travel tools as ice anchors, pushing poles, ice saws, pickaxes, and dynamite. Chum amused himself by padding down the ship's ladder to explore the ice. Then he bit Comer's hand. Pickels had one of his men shoot the dog. "There was nothing else to be done," Hovey shrugged.

Early September found the *Cluett* at Cape York, 150 miles from Etah. Comer doubted they would make it. Pickels didn't care how far north they went so long as he got home before winter.

Pickels turned inland at Cape Atholl, the rocky outcropping that marked the entrance to North Star Bay. Hovey's heart leapt when he saw two boats dodging through the floes. A tall white man materialized, bareheaded and clad in skins. His long beard gave him "the appearance of a Norse Viking of the older times." There were only a few whites in this part of the world, so Hovey guessed the man's identity.

"Are you Peter Freuchen?" Hovey shouted.

He was.

"Oh, thank goodness, we are saved at last!" Hovey exclaimed.

The Dane was towing his employer Knud Rasmussen's ship, the 35-ton *Kap York*, behind his motorboat, the *Ingerlis*. The *Kap York* had just departed for Europe after a brutal run up from southern Greenland when its screw shaft snapped against the ice.

Hovey asked about taking the *Kap York* to Etah. Out of the question, Freuchen replied, noting its damaged condition, but he was willing to pilot him up there in the *Ingerlis*. If they left in a few hours, they could be back by the following night. Freuchen had to hurry so he could drag the *Kap York* south for repairs before ice sealed the ports.

Overjoyed by his good fortune, Hovey lunched with the explorer and his Inuit wife Navarana. The American displayed a collection of empty brass cartridges he intended to use as trade goods. "When they polish them the brass will shine, which is what the Eskimos like," he explained. "I could not understand how an internationally known scientist could be so lacking in the understanding of human nature," Freuchen sighed.

Hovey, Freuchen, Sigluk (one of Peary's North Pole companions), and Freuchen's friend Hendrik Olsen, the West Greenlander who had misplaced the dog biscuits and fuel during the previous year's mail run, steered north in the *Ingerlis*. They made a quick stop to deliver Uutaaq's Victrola. Twenty-five miles from Etah the motor died. Olsen repaired the engine, but a northeasterly gale pinned them down. Hovey spent his fifty-third birthday in "a wretched and precarious situation." He was afraid that the wind would dash them into the rocks, or that a chunk of granite falling from the 700-foot cliffs might crush them.

At 6 a.m. on September 14, the fourth day of what was supposed to be a one-day round trip, the *Ingerlis* puttered past Allen and Green's hut on Starr Island. It reached Borup Lodge a half hour later. Tanquary saw it first. The zoologist hobbled down the steep path toward the shore. Freuchen's shout, "Dr. Hovey is with me!" caught him by surprise. He gave the deerskin-coated figure on deck a double-take before recognizing his fellow scientist.

Allen, Ekblaw, and Green joined Tanquary. We can pick up MacMillan and Small at Neqi on our way south, they explained. But Hunt had headed north the previous day to shoot caribou, and no one knew where he was.

Hovey insisted on leaving immediately. The Americans tossed records, photographs, specimens, and personal effects onto the *Ingerlis*. Nukappiannguaq dashed off in Hunt's general direction. The Inuk returned around midday. Hunt was too far away to retrieve in time, he said. Ekblaw made a snap decision, dashing off a note for the doctor. "If Mac does not stay," he wrote, "I shall do so, so you will not be abandoned entirely, old man." This noble gesture was typical of the geologist who, two years earlier, hadn't the foggiest idea about preparing for an Arctic expedition. Hovey added his own message: Freuchen said they couldn't wait for him.

Twelve hours after arriving, the overcrowded *Ingerlis* pulled away from Borup Lodge. Four Americans—a radioman, two scientists, and a murderer—watched their home recede into the distance. All had left New York with visions of immortality. Now, with their dreams turned into mist, they set their sights toward the south.

MacMillan and Small absorbed Hovey's story. We must get going, Hovey urged. MacMillan refused to leave Hunt. He had been angling for another year in the Arctic anyway, so the doctor's misfortune was his gain. Small also volunteered to stay, an impressive commitment from a man who had been certain he wouldn't survive his first winter in the north.

Hovey voiced his displeasure with MacMillan's performance. For some reason, he blamed MacMillan for the *Cluett* fiasco. He attacked the explorer for not mentioning the expedition's sponsors in his correspondence. What bothered him most, however, was MacMillan's failure to preserve any walrus skins. Before the *Diana* left port, Hovey and Osborn had tasked Mac with collecting as many exotic pelts as possible. Selling Arctic rarities was a good way to finance expeditions. Mac had traded food and other goods for a few hundred fox pelts, much to the other Americans' dismay, but Hovey demanded more valuable specimens.

MacMillan walked away—he wanted to write a letter to his sister. Hovey, cooling down, handed over a bundle of mail, a rifle, some ammunition, and half a box of oranges, and promised to cache the supplies Mac had ordered at North Star Bay. They shook hands and parted two hours after the *Ingerlis* arrived at Neqi.

The seven-man expedition was whittled down to three, one of whom had no idea that the majority of his companions were on their way home.

A southeasterly breeze caressed MacMillan's cheek. This wind won't do the *Cluett* much good, he sighed. Allen, Ekblaw, Green, Tanquary, and Hovey had been gone for a week. Besides checking the wind on occasion, Mac hadn't thought much about his former teammates. He was having too much fun. The fearless Aqqioq, his arm scarred from the time a walrus impaled him—the tusk passed clean through—was dashing into the middle of a herd of walruses with harpoon cocked. Mac charged after him. This was living.

Still, duty called. Leaving Jot Small at Neqi, MacMillan boarded his punt for a 48-mile pull through the autumn twilight to Etah. He had to tell Hunt what had happened.

Eighteen hours of rowing brought him to the lodge. His cramping legs quivered. Viivi and Aleqasinnguaq burst from their igloos, surprised to discover that he had not left with Hovey. Together they whipped the damp, cheerless house into shape. The women exhibited boxes and boxes of presents which the Crocker Landers had given them. From the Americans' perspective, it was all stuff not worth taking home. Viivi and Aleqasinnguaq had more material goods than they had ever owned.

Hunt paddled his kayak down the fiord a few days later. Mac walked into the dusk to greet him. They chatted about the doctor's success bagging caribou. The doctor was almost at the door when Mac broke the news.

"Well, Hunt, the boys have gone."

A puzzled look crossed the doctor's face.

"They've all gone. Just you, Jot and I remain," Mac continued. "Dr. Hovey has been here in a power boat. The ship reached North Star Bay."

Resentment coursed through Hunt, who was condemned to another year in the Arctic because he had gone hunting one day too soon. MacMillan sensed his distress. He promised the doctor an important role in his spring exploration trip, as if that were any consolation.

Hunt prowled the house "like a stray cat" for a week before asking whether he could sledge to South Greenland that winter to catch the first spring steamship to Copenhagen. MacMillan saw no reason to keep the moody physician at Etah. Within ten minutes Hunt had pulled his suitcase from the attic and was throwing clothes inside, even though he couldn't leave for another two or three months.

"Mac's attitude has discouraged scientific work, and little has been done," Hunt asserted in a letter home. "Unwise use of the food supplies has reduced them to unsafe limits, and there has been dishonest use of them in trading for fox skins." The doctor professed "no bad feeling among us, but a desire to be quit of the expedition." Hunt was a strong-minded man who did not suffer fools lightly. He respected MacMillan's gift for organization, a talent he lacked, yet worried that his leader had lost sight of their most important priority—staying alive.

The two men reached an unspoken, uneasy accord. Mostly they avoided each other. Hunt made soundings on the fiord in an attempt to bolster the expedition's paltry scientific record. MacMillan played with his camera, making multiple-exposure plates of the sun rolling along the southern horizon.

MacMillan acted with little urgency. With his party dwindling and few natives around Etah, he had less to worry about. There was no need to round up dozens of dogs or mountains of food for a spring expedition. For years he had pored over details, wrestled figures, and managed personnel. Now he was free to enjoy himself.

To do that, he needed the supplies Hovey had stashed at the North Star Bay trading station. MacMillan and ten Inughuit left Etah on Halloween. On November 4 they approached the camp at Qaanaaq, where, much to MacMillan's surprise, the great Uutaaq rushed out to meet his *qamutit*. Mac installed him up front so he could report the news while they drove in.

Uutaaq spoke about this and that person, about this hunt and that trip. He mentioned that MacMillan's supplies were at Issuissuup Paava, or what Westerners called Parker Snow Bay, 40 miles south of North Star Bay. Mac wondered why Hovey had deviated from the plan. Perhaps ice had forced the *Cluett* out of North Star before the crew unloaded his goods, so they dumped them in the next available port.

Onward they rode. Uutaaq offered his next piece of information. Fitzhugh Green was heading for Etah from the south, he said, and would probably reach Qaanaaq tomorrow.

MacMillan, thinking his unsteady grip on Inuktun had caused an error in translation, asked Uutaaq to repeat himself. Then he asked again. He still didn't believe it. Mac figured Green was in New York, indulging in ice cream and chocolate cake.

"And the men?" MacMillan inquired.

"Oh, they are all there," Uutaaq replied.

MacMillan pieced together what was happening. The *Cluett* was iced in, and the men were trapped somewhere near Parker Snow Bay, perhaps with insufficient food, clothing, and shelter. Green was out searching for him. The Crocker Landers' rescue mission needed rescuing.

Mac felt "like a squashed tomato." He had been considering an ambitious trip out beyond Ellesmere Island's western shore, where he might encounter the undiscovered land that scientists said was out there, before sledging home through either Alaska or northern Canada. Hunt and Small would remain at Etah to protect their possessions and await another relief ship. "My two year plans were of no avail now," he wrote in his journal that evening. "They must all be given up. This was the hardest blow of all."

Mac pitched his tent on the ice, preferring to sleep alone rather than between lice-ridden natives in an igloo. There was nothing to do but sleep, wait for Green, and decide what came next.

"To be opened when every thing's gone dead wrong," read the sealed envelope at Etah. Everything hadn't gone dead wrong, but as MacMillan snuggled into his caribou-skin bed, he had a hard time coming up with many things that were going right.

"Well Mac," Hovey wrote from North Star Bay two days after their conference at Neqi, "may you, Dr. Hunt and Mr. Small have a comfortable and satisfactory time this year." Hovey was finished with the open seas, which had almost swamped the *Ingerlis* during its return trip. He was finished with the "lazy, good for nothing" Inughuit. He was finished with the incompetent Captain Pickels. New York, the museum, and his comfortable office beckoned. The *Cluett* must leave "without delay," he said, for "we cannot afford to get caught here now!"

The *Cluett* put North Star Bay behind it forty-eight hours later. Pickels could run his faulty engine only in an emergency, so the captain exploited the benevolent winds pushing them around Cape Atholl. With help from Allen, the ship's engineer got the engine purring, and the *Cluett* made 75 miles through the ice pack in less than a day. Low-riding fog suggested open water nearby. One more good run would break them free.

The weather shifted. A southwesterly gale shoved the helpless craft back north. Pickels crashed into floes, never once consulting his ice pilot. Hovey cringed at a grinding noise from below. An examination revealed a bent crankshaft.

Pickels called a strategic retreat to Parker Snow Bay. On the way into the harbor, he snapped his rudder against a cake of ice. A second collision stove in a plank amidships. Seeking shelter from the storm, Pickels guided the wounded vessel alongside a 1,000-foot cliff. When the weather calmed, he made two halfhearted break-out attempts before waving the white flag and dropping anchor 150 yards from the bay's northeast shore. A snow-speckled, table-topped cliff rose behind them. Ice floes merged and thickened until they locked the *Cluett* in place for the winter. The *Cluett*'s ragtag crew banked the ship partway with an insulating mound of snow, but quit before finishing the job.

Comer and Hovey explored the hold. They discovered that their food reserves were much lower than expected. Pickels should have laid in at least a year's worth of food in case they had to overwinter. Instead, he had brought only about two-thirds of what he needed to feed his sixteen-man crew. Pickels never explained the shortfall.

The Crocker Landers assumed he had sold some provisions for personal profit on the way north.

Hovey allowed Allen, Ekblaw, Green, and Tanquary to crack into MacMillan's supplies. "The ship is going to be in dire straits before the winter is over," he worried. Scurvy and starvation seemed likely.

Pickels nearly killed Ekblaw when he discharged his Winchester rifle while cleaning it. Echoing MacMillan's wounding six years earlier, the bullet tore through a partition, passed into the mess, grazed Ekblaw's left sleeve, threw splinters into his face when it blasted through another wall, then embedded itself in the corner of Tanquary's room. Had Ekblaw not been leaning back on his stool, the shot would have struck him in the chest.

"How *could* you recommend that we take" an auxiliary steamer, Hovey wrote in an angry letter to MacMillan. "I cannot tell you how much my personal, museum and other affairs will suffer from this long and unexpected absence."

Hovey sent a more conciliatory message to Peter Freuchen, who had been happy to see the meddlesome Americans leave. Hovey begged him, "for the sake of humanity," to give the refugees on the *Cluett* all the food, clothes, stoves, fuel, and blankets he could spare, along with enough sledges and dogs to carry himself and the Crocker Landers to either Upernavik or Holsteinsborg (present-day Sisimiut), where they might catch an early steamer for Copenhagen. He also wanted Freuchen to volunteer as a guide for the trip. "If you can only take one from our party," Hovey added, "*I must be that one.*"

Hovey made an additional request. "Mr. Freuchen," he wrote, "please treat *me* as the authorized leader and head of this party—i.e. the Crocker Land Expedition party."

Hovey dispatched Green and a native chaperone to North Star Bay to deliver the letter. The ensign returned to the *Cluett* with Freuchen and enough sledges to transfer Hovey, Comer, the Crocker Landers, and their gear to North Star. Hovey demanded that

Freuchen take himself, Allen, Green, and Tanquary south as soon as the winter ice formed. Ekblaw would stay at North Star Bay until another relief ship arrived in the summer of 1916, and Comer belonged with the *Cluett*.

Green and Freuchen repeated this information when they found MacMillan at Qaanaaq in early November. Green also handed over Hovey's intemperate notes. MacMillan hadn't received such a scolding since his mother caught him hopping ice floes in the waters off Provincetown. "From what I have heard thus far it seems to me that the scientific results of the Crocker Land [expedition] are far below what were justly planned for and expected by the organizing institutions and supporters of the enterprise," Hovey grumbled. MacMillan hadn't made any contributions to geography, and had performed shoddy ethnological and archeological work. Hovey ordered him to gather his possessions from Etah and head for Parker Snow Bay, presumably for a final tongue-lashing before the curator followed Freuchen south.

Mac argued with Hovey for six weeks via native courier. He and Green finally left Etah for North Star Bay in mid-December. Green complained about his aching jaw all the way down. They arrived to find no Americans, no Freuchen, and no note explaining their absence. The two spent Christmas night in Freuchen's empty house. It was a relief to be inside, even if "inside" meant a two-room wind trap on a dismal, rocky plain backed by low, uninspiring hills. The past few days had been so cold that the men had to warm up their alcohol fuel before it would ignite.

Mac discovered some boxes with his name on them—a fraction of the order he had placed the previous year. Within was a treasure trove of reminders that civilization still existed. He pawed through jars of honey and jam, hefted cans of fruit, and tore into a cache of cookies. Ezra Fitch, of outfitter Abercrombie and Fitch, had sent a pair of boots better suited for summer wear.

Freuchen arrived the next day with Hunt and Comer in tow, after a Christmas spent shivering atop a windblown glacier. The

Dane had not yet thawed before MacMillan lit into him about his half-baked plan to take the Americans south. When pressed, Freuchen confessed he had no idea how much dog food was on hand. Alarmed, Mac pushed on to Parker Snow Bay, where he found Allen, Ekblaw, and Tanquary on the *Cluett*, looking fit and hale, and Hovey "looking to be at least 80 years old," shivering in the feeble warmth of a primus stove.

MacMillan and Hovey renewed their argument, this time with the hot intensity of face-to-face combat rather than the cold fury of a paper war. Hovey parried MacMillan's argument that he was unfit for travel by waving a medical release from Hunt. This letter says that you should engage in "no severe physical exercise," Mac observed. No one can make a 1,200-mile sledge trip without "severe physical exercise." Hovey shifted his approach, assaulting MacMillan for botching his mission to make soundings on the polar sea, missing opportunities to map the coast of Axel Heiberg Island, failing to search for land north of the Parry Islands, and canceling a proposed trek across the Greenland ice cap.

Then they bickered about fox skins. Hovey had promised Freuchen a large bundle of skins—about three times as many as necessary, by MacMillan's accounting—as payment for his clothes and food. MacMillan was outraged. Those skins represented a way out of debt, with something left over for himself. Hovey maintained that selling at a discount would "remove any stigma of 'trade' from a scientific expedition."

MacMillan was ready to wash his hands of the entire mess. He wrote orders granting his men permission to catch the next steamer out of Greenland. Again cautioning Hovey against making the trip, he hitched up his ravenous team and headed north. MacMillan had stayed in Parker Snow Bay for less than twenty-four hours. "I'm afraid they will be hungry," he said as he took a last look at the *Cluett*.

The Crocker Land expedition, once a tight-knit group of seven adventurers, had fractured into six quarrelsome units. Allen,

Green, and Tanquary were heading south with the next full moon. Freuchen had neither the food nor the dogs to bring anyone else. Comer, an accidental Crocker Lander, was marking time at North Star until something better came along. Hunt floated between several hunting grounds, various stone houses, and improvised medical offices on board the *Cluett*. Ekblaw conducted scientific work at his own discretion. Small waited at Etah for whatever came next. And MacMillan was living the life of an Arctic drifter.

MacMillan expunged the other Americans from his mind. "I feel that I am home now," he smiled while his dogs plied the icy road from North Star Bay to Etah.

In New York, on November 6, 1915, a few hours after Green's unwelcome reunion with MacMillan in Qaanaaq, George Sherwood sat down at his desk to read his mail. Reinstalled as head of the museum's Crocker Land Committee in Hovey's absence, he studied an envelope postmarked Highland Park, Illinois. He had a pretty good idea what the letter inside said.

Sherwood opened the envelope and read Augusta Krieger's penciled lines. Her handwriting looked agitated, hurried. "Where's the ship?" she demanded. "What's the news?"

Many similar pleas had reached New York in the past few weeks. Ekblaw's fiancée was a regular correspondent, as was Mrs. Hunt, MacMillan's sisters, and other loved ones. Sherwood, who had no Arctic experience and no clue as to the expedition's whereabouts, tried to be comforting. "I do not think we should feel any anxiety at the present time," he replied.

Four days later, Sherwood received a cable from Knud Rasmussen in Copenhagen. The *Kap York* met the *Cluett* at North Star Bay, it read. Rasmussen was not sure whether the men had escaped Etah, but he was certain they had been safe two months ago.

Rasmussen's update calmed the families' worst fears, but not their frustration. "All the scientific data in the world is not worth his being from us another year," MacMillan's sister Letitia said. Sullen resignation permeated their correspondence with the museum, which had done such a poor job of keeping them informed over the past two years. "I am hoping for the best for next spring now and trying to forget what might have been this fall," Marion Hunt sighed. "I did look for the party so surely this fall."

"It does seem hard all round," she added, thinking not only of herself and her daughter, but also of her husband, the other Crocker Landers, and the war-torn world.

"We [are] not a happy party," Hovey reported from his damp, miserable cabin on the *Cluett*. Meals consisted of little more than oatmeal and beans. Ice coated the ship's interior walls. Crewmen scratched at the lice covering their bodies. There was neither soap nor, perhaps worse, tobacco. The first mate tiptoed around lest he arouse the ghosts he had seen on board. He also believed in mermaids.

Pickels was a hated man on board. When Freuchen gave him a discount price on a load of fur clothes, the captain promptly "sold it to the crew charging about twice what he was to pay Peter." On another occasion, Comer caught Pickels eating a hunk of hoarded bread and drinking hot chocolate with sugar. Hovey wasn't much better; Allen and Tanquary found him prying open a box of peanut candies addressed to them. Hovey insisted that the candies were expedition property.

Hovey circled January 16, the next full moon, for his escape from *Cluett* prison. As the big moment neared, both he and MacMillan composed alternate versions of events for AMNH president H. F. Osborn's consideration. Hovey blasted MacMillan's "unwise and extravagant expenditure of supplies" and his lack of a "consistent and cooperative plan of scientific work." MacMillan admitted that "the boys" had not done much work but blasted Dr. Hovey as "absolutely incompetent." Promising to "put new land on the map," he outlined a spring trip to King Christian Island, which had 300 miles of uncharted coastline. Along the way, he would no doubt find "undiscovered islands."

Hovey and MacMillan agreed on one thing: the remaining expedition members must be rescued in the summer of 1916, when food supplies would reach critical levels. Pickels had given up on the people at Etah and was heading home as soon as he could. It is "absolutely necessary" that the museum send another rescue ship, MacMillan urged, perhaps with Peary in command. Whatever you do, he beseeched Osborn, do not put Hovey in charge.

Hovey awoke early on the morning of January 16, 1916. Poking his head abovedecks, he smiled at the clear winter sky. A full moon set the frozen harbor twinkling. A million icy reflections lit his way home. The air was cold and still, and the thermometer registered –15 degrees, "just right for sledging."

"Personally, I advise you not to go south this winter by sledge across Melville Bay," Dr. Hunt had warned. You might "jeopardize the safety of the party," MacMillan cautioned, "being ignorant of Arctic ways and inexperienced in Arctic sledging." Mac added that "there are so many serious faults in the general plan of getting you south that I have grave fears as to its success."

Nonsense, Hovey sniffed. MacMillan criticized Freuchen's leadership abilities, yet there was the Dane, loading pemmican, biscuit, chocolate, and extra clothes on the party's seven sledges. And Hovey was feeling strong. Daily hikes had prepared his fifty-three-year-old body for the long road ahead.

Hovey pulled a sweater and a vest over his flannel shirt, wriggled into a caribou *qulittaq* and polar bear pants, and snugged a wool cap over his head. Hareskin socks, sealskin boots, and bearskin mittens completed his ensemble.

Allen, Green, and Tanquary joined the scrum of *qamutits*. Their weathered faces spoke of two rugged years in the Arctic. All of them had suffered. Northern life had pushed Green beyond his limits and nearly done the same to Allen. Tanquary's scars became obvious the moment he took off his boots. Although none of them were close, they shared a bond that excluded Hovey. Their relationship with the latecomer was distant, if proper. Only Green had reached out to him, having decided that the well-connected curator could do more for his future prospects than the discredited MacMillan.

Freuchen kicked his runners free of snow, checked his traces, and secured Hovey atop the load before barking a "Huk! Huk!" to his dozen dogs. Off they went, leaping away the first few feet of a 400-mile journey across Melville Bay and on to Upernavik. From there it was another 800 miles to Holsteinsborg, and freedom.

"Godspeed for the long sledge trip southward," Ekblaw had told Hovey the day before. "At first the trail will seem extraordinarily hard; but as you become accustomed to it, and as the sun returns to brighten the way, you will find the days pleasanter and more enjoyable." The scientist betrayed no envy that Hovey was leaving while he must remain apart from his love.

"I am feeling very fit," Hovey crowed, "and I shall start across Melville Bay without fear that I shall retard the march of my party."

Whatever was waiting out there, it had to be better than wintering with Pickels's bungling crew in Parker Snow Bay.

24

FLIGHT

"Tired but happy," Hovey reported after his first day atop Freuchen's *qamutit*. Sledging conditions were as perfect as anyone could hope for. Ample moonlight and a few beams of refracted sunlight illuminated the frozen road. The sea ice proved smooth and consistent. Only a handful of small leads slowed the party's progress.

Hovey had even done some real explorer work, much to his delight. For months he had scanned nearby glaciers through binoculars from the *Cluett*'s deck. Now he got a close-up look at the craggy behemoths from his sledge. One massive specimen struck his fancy. Shouting back to Freuchen, he asked what it was called. No one had ever named it, the Dane replied. Hovey seized that right for himself, dubbing it Ekblaw Glacier.

The party trotted for five hours before halting for lunch. Drivers untangled traces and fired up primus stoves. Hovey absorbed the sights and watched Green lead a line of hand-walking natives around the ice. Their furs billowed like a parade of inverted cones. Coffee and biscuits made for an appropriately spartan meal before they remounted the *qamutits*.

"Cheer up, doctor, only an hour more!" Freuchen yelled a few hours later. Hovey was sagging. To his great amusement, ten minutes later the caravan stopped at a cluster of stone-and-turf huts. Freuchen had been pulling his leg, as if he were one of the boys. Hovey asked how far they had come. Fifty miles, Freuchen answered, marvelous progress for nine hours of travel. At this pace, the intimidating cliffs around them would soon be replaced by a row of buildings in New York City.

Hovey supped on frozen auks while the dogs devoured walrus meat. He viewed an offering of dried narwhal with trepidation until Freuchen assured him that its flavor resembled Roquefort cheese. He tried it, and even kept it down. Feeling weary yet exhilarated by his newfound prowess, Hovey removed his outer layer of furs, climbed into the middle position of a sleeping platform, and rolled himself in an army blanket. Natives stripped off their clothes and flopped beside him.

The scientist awoke expecting a lazy day. Freuchen planned on resting the dogs, who were still working themselves into condition. Hovey puttered around camp until noon, then joined Tanquary for a walk in the –35° weather. The pair made it barely 100 yards before Hovey bent in pain and clutched his chest. A "hand of steel" squeezed his heart. He wheezed for breath. Tanquary nursed him back to the huts. Freuchen joked about Hovey's nose being frozen before grasping the seriousness of the situation. The curator collapsed on a pile of skins. Someone lit a primus stove. Others began rubbing warmth into his extremities.

Hovey belonged in a hospital, not on a sledge. His symptoms indicated a heart attack. Blood vessels constrict in extreme cold, forcing the heart to pump harder to distribute blood. When combined with moderate exercise, the strain can overwhelm people with high blood pressure, which Hovey had.

Hovey rested. Allen, Green, and Tanquary discussed his fate. None of them had wanted him along in the first place. He was too old and too inexperienced for such a demanding trip. His presence endangered everyone. He had to go back.

The Crocker Landers presented their verdict when Hovey woke up. His face sank with the realization that he was in the Arctic for the long haul. All he could do was accept their decision with grace. "Nature's laws are inexorable and cannot be infringed upon with impunity," he said.

The men dispatched an Inuk to the *Cluett* with a request for either Ekblaw or Hunt to come fetch the curator. Hovey was a defeated, resentful man. "This year has been and continues to be a bitter experience," he wrote. First his wife's death, then this. "The prospect is not good for either me or the men who will have to share their already inadequate provisions with me."

Freuchen's party loaded up the next afternoon. Hovey handed over a batch of spiteful letters informing the museum that he would not return on the *Cluett* next summer because he doubted "her ability to get across Melville Bay . . . in her present condition and under her present master." A second ship was needed. He again criticized MacMillan's prodigious fox-skin collecting, and complained that the explorer "has turned the object of the expedition from science to trade and has interfered with doing some of the things for which the expedition was sent up."

Green, in a foul temper because of a persistent toothache, snapped that the curator should have stayed on the ship. With this minor chord hanging in the air, the traveling party sorted the snarling dogs, mounted their *qamutits*, and readied their whips. The sledges lurched into a field of soft, deep snow. Hovey would have given anything to be with them.

Ekblaw eased Hovey back to Parker Snow Bay. Two unwelcome sights greeted him: the decrepit *Cluett* and the disbelieving mug of Captain Harris C. Pickels. Feeling old and useless, Hovey occupied himself by writing long, self-serving letters with no immediate prospects of delivery. "I shrank from making the trip even for the summer months," he claimed. "Now the Museum is the worst sufferer of all, through the great inconvenience and anxiety now being suffered by its officers and the heavy extra financial burden entailed upon it by the failure of the '*Cluett*.'"

Hovey contemplated the party he had sent north two and a

half years earlier. Hunt was a competent physician, and Ekblaw "the salvation of the scientific side of the Expedition's program." The others had disappointed him, and Hovey did not handle disappointment well. Tanquary was too passive for fieldwork. Allen had shut down after abandoning the radio project. Small was annoying rather than helpful. Green was "excellent on the trail" but demonstrated "no interest in or liking for science or scientific work." Perhaps a stronger leader would have inspired a better performance from him. Rather than hire Green to work at the museum, something Hovey had considered years earlier, the curator planned to get some final reports from him ("they will necessarily be brief") before cutting ties forever.

MacMillan was the biggest disappointment. Hovey had never viewed him as a protégé, or as a long-term asset. Nothing that he had witnessed since arriving in the north changed his mind. MacMillan "had enthusiasm for and great energy in Arctic work," he concluded, but was "fundamentally lacking in scientific spirit and in knowledge of what constitutes truly scientific work." His methods showed an "absence of system," and his results were of "subordinate value." The museum should never work with him again.

Hovey's evaluation conflicted with MacMillan's self-image. MacMillan relished the glory that came with discovery but, unlike Peary, he viewed himself as a scientist rather than "just" an explorer. A combination of circumstance and ineptitude limited his team's achievements. Crocker Land's disappearance proved devastating. Even had it existed, Mac's slimmed-down traveling party could not have accomplished much there before the polar sea broke up. Following that disappointment, Mac seemed content to hang around with the Inughuit and let the expedition take whatever course it might. He talked about resuming the search for the continent that must be there but had mounted no major campaign to search for it out on the polar sea. The widespread starvation of 1914 diminished his opportunities for far-flung scientific ventures because there weren't enough able-bodied dogs to go around. At the same time, he allowed his men too much freedom in their work, even when they were accomplishing nothing. In 1915, the prospect of putting new land on the map excited him more than methodical investigations of local archeology or ethnography.

Hovey's gloomy, haughty nature made him an outcast on the *Cluett*. "He is an impossible man and a great trouble maker," the exile complained about Pickels. "You have caused me enough trouble . . . to last a voyage," the captain retorted. The two antagonists bickered about how to divide the precious "tobacca," as Pickels called it, and about Hovey's role aboard ship. Hovey bristled at the captain's insistence that he was a mere passenger. I represent your chartering organization, Hovey retorted, and therefore have some say over who is allowed on board, how we use supplies, and where we go when the ice recedes. Eventually they stopped speaking to each other, instead communicating through angry letters exchanged with a scowl.

"Melville Bay in January is the vaguest thing in the universe," Green mused soon after leaving Hovey. "No landmarks in sight, no trail to follow; moon and stars and pale twilight deep in the night fog of unspeakable cold; vast looming icebergs without outlines or limits; no single shadows, but one deep, meaningless, oppressive, suffocating shade which chokes and blinds and crucifies." The constant dark eroded his sanity, as it had in 1914 and 1915. Pain radiated from his aching jaw as he guided his team between gloomy pyramids of ice. "Alas, the sun never rises!" he complained.

"We [are] idiots to be traveling without a good chart," Green wrote. Land, ice, and fog merged into a single, indistinct blur. Freuchen sent scouts this way and that with a bluster that failed to hide how lost he really was. The natives contradicted each other at every turn. Every peak looked familiar to someone and strange to everyone else. The Dane beat his dogs in frustration when he thought no one was looking. The Americans were no help, because their compass wasn't working properly. Leads widened and ice grew patchier as the party blundered south. One false step in the twilight could land someone in a potentially fatal saltwater bath.

Spirits soared when they spotted the glow of a soapstone lamp through a seal-bladder window. It was Cape Seddon, home to three Inughuit families.

But grim tidings hung over the settlement. Miteq writhed in agony from rheumatism. Green injected him with morphine. A boulder had crushed Ittukusuk's foot (Ittukusuk II, not the one who had made the Crocker Land trip). And Inutaq had drowned in his kayak several months before. Three families, three disasters.

The arrival of such unusual guests brightened the mood. The Crocker Landers gorged themselves on seals and narwhal before packing up for the next stage of their trip. A bit of tobacco bought them enough meat to last several days.

Their supplies inevitably ran out, and the dogs started dropping. The men tossed extraneous weight from their sledges. They breathed a collective sigh of relief when they sighted the Devil's Thumb, an 1,800-foot spire signifying the northern boundary of Danish territory. From here, the men would encounter Europeans, and perhaps European comforts, at every settlement.

Another 50 miles brought them to their first south Greenland village, a community of forty natives living in a half dozen wood-and-sod shelters. The Inughuit muttered among themselves. Northerners had no great love for these people, who could neither build proper houses nor craft soapstone lamps, and who wore trousers made of sealskin because they sold their bearskins at trading stations. Useless beads adorned the women's clothes. Their language sounded rough and unpolished.

"I am Itué," the chief declared, scrutinizing the Inughuit Taitsiaq's *qamutit*. "Surely you have heard of me."

"Not yet," Taitsiaq purred, "but do not grieve, for my ears are very small." The Inughuit recognized no chiefs, and they learned modesty at a young age.

Allen, Green, and Tanquary dipped their toes into the waters of civilization. Villages became combinations of squat, stone huts and snug wooden houses. More people spoke Danish, and fewer drove sledges. The Americans' heavy furs looked out of place in communities large enough to support a doctor and a minister. The men bathed, cut their shoulder-length hair, ate with forks and spoons, and slept between sheets. Green found temporary relief from his toothache when a physician shot his gum full of cocaine. "Life was once more worth living," he sighed. Five-month-old war news felt fresh. In Upernavik, where all 250 residents turned out to greet them, they danced with a bevy of native women.

Racial intermingling, rare in the United States, was common in south Greenland, where many European men took Inuit wives. The Americans understood the urges behind these relationships yet recoiled at their genetic implications. "This intermarriage encourages greater familiarity between races," opined Green, the best versed in contemporary literature on scientific racism and racial hierarchy, "but besides slightly elevating the brown it naturally lowers the white man's born propensities for civilized environment." As Freuchen later remembered—and he had a flair for exaggeration—Green boasted that he had studied the natives for three years without finding one "who had risen above the level of a dog." Dr. Hovey had expressed similar views in the presence of Navarana, Freuchen's native-born wife.

The Dane gritted his teeth and pointed the Crocker Landers farther south. A few hundred miles of tough sledging brought them to Uummannaq. Freuchen left the expedition there so he could get home before the ice melted. The Americans bid Freuchen farewell, paid off their remaining native guides in spoons, cigars, some flannel, and a coffee mill, and continued their flight. "I was relieved when I was finally able to leave them," Freuchen later recalled.

Allen, Green, and Tanquary staggered into Egedesminde (present-day Aasiaat) on March 21, 1916, two months after separating from Hovey. They were more than 1,000 miles from Etah and less than 200 from their destination, the port of Holsteinsborg. From here the road south was blocked. The sea ice was too thin for *qamutits* and too thick for kayaks. An overland passage would be both dangerous and expensive. Dog food was even scarcer than human food.

The tiny party's journey exposed the fragility of Danish Greenland's socioeconomic system. Their presence strained limited food supplies and inflated prices of essentials in towns along the coast. Overhunting, and diminished hunting skills resulting from the southern Greenlanders' interaction with Europeans, had reduced fresh meat stocks. Wartime travel complications and unusual ice conditions discouraged supply ships from calling. With starvation a real possibility, Danish colonists welcomed the visiting Crocker Landers into their homes, then inquired as to how soon they would be moving on.

Splitting up was their best option. Two men would stay behind, allowing the third to push on for Holsteinsborg and the first steamer for Europe. Green volunteered himself for the mission. Tanquary objected. Their discussion turned rancorous as each man explained why he should go home first. Green claimed it was his duty as leader to undertake the trip. Tanquary was engaged to be married and had a teaching position waiting for him at Kansas State Agricultural College. Green backed down, mumbling that his appendix was hurting and he didn't feel like traveling anyway.

Tanquary made Holsteinsborg on April 20. The sight of a tree—a real tree, three feet high—amazed him. He paid each of his guides eight Danish kroner, or a little less than three dollars. A letter of credit from Hovey ensured him a clean room and decent food.

Knud Rasmussen motored into the harbor a week later. Rasmussen had taken the steamer *Hans Egede* from Denmark to Greenland. The ship was still working its way north; Rasmussen had transferred to his motorboat south of Holsteinsborg and was heading up to his trading station. Eager for advice from an expert, Tanquary laid out the expedition's situation. Rasmussen suggested asking his associates in Denmark for help chartering a second relief ship. As a last resort, he might be able to bring MacMillan and the other refugees south in the *Kap York* next summer. Tanquary accepted his offer, pending the museum's approval.

The two-masted, 900-ton *Hans Egede* chuffed into Holsteinsborg a few days later. Tanquary purchased a ticket for Copenhagen with borrowed money. The entomologist had arrived in Greenland as part of the best-equipped expedition ever sent north. He began his 8,000-mile trip home with little more than the clothes on his back. Most of his personal belongings were on the *Cluett*, and his specimens, the fruits of three years in the Arctic, were boxed up at Etah. Josephine Perry, his anxious fiancée, had no idea he was coming home. A new job was waiting for him. But these were obligations for an aspiring, middle-class American. Before embracing comfortable domesticity, he must first deliver his comrades from exile. He must tell the world that the Crocker Land expedition needed saving.

A few weeks later, Tanquary stood at the rail of the *Hans Egede* watching Thorshavn emerge from the surrounding hills. The dismal little town was the capital of the Faroe Islands, an aloof, T-shaped spray of basalt lumps 200 miles north of Scotland, 300 miles east of Iceland, and 400 miles west of Norway. Tank had exchanged one of the loneliest places on earth for another. Unlike Etah, however, Thorshavn was in communication with the outside world.

Tanquary hopped off the vessel with a few kroner jingling in his pocket and a few hours until the *Hans Egede* resumed its voyage. Finding a telegram office, he penciled two messages in the terse lingo of the medium. First he copied a missive Hovey had sent with him. "Food supply inadequate charter violated," he wrote. Send "reliable steamer competent experienced master adequate accommodations full years provisions." Tank's own message sketched out his southern trip and parroted Hovey's demand: "realizing seriousness of second failure to relieve expedition strongly urge reliable steamer full years provisions." Cable me instructions at Copenhagen, he pleaded.

Much to his surprise, Tanquary found no replies waiting for him when the *Hans Egede* arrived in Denmark. Nearly penniless in an unfamiliar city, he checked into the Hotel Dagmar and waited. It was late May. The window for chartering a ship was closing. He marched into American ambassador Maurice Egan's office and asked for advice. Egan suggested resending the telegram. Tanquary had not thought of that.

George Sherwood had received the scientist's earlier cables at the museum but did not respond. He had been dreading a request such as Tanquary's. Sherwood had no idea how to pay for another vessel.

The only person excited by the prospect was Colonel H. D. Borup, who pleaded for a spot on a second relief ship. Borup had been checking in throughout the spring in case the museum needed his services. "I am in daily training at the gymnasium, besides walking, regardless of weather," he advised museum president Osborn.

Sherwood at last broke his silence, ordering Tanquary to scour Copenhagen for a steamer. Knud Rasmussen's agent Marius Nyeboe, who had a vested interest in getting the Americans out of his employer's trading zone, volunteered to assist the zoologist. Even with Nyeboe's help Tank found few prospects, none of them bright and all of them expensive. The expedition's best shot was the Greenland Mining Company's *Danmark*, a wooden steamer. The firm demanded a charter fee of $18,300. Extra supplies and other expenses lifted the total cost to around $35,000. When Sherwood checked, he found that the Crocker Land expedition fund had a balance of $8,880.19.

Sherwood contacted potential donors. "The emergency is very great, and the Committee will appreciate any contributions that the friends of the expedition will make," he wrote. Contributions for the "Hovey relief expedition" trickled in. "It is a very difficult time just now to get money for anything, and particularly for anything scientific," University of Illinois president Edmund James noted. "The world seems to have gone crazy on the war; one continent killing, maiming and destroying everybody they can, and the other continent being called upon to take care of the people who suffer as a result of the fighting."

Lacking palatable alternatives, the museum engaged the *Danmark*. At this dark moment, it absorbed another blow when H. D. Borup died in a sanitarium following a brief illness. The colonel was sixty-two years old, and utterly alone. His beloved wife and son were dead. His daughter, Yvette, had left for Asia a few months earlier with her husband, George's dear friend Roy Chapman Andrews, who still hadn't found a good place to display the whale skeletons piled behind the museum's tennis court. Until the end the colonel had expressed the hope that MacMillan would bring back a boulder to use as a headstone at George's grave.

Tanquary rode the *Hans Egede* back across the Atlantic, missing a telegram from the museum asking him to return to Greenland in order to represent the institution aboard the *Danmark*. Fortunately, the Germans had moderated their U-boat activity in the North Sea in recent months, so the *Hans Egede* faced little threat of a surprise attack.

Maurice Tanquary arrived in New York on June 21, 1916, a few days shy of three years after setting out on the *Diana*. His bronzed face lent him a travel-worn appearance, but otherwise he looked well. Tank gave reporters little information about his experiences, on the grounds that MacMillan should speak for the group. He stayed three nights in a hotel near the American Museum of Natural History, which covered his $6.12 bill, sat through a few meetings with museum officials, and hopped a train for Illinois to see his fiancée. From there he went on to Kansas, which must have seemed startlingly flat after three years tucked under Greenland's mighty cliffs, and began preparing for his fall classes.

One Crocker Lander was home. Six more were scattered across the enormity of Greenland.

DISCOVERY AND DISAPPOINTMENT

"WHAT GLUTTONS WE ARE!" MacMillan laughed, sucking the marrow from another musk ox bone. A hollowed-out skull lay nearby. The brain it once held filled the explorer's belly. Some of Mac's favorite Inughuit—Akumalinnguaq, Aqqioq, Agpaler-suraassuk, Ittukusuk, and Nukappiannguaq—lolled around the enormous snow house Nukappiannguaq had built 350 miles west of Etah, on the southwest tip of Axel Heiberg Island. MacMillan pondered the last time he had been this far from home. "Every-thing was an uncertainty," he remembered of the 1914 Crocker Land fiasco, "my supporting party, my food supply, the location of Crocker Land, the condition of the ice." Tonight, April 10, 1916, he had plenty of food, healthy dogs, and good company. It was the group's twentieth day in the field.

The expedition's prospectus had promised exploration of the remote region west of Axel Heiberg. The Norwegian Otto Sver-drup's 1898–1902 party had discovered Axel Heiberg, Amund Ringnes, and Ellef Ringnes islands while marooned on their ice-bound ship, the *Fram*. MacMillan saw the peaks of Amund Ringnes over the frozen ocean to the west whenever he looked up from his musk ox bone. MacMillan's destination, King Christian Island, also known as Finlay Land, lay 60 miles beyond that. Sverdrup's men had spotted that sideways-comma-shaped island in 1901 but never trod its shores. Mapping it would give MacMillan a minor geographical victory to offer his masters at the museum. Other discoveries might present themselves along the way. Crocker Land was still out there, just not where Peary said it was. He'd brought several Bowdoin flags, a Harvard flag, a Yale flag, and a silk American flag with him in case he found something worth claiming.

Mac was on a journey of pure discovery, with no pretense at science. Even if he had brought a scientific staff, his breakneck pace would have prevented them from collecting specimens, examining geological features, or making precise maps. He had left too late in the year to linger in any one spot, and needed to be back at Etah by June 1 or else face getting trapped on Axel Heiberg or Ellesmere when the ice broke up. MacMillan hoped only for an opportunity to put his foot on new land, or at least uncharted land, before retreating.

MacMillan's brains-and-marrow feast was the last easy moment of the trip. As planned, Akumalinnguaq and Agpalersuraassuk turned back. Mac paid each of them two sticks of tea, five cans of milk, four gallons of oil, three boxes of matches, some tobacco, and two packages of cigarette papers for their services. The three remaining Inughuit hinted that they were also ready for the trip to end. Their hunting trips stopped producing kills. Forced onto a diet of pemmican, both dogs and men began to tire. MacMillan was philosophical when Pe-see-ah-too,* one of his favorite dogs, died. In its final hours the animal was too weak to drink the bear soup its master offered. It curled up in the snow and refused to move. "He is now where there are no sledges, nor long, long trails, nor cruel whips," MacMillan wrote.

The party reached its destination on April 19. "King Christian

---

* Probably MacMillan's version of *pitsiaqtoq*, meaning "one who is good."

Island is mine," MacMillan exulted with Pearyesque bombast.
Hoping to extend his stay, he again sent his guides hunting. They
found nothing.

MacMillan was 500 miles from Etah, with little food and a
grumpy party. He blew his harmonica while the Inughuit played
cards in their snow houses. Aqqioq sat nearby, mending a harness.
Then the Inuk's knife slipped, and MacMillan looked up to see the
handle protruding from between the man's nose and left eye. To
Mac's disbelief, Aqqioq removed the knife, blinked through the
flowing blood, and held still as his tribemates sealed the wound
with adhesive. Miraculously, he kept both his eye and his life.

It was time to retreat. On April 22, while Tanquary was waiting
for the *Hans Egede* at Holsteinsborg, MacMillan stepped back onto
the polar sea to begin the long haul to Etah. Heavy snow obscured
his view of King Christian Island, and anything else more than a
few feet away. The Arctic had again robbed him of a vision of land.

The group perked up as they headed east. MacMillan observed
some specks of land that did not appear on Sverdrup's rudimentary
charts. At least they looked like land, but they were low enough that
they might be ice floes. "We are putting new land on the map," he
exclaimed nevertheless. Most of these finds encompassed only one
or two square miles. He claimed some bigger islands before deciding that Sverdrup had already grabbed them. These "new lands" did
not rate a mention in the cairn notes he left along his path.

More important, the natives started bringing down musk oxen
and polar bears. Hunting success bought MacMillan enough time
to sketch the north, east, and south coasts of Cornwall Island, a
900-square-mile rectangle about 40 miles off Axel Heiberg Island's
southwest coast. From the top of a 1,300-foot peak that he dubbed
McLeod Head he saw three uncharted islands, none of them more
than a mile or two across.

He couldn't explore these dots. The party was hundreds of miles
from Etah, and the spring breakup was coming. With Ittukusuk,
Nukappiannguaq, and the wounded Aqqioq leading the way, the

quartet rode across Smith Sound and into Etah on May 16. They had been in the field for fifty-seven days.

Viivi, a four-foot-four-inch bundle of energy, shared the news from around the lodge. Inutaq had drowned in his kayak. Taitsiaq had shot a boy by accident. Aleqasinnguaq, Piugaattoq's widow, had married Ulloriaq. "Thank goodness," sighed MacMillan, who was no longer responsible for her care. He did keep her sixteen-year-old son, Anaakkaq, whom he called Sammie, under his charge. "His father was lost on my first trip," he explained in his diary, feigning ignorance of the fact that the young man was Peary's child.

MacMillan had participated in a remarkable trip that logged over 1,200 miles in less than two months. Along the way he refined the maps of what are now known as the Sverdrup Islands and sketched a few hundred miles of uncharted coastline. He also answered some of Hovey's doubts about his leadership abilities. Explorers needed achievements if they hoped to keep exploring. No longer a mere disciple of Peary, MacMillan had conquered new lands.

But, as he looked around the lodge, he saw a mess requiring his attention. Specimens, photographs, and equipment all needed packing. A ship would be here soon. It might be the *Cluett*, freed from its icy chokehold. It might be another steamer chartered from New York. Peary himself might be on board. Whatever form deliverance took, it was time to get ready for home.

"Boat coming!" came the cry early in the morning of August 17, three months after the sledge party returned from its western trip. "Nothing good comes out of the south," MacMillan had muttered when a strong southerly wind almost swamped his dory a few weeks earlier. Now something else was coming from the south. He and Small walked outside. MacMillan ran through a mental list of possible relief steamers, wondering which one was here to whisk him home.

To his surprise, the motorboat from North Star Bay was puffing toward the lodge, bearing Freuchen, Rasmussen, Captain Comer, and, he groaned, Hovey. Mac had assumed that Comer, Hovey, and the others had left Greenland aboard the *Cluett*.

The two parties swapped stories. MacMillan described his King Christian Island trip. He recalled an amusing moment when Viivi's little boy carried around a stick of dynamite in his teeth—Green had left a crate open. Etah had otherwise been quiet.

Hovey told a more involved tale. Dr. Hunt had essentially forbidden him to travel after diagnosing "temporary heart weakness." The curator was nevertheless talking about sledging south from the rickety *Cluett* if no rescue ship came in the summer. A couple of tentative hikes had provided cause for optimism until, a few weeks previously, he seized up during a two-mile walk. He popped an aspirin and straggled back to the ship. His chest and back ached for several days.

Meals aboard the *Cluett* consisted of oatmeal, beans, bread, some salt beef, and whatever bits of fresh meat the crew scrounged from the Inughuit, who were short on food themselves. With supplies running low, Hovey, Ekblaw, and Hunt agreed to ride the *Cluett* south if it broke free before another relief ship arrived. Then Hovey changed his mind. Trusting neither the vessel, its captain, nor its crew, he figured he would get home sooner by waiting for another rescue boat. The only person who believed in the *Cluett* was Minik, who stunned everyone when he decided to ship out with Pickels. "I do not approve of the matter at all," Hovey complained. The curator believed that unhappiness awaited the Inuk in the United States. Worse, Minik's return might dredge up old stories of his mistreatment and embarrass the museum.

Captain Comer also had a woeful story. With food and space short on the *Cluett*, he had whiled away the past several months in a 16-by-20-foot room near Rasmussen and Freuchen's trading station. A rotating band of Greenlanders occupied an adjoining room, as did their dogs, whose howling constantly interrupted the captain's sleep. The natives are "destructive and wasteful," Comer grumbled. He could not communicate with them, so he kept to himself, except when the Inughuit engaged in a game of culinary cat and mouse. "The natives seem to make it a point to come in at meal times no doubt hoping to get some thing to eat or drink," he groaned. "In order to avoid them I have to eat rather irregular."

Everything about his surroundings was grim. Canned goods became cylindrical hunks of ice. His quarters were so cold that just-washed dishes froze to the table before he could wipe them dry. Hungry visitors dug out moldy beans from the ash heap.

The captain wrapped himself in blankets, updated Freuchen's weather records, and waited. He carved napkin rings from walrus tusks, made plaster casts of the natives' faces, and photographed the string animals children made playing cat's cradle. Hunt or Ekblaw checked in every few weeks. Freuchen drifted through before disappearing again. Uutaaq and his brother Iggiannguaq came by to grouch about Peary, who hadn't paid them everything he had promised, although he had sent a Victrola with Hovey. "The Gramophone is not so useful," Comer admitted. His primary contact with the outside world was Minik, who stopped by several times with reports and supplies.

With everyone up to date, Hovey described his new plan. All four of them—himself, Comer, MacMillan, and Small—would sail Freuchen's motorboat, the *Ingerlis*, to North Star Bay, where they would hole up until a second rescue ship arrived. If ice conditions allowed it, the relief vessel would zip up to Etah for the expedition's equipment and specimens before taking everyone home. If the ice made a run to the north impossible, they would leave their gear at Etah and head straight home. If no ship came, they would navigate the motorboat across Melville Bay and on to Holsteinsborg.

Jot and MacMillan were unimpressed. It was foolish to challenge Melville Bay in a small, overcrowded boat, Jot said. Mac rejected the idea of leaving his house, equipment, and specimens "unprotected and in the hands of the Eskimos" when a ship was likely to reach Etah within a few days. Hovey's scheme reeked of panic.

Mac got excited when Rasmussen relayed word of Vilhjalmur Stefansson, whose party had been missing for two years. Peary had received an ambiguous letter Stefansson sent from Banks Island, far northeast of Alaska. As far as anyone could tell, the Canadian had been marooned on Alaska's north shore for a significant time before sledging east with a handful of men in search of Crocker Land. He was aware of MacMillan's inability to find the continent but reasoned that "MacMillan can not be sure that there was not some land within twenty miles of where he turned back."

Stefansson was closer to Etah than any of them imagined. Less than two months earlier he had gone caribou hunting on Amund Ringnes Island and conducted tidal observations off Ellef Ringnes Island. He had even located a record from MacMillan's western trip.

Ignorance was a way of life in the Arctic. Explorers had no way of knowing whether someone was over the next glacier, much less several hundred miles away. Without the constant stream of Inughuit couriers, MacMillan would have had only the barest awareness of where his own men were, much less Stefansson. He had made little effort to follow his team's movements or guide their activities since the expedition splintered. Ekblaw and Hunt hunted, conducted scientific work, and dispensed medical care as they pleased. MacMillan heard rumors that Allen, Green, and Tanquary had reached southern Greenland but had no other information concerning their whereabouts.

Most amazing, none of the men at Etah were aware that the *Cluett* was on its way home. Captain Pickels broke out of Parker Snow Bay on July 29, less than three weeks after Hovey abandoned the vessel for North Star Bay. As promised, the captain sailed for home without attempting to reach North Star Bay or Etah. While Mac and Hovey were talking, the *Cluett* was shambling toward Battle Harbor, where it would send an "all's well" telegram to the museum—collect—when it arrived in early September. Hovey had underestimated Captain Pickels, or at least his luck.

———

MacMillan watched the *Ingerlis* motor out of Etah. All his visitors were aboard. So was Jot Small. Everyone expected a relief ship at Etah within the next ten days, so they planned on a short separation.

"They went leaving me to my Robinson Crusoe life," Mac wrote. Ominous clouds rolled in while the solitary explorer was busy marking crates. The sun dipped below the horizon for the first time in 123 days. Mac eyed the waning reserves of flour, sugar, molasses, and canned goods in the pantry. "I shall be living like an Eskimo," he thought with a mixture of joy and dread. He confessed that "the hours are the longest I have ever experienced because of the uncertainty." Remembering Hunt's untimely absence the previous summer, he remained within sight of the house.

On August 28 he sat down with his thick, hardbound diary. It was the fourth volume in the series. Embossed on the front were dates that at one time held great meaning: "1913–1915."

MacMillan opened the book to the first clean page. "Three or four days more will decide my fate," he wrote.

26

WAITING

Fitzhugh Green sat at a writing table with his tortoiseshell notebook and a pencil, as he often did. The ensign had awoken between sheets, not skins, on that summer morning in 1916, around a month after Tanquary had left him and Allen for the south. The two navy men were dividing their time at Egedesminde between the homes of the governor and a local missionary. With a population of 1,500, mostly Inuit, Egedesminde offered little in the way of amusement. It resembled most of southern Greenland's other settlements. A small clump of neat, wooden houses with steep roofs and square windows clung to the rocky hillside. From a distance the structures resembled child's toys set atop a gravel pile. The Americans enjoyed the Danes' company, especially of those few who spoke English, but otherwise found it a dreary place—"somewhat offensive," as Green put it. They had no purpose or mission besides waiting for the ice to break, opening the harbor for a ship from Copenhagen. "Months of *not much*," he remarked.

Green had reflected a great deal about the end of his three-year journey. "I don't want to get home," he had declared in the fall of 1915. "Why should I go home anyway? The war interests me only that it touches my morbidity." With home so tantalizingly close, he dropped his insouciant mask, filling his journals with diatribes against the villains who had imprisoned him in the north. Museum officials should have purchased a strong ship rather than chartering the woeful *Diana*. They should have sent a decent cook. They should have planned better. They should not have hired the underpowered *Cluett*. "If there is a divine compensation for making other people suffer," he seethed, "the Am. Mus. will pretty nearly be compensated out of business."

Green poured out his emotions in marathon writing sessions. Life was but a "monotonous drudgery," he complained. "Bah! The futility of it all! The vast imbecility of it all!" His Arctic travails had undercut whatever emotional stability went north with him. The young man who glided between toady, able administrator, and borderline psychopath was desperate to learn who he really was.

Green's narratives flitted between literary genres, sometimes stream of consciousness, sometimes fictionalized autobiography, sometimes proto-science fiction, and sometimes all of them at the same time. He wrote about the beauty rituals of Inuit women, a father and son flying in an aeroship, and the glories of sharpening a pencil. He wrote stories about brilliant Arctic explorers and tales of betrayal by trusted friends. He wrote about dead men whose cold eyes accused the living, and about good men who murdered their companions. It is impossible not to see Piugaattoq's ghost percolating through Green's ramblings.

At one point Green the author has a mysterious stranger give one of his characters, named "Green," some advice about coping with a troublesome past. "Why not take truth into our own hands and cover the nicks and scars . . . with healing balms of effective tho fictional character," he suggests.

Green—the real Green—could reinvent himself yet again. Americans wanted their explorers pure, manly, and honorable. If he got home, he would parlay their expectations into everlasting fame. He closed his notebook, the day's work over.

———

Green and Allen found their purpose in late June 1916, when the *Hans Egede* docked at Egedesminde for the second time that year, having dropped off Tanquary in Copenhagen during its previous transatlantic run. Its crew confirmed Tanquary's return and informed the Americans that the museum had chartered the *Danmark* for a rescue operation. The *Hans Egede* also delivered a telegram from AMNH president Osborn ordering Green to assume command of relief operations until the *Danmark* reached Hovey. Green wasn't sure what that job entailed, and the prospect of hanging around in Greenland displeased him, but he saw no way around the directive.

Allen and Green moved aboard the *Hans Egede*, much to the provision-poor Greenlanders' relief. Ending their three years of abstemious living, they cut loose like the sailors they were. Green called his *Hans Egede* residency "the *best* [time] since I came up North." Governor Knudsen "nearly annihilated us by several rum parties," he laughed. One bacchanal concluded with the governor falling overboard. Days slipped by in a haze. "Rain all the time—at least I *think* so," the ensign wrote. Etah seemed a million miles away. "I hope Tanq remembered to send Mac some unalcoholic grape juice," Allen mocked.

June passed without a *Danmark* sighting. The Fourth of July came and went. So did Bastille Day. Green and Allen assumed the vessel was caught up in the war. Maybe it was quarantined. Maybe it was on the ocean floor.

Whatever the ship's fate, there was no reason for Allen to linger at Egedesminde. He sailed with the *Hans Egede* to Copenhagen, leaving Green facing the "highly distasteful" prospect of another winter with the Danes and the Inuit.

The arrival of the *Godthaab* in late July gave Green an opportunity to follow Allen to Copenhagen. The ship reeked of sealskins and animal oils, but to Green it smelled like freedom. He deserted his responsibilities at the first opportunity. "I seem to have done what I could do for you in the North," he explained in a letter to Hovey. "Best wishes for a good voyage home." Fair skies and gentle breezes accompanied the *Godthaab* out of port. Greenland, the ensign's prison for the last three years, faded into the distance. The steamer slid through the foggy North Atlantic without sounding its horn. It was safer to navigate blind than to alert British contraband patrols or German raiders to their presence.

Green caught his first glimpse of Copenhagen on August 15, two days before Hovey, Freuchen, Rasmussen, and Captain Comer reached Etah in the *Ingerlis*. He checked into the Hotel Dagmar, took in a few shows, found a good tailor, and wired the museum.

His brief, vague message sparked confusion. Officials wondered why he was in Denmark rather than Greenland. "I feel quite certain that [the telegram] has simply been forwarded and that Fitzhugh has remained in [Greenland] to carry out his instructions," Sherwood informed the ensign's mother. If Fitzhugh was in Copenhagen, Mrs. Green replied, it must be the result of "some action of the Navy Dept." She was already angry at the museum because it had given her son command of the relief expedition only until it found Hovey, rather than for the duration. "I wonder if you know anything of his service record," she spat. "I wonder if you thought he could not be trusted to continue his modest, unassuming self on the return trip."

"Where is *Danmark*?" Sherwood cabled Knud Rasmussen's Danish headquarters. "Has Green or Allen arrived Copenhagen?" Green soon clarified his location but had no information on the relief ship's whereabouts. Perhaps it had bypassed Greenland's southern ports and headed straight for Etah, he replied. There might have been an accident. Maybe heavy ice had trapped the vessel. Jerome Allen's arrival in New York on August 21 left the mystery intact, as the radioman had no news of the *Danmark* either. "We are at a loss to understand this delay and also the reason for Green's return by way of Copenhagen," Sherwood shrugged.

Green's cable, along with a brief transmission he sent to the navy and a few bits of information from Allen, gave the *New York Tribune* enough material to fabricate a tale of manly resolve that upheld American myths about explorers. In its rendition, which other papers reprinted and embellished, Green emerged as a gallant, clean-cut, small-town boy imbued with both a pioneering spirit and a talent for modern science.

"It was Ensign Green who was responsible for the almost super-human efforts made by the expedition to find the supposed land," the *Tribune* claimed. "Starvation threatened the expedition," it continued, "but urged on by Green they pressed northward." The *Washington Times* picked up the story from there: "Green persisted in the search, even after almost insurmountable obstacles broke up the party and threatened it with starvation." Then the *New York Sun*: "He felt that he was under orders to find [Crocker Land] if possible, and kept up the perilous sledge journeys even under the most unfavorable conditions." Piugaattoq's death never entered the picture. Even MacMillan faded from view. Green was the sole hero.

The man himself walked down the gangway of the steamship *United States* on September 5, two and a half months after Tanquary's return. "Heat is unendurable!" he complained. A few hours later he was holding court at the New York Yacht Club, reminiscing about –60-degree days, vicious sledging conditions, and life among the Inughuit. "I was sure I saw land," he told a reporter from the *Tribune*. "It looked like a low-lying coast covered with ice. . . . I have seen mirages on the sea often, but I never saw any like those of the far North." Before stepping into a taxi hired to whisk him to Grand Central, he assured the world that the expedition had been a tremendous success. MacMillan was coming home with invaluable collections of furs, minerals, and artifacts.

Green's reappearance touched off a new round of "no Crocker Land" stories. Dr. Cook's partisans seized on the ensign's report as further evidence against Peary's North Pole claims. Cook's allies in Congress launched an unsuccessful bid to strip Peary of his rank of rear admiral and cancel his annual pension.

Peary's allies defended the commander's integrity. "It will be charged that Peary invented Crocker Land," the *Washington Times* observed. "Why should he have done that? The very fact that he made and published such an error is really proof of his straight-forwardness. If he had invented this new land . . . he would have been perfectly certain that sooner or later the truth would become known, and he would be discredited." Otto Tittmann, president of the National Geographic Society, which sponsored Peary's final trip, argued that Crocker Land's disappearance in no way affected Peary's case for the Pole.

"It may be that MacMillan and I were both misled by the nearly permanent clouds of condensation over persistent lanes of water," Peary allowed. Or, the admiral continued, "unusual refraction, which occurs in the Arctic regions, may have lifted into view land that was in reality well below the horizon, and my estimate of the distance of Crocker Land may have been too moderate." Future discoveries might yet vindicate him.

Back with the navy, Green tried to leverage his notoriety into a plum assignment in London rather than another tour on a bat-tleship. Arctic service "carries with it a certain prestige among Englishmen whose intense interest in such things seems second only to their duty," he explained to personnel officers. The navy would benefit from his reports, and "the professional advantage to me personally would of course be immeasurable."

The navy instead sent him to meet the *Danmark* at Sydney, Nova Scotia and take charge of any government-owned equipment the steamer brought back from Etah. A month passed with no sign of the ship. Green used his idle time to pursue future prospects. He requested a fast-track promotion to lieutenant, which the navy denied. He toured mills and munitions plants in anticipation of a post-navy career running a shipyard. And he cultivated Robert Peary. "We had a wonderful experience in the north," he gushed in a fawning letter. Green suggested that he visit the commander to share the details.

On October 2, with the *Danmark's* whereabouts still a mystery, the navy reassigned Green to the battleship *Texas*. "I am delighted with the prospect," he said. A few hours later, he requested a five-week leave. His reasons soon became clear. On October 8 Green announced his engagement to Natalie Wheeler Elliott, a society belle who was the sister of one of his classmates at Annapolis. His copious Crocker Land diaries never mention Natalie, nor do his papers contain any correspondence to or from her during the Crocker Land years. It is possible that Natalie is the "Anna C." of his befuddled late 1914 letters, but there is no direct evidence of this.

Fitzhugh and Natalie married on November 27. Two days later the couple left for an extended honeymoon in Bermuda. Green had gotten away with the glory and the girl.

America soon forgot both Green and the remaining Crocker Landers, whose greatest achievement was subtracting land from the world map. It is hard to win lasting fame for finding "empty" space. Unlike 1909, when Peary made his well-publicized return, in 1916 Americans were distracted by external affairs. "In the greatest war the world has known, polar expeditions receive scant attention," Arctic enthusiast and Peary supporter Herbert L. Bridgman noted in the *American Museum Journal*. "Were it not for the shadow which falls from the East the world would be alert to learn the fate of the absent, and if necessary, to succor them." When Green arrived in New York, the horrific Battle of the Somme was entering its third month. Arabia was in revolt against the Ottoman Empire. Italy and Romania had joined the conflict. Germany's on-again-off-again policy of unrestricted submarine warfare put American ships and American lives in the crossfire. Woodrow Wilson was campaigning for a second term on a dubious promise to keep the country out of the war. With the world in flames, Americans devoted little attention to a few hardy souls trapped in a land of ice.

"I suppose if we had discovered Crocker Land there would have been no difficulty whatever in raising the full amount,"

H. F. Osborn groused. Museum officials assumed the tough fund-raising environment would get even worse if donors learned the truth about the expedition. No one in New York knew the exact situation in northern Greenland, but the hemming and hawing by Tanquary, Allen, and Green about "the management of affairs" suggested that all was not well.

Anticipating trouble, Osborn sent a letter on September 8, 1916 that he hoped would find Hovey and MacMillan somewhere between Etah and the United States. It is *extremely important* that no suggestion of any lack of harmony in the management or administration, or among the members, should be made public in any way," he warned. In a few weeks, when everyone was home, they could create an upbeat cover story.

REUNION AND SEPARATION

NEARLY 2,500 MILES NORTH of New York, MacMillan sat on a hill behind Etah one chilly night with Panippak, one of his favorite companions. At about sixty years old, Panippak was among the oldest of the Inughuit and a fount of tribal lore. He was also a grandson of the great Qillarsuaq, a powerful shaman who, guided by a vision, led several families on a migration from North Baffin Island to northwest Greenland around 1850. During their multi-year stay Qillarsuaq's people reintroduced the kayak, the bow and arrow, and the fish spear—technologies the Polar Inuit had lost when the eighteenth-century Little Ice Age disrupted traditional hunting and fishing patterns.

Panippak was in a mood to talk. MacMillan listened with rapt attention. Panippak discussed his famous grandfather and pondered the skies. They looked very different here than they did in Maine, or anywhere else in the continental United States. Astral landmarks such as Scorpius and Sagittarius never broke the horizon at Etah's latitude. Polaris, the north star, was too high in the sky for navigational purposes. It had no significance for the Inughuit, who didn't have a name for it.

MacMillan named constellations while Panippak described what he saw. The Big Dipper became a herd of reindeer. Cassiopeia became three stones supporting a lamp. What MacMillan interpreted as Orion's belt was to Panippak a staircase cut in a steep snow bank. The seven sisters of the Pleiades transformed into a team of dogs pursuing a bear. "They are the spirits of our people," Panippak said of the stars. "It is a wonderful world up there. We shall all be together with those we love."

Panippak wasn't talking about heaven, at least not the one a devout Christian like MacMillan believed in. The Inuk saw spirits all around him but would never have considered asking for guidance from an all-powerful God. Although *angakkoqs* wielded some small influence over the mystical world, for the most part good spirits did good things and bad spirits did bad things.

The astronomical features looming over Mac and Panippak told many stories. The northern lights were the spirits of stillborn children dancing with their afterbirths. The moon, moving beyond its first quarter, was the sun's lustful older brother, whose desire for his sister was so intense that he forever chased her across the firmament. Venus was once an old man who was about to harpoon a seal when a crowd of noisy kids scared off the animal. The outraged hunter shouted loud enough to cause a rockslide, burying the children. Their parents attacked the man, who ran for his life before shooting into the sky, where he became Naalgsartoq, "he who stands and listens." He appeared in the west when spring approached, staying low on the horizon so he could hear seals under the ice.

The stars, which were as brilliant here as anywhere on the planet, informed Panippak's life in practical as well as supernatural ways. MacMillan's friend read them like a sky map that indicated location and heading. Starlight provided a means for evaluating one's surroundings during the dark Arctic winter. Open leads of water threw dark, streaky reflections on the clouds. Frozen seas cast up an expanse of dull white. Bands of snow showed as brighter white reflections.

Unlike the eighteenth-century missionary Hans Egede, who

deplored "false" *angakkoqs* whose "silly tricks and wicked impostures" kept southern Greenlanders from embracing true religion, the Crocker Landers neither denigrated the Inughuit's spiritual beliefs nor tried to convert the tribe to Christianity. MacMillan saw the natives as essentially Christian in morals if not in ritual. They protected the weak, sacrificed their comfort for the welfare of others, and viewed material objects in communal rather than individual terms. Crime and violence were rare.

MacMillan loved his conversations with Panippak and other elders. Although the American considered himself an explorer and an ethnographer, what he enjoyed most was absorbing native lifestyles. The boy who had bounced between homes grew into a man who found a home at the edge of the world.

Forty-eight hours after Fitzhugh Green disembarked in New York, MacMillan was working outside Borup Lodge when he heard a thrumming to the south. It was September 7, late for a relief ship but still early enough to get everyone home. Icebergs bobbed in Etah harbor like bluish-white pyramids. MacMillan sighed with the expectation that his Arctic adventure was coming to an end.

It was not a relief steamer, but rather Peter Freuchen's *Ingerlis*. Here to transfer him to a vessel waiting at North Star Bay, MacMillan assumed. Peering through his binoculars, he discerned Comer, Ekblaw, Hovey, and Small on the deck. A horrifying realization dawned on him. These men were not coming to take him away, but rather to live with him. "I am not to be favored with a solitary winter," he moaned. "I shall have more company than I want or can take care of properly."

MacMillan donned a welcoming mask. Four unhappy Americans piled into the lodge. Comer was tired of Hovey's incessant talk of escape. The curator is "quite variable, first proposing one thing then another," the captain sneered. "All lack confidence in him and all wish to be free of him." Ekblaw resented MacMillan for selling their food and for stifling his scientific work. He rode along on the *Ingerlis* so he could pick up a few things from Etah before scuttling back to the Danish trading station, which was almost out of food but still preferable to the lodge. Dr. Hunt wanted no part of Etah and hadn't bothered to make the trip.

Hovey settled into Hunt and Allen's old room. Comer took over Ekblaw and Tanquary's. Arguments began almost immediately. Hovey browbeat MacMillan about the fox skins—again. Mac finally confessed to acquiring them for his own monetary gain, not the museum's. This wasn't much of a revelation, as other party members had often voiced frustration about this practice. The furs had assumed an almost symbolic value. Control over them represented control over the fractious expedition. Hovey impounded eight dog biscuit crates stuffed with pelts. Then the man who criticized MacMillan for overcommercializing the expedition asserted his intention to buy as many skins as possible from the Inughuit.

An uneasy détente settled over the Etah four. Writing, card games, and music killed some time. They talked about loved ones, mulled the *Cluett's* whereabouts, and wondered when someone would bring them home. On November 7 they debated who America had elected president, unaware that Woodrow Wilson's anti-war pledge had secured him a second term. Comer sang songs and related stories about the Strait of Magellan and Antarctica's Desolation Island. Old memories distracted the grizzled captain from his fears that his wife was facing destitution without his salary.

Everyone maintained a busy front even though no one had much to do. Small resumed command of the kitchen. Hovey put on hip boots and collected jellyfish and other aquatic animals with a long-handled net. When the fiord froze over he refocused his attention on the crates containing Green's unused seismograph. Even though the ensign had never opened some of the boxes, he had somehow lost the assembly instructions. Using a picture from a catalog as a guide, the men assembled the machine in one of the back rooms. Meanwhile, Comer hobbled outside twice a day on his gimpy right knee, which he had wrenched in an ice crack years earlier, to read thermometers and measure the thickness of the ice. The captain also drew water from a nearby stream. When that froze, he tethered a small iceberg to the shore with a piece of kite wire—finally useful!—and melted chunks of it on the stove.

Food was holding out, if barely. Sugar, canned goods, and molasses were gone before Thanksgiving. They had some "slightly putrid" remnants from the summer walrus hunt. MacMillan had a few hundred eggs stashed away. Dog biscuits were fairly plentiful. They "[do] not taste bad," Comer reported, "but are hard on account of the bones as it is horse meat and bones mixed with flour." The men survived because the Inughuit brought them meat, and because of the supplies MacMillan had had sent up on the *Cluett*.

Winter's arrival exacerbated the animosities. Small deteriorated when the summer sun disappeared, as he always did. All of his teeth had fallen out. Hovey fretted about his long absence from the museum and worried that the faltering expedition might tarnish his professional reputation. Comer's lungs burned from the house's greasy, smoky air. He found Hovey unreliable, MacMillan unreasonable (refusing to trade Viivi some dog biscuits for a pair of rabbit-skin mittens for Comer's freezing hands), and Small just plain filthy. Jot "blows his nose with his fingers," Comer complained of the cook, and he combated body lice by dumping bedbug powder down his shirt. Even MacMillan wilted under the pressure. "Great heavens," he wrote a friend, "what a country. . . . There are times in June and July, when the birds are back, when the sun is high . . . when we think it is beautiful, but we deceive ourselves. It follows a long, cold, dark period of one hundred and eighteen days; our pleasures are but contrasts."

Trivial matters sparked heated battles, often instigated by Small. The misguided wisdom of the brash, rough-hewn jack-of-all-trades infuriated Hovey, who engaged him in absurd shouting matches over the difference between corned beef and salt beef, or what would happen if all the world's springs stopped flowing. Hovey would never have crossed paths with Small in the outside world. Confined in a physically and emotionally stressful environment, and separated from their accustomed social spheres, the members of this involuntary micro-community struggled to cope with reality.

Twenty inches of ice blanketed Etah harbor by early November. Traveling season had come. Time for another desperate mail run, this one even more crucial than the previous year's grind across trackless, fog-shrouded Melville Bay. Mac and Hovey penciled letter after letter in anticipation. Comer and Small talked about the people to whom they should be writing. MacMillan struck an upbeat tone in his correspondence. "A third ineffectual attempt [at relief] would prove a bit unpleasant, but not seriously so," he told one friend. He gave the museum a different story. "Our relief must be made certain in 1917," he advised Osborn. Send Peary or some other competent man.

Hovey had run out of optimism. "Relief must come next year, or we shall be in serious straits," he wrote his superiors at the museum. "We shall be unable to heat the house. . . . Our supply of white man's food will be extremely limited, if not exhausted, and we shall be obliged to distribute ourselves among Eskimo igloos here and elsewhere and live with and like the natives." That last indignation, the prospect of adopting savage ways, rankled Hovey. Men like him did not accept charity, especially from inferior peoples. "It is of great importance to me to get home," he declared.

On November 23, Agpalersuraassuk and Sammie stacked the precious mail atop two sledges bound for North Star Bay. From there, Ekblaw and Hunt would carry the letters to one of the ports 1,000 miles south. At least, that was the plan. No one had heard from either man in two months.

The drivers returned two weeks later with fresh mail and startling news. A ship called the *Danmark* was frozen in at North Star Bay. For a second time, a relief expedition needed relief.

"Where is it?" Ekblaw's fiancée Augusta Krieger demanded. "Where is the party?" George Sherwood had no answer. He urged patience, as he did with all the Crocker Land families. There was no need for worry until early December, he said.

"I am greatly worried about the Crocker Land situation," Sherwood informed Herbert L. Bridgman, in strict secrecy.

Captain Christian Jansen of the *Danmark*, an experienced Arctic navigator, had never encountered an ice pack like the one he found in Melville Bay. Jansen had headed north later than planned because the Greenland Mining Company, with the museum's consent, dispatched him on a side trip to deliver 200 tons of graphite before steaming for Etah. The *Danmark* raced the ice up to the south Greenland port of Upernavik. Confident in his vessel, the captain challenged Melville Bay only to get locked in. The ship drifted with the pack for seven weeks before breaking clear. On September 23, 1916, two weeks after Hovey's crew relocated to Borup Lodge, Jansen powered the steamer through two and a half inches of ice in North Star Bay so he could drop off some supplies for the trading station.

Southerly gales blew more ice between North Star Bay and Etah. Inexplicably, the *Danmark*'s crew unloaded its cargo at a crawl, giving the floes time to interlock. Jansen stabbed at the pack without breaking through. Ice held the *Danmark* fast. Worse, the ship had burned so much coal that Jansen did not have enough to reach Etah the following summer. His rescue operation had failed. The only good news was that the *Danmark*, unlike the *Cluett*, carried sufficient food for the winter.

Jansen invited Ekblaw and Hunt aboard the marooned *Dan-*

mark. Conditions on board were "rather difficult and unsatisfactory." Their quarters were tight, dark, cold, and stuffy. There was no fresh meat, only unpalatable salt beef. Without fresh food, the chances of a scurvy epidemic were high. Ekblaw and Hunt also suffered from isolation. "I am not very perfect in the English language," Jansen said. Ekblaw remembered a sprinkling of Danish from his childhood, but Hunt had no idea what anyone was saying. The doctor sulked, convinced the *Danmark* could have gotten him home if not for its crew's incompetence, and outraged that the museum had sent another underpowered vessel. "Why couldn't they send a properly equipped ship?" he seethed.

"Already I am so heartily sick of the ship that any relief or escape seems desirable," Ekblaw complained in mid-October. He disliked the Danes. Shipboard life was "exceedingly monotonous and wearisome." The scientist was unsure of his next move. Mac would probably send him south for help, but the *Danmark*'s presence might have changed the situation. At this point Ek didn't even know who was in charge of the expedition, Mac or Hovey.

Receiving little direction from Etah, Ekblaw decided his own future. "We assume that the Museum has done its utmost to get the Crocker Land Expedition home this year and has used all the means at its disposal within reason," Ekblaw wrote. "These means have failed through no fault of the Museum, it is unlikely that better means will be available next year, and there is always the possibility that the *Danmark* can not get out safely, so we feel justified in attempting the journey to South Greenland where we can be reasonably sure of getting a ship to Denmark, and thence home." Hunt expressed himself more bluntly. "How I wanted out," he later said. "We were eager to be off, to be shut of the whole expedition."

Ekblaw and Hunt boxed up nonessentials for storage on the *Danmark*. Ekblaw hired four Inughuit guides and persuaded Knud Rasmussen to accompany them part of the way south. They loaded *qamutits* by the pale light of a waning, fingernail moon. Rasmussen secured furs atop his vehicle. Seventy dogs nipped, fought, and howled.

With a "Huk! Huk!" the dogs took the first steps of a 1,100-mile journey to save the Crocker Landers. The *Danmark* could not rescue the men at Etah. New York could only guess at their condition. Word of their plight needed to get out. The expedition's fate lay in the hands of a Midwestern geologist and a backwoods physician with a paralyzing fear of the cold, neither of whom was any good on a *qamutit*.

28

OFF THE MAP

"I FULLY REALIZE THE DIFFICULTIES in getting a suitable ship and the enormous expense involved," Mrs. Marion Hunt wrote in a February 1917 letter to George Sherwood, "but the men have been there four winters, the last two in difficulties short of food probably and I feel that the Museum should make their biggest effort this year and take the surest way to bring the men out." No more three-masted auxiliary steamers. No more underpowered vessels. Regardless of the expense, "they just *must* get home *this* summer."

The families with loved ones in the north were suffering from a collective case of jangled nerves. Elmer Ekblaw's mother panicked when she read a newspaper report of a German submarine sinking the *Danmark* off the west coast of France. It turned out to be a different *Danmark* from the one the museum had hired, although no one in New York had any idea whether the relief ship was above or below the ocean's surface.

Knud Rasmussen promised Ekblaw and Hunt good sledging and abundant meat. Bent on getting home whatever the risk, Hunt demanded his own sledge in case he decided to split from the rest of the group. As extra insurance, he persuaded his friend Ukujaaq, a veteran guide who had accompanied Peary on his polar run, to join him on the first leg of the journey.

Storms on Melville Bay halted their progress. Howling winds buffeted the drafty canvas tents they had erected in the lee of an iceberg. Ekblaw's big toes, wrists, face, and fingers were frostbitten. Black splotches covered his body. Fluid leaking from ruptured blisters froze in his socks. His clothes were wet with sweat. He could not stop shivering. Hunt's ankles screamed after ten hours of snowshoeing through the soft snow blanketing the ice. It was two feet deep, with a thin crust on top and slush at the bottom. The Inughuit said it was the worst possible surface for traveling. Hunt took a step, knocked ice from his snowshoes, and then took another. Overloaded sledges sank in the sludge. The dogs were hungry. In the darkness, people kept tripping over uneven surfaces and banging into icebergs. With no land in sight, the guides were unsure of their location and direction. Hunt estimated the temperature at –50 or –60 degrees.

Someone remembered it was Christmas Eve. Ekblaw produced a box of dates his fiancée had sent up on the *Cluett*. Rasmussen located two cans of pears in his bags. Ukujaaq had some bear meat from one of his old caches. With this feast in their bellies, the exhausted travelers crawled into caribou-skin bags for another miserable sleep. Ekblaw started whistling "Silent Night." Rasmussen added Danish lyrics. The natives hummed along. "I hoped that the morrow would not be so cold, nor so wearisome, nor so discouraging," Ekblaw wrote.

Unfortunately, Christmas Day proved exactly that. So did the next day, and the next one. Rasmussen decided to make a dangerous solo run for help. He thought they were somewhere near Cape Seddon, Melville Bay's southern terminus and the site of a village, so he hitched the best dogs to an empty sledge and set off in what he hoped was the right direction.

The Dane melted into the darkness. Hunt unfurled his sleeping bag. A week of breaking trail had broken him. Ekblaw shook the doctor awake after what felt to him like a few seconds of slumber.

"Hal," he said, "we had better be going somewhere. Knud has not come back, and I am worried. The dogs are dying."

Hunt rolled over. "Don't worry," he mumbled.

"Hal," Ekblaw persisted, "you have been sleeping for two days, and we have no food left. We must go on. I think the other team is lost."

Startled, the doctor crawled from his bag. The Inughuit wanted to retreat before their dogs died. Keeping them there had taken all of Ekblaw's powers of persuasion.

Clouds, a little thinner than in past days, turned everything a dull, soggy grey. Hunt and Ekblaw hobbled to the top of an iceberg. From the summit, the Americans scanned the smudgy expanse for anything resembling land. A dark blob to the north looked promising.

Ukujaaq joined them. "I know where we are," he half spoke, half pantomimed. Neither Hunt nor Ekblaw understood much Inuktun. "I lived in that country one or two seasons," he continued. "We'll be at the settlement within an hour." Had they not stopped when they did, or had the storms continued, they might have missed their spot.

Hunt strapped on his snowshoes while the others dumped goods onto the ice. The doctor resumed his agonizing march. The dogs dragged the empty *qamutits*. Despite Ukujaaq's prediction—perhaps there was a problem of translation—it took seven excruciating hours for the villagers to see the party and dispatch a relief squadron under the command of Uutaaq. Rasmussen was among them, with fewer dogs than he had left with. He had just reached the settlement, having first set off in the wrong direction.

Hunt staggered toward the nearest hut. "Call off the dogs!" he roared as he shimmied through the entrance tunnel. Shoving aside the sleeping inhabitants—a perfectly acceptable practice—he collapsed. Ekblaw, his entire body aching, was close behind. They slept the sleep of relieved men, confident they had survived the worst of their troubles.

The team rested for a few days before striking out for the trading station of Tasiusaq, 150 miles to the south. The group had entered Danish territory. At midday sunlight seeped up from below the horizon.

Holsteinsborg, the south Greenland port where the Americans planned to catch a ship, was over 500 miles away by air, and dogsleds didn't fly. Ekblaw could not make it that far. The geologist's feet were ruined and his spirit shattered. Soaring blood pressure gave him uncontrollable nosebleeds. "I had lost nearly a six-pound pemmican-canful of blood, and was weak as a cat," he reported. He resolved to go as far south as possible, perhaps to Godhavn, a smaller port halfway between Tasiusaq and Holsteinsborg, and wait for help.

He kept his decision private. The two Americans were operating on a need-to-know basis. Ekblaw disapproved of Hunt's hostility toward the expedition, especially toward Hovey, whom the geologist viewed as a future benefactor. Homesickness would drive the doctor onward no matter what, he reasoned, so there was no point in ruffling any feathers at this moment of incredible stress.

Rasmussen turned back at the small island community of Prøven (present-day Kangersuatsiaq), a few days south of Upernavik. Ekblaw and Hunt were happy to see him go. Neither of them trusted the quixotic adventurer–businessman. Losing Ukujaaq was a different matter. Ukujaaq called Hunt *nanorsuaq*, great bear. Hunt referred to Ukujaaq as his blood brother. The stocky, sturdy, fun-loving Inuk treated the doctor as a loving son would his father (Hunt was thirty-eight, Ukujaaq was in his mid-twenties), nursing him through tough days on the trail without mentioning his own burden, a partially paralyzed right leg that the doctor attributed to polio. Hunt gave Ukujaaq every material item he could spare, keeping not much more than a sleeping bag and a volume of Robert Browning's poems. Both men knew they would never see each other again.

At 72° 22′ north, Ekblaw and Hunt were far above the Arctic Circle and several hundred miles from their destination. A quick hop across the bay brought them to South Upernavik, where their luck soured again. Warm temperatures, rough seas, and southerly gales discouraged ice formation, trapping them in town. By mid-February, following weeks without progress, Ekblaw gave up on reaching a ship. Hunt insisted he could make it. No one had ever scaled the mountains behind the village and pushed south via an overland route, but he was desperate enough to try.

Ekblaw pointed out the obvious drawbacks. The route was dangerous, good sledges were scarce, and decent dogs rare. His arguments had no effect. "I was determined to get out and willing to make any personal sacrifice in an attempt to do so," the doctor wrote. Faced with implacable resistance, Ekblaw gave his reluctant blessing. There weren't enough dogs for them both, so the scientist volunteered to stay behind.

Hunt gathered three sledges and enough adequate dogs to give him a chance at success. Three Inuit charged twice the going rate to guide him into the unexplored territory.

Villagers dragged Hunt's sledges up the cliff using coils of sealskin line and every able-bodied dog in town. At the top, Ekblaw handed the doctor their precious batch of letters and cables.

Hal Hunt, who barely understand the local language, who had almost exhausted Hovey's line of credit, who had gone nearly deaf from three and a half years of Arctic winds, was the sharp end of the spear. The doctor despised Hovey, considered MacMillan a weak and foolish leader, and believed the museum had shirked its responsibility to bring him home. So far as he knew, the fate of his entire party rested in his capable hands.

———

Hunt and his guides pushed through the deep powder covering the hills. Their daily existence read like a list of Arctic woes. Hungry dogs. No fresh game. Ear-piercing blizzards. Ice crystals whipped into the eyes. Starvation. Depletion. Exhaustion.

Isolation consumed the outdoorsman who had savored days alone in the Maine woods. He hadn't seen another white man since South Upernavik, and he yearned for someone to talk with. Moreover, he was getting nervous about making the boat, which typically arrived in late April.

He found some respite on March 8 when his squadron shuffled into Jakobshavn (present-day Ilulissat), a small village dominated by the massive Sermeq Kujalleq glacier. Hunt was too tired for sightseeing, but he perked up when his guides delivered him to Governor Anderson's tidy wooden home. Two attractive Danish women greeted the weary traveler.

"We have just finished a banquet, and the food is still on the table," one of them said, "so please come and eat and have some coffee with us." Hunt thought they were beautiful. "I had seen no white girls for four years," he explained. What should have been a familiar environment was alien and uncomfortable. Hunt stank. Lice were crawling over his body. But he set aside self-consciousness long enough to wolf down everything his hosts put in front of him.

Governor Anderson escorted him to a guest room. Hunt's eyes widened. Steam rose from a wooden bathtub. There was soap, a feather bed, and towels as snowy white as the hills he had crossed to get here. "Feathers under me, feathers over me," he sighed as he burrowed into bed.

By the time he awoke, some kind soul had killed the lice in his furs with gasoline. Anderson suggested that he stay a while, maybe do some caribou hunting. Charming though his hosts were, the doctor insisted on heading south. He stayed long enough to hire new guides and test the governor's skills at chess, which, like those of most people, fell short of his own.

It was "the worst year for sledge travel the people have ever known," Hunt recorded in his diary. Because there was no sea ice between Jakobshavn and Egedesminde, his next port of call, he again pointed his *qamutit* into the jagged Greenland interior. Every team of dogs he hired was in worse shape than the previous one. More expensive, too. Money, useless among the Inughuit, became a real concern. He hoped to scrape by to Holsteinsborg. "They surely expect some member of the Expedition there," he reasoned, so the museum would send a letter of credit.

Hunt was penniless by the time he reached Egedesminde, where he waited out a week of warm weather. The few Danes in town told him he would probably miss the ship.

He exchanged his sledge for an *umiaq*, also called a "woman's boat" because it was typically used for transporting women and children. Hunt and the Inuit paddled through whitecaps and drift ice littering the maze of islands fronting Greenland's west coast. March 21 found them in Agto, a two-mile-wide hunk of rock and marshes populated by eight families and a Danish storekeeper named Hansen, who had never learned how to play chess. Hunt was about 100 miles short of his goal. The ship was due any day.

Hunt's guides rowed for home, leaving the doctor alone and unsure of how to proceed. Agto had neither motorboats nor *umiaqs* capable of withstanding the ferocious tides, powerful winds, and harsh seas pounding the scores of uninhabited islands between the settlement and Greenland's ice cap 80 miles to the east. If he some-how reached the mainland, there were no dogs there to carry him south. Compounding his problems, the community's food supply consisted of the few cod villagers pulled from the ocean each day. One extra mouth was one too many.

Days ticked away. Ice formed along the shore, preventing large boats from reaching Agto. Then storms dispersed the ice but cre-ated unsafe seas for *umiaqs*. Then more ice. Then more storms. Hunt surveyed the harbor from Hansen's front room. He went sledding with the Dane's four-year-old daughter, who was around the same age as his own little girl. He commissioned a kayak, thinking he could paddle to Holsteinsborg if the weather and water improved.

Hunt finally located an *umiaq* crew willing to lead him south. The party left Agto on April 19. A ship might be docking at Holsteinsborg at that moment. Hunt donned waterproof sealskins and wedged himself into the kayak's eighteen-inch-wide opening. Loose ice bobbed around the harbor. Fastening his coat to the rim of the opening, he shivered at the possibility of a wave tipping him over. A talented kayaker could right his craft. Although competent, Hunt wasn't a talented kayaker. His aching hamstrings stretched into an unfamiliar position. Inuit, who grew up without chairs, bent at the waist when they sat, creating an L-shape that all the Americans except MacMillan found uncomfortable.

Pushing aside his fears and discomfort, Hunt dipped his paddle and followed the *umiaq*. The boat knifed through the thin layer of ice. Thicker pans sent the tiny flotilla scrambling for detours. Hunt dislodged ice accumulating on his kayak with a caribou antler. He couldn't do much about the ice on his paddle or the icicles drooping from his bow and stern.

Onward he paddled, pressing his guides through eighteen-hour days and cruel northern winds. Nighttime temperatures fell below –30 degrees, cold for April.

Hunt awoke on April 22 just 15 miles from his goal. Sliding into his kayak at 7:30 a.m., he pulled with more vigor than he had felt in a long time. Up ahead, the *umiaq* plodded through the ice. The 1,200-foot cliffs overlooking Holsteinsborg's northern fringe loomed from behind a warren of small islands. Accelerating his pace, Hunt shot past the *umiaq* into open water.

Each stroke drew Holsteinsborg into sharper focus. Its 1,500 residents occupied a hilly slice of one of the innumerable peninsulas jutting from Greenland's west coast. Rows of colorful houses with double walls and steep roofs lined the snow-powdered land beneath the cliffs. Hunt scanned the harbor for the *Hans Egede*. The Danish steamer was not there.

The town rushed out to meet the doctor at the shore. Pastor Frederiksen pumped his hand. Governor Binser introduced himself and his wife. Hunt inquired about the *Hans Egede*. It was en route, the Danes said, and expected any day. After snowshoeing, sledging, and paddling something like 1,500 miles, the doctor could relax. His passage had taken three months longer than expected, and he had lost Ekblaw along the way, but the road home remained open. Relieved beyond words, he submitted when the crowd lifted him from his kayak.

A pungent aroma greeted him the next morning. It was coffee, strong coffee. A maid brought a cup. The doctor wandered into the governor's dining room for a breakfast of oatmeal, warm bread, and home-brewed ale. There were rich jellies, delicious fish, and a bottle of schnapps. It was perfect, except that it wasn't Maine.

Hunt hated inactivity. Every day he climbed a peak to watch for the *Hans Egede*. He attended a typhoid victim at the local clinic. Binser and Frederiksen shared fond memories of Tanquary, who had passed through Holsteinsborg the previous year. Binser played chess but was "not in good practice," so Hunt tracked down the local champion, a hunchbacked Inuit who placed a thick cushion on his chair so that he could see the board. Hunt checkmated him again and again. "He was a good sport," the doctor allowed.

The Danes speculated that the war had delayed the ship. Perhaps it wasn't coming at all. Denmark might have entered the conflict.* There was no way of finding out.

"Had I fought my way south only to be balked again?" Hunt asked. He meandered around the bay in his kayak, half for the practice and half for something to do. Every far-off blur became the ship for a few thrilling moments before floating away. Growing

---

* Denmark remained neutral throughout the war.

desperate, the doctor considered purchasing one of the weather-beaten dories lining the bay, rigging it with sails, and navigating down the treacherous Labrador coast to Battle Harbor, St. John's, or some other port offering passage to the United States.

"*Umiarsuaq! Umiarsuaq!*" came the cry on the evening of May 12. "A great ship!"

It was the *Hans Egede*. The steel-clad steamer had avoided both the Kaiser's U-boats and the British destroyers that were waylaying neutral vessels. Hunt interrogated the crew, who told him that the United States had entered the war a month earlier. "This may prevent my getting home by way of Denmark," he worried. To his dismay, the ship brought nothing from the museum—no updates, no advice, and no letter of credit.

The doctor talked the captain into letting him aboard. Two weeks later, following a vicious bout of seasickness and many spirited chess matches against the ship's physician, he stepped onto the grim shores of Thorshavn, the dismal outcrop Tanquary had visited in 1916. The local fleet was bottled up in the harbor. Fishing, the community's lifeblood, was at a near standstill because of the U-boats prowling offshore.

Hunt found his way to the telegraph office. Handing the clerk his last coins, he wrote out a terse cable:

MACMILLAN COMER SMALL AND HOVEY ETAH

DANMARK NORTH STAR BAY

EKBLAW GODHAVN

HUNT HANS EGEDE

ARRANGE CREDIT PASSPORT COPENHAGEN THROUGH AMERICAN

MINISTER

HUNT

He then hustled to the British consul's office for advice. The trip to Denmark was too dangerous, he was told. What about getting home via Great Britain, the doctor asked. Bad idea, came the answer. Hunt lacked a valid passport, so British officials would probably arrest him as a spy. Faced with two bad options, the doctor decided to take his chances with the *Hans Egede*.

"I am so happy," Marion Hunt sighed when the museum forwarded her husband's telegram from Thorshavn. George Sherwood was relieved as well. Fishermen had spotted the *Danmark* in Melville Bay in August 1916. Beyond that, he knew nothing about the rescue ship's location or condition. In public he insisted the vessel might return with the Crocker Landers at any moment. "Even should she be caught in the ice and be compelled to winter in the north," he clarified, "no anxiety need be felt for the safety of our party." Sherwood told a different story in private. "We have grave fears for their safety," he told British ambassador Sir Cecil Arthur Spring-Rice. "Our gravest anxiety is for Doctor Hovey, because of his physical condition."

Sherwood gave up hope of their immediate return in January 1917, around the same time that Ekblaw and Hunt got trapped in South Upernavik. With the *Danmark* either iced in or resting on the bottom (an unlikely but possible scenario), the question became what to do next. His instincts told him to get another ship. His ledgerbook argued otherwise. In 1911 Hovey had proposed contributing $10,000 toward Borup and MacMillan's venture. As of January 1917, the museum had spent $95,000 on the Crocker Land expedition. Pending expenses such as salaries and unpaid bills would add an additional $44,000, not including the cost of chartering another ship. Neither of the other major sponsors, the American Geographical Society and the University of Illinois, were willing to give any more.

Allen, Green, and Tanquary urged Sherwood to hire a third ship. Their arguments persuaded him. Finding a worthy boat, however, was no simple matter. Peary's old stalwart, the *Roosevelt*, was steaming toward Alaska on a special mission for the government. The Bureau of Fisheries couldn't recommend a suitable vessel. W & S Job and Company, owners of the *Diana* and other Arctic veterans, wouldn't even discuss a charter until the sealing season ended in March. American diplomats in Copenhagen advised that the Danish government had suspended cruises to Greenland because of the war. Sherwood was so desperate that at one point he considered inquiring about the disgraced *Cluett*. "I am rather staggered by the difficulties that confront me," he wailed.

Sherwood didn't have a ship, but he did have a captain. More than five years had passed since Bob Bartlett stormed out of museum director Frederic Lucas's office when the museum denied him command of the Crocker Land expedition. In early 1917 the museum turned to him as their best hope of saving the beleaguered party.

The forty-one-year-old captain was a legend within the exploration community. "In spirit and in deed he was . . . truly a child of the Homeric age," one admirer said. "He was in fact a modern Odysseus who wandered far by land and sea." Though Bartlett's mother had begged him to become a minister, the Arctic Ocean's frigid waters coursed through his veins. His birthplace, the windswept rockpile of Brigus, Newfoundland, was a waystation for hardy men who devoted their lives to the sea. His father was a captain, as were his uncles and his great-uncle. He claimed that his distant ancestors included Iberian survivors of the Spanish Armada.

Bartlett was working on sealers before he turned seventeen. His uncle John made him first mate on the *Windward* for Peary's 1898 expedition. He captained the *Roosevelt* in 1905 when it delivered Peary to Ellesmere Island, then repeated the trip three years later before accompanying the commander beyond 87° north latitude. Bartlett was as sure a bet as existed in the dicey game of Arctic navigation.

The captain stood five feet ten and a half inches tall and weighed a rock-solid 174 pounds.* Piercing eyes and high cheeks reddened

---

* 2.46 pounds per inch, within Peary's preferred range.

by exposure suggested a man who took no nonsense. Broad yet sloping shoulders gave him a deceptive semi-slouch that concealed catlike reflexes.

The paradoxes extended beyond the physical. Bartlett was as profane as one would expect from a rough-hewn man of the sea. He was also a lover of literature who read and reread the *Odyssey*, the *Rubaiyat of Omar Khayyam*, and Shakespeare, and who was capable of eloquence when the spirit moved him. Bartlett chided superstitious sailors but snapped at anyone who whistled on board, because whistling brought ill winds. In his cosmology, bad luck struck any ship carrying women or horses, cows all faced the same direction before a thunderstorm, and cats washed their faces in front of the fireplace when visitors were on their way.

Early 1917 found Bartlett at loose ends. For years he had aspired to lead his own expedition, but no one would finance him. A proposed trip to the South Pole went nowhere, as did his ambition of flying an airplane to the North Pole. Feeling unappreciated, he had signed on with Stefansson's ill-fated bid at reaching Crocker Land from the west. When the *Karluk* sank in 1914, Bartlett cued up Chopin's funeral march on the Victrola and joined the other sailors on the ice. It took him until 1916 to get home.

"I am fit only for the Arctic," he sighed. Bartlett's appointment book was empty when Sherwood asked him to pilot the relief operation. He accepted without hesitation. The museum agreed on a $500 salary for his services.

In late May, just as Hunt arrived in Thorshavn, Sherwood landed a ship when W & S Job offered its largest sealer, the *Neptune*. It didn't come cheap. In 1913 the museum had paid $3,500 per month for the *Diana*. In 1917, with the war boosting insurance rates and creating lucrative shipping opportunities, the Job brothers insisted on $15,000 per month for the *Neptune*. "This price is staggering," Sherwood complained. He signed a contract anyway, having no other options besides praying the *Danmark* would bring his people home.

Christened in 1873, the *Neptune* was a venerable vessel with a proud record of Arctic service. Its squat profile and stubby stack gave the two-masted steamer a clunky, hulking appearance. Finesse wasn't its game; the *Neptune* was designed for brutality. Its 18-inch-thick hull was constructed from heavy oak timbers faced with oak planks and tough greenheart. A layer of iron plates sheathed the bow. Impact-absorbing rock salt filled the gap between the hull's inner and outer walls. With a skillful captain at the helm, the *Neptune* decimated ice that crippled weaker ships.

Filling the *Neptune*'s hold with an extra year's worth of supplies, a necessary precaution in case Bartlett got frozen in, added several thousand additional dollars to the already astronomical cost of sending the relief mission north. Sherwood figured that the museum would end up around $75,000 in the red unless some generous donors stepped forward.

On June 1, following an uneventful voyage, Dr. Harrison Hunt took his first steps on European soil (he had hidden in the hold for part of the trip in case Germans boarded the ship). Wartime Copenhagen seemed as bizarre as Etah had four years earlier. Hunt spoke no Danish and hadn't a krone to his name. Lice infested his tangled beard and wild hair. Sweat dripped down his body. His sealskin outfit was too heavy for the climate and out of place in the city, but he had no other clothes.

He looked up and down the dock, waiting for some representative from the museum. Nobody came. "I confess to a feeling that I was not out of the woods yet," he later remembered.

Hunt bummed some change from the *Hans Egede*'s captain and telephoned American ambassador Maurice Egan. Hunt explained who he was, then explained again, until Egan agreed to help him. A taxi deposited an attaché who took him shopping for shoes, shirts, collars, and ties before checking him in at the Hotel Dagmar, where Maurice Tanquary and Fitzhugh Green had stayed. Hunt purchased a *Ladies' Home Journal* from a newsstand ("for the advertisements") before settling in for the night.

George Sherwood, finally able to contact the doctor via telegram and hoping for an excuse to cancel the punitive *Neptune* charter, sought advice about whether the remaining party members needed another relief ship. Hunt had no faith in the *Danmark*. "It is always more sure to have two ships than one," he replied, "and the Crocker Land expedition must not remain in Greenland any longer."

Egan and Sherwood worked their contacts for an emergency passport for Hunt. Reconfirmed as a citizen of the civilized world, Hunt took a ferry across the Skagerrak, the channel separating Denmark from Norway, before taking a short train ride to Oslo, where he handed a ticket-taker his boarding pass for the *United States*, the same ship Green had taken home. The liner slipped out of port on June 8, eluded the German blockade, and chugged into the Atlantic Ocean. Six months after leaving North Star Bay, Hunt was going home.

Uncomfortable in his new clothes and perspiring in the heat—temperatures in the mid-seventies were lovely for New York in June, but steamy compared to northwest Greenland—Hunt scanned the quay for the woman he had so readily, almost eagerly, left four years ago.

Amid the hundreds of reunions accompanying a transatlantic ocean liner's arrival, a lone figure caught his eye. Marion looked exactly like he remembered her. Self-consciousness washed over him; he looked nothing like he did in 1913. His skin was leathery and weatherbeaten. His wife had never seen him with a beard.

Marion threw herself at her husband when he stepped off the gangplank. She sensed his unease. "I'll always know your eyes," she assured him. Hunt couldn't hear her. He was too deaf. It didn't matter.

Hunt's adventuring days were over. His Crocker Land ordeal wasn't. He and Marion dashed across town for a press conference at the museum. The building's exterior was basically unchanged from the last time the doctor had seen it, as the war had halted its planned expansion. Inside, however, an unfamiliar martial air suffused the premises. There were fewer young men around in 1917 than in 1913. Promising mammalogists, paleontologists, and botanists were off drilling at army bases. Some staffers were on their way to the front. Those who remained performed military maneuvers three days a week among the exhibits in Philippine Hall. Handbooks on public health and food conservation sat on desks. Offices buzzed with talk of the new American Museum War Relief Association, which had adopted two war orphans.

Hunt offered reporters the story both the museum and the public wanted to hear. With a modesty befitting a true American frontiersman, he downplayed the significance of his remarkable journey. Nevertheless, he provided enough anecdotes about starvation, daring escapes, and Herculean labors to set his audience's hair on end. Even without embellishment—the doctor was too levelheaded for exaggeration—it was an amazing tale.

Hunt proved a loyal trooper. "From the scientific point of view the Crocker Land expedition . . . has obtained excellent results," he said. MacMillan was a tremendous leader who had accumulated mountains of scientific data. Hovey was "the best equipped geologist who has ever gone into the Arctic." None of it was true, at least not from his perspective. These were necessary lies. The dysfunctional expedition needed donations. Besides, he didn't want enemies. He wanted to go home.

The museum hoped that the doctor's return and the *Neptune's* departure would renew interest in its expedition. Sherwood informed friendly reporters that MacMillan had discovered rich coal deposits, new islands (not mentioning how tiny they were), and unspecified botanical and zoological treasures. But the bally-hoo did not help fundraising. "It is difficult to sell any news now in view of the war and other important matters which are absorbing the public's attention," *New York Tribune* publisher Ogden Reid informed AMNH president Osborn.

Millions of armed men were slugging out the fate of Europe and much of the rest of the world. Woodrow Wilson, Black Jack Pershing, Marshal Ferdinand Foch, and Kaiser Wilhelm were in everyone's minds and on everyone's lips. Donald MacMillan, George Comer, Edmund Otis Hovey, and Jot Small were not. The exploits of heroic explorers, and the unpaid bills of their sponsors, were irrelevant to a society whose faith in mankind's goodness, wisdom, and idealism had dissipated as thoroughly as the illusion of Crocker Land.

Even a single night in New York was too long for the home-sick Dr. Hunt. He and Marion headed for Grand Central Terminal almost as soon as he answered the final question. He was on a train to Bangor before the morning editions containing word of his return hit the streets. The national media soon forgot about him.

LAST DAYS

JOT SMALL WAS PRETTY SURE he was going to die within the next hour or two.

It wasn't supposed to end like this. Small was the handyman who mended the expedition's boats, jury-rigged broken equipment, and cooked godawful meals. He was comic relief, the wild man of the chessboard, the one who cowered indoors when the autumn sun disappeared. And he was facing his own slow, awful demise.

Small never acquired his friend MacMillan's taste for Arctic living. The mechanic's idea of fox hunting was depositing a hunk of poisoned meat in a heavily trafficked spot. His first serious try at dogsledding came in late 1916, three years into the expedition. His first trial run lasted less than half a mile before his team dumped him. Small waved his whip and swore before lowering his head and trudging after them. Subsequent attempts were similarly futile. Small wrapped his whip around his neck. Dogs pulled in contrary directions while their red-faced master, snot dripping from his nose, screamed at them to work together. They stood stock-still when he urged them forward. They followed him when he told them to stay. They dragged the sledge over his hand. They were his worst nightmare.

Until today. Death assumed many guises in the Arctic. Stray bullets, starvation, hypothermia, polar bears, walruses, slippery glaciers, and tipping kayaks might all prove fatal. Small was enter-taining happier thoughts as his party sped toward Etah. They had killed sixteen seals, and his other trophy—a pair of gyrfalcon eggs—would excite MacMillan more than the meat.

Small was walking along the ice foot skirting Rensselaer Bay, a bit up the coast from Borup Lodge, when a thin layer of surface ice gave way. He fell several feet before catching himself by his arm-pits with his lower half dangling in the frigid ocean. Terrified, he peered up through the icy cylinder for a friendly face. Nothing. He screamed. Orfik, his guide, was out of earshot.

Small faced an endgame worthy of an Edgar Allan Poe story. The incoming tide would drown him, if the cold didn't kill him first. Bearskin pants couldn't protect him forever. His grip was slipping.

Each wash of the waves crept higher on his body. Flocks of little auks soared above his narrow line of sight. He screamed again.

A face appeared over the rim. It was Anaakkaq, Admiral Peary's son. The Inuk made a reassuring gesture and disappeared. He returned a moment later with some tribemates who lowered a line and heaved the dripping American up through the crack.

Aqqioq guided Small back to the lodge. Dry yet still rattled, the mechanic described his ordeal to MacMillan in as few words as possible. A look of revelation crossed his face. "To hell with it," he said, tromping inside. "I'm going to stay home!"

"The sum total of our work in a day is surprisingly and disappoint-ingly small," MacMillan confessed in early 1917. The men plowed through the books in their library. Comer whiled away mindless hours carving ivory. Hovey plotted his escape from Etah. MacMil-lan flipped through stacks of Victrola records. Red seal after red seal—those were opera, "mostly sung in Italian, high class, and a bit heavy for our fourth year in the Arctic." Comer, Hovey, and Mac-Millan riled Small with gloomy predictions that Germany would lose the war. Jot defended the Kaiser's regime. It had overseen tre-

mendous progress in the arts and sciences, he said, and revolutionized Germany's educational system.

On Sundays MacMillan shaved, donned a clean shirt, listened
to hymns, and avoided unnecessary work. "I want the day to be
different from the other six days of the week," he explained. "The
loss of Sunday to a civilized people would be irreparable; its lack to
an uncivilized is a blessing long delayed." Observing the Sabbath
became a means of maintaining moral superiority over the Inughuit. "Of course the natives go ahead as they have no Sunday or
pretense of religeon [sic]," Comer chipped in.

For all their smug self-assuredness, the Americans' survival
depended on the natives' willingness to exchange fresh meat for
oil, bullets, and other goods from the expedition's diminishing
reserves. Comer, MacMillan, and Small did little hunting. Hovey
did none.

Even that source of food was drying up. Hunting parties
encountered wide lanes of open water blocking them from their
southern caches and killing grounds. "During our three and a half
years here I have never known them to be in such straits," MacMillan wrote in early 1917. "Some of the dogs are merely shadows."
Frustrated, the natives began grumbling about the Americans'
stinginess. Unless the situation changed, they might lose interest
in the party's well-being. MacMillan had no idea whether the next
team of hunters would be willing to sell them hunks of meat.

News of the outside world arrived in dribs and drabs. On election day of 1916 Hovey speculated, with great displeasure, that
Woodrow Wilson had won reelection. Comer insisted that New
York senator Elihu Root had taken the prize. You're both wrong,
MacMillan and Small declared; Teddy Roosevelt, the ideal wartime leader, had triumphed. A month later they learned via sledge
from North Star Bay that Wilson, Roosevelt, and Supreme Court
justice Charles Evans Hughes were the probable candidates, at
least as of the previous summer. The Americans predicted Hughes
would be "undoubtedly our next President of the United States."

On inauguration day Hovey toasted President Hughes with a cup of fermented stewed prunes.

A December visitor delivered a ten-week-old letter from Ekblaw advising them that the *Danmark* had been marooned at North Star Bay for the past three months. Ekblaw assumed that the Etah bunch would relocate to the dank, cramped ship. Rather than abandon equipment and supplies, however, MacMillan and the others opted to stay put until the *Danmark* picked them up in the summer of 1917. Ekblaw did not mention that Captain Jansen didn't have sufficient coal for the trip north.

The fragile bonds joining the men frayed. Comer, whose rheumatic right knee and respiratory problems put him in a perpetually foul mood, loathed MacMillan, whom he blamed for the expedition's meager results. Hovey agreed with the captain on the leadership issue but was also tired of everyone mocking his obsession with going home. The curator almost came to blows with Jot Small when the handyman tried to explain the American transportation system to a few puzzled Inughuit. Waving a city transfer ticket Hovey had carried north for some reason, he tore it in an imitation of a conductor collecting fares. Hovey went ballistic. Apparently he considered this piece of pocket detritus a prized artifact. Small and Hovey rarely spoke anyway; this incident merely confirmed their mutual hatred.

MacMillan appeared unconcerned by the breakdown of his tiny community. The fates of Ekblaw and Hunt never crossed his mind, or at least never concerned him enough that he mentioned his former companions in his journal. He dismissed the fights as harmless examples of boys being boys. Whenever possible he slept outside rather than in the lodge, in part because he enjoyed living like the Inughuit, at least up to a point, and in part because he was sleeping through the daytime hours so that he could record temperature data at midnight. As a result, he was a near-stranger to the people under his command.

———

MacMillan stood at the summit of Thermometer Hill on February 17, 1917. "The sun at last!" he cried after 116 days of darkness. It was the fifth time he had experienced spring in the far north, and the fourth on this expedition. Large pans of ice studded the sea below. Cold temperatures and gentle winds were again fusing them into a solid sheet following the freak open waters of the past several weeks. Soon it would be time for traveling.

MacMillan was bored. He studied maps and reviewed Arctic narratives until he unearthed a decades-old address in which British adventurer Sir Clements Markham stated that "next to northern Greenland, the most interesting part of the unknown region is the land . . . between Jones Sound and Smith Sound." This was the southern half of Ellesmere Island's east coast, a roughly 300-mile stretch of coastline cut by deep fiords and ringed by snowy mountains.

"I decided that this should be my fourth year's work," MacMillan said. He plotted a trip from Cape Sabine, the site of Adolphus Greely's starvation camp, down to Clarence Head. Previous explorers had compiled reliable charts of the coastlines above and below these points. The area in between, which MacMillan proposed to survey, had been mapped only from ships passing several miles away.

Aqqioq, Agpalersuraassuk, and Ittukusuk agreed to come along. MacMillan figured that his failing hardtack, pemmican, and oil reserves could sustain them so long as they found fresh meat along the way.

Hovey was preparing his own expedition, this one aimed at Greenland's southern ports and, somehow, home. The curator was exercising every day, and he was more fit than he had been in 1916, when his bid for freedom nearly killed him. Qulatannguaq, an expert dog driver and a good man in a pinch, signed on to guide him, as did Qulatannguaq's son Imiina, and Tautsiannguaq, the man MacMillan had almost suffocated in a snow house in 1909.

Hovey got away before MacMillan. On March 24, a dull, grey day, he watched his helpers load three *qamutits* lined up outside the lodge. He couldn't have offered any suggestions even had he wanted to, as he knew only about a dozen words of Inuktun. Comer, MacMillan, and Small stared in silence. None of them believed any good would come of this trip. Comer had tucked away Hovey's "in case of my death" letters.

Everything was ready by noon, when Hovey climbed onto a sledge—he would ride rather than drive or walk. Conditions were perfect. The thermometer read –11 degrees, and the strong winds of the past few days had settled into a light northeasterly breeze.

"Huk! Huk!" Qulatannguaq shouted. Three teams of snarling, panting dogs barreled away from the lodge. They passed Provision Point and the radio hut on Starr Island before disappearing around the cape.

MacMillan shrugged at Hovey's departure. Comer did not share his apathy. "Now that he is gone," the captain wrote, "I feel it more strongly that he should not have done so." Comer worried not only for the curator's health, but also for the expedition's reputation should something awful happen to him.

A few weeks passed before Hovey sent word from North Star Bay. "I had a fine trip down," he wrote, "a surprisingly comfortable and really enjoyable trip." Knud Rasmussen, just returned from south Greenland, acted as his host. Hovey never mentioned the Dane's grueling journey across Melville Bay with Ekblaw and Hunt in his letter to Etah. He never mentioned the departed Americans at all. Instead, he focused on himself, his continued good health, and his satisfaction with the natives' performance so far.

MacMillan wasn't at the lodge to receive the curator's message, having departed Etah with Aqqioq, Agpalersuraassuk, and Ittukusuk on his mapping expedition the day after Hovey left. He expected to be away for as long as two months. His first round trip lasted two weeks. MacMillan lost his nerve when a blizzard stranded him alone on the middle of Smith Sound. A second storm blew out most of the ice from their proposed route, forcing them home after charting only a single inlet. Ittukusuk did locate a cairn with letters from the 1875 Nares expedition, and MacMillan plucked some souvenirs from Greely's starvation camp at Cape Sabine.

The party tried again in early May, too late in the travel season to accomplish much. This time MacMillan discovered a few specks of land (the Inughuit often used them as campsites, they told him), named a few glaciers, and mapped a fragment of coastline before calling a retreat on May 15, the day Dr. Hunt left Greenland on the *Hans Egede*.

MacMillan barreled into Etah early on the morning of May 25. Comer was unimpressed with his achievements, complaining that his team's arrival "broke up what sleep I would have had."

Comer, MacMillan, and Small were reunited for what they assumed was the last time. "After four years," MacMillan wrote, "we felt that a ship must surely come."

Six weeks later, MacMillan distributed parting gifts among the Inughuit before dashing off to enjoy a few mild July days amid the bald, craggy hills of Littleton Island, without telling Comer where he was going or when he would be back. The captain, who had grown accustomed to unexplained departures, barely looked up from packing the seismograph.

MacMillan wanted a last peek at the eider ducks and other birds inhabiting the sanctuary. He also wanted time to think. A painful sense of nostalgia gripped him. He, Borup, and Bartlett had slept under an old sail on Littleton Island one night in 1909. "Poor George is dead and Bartlett is some two thousand miles away," he said. They should have been here together. They should have explored Crocker Land together. It wasn't supposed to be like this.

MacMillan's adult life revolved around a search for a stable home and a father figure to replace the one who sailed away when he was a boy. He found a surrogate parent in Peary, the stern, remote, charismatic monomaniac with a soft spot for his eager apprentice. Although the commander never loved MacMillan like he did Borup, his cool affection inspired unswerving loyalty.

What constituted a home remained less clear in MacMillan's mind. He considered himself a man of the Arctic. With his time in the north drawing short, he wondered how he measured up against his heroes. He considered Kane and Greely to be great leaders who lacked his own understanding of the natives. He pitied Kane's starving men, dying in a hovel not far from Borup Lodge, and Greely's crew, shriveled to skeletons a few miles from abundant food sources. "One Smith Sound Eskimo could have saved the entire party," MacMillan believed.

He respected the Inughuit's ways and valued their opinions. At the same time, he was never sure whether he was part of their group or merely an employer, a passenger, a piece of baggage. Hunters came and went without informing him of their whereabouts. Guides blazed paths for him without soliciting his input.

"It is my ambition to know these people thoroughly," MacMillan had told H. F. Osborn a few years earlier, yet he did little to understand the tribe in any systematic way. His grasp of the Inuktun language, a difficult one to learn, was tenuous. His research methods were so lackluster that Hovey sarcastically inquired, "What has become of the ethnological work . . . ? I have not heard a word about that since I have been up here." Mac largely ignored the remarkable archeological surveys Comer had conducted over the past several months. The captain, who owned an impressive collection of artifacts from the Inuit living around Hudson Bay, had spent countless hours prising cultural treasures from old trash piles and abandoned houses.

For all of MacMillan's jaunty diary entries about the joys of Arctic life, the lure of a quiet existence in the United States nagged at him. "One can't get away from the haunting desire to have at some time a home and wife, and children, and secondary to that longing a place where one can have his friends to entertain," he wrote.

Years of deprivation in unfamiliar surroundings revealed the inner character hidden beneath the Crocker Landers' civilized façades. The far north exposed Fitzhugh Green as a borderline sociopath. It forced Ekblaw to discover competencies hiding within him. It inspired Hal Hunt to confess his passionate love for his family. MacMillan was still wrestling with what the experience had done to him. He recognized that he was a different man than he had been in 1913. Exactly who that person was remained unclear. So where was home? And what was home? Was it a picturesque New England cottage? A sturdy lodge in Etah? A snow house in Greenland? The answers to these questions eluded him as he watched the birds on Littleton Island. His nostalgia trip produced no revelations.

Summer came to Etah. Blooms of saxifrage made purple carpets on the hillsides. Waves dissipated the ice covering the fiord. The trickle of water issuing from the frozen stream behind the lodge widened into a steady flow.

Comer, MacMillan, and Small were ready to leave. They invented excuses to go outside and check the harbor for a ship. Conversations revolved around what to eat once they got home. Their food would last for a while, but not for long. Fuel was running low, too. Snowmelt uncovered some coal worth gleaning. Mostly the men burned old crates.

Mac and the others packed equipment, supplies, and specimens into several hundred boxes and gave the Inughuit the scraps. They stared at the harbor, and waited, and hoped. Each southerly blow had the potential to smash the ice in Smith Sound into an impenetrable field. July crawled past without a ship. "A little strain on the mind," Comer acknowledged.

July 31, 1917, was a brilliant summer day. The omnipresent sun lifted temperatures into the upper forties. A northerly breeze wafted down from the hills. It was an ideal time for photography. MacMillan lugged his heavy moving picture camera and tripod to the falls behind the house.

He had started cranking when Inaluk wandered over. She watched in silence for a moment before asking whether he had seen the ship.

"Not yet," MacMillan replied, continuing to shoot.

A surprised expression crossed her face. She approached her husband, Akumalinnguaq, who was standing nearby. A ship is coming, she said.

The cry went up a few seconds later. *"Umiarsuaq! Umiarsuaq!"* A big ship!

MacMillan released the crank and spun to face the sea. An unfamiliar vessel was bucking a headwind and rough waves. Its profile didn't match the *Danmark*. Two masts, widely spaced. A battleship-grey hull. MacMillan recognized it as the *Roosevelt*. Peary had come for him!

The ship blew its whistle when it neared Provision Point. Comer thought it was a distress call; it might have hit an under-water ledge. MacMillan leapt into the punt. He rowed close enough to read the name on the bow: *Neptune*.

MacMillan heard a familiar voice on deck.

"Is that you, Bob?" Mac yelled.

"Of course!" came the reply. "Who in hell do you think it is?"

MacMillan climbed aboard. Bartlett, red-cheeked as ever, gave him a hearty greeting. They dispatched the essentials within a few minutes. Woodrow Wilson was president. The United States was in the war. Dr. Hovey was missing.

The *Neptune* had endured the worst ice Bartlett had ever seen in Melville Bay. Bartlett passed the *Danmark* at North Star Bay, took on the expedition's boxes it had aboard, and gave Jansen permission to head home, which the captain was going to do regardless.

Bartlett needed time to make repairs. As if on cue, the next day storms rolled into Etah, preventing much work from getting done. Comer scrounged through the crates in the *Neptune's* forehold until he located some underclothes to replace his threadbare set. Comer, MacMillan, and Small loaded specimens, equipment, batteries, their powerboat, and anything else moveable onto the ship. Somewhere in that vast collection was a well-handled envelope that remained unopened; for all his travails, MacMillan was escaping without everything going dead wrong. MacMillan also found space on the *Neptune* for several of his favorite dogs.

The Inughuit milled about, making last-second trades. "They are all apparently sorry over our leaving," MacMillan wrote. Still, parting seemed more difficult for him than it did for them.

Bartlett rang the ship's bell at 3:30 a.m. on August 4. Borup Lodge, a snug home for the past four years, slipped into the distance. MacMillan had often mused about turning it into a permanent facility for Arctic researchers. His practical side knew better. Natives soon tore down the building for its valuable wood. Today there is almost no evidence that it ever existed.

Southerly winds pushed ice around the harbor. Blankets of snow from the recent squall obscured the floral carpets layering the grey-brown cliffs. The *Neptune*'s engines chuff-chuffed at a steady rate as the ship passed the radio hut on Starr Island and cleared the fiord. Turning to port, Bartlett put the bird sanctuary of Littleton Island at his rear and Ellesmere Island to starboard. Etah slipped out of view.

It took twenty-four hours for the *Neptune* to find trouble. Prevailing southerly winds shoved an icy roadblock across narrow Smith Sound, the only path home. Bartlett climbed to the crow's nest. Tobacco juice sprayed from his mouth as he shouted commands. Thick fog, heavy seas, and driving snow reduced visibility to near zero. Bartlett poked and nudged all day without making much progress. The next day brought more of the same, as did the next.

Another captain—Kehoe of the *Erik* or Pickels of the *Cluett*—might have retreated to a safe harbor for the winter, resulting in a fifth year for the expedition. But Captain Bartlett did not quit. He kept testing the pack, banging the *Neptune*'s prow into floes, squeezing into narrow leads, daring the ice to stop him. Past North

Star Bay. Past Parker Snow Bay. Past where the *Danmark* and the *Cluett* had surrendered.

It took more than a week for the *Neptune* to reach Cape York, the gateway to Melville Bay. Bartlett made countless sallies into open lanes of water that proved to be dead ends. Mostly he held his position and hoped the ice would clear. He prodded and prodded, trusting his instincts and his ship's sturdiness. On August 13 the *Neptune* broke into clear seas. Three days later Bartlett slipped past the anti-submarine chains protecting the town of Godhavn from a surprise attack. The Americans breathed a collective sigh of relief.

Governor Ohlsen greeted them at the pier. Comer wandered off to visit friends. MacMillan and Bartlett accepted Ohlsen's invitation to coffee and cigars at his home. Another guest arrived a few hours later: Elmer Ekblaw. The scientist was in poor health, and was overjoyed at the prospect of going home. He had been living with Danish families in South Upernavik and Godhavn. Ekblaw hadn't done much scientific work since splitting from Hunt. Heavy snow and skyrocketing blood pressure kept him out of the field.

Ekblaw transferred his things onboard the *Neptune*. The crew renewed their voyage. Rolling seas confined Ek and MacMillan to their beds for several days. Seasickness was a small price to pay for open water. The *Neptune* arrived at Sydney, Nova Scotia, on August 26. A train ran from there to New York. Four years into their two-year mission, the Crocker Land expedition was home.

There was only one cloud on the horizon. A bundle of letters contained a month-old communiqué from AMNH president H. F. Osborn. "Bring back only *the good news* and say nothing of the troubles of any kind until you see me," he warned. MacMillan paid more attention to the dispatches from his friends and family. Against incredible odds he had brought his men home alive. He was ready to bask in the glory that came with being an Arctic adventurer.

30

NO HERO'S WELCOME

"SO MANY AND SO STRANGE THINGS have happened that we seem to be returning Rip Van Winkles," MacMillan wrote from his berth on the *Neptune*. Back issues of the *Christian Science Monitor* revealed an America that was foreign to him. "The world has moved on and left us behind," he said. Civilization promised easy access to food and shelter, such underappreciated luxuries as trees, and a whole new set of challenges. Life-and-death concerns—the seasons, the tides, the thickness of ice, the direction of wind, the location of game, and the health of dogs—were meaningless in the United States in 1917. What mattered were the war, the dollar, and the dramatic changes reshaping society.

The Crocker Landers had been almost unbelievably fortunate. For all that went wrong, so much went right. No one broke a leg far from camp or plunged into the water without a rescuer nearby. Seals or walruses appeared whenever starvation loomed. The Inughuit deserved a large share of the credit for their survival. At the same time, MacMillan, with contributions from Hunt and others, had kept the natives loyal enough to keep supplying the Americans with food and skins.

MacMillan was wise to request that extra supplies be sent up in 1915, although at the time he was more interested in extending his own stay than in feeding the entire expedition. On the other hand, the trading station at North Star Bay provided an essential, and unexpected, safety net. Had Rasmussen and Freuchen set up shop a few years later, or not at all, the expedition might have faced disaster. Had Hunt not been such a good provider, had Ekblaw not overcome his initial ineptitude, had Allen not massaged the generator through its travails—the list of "what if"s is long.

None of that mattered. MacMillan was on his way home. After worshipping Arctic explorers most of his life, he was ready for his turn in the spotlight.

A reporter from the *New York Tribune* boarded the *Neptune* in Sydney. MacMillan greeted him in a sealskin cap, flannel shirt, and weatherproof boots. The *Tribune* had an excellent relationship with the expedition and the museum, so the explorer sat for a lengthy, exclusive interview. Mac played his role to a T, attributing his survival to "good luck" while emphasizing the dangers of remaining in the north any longer. Exotic foods made good copy, so he recalled meals of raw meat, fertilized duck eggs, and other local delicacies. "A taste of real bread was certainly welcome after eating dog biscuits for two or three months," he said.

Mac closed up tight when asked about the expedition's shortcomings. "It was a wonderful image," he said of the Crocker Land mirage. "Don't think, however, that Peary was faking." It would have fooled anyone, "no matter who he was." The reporter asked whether he had surveyed the Greenland ice cap, the expedition's number two priority. Falling silent for a moment, MacMillan replied that he should report to the museum before discussing his discoveries.

MacMillan's interview hit newsstands on August 27, 1917, the same day a tanned and rested Edmund Otis Hovey stepped off the Scandinavian-American Line steamship *Oscar II* following an uneventful passage from Copenhagen to New York. His foolhardy journey from Etah to south Greenland got him home a few days before his lodgemates. The curator, who received his own "tell only the good about the Expedition" letter from AMNH president Osborn, obliged reporters with a harrowing description of his sledge trip. Hinting that MacMillan had discovered "valuable mineral deposits," he left for his Upper West Side home, a three-block walk from the museum.

These twin returns prompted a spate of celebratory articles. "Month after month of cold, starvation, sickness, and fatigue mean nothing to these twentieth century Vikings," George Brakeley gushed in the *New York Sun*. "To them hardships are merely part of the game, objectionable more for the hindrance they are than for the suffering they entail." Brakeley reduced the seven-man expedition to a lone hero who personified rugged individualism and frontier ingenuity. Praising MacMillan's "superhuman exertions," he claimed the explorer "could have found ample excuse for a return to civilization and safety" the moment Crocker Land vanished, but instead volunteered for two extra years in the north.

"The remarkable thing about the MacMillan expedition which sets it apart from many others of the sort is that not a single fatality attended it," Brakeley observed. Others made the same assertion. "The expedition was carried through without the loss of a man," marveled the *El Paso Herald*.

Public interest in the Crocker Landers had waned by the time these stories reached the hinterlands. A *New York Sun* reporter who interviewed MacMillan in Freeport stumbled on one reason why. "What was your most valuable find?" he asked. "I suppose it was our securing two complete sets of knot's eggs," MacMillan answered. Notable as this find was for science, it was not the stuff of legend. Journalists couldn't spin heroic dramas around eggs.

I also found the lining of Elisha Kane's hat, MacMillan said.

On October 10, 1917, about 400 scientists, donors, and friends came in from a cool New York evening for the American Museum of Natural History's invitation-only welcome-home reception. Ongoing exhibits, including fossils of prehistoric hominids and murals depicting early humans, shared space with Kane's cap lining, the knot eggs, and a series of Inughuit drawings in the unfinished Hall of the Age of Man. MacMillan pointed out his favorite photographs from the expedition. Guests leaned in for a close look at native clothes, *qamutits*, and kayaks.

The gathering marked the first time the Crocker Landers had been together in more than two years. Maurice Tanquary rode the train to Manhattan from his teaching job at Kansas State Agricultural College (present-day Kansas State University) in Manhattan, Kansas. Life was on an upswing for the entomologist. He had married within days of his return, and nine months later became the father of a lovely daughter.

Elmer Ekblaw had been loafing around a rental house in Rantoul, Illinois, a short commute from the university. He and Augusta Krieger were set to be married in February 1918. Beyond that, he was waiting for confirmation of the research fellowship Hovey had promised, and soon delivered, while puzzling over the changes to his beloved campus. With 7,000 uniformed men marching around, his alma mater seemed more like a military base than a university.

Jerome Allen experienced the war more directly. He had reenlisted in the navy but couldn't discuss where he was stationed or what he was doing. "Secret military work," he said, hinting at his involvement in a covert anti-submarine program. The radioman was more eager to discuss his 1917 Indian motorcycle, complete with a sidecar for the new Mrs. Allen. A lifelong gearhead, he loved driving way too fast "when the cops are scarce."

Fitzhugh Green also arrived in uniform. Recently minted as a junior-grade lieutenant, Green had devoted the past year to his tireless quest for personal advancement, whether in the form of extra pay, a cushy shoreside post, or duty as a traveling celebrity-cum-recruitment officer. The brass rejected request after request.

Green's work as an ordnance officer on the *Texas* bored him. Following cruises in the West Indies and a brief deployment near

Hampton Roads, the *Texas* was moored in the New York City area, where Green passed dull days "playing golf and cutting fifths of seconds off my turret loading time."

Green's contract with the museum forbade him to write about the trip until MacMillan had completed his own book. The lieutenant nevertheless composed a series of Crocker Land articles for the United States Naval Institute's *Proceedings*. The first installment of "Arctic Duty" appeared in the publication's September 1917 issue. Hovey, Osborn, and Sherwood protested. Green insisted that he had no intention of stealing MacMillan's thunder, despite the fact that his florid language, fast-paced narrative, and he-man sensibilities targeted a wider audience. "For a man to quit his work completely at the end of one year, rush home and get into print with the first story of the work, while I stick to my job exploring and collecting for four years . . . does not savor of loyalty, or, in fact, honesty," MacMillan seethed. MacMillan nursed a host of other grievances, including the museum's inept selection of ships, its contradictory messages about collecting fox skins, and its decision to send Hovey on the *Cluett*. Although he played nice at the reception, MacMillan was also fed up with his former companions, excepting Jot Small, who retained his affection even though he was "not a success as a cook." MacMillan considered Tanquary a lazy ignoramus and disparaged Ekblaw for questioning his commitment to science. Green was a troublemaking coward. Dr. Hunt "was not at all enthusiastic" about the mission. "There is nothing to do but forget and forgive," Mac sighed. "Not ten percent of all men, enthusiastic with the thought of going [north], find the work really enjoyable."

Hal Hunt, who had no use for either MacMillan or Hovey, was in Bangor reading medical journals on the evening of the reunion. "The pleasure of meeting the other members of the expedition would have been great," he informed Osborn, "with the exception of MacMillan." Blasting the expedition as "a National disgrace," the doctor prayed that, "for the good name of the United States," MacMillan would never command another team. Hunt had mistrusted the museum from the moment Hovey bullied him into signing a punitive contract on the deck of the *Diana*. His time in the north disrupted his career and forced his wife to make ends meet by working as a camp counselor on Cape Cod. He blamed Osborn and other museum officials for extending his exile by two years, and he wanted recompense.

Osborn offered Hunt a $500 bonus. "I am not convinced that my treatment by the Museum has been either fair, or square," the doctor retorted. "He was terribly homesick," Hovey shot back in a message to Osborn, "and his view of almost every act and word was warped and unreliable." Their dispute stretched on for months before both sides exhausted themselves without reaching any real resolution.

Few of the people circulating around the Hall of the Age of Man had any idea that the honored guests were so embittered. Arctic living splintered the seven men who had forged tight bonds during their first days together. Rather than a life-defining moment, the Crocker Land expedition was something most of them would have preferred to forget.

Captain Comer summed up their feelings better than anyone. "Do not draw a veil over the whole voyage," he said. "Bury it deeply and cover it with concrete."

Evidence of the Crocker Land expedition faded fast. The museum put a few relics under glass, including the swatch of Peary's silk American flag that MacMillan found at Cape Thomas Hubbard, and piled many more into haphazard exhibits. MacMillan discovered his expensive camera buried under a musk ox skin. He never found the field glasses someone snatched from a display.

Specialists at the museum, including Yvette Borup's husband, Roy Chapman Andrews, sorted through hundreds of crates, each containing close-packed wooden boxes with handwritten labels.

Most of the specimens were useless. The museum kept a few seal and walrus pelts. It already owned more musk ox and caribou skins than it wanted. Some skins went to the University of Illinois, along with most of the plants Ekblaw and Tanquary had collected. Inferior skins, those missing hoofs or heads, were shipped to expedition members and friends of the museum. Cairn records went to the American Geographical Society. Hunt asked for and received a kayak. MacMillan sent a stuffed polar bear to Bowdoin. He donated two of his sled dogs, Al-ning-wa (Baby Girl) and Kai-hoc (White),* to Boston's Franklin Park Zoo.

Disposing of the expedition's financial deficit was more complicated. By Sherwood's accounting, the museum's total expenses amounted to $192,580.11. A few favorable insurance adjustments helped (the museum paid $2,000 on the *Cluett's* claim, rather than the $6,981 originally requested), as did MacMillan's waiving of his salary, but the expedition was $80,000 in the red, including loans taken from the museum's general fund.

The debt came at a bad time. The museum needed at least $2 million for new buildings to house the skeletons and prepared specimens in its basement. Repeated bailouts of the Crocker Land expedition drained the general fund. Officials had to tap their credit lines just "to make it possible to carry on the business of the Museum."

Osborn and Hovey pleaded for donations, but no financial angel appeared. Over the next several years they paid down the expedition's expenses in dribs and drabs. As of late 1921 they owed more than $20,000. At that point the Crocker Land Fund disappears from the museum's records. Possibly some deep-pocketed donor made up the difference. More likely, the museum wrote off the remaining debt owed to the general fund as a lost investment.

---

* MacMillan had such a poor grip of Inuktun that the dog he thought was named White was actually named Brown (*kajoq*). The Inuktun word for white is *qaqortoq*.

———

Reminders of the expedition's shortcomings arrived like the steady beat of a dirge. In January 1918, Dr. Rollin A. Harris, the scientist who popularized the idea of an undiscovered Arctic continent, was found at the side of a road in Washington DC, dead of a heart attack. None of his obituaries mentioned his role in sending the Crocker Landers on a wild goose chase.

Robert Peary died two years later of pernicious anemia, a condition first diagnosed in 1901 by his nemesis, Dr. Frederick Cook. The commander rarely spoke of Crocker Land after 1917, but when he did, he held fast to his tale of a realistic mirage. MacMillan was an honorary pallbearer at Peary's funeral and remained a devoted admirer for the rest of his life. He never expressed any doubt about the commander's Crocker Land story. None of Peary's obituaries mentioned the disappearing continent.

Crocker Land received a final ripple of publicity with the 1918 publication of *Four Years in the White North*, MacMillan's narrative of the expedition. MacMillan began working on the project the moment the *Diana* left New York in 1913. From the start he viewed daily diary entries as rough drafts of passages in the book. He spent hundreds of quiet hours writing in and revising his journals at Etah, becoming so engrossed with the project that his colleagues smirked behind his back when he pontificated about what incidents might or might not make it into the Book. When he got home MacMillan bolstered his notes with additional reflections and quotations from other Arctic travelogues. Peary's books had taken shape in much the same way.

Four Years in the White North employed the literary flourishes readers expected from the genre. A pedestrian two-day sledge from Etah to Neqi became a trip "replete with thrills from start to finish" that "nearly cost us our lives." Hillsides were "fairly crawling with Arctic hare." His "faithful helpers," the Inughuit, were, with the exception of the traitorous Minik, devoted, kind, and wise, as well as being dead-eye marksmen. Exclamation marks riddled the text. The chipper tone never flagged. No arguments or miscues disturbed his version of the expedition.

MacMillan wrote for a mainstream audience. Big sales of *Four Years in the White North* could finance future expeditions and seal his reputation as Peary's heir. Instead, the book received polite reviews and sold few copies. In 1918 war news provided the reading public with ample heroes, exotic locations, and noble crusades. And in the dismal climate that followed the war's depressing conclusion, few people were interested in those things anymore.

MacMillan's narrative enthusiasm sagged at a crucial moment in *Four Years in the White North*. "The story was quickly told," he wrote. "Green, inexperienced in the handling of Eskimos, and failing to understand their motives and temperament, had felt it necessary to shoot his companion." MacMillan offered no further insight into Piugaattoq's murder.

Green, on the other hand, embraced the killing in his writings about the Crocker Land expedition. There was never a question of remorse. Instead, the act became part of the officer's delusional, triumphant self-narrative. He included an extensive description of the incident in "Arctic Duty." In his recounting, MacMillan "magnanimously" sent the ensign and Piugaattoq west following the futile run across the polar sea. "All the adventurous blood in my veins boiled up at the prospect," Green blustered. He mapped virgin terrain while Piugaattoq fretted about weak dogs and food shortages. "From this," Green asserted, "he turned to abuse of MacMillan and his methods, then to the deceitfulness and weak natures of white men in general."

Next, Green described being in the igloo for two days. Maintaining his cool, he rallied the devious Piugaattoq, who then betrayed him by speeding off in their remaining *qamutit*. "He sullenly refused to go slowly," Green explained. The American grabbed his rifle (from the sled he couldn't keep up with), "pumped in my last cartridge, knelt, and shot for my life."

"He toppled drunkenly and rolled into the snow."

In his next chapter, Green frames the murder as evidence of mankind's innate desire to satisfy subconscious cravings for survival. "As I stood there with [an] empty, smoking rifle in my hand something of that gratification of sense held me," he wrote. "At last I tasted of pleasure for which I starved. A moment before I had faced the end of everything. Now I beheld the beginning. I had seen dogs, clothing, fuel, food, vanishing in the gloom ahead. Here they were—mine to keep, to drive, to wear, to burn, to eat. He that had loomed hostile . . . now crumpled and inert in the unheeding snow.

"For once fate was balked," Green concluded. "I gloated over my victory, not the man—he like myself was but a pawn in this game of the gods."

Mystical and self-aggrandizing, Green asserted victory over the human and natural foes conspiring against him. His language echoed contemporary beliefs about so-called inferior peoples. The Inuk was an emotional child harboring irrational feelings of superiority over white men. In contrast, Green was a red-blooded hero, a Teddy Roosevelt for a new generation, a philosopher–warrior as comfortable in a drawing room as in the savage wilderness. Four years in the north hadn't changed him. He was the same insecure braggart he had been in 1913.

The issue of Piugaattoq's death reemerged in January 1921, when, in response to inquiries from Danish authorities, Knud Rasmussen offered his take on the incident. Rasmussen remembered hearing in 1916 that an avalanche had buried Piugaattoq. A conversation with Green several months later sparked his first doubts about the story. "At my question," Rasmussen wrote, "Mr. Green's face suddenly changed color, and in evident confusion he replied that this was a matter which Mr. MacMillan had told the members of the expedition not to talk about."

Rasmussen chalked up Green's dissembling to ruined nerves. At some point he learned the truth. In his version, MacMillan's companion Ittukusuk had told the other Polar Inuit what really happened, and years later someone passed the information on to him. Rasmussen saw no reason to prosecute Green, who was "most certainly at that time a nervous wreck, who can not be regarded as responsible for his act," but thought Piugaattoq and Aleqasinnguaq's children deserved an apology, along with material support until they reached adulthood.

Rasmussen held no great fondness for the Americans, who had denuded his stocks and muscled in on his market, but there is no reason to doubt his assertion that at least some of the Inughuit saw through Green's lie about an avalanche. This makes Green's relationship with Piugaattoq's wife, Aleqasinnguaq, even more mysterious. Why would Aleqasinnguaq moon around the ensign if she knew he had killed her husband? On the other hand, Green's abusive behavior toward her fits his character. His disdain may have been an emotional bluff, a way of demonstrating mastery over her. Rasmussen's statement also raises the question of why the explorer waited so long before sharing the truth.

MacMillan had briefed AMNH president Osborn on the murder and the cover story when he got home. "In telling [Ittukusuk] part of the facts and then letting him draw his own conclusions," he added in the wake of Rasmussen's statement, "I must admit that it was plainly our intention to deceive. Since the lives of the whole party because of the act of one man would be henceforth in danger, I feel, and I think you will agree with me, that we were justified in acting in the way in which we did." Now that the Danish government and the American State Department were involved, MacMillan wanted nothing to do with a seven-year-old murder. The expedition had cared for Piugaattoq's family, he told Osborn. Besides, the children were old enough to take care of themselves. MacMillan accused Rasmussen of reviving the case not out of concern for the Polar Inuit, but rather "for trade monopoly and with the determination to keep all Americans henceforth out of what he regards as his rightful domain."

If Green, now a full lieutenant with a silver star for service during the war and a comfortable post at the Indian Head Naval Proving Ground in Maryland, made any response to Rasmussen's charges, it does not appear in the archives.

The Danish investigation went nowhere. In a bizarre twist, the debate over Piugaattoq's death resumed in 1926, when the Inuk Qillugtooq confessed to murdering Ross Marvin during the 1908–09 North Pole expedition. At the time, Qillugtooq told George Borup that Marvin fell through some thin ice. This was not true. Qillugtooq had shot and killed Marvin because the American was determined to push the group through a dangerous section of new ice. Marvin's stubbornness endangered Qillugtooq and his cousin, known as Harrigan, so the Inuk shot him in self-defense.

Green, by this time a lieutenant commander, popped by the *New York Times* office to comment on the matter. Marvin's murder should surprise no one, he said. "It is quite true that Eskimos are kind, generous and peace-loving people," he explained, "but the brown native of the Far North has certain childlike qualities. Under pressure of hardship and anxiety he becomes panicky. . . . As a result the Eskimo will under such circumstances behave in an altogether unnatural way. He will steal, mutiny, or desert." Marvin must have died during one of these "fits of despair."

Like Green, Qillugtooq escaped punishment. The twin murders became an Arctic quid pro quo, in which the white man took revenge for the killing of one of his own. Of course, Green did not have Ross Marvin in mind during those terrible days in April 1914. But no one showed much interest in pursuing either crime. If the situation called for a tradeoff, then that's what would happen.

"You have no idea how impatient I am to go north," MacMillan wrote to his friend Jerry Look in May 1918. "The thought is with me morning, noon, and night. I think I am insane on the subject."

Of all the Crocker Landers, only MacMillan was interested in becoming a full-time explorer, if he could find the money. *Four*

Years in the White North had been a relative bust. MacMillan threw himself onto the lecture circuit. Life on the road assumed a demoralizing sameness that contrasted with the unpredictability of life in the Arctic. Catnapping in rattling trains, gladhanding welcoming committees, chatting with vague acquaintances, delivering the same old speech with fresh enthusiasm, and treating familiar questions like revelations required a different kind of patience than did stalking a seal's breathing hole or waiting out a blizzard. Mac ground through it, entertaining audiences across the northeast with his motion pictures, lantern slides, and easygoing descriptions of a world few of them would ever see.

The high latitudes kept calling. In 1918 he considered flying to the North Pole and back. "No joking," he told Jerry Look, "it could easily be done in two months and would create a great sensation as well as interest in scientific circles." He discussed opening a trading station at Jones Sound, the channel separating Ellesmere Island's southern coast from Devon Island. He planned a cruise to circumnavigate Greenland. None of these ventures panned out.

Desperate, he accepted a second mate's spot on a fur-trading vessel bound for Baffin Island. Bowdoin College, which had hired him as an anthropology professor, granted him leave. Technically, he was also on leave from Worcester Academy, where he hadn't taught since 1908.

Mac wanted more. With support from the MacMillan Arctic Association, a group of Bowdoin alumni dedicated to advancing his career, he designed the 88-foot schooner *Bowdoin*. Like Peary's *Roosevelt* and Fridtjof Nansen's *Fram*, it featured a crush-resistant, egg-shaped hull. Ironwood sheathing reinforced its tough exterior. Still smarting from the *Cluett* and *Danmark* disasters, MacMillan supplemented the *Bowdoin's* twin masts with a powerful oil-burning engine capable of pushing the ship through the ice in Melville Bay, or wherever else he pointed it. Construction costs totaled around $35,000, a few hundred dollars more than the museum paid to hire the *Neptune* for two months.

Osborn and Hovey were not interested in backing MacMillan's new enterprise. The feeling was mutual. MacMillan characterized his relationship with the institution as "very unsatisfactory."

About 2,000 people, nearly the entire population of Wiscasset, Maine, gathered at the pier on July 17, 1921, to watch the *Bowdoin* embark on its maiden voyage, a one-year expedition to map the west coast of Baffin Land. Men in straw boaters chatted about MacMillan's prospects. Boys in soft caps climbed wooden crates for a better view of the proceedings. Governor Percival Baxter, an alumnus of Bowdoin, worked the crowd. A handful of dinghies and punts dotted the Sheepscot River, the waterway connecting Wiscasset with the Atlantic Ocean some 60 miles downstream. The air was mild and the mood festive. An American flag waved from the ship's forward mast. A Bowdoin College banner adorned the aft mast.

MacMillan's six-man crew mingled with wellwishers strolling among the piles of lumber on the ship's deck. Jot Small had decided to come along on the trip. Ekblaw declined Mac's invitation. "Though he is going into a most promising territory for valuable work, I cannot forget that in an even more favorable field he failed to achieve the success that he should," the geologist confided to Sherwood.

MacMillan had checked and rechecked everything. Food, clothes, and fuel stuffed the lazarette. Markings on crates told him where to find his two movie cameras and four miles of film. His radio was tiny compared to the one Allen had battled. A library of Arctic books lined the shelf over his bunk. Kane's *Arctic Explorations* occupied a special place of honor. New toys, such as a fathometer for reading the ocean's depth and a radio direction finder that plotted the ship's location, rested on the chart table.

MacMillan laid two additional items next to them. He treasured the watch Peary had given him before they headed north together. The commander was gone, but his gift was returning to the Arctic.

Beside it MacMillan set an envelope. It looked a little the worse for wear than when he had received it eight years earlier, but the words across the front remained legible: "For You, To be opened when every thing's gone dead wrong. Hope you'll never have to open it!"

"I hold it that we should explore every land, however remote, however desolate," MacMillan told a *New York Tribune* reporter. "That we should lay down its coastline accurately, inform ourselves of its physical characteristics, study its bird life, classify its botanical species, know its people; that we should substitute facts for ignorance, conjecture, guesswork, and absurd theory." Mac's previous voyage was a step in that direction. It replaced the theory of Crocker Land, a continent built on dreams and lies, with the unwelcome fact of choppy ice fields extending to an empty horizon.

Family, friends, summer tourists, and local dignitaries cheered when MacMillan emerged on deck. Church bells rang. Harbor craft sounded their whistles. Loosing a blast of its own, the *Bowdoin* eased into Sheepscot Bay. Onlookers waved until the ship passed Davis Island and slipped out of sight. Like the brant and gyrfalcons whose instincts drew them to northern Greenland every summer, Donald MacMillan, the son of a sea captain, was returning to the place he called home.

31

ENDINGS

DONALD BAXTER MACMILLAN, the world's most famous living
Arctic explorer, eased into a chair in his blue-grey, wood-shingled
home on Commercial Street in Provincetown, Massachusetts. Like
the auks returning to their nesting grounds, he was back in the place
of his birth, a few minutes' stroll from the modest home the Mac-
Millan family occupied before his father died. Cool breezes wafted
against the window. It was a few degrees above freezing outside,
typical of early spring, almost balmy for a veteran of the upper latitudes. Mac would have flung open the windows of Borup Lodge on
a day like this.

He inserted a sheet of paper into his typewriter, advanced the
roller, and pecked out the date: April 7, 1966.

MacMillan was remarkably spry for a ninety-one-year-old man
with more than two dozen voyages above the Arctic Circle to his
name. Cataracts and glaucoma muddied his eyesight. Poor hearing
kept him off the telephone. He tired easily. Otherwise he was in
good shape.

The house on Commercial Street was a masterpiece of Arctic
chic. Around 5,000 books, most of them about exploration, weighed
down bookcases. Miniature kayaks and sledges served as conversation pieces. A narwhal horn lamp stand with a base made from
walrus tusks stood by his chair. Stuffed puffins and auks adorned

the piano. Mounted cod, salmon, and trout gaped at framed photographs of the *Bowdoin*. Downstairs, a polar bear pelt guarded the fireplace. The ocean was a few steps from Mac's back door. He liked watching ships come and go from his third-floor attic window.

MacMillan was childless, but his wife of thirty years, Miriam Look MacMillan, was around somewhere. They had met in 1912 or 1913 when her father, Mac's friend Jerry Look, invited him to lecture about his travels with Peary. Eight-year-old Miriam fell in love with the adventurer. *"I'll* be Donald MacMillan," she insisted when playing North Pole with her friends (an ash heap with a broom stuck in it served as ninety north).

"Miriam has grown very much attached to her 'Uncle Dan,'" her mother observed in a letter that traveled north with the Crocker Land expedition. Uncle Dan epitomized Miriam's childish ideal of masculine ruggedness and gentility. He was a pioneer who never smoked, a frontiersman who delivered boxes of candy. Their intergenerational friendship blossomed into a courtship. The couple married in 1935. He was sixty. She was thirty-two.

MacMillan worried that his long absences might create tension within the marriage. Miriam offered a simple solution: she would accompany him aboard the *Bowdoin*. He consented to a trial run. Miriam proved her seaworthiness and became a permanent member of the crew. She was also a talented author who wrote an autobiography (1948's *Green Seas and White Ice*) and two novels with Arctic themes (1950's *Etuk, the Eskimo Hunter* and 1953's *Kudla and His Polar Bear*). Mac's pet name for her was Aglaliortok, "the one who makes books."

MacMillan pushed the *Bowdoin* north on numerous ethnographic, geographic, and geological missions before retiring in 1954, when he was nearing eighty. Several times the ship nosed into Etah, where its captain reconnected with Ittukusuk and other former companions. During World War II he donated the *Bowdoin* to the U.S. Navy, which kept him at the helm and tasked him with improving existing charts of the Arctic. He retired from active duty in 1946 with the rank of commander, the same grade Peary held when they first met. In 1954 the navy promoted him to rear admiral in honor of his lifetime of mapping and exploration work.

MacMillan relied on income from his incessant speaking tours, which is what occupied his mind on that brisk April morning. He was thinking of composing a talk about the first expedition he had ever led, but the details escaped him. Perhaps his addressee, National Geographic Society president Melville Grosvenor, might help him.

Aged fingers sought the correct typewriter keys. Mac explained that he had just reread the section of Peary's *Nearest the Pole* describing the commander's 1906 trip west from the *Roosevelt*. MacMillan imagined himself standing with the commander atop Cape Thomas Hubbard, contemplating the mighty peaks of a continent looming over the frozen polar sea. He knew Peary's words practically by heart: "My heart leaped the intervening miles of ice as I looked longingly at this land, and in fancy I trod its shores and climbed its summits, even though I knew that that pleasure could only be for another in another season."

MacMillan was that "other," the successor who fought those intervening miles of jagged ice separating him from the illusion dancing on the horizon. Examining his journey through the haze of fifty years, he realized that Peary's ephemeral vision was not the only thing that had disappeared.

"Who was Mr. Crocker," MacMillan asked, "and what connection did he have with Peary?"

MacMillan had forgotten about George Crocker, the banker whose deep pockets inspired a lie that sent him and his men to the edge of the world. Ironically, Peary's fable launched MacMillan's long career by confirming the younger man's desire for Arctic living, and by teaching him how—and how not—to lead an expedition. In ways both large and small the Crocker Land myth changed every-

one it touched, the Americans who went north and the northerners who adapted their lives around the Americans' presence.

Most of the Crocker Landers lived quiet, almost pedestrian
lives. MacMillan and Small's lifelong friendship aside, none of them
stayed in touch with the others who had shared their ordeal.

E. O. Hovey was the first to go, passing away in 1924 while
working on a book about his true passion, volcanoes. He stayed
with the American Museum of Natural History until the day he
died. The curator's relationship with MacMillan remained toxic
until the end.

George Comer died thirteen years later. He made one more trip
north, in 1919, before retiring. The captain served a single term in
the Connecticut state legislature, but otherwise devoted himself to
his studies of the Inuit, and to his long-suffering wife, Julia, who
had been forced to beg money from the museum while her husband was trapped in Greenland. Present-day travelers to Hudson
Bay can sail through Comer Strait, a narrow passageway separating Southampton Island from White Island.

Bob Bartlett died in 1946, at the age of seventy, of heart and
kidney disease. He remained a legend in Arctic circles and a master
of the high seas until the end. During World War I he captained a
troop transport and an ammunition ship. In the next war he helped
establish military bases in the far north. In between he steered the
Effie M. Morrisey, a 120-ton, two-masted schooner, on a series of
expeditions into the high latitudes. Bartlett figured he sailed about
300,000 miles on the *Morrisey*.

Like MacMillan, Bartlett never lost faith in Peary. In 1945 the
two former Crocker Landers reunited in Boston Harbor to receive
Congressional Peary Polar Expedition Medals for "outstanding service to the Government of the United States in the field of science
and for the cause of polar exploration." Following the ceremony,
Bartlett asked for permission to speak. "A medal is a wonderful
thing," the white-haired captain bellowed, "but there is something

beyond medals, something transcendent—the memory of the greatest explorer who ever lived, Admiral Robert Edwin Peary."

Maurice Tanquary taught at Kansas State Agricultural College for a few years before becoming Texas's state entomologist. In 1924 he launched a new career as a professional beekeeper, in the process pioneering many techniques for commercial apiaries still used today. "He likes thrills and snappy stuff," declared a profile in the *Beekeeper's Item*, "so several years ago, he climbed the north pole and after staying three years got tired of waiting for Dr. Cook any longer and walked home" (never get your history from an apiarists' journal). Tanquary returned to academia in 1928, accepting a post at the University of Minnesota, where he researched bees until he died in 1944.

Elmer Ekblaw, Tanquary's fellow University of Illinois graduate and the man responsible for recruiting him to the expedition, died five years later. Following a brief stint in private industry, he migrated to MacMillan's former home of Worcester, Massachusetts, to become a geology professor at Clark University. His expertise in soil conservation put him in high demand in the early 1930s, when the Dust Bowl devastated the American heartland. Ekblaw split his time between teaching and preaching the importance of good environmental stewardship.

Jot Small became an institution in the seafaring village of Provincetown. For a time he ran a business turning out high-end sailboats. Then, in what must be considered an ironic move, he opened a restaurant, Jot's Galley, at 490 Commercial Street. MacMillan probably ate there, as it was less than 500 feet from his house. Locals revered Small as a salty-tongued raconteur who liked everyone and was always good for a laugh. Jot was Jot, and that's all Jot would ever be. When he died in 1952, the *Provincetown Advocate* offered further evidence that time blurs memories. "With his natural talent as a cook he proved a valued member on MacMillan['s] explorations," it claimed. The mighty Cook-soah, perhaps the worst chef to ever man a stove in the Arctic, would have chuckled at that one.

Jerome Allen stayed in the navy through World War II, serving as an electrician, a wireless operator, and the commander of a destroyer. He retired with the rank of captain. Along with his wife Victoria, he settled in La Mesa, California, a lovely hilltop town near San Diego. He died in 1955.

Harrison J. Hunt was still alive and well when MacMillan inquired into Mr. Crocker's identity. Although his legs were wobbly, his eyesight failing, and his ears encased in hearing aids, he remained a legendary figure in Maine. The doctor got past his anger at the museum and rededicated himself to medicine. He specialized in venereal diseases, something he had encountered far too often in the north. Hunt remained an outdoorsman who dashed into the north woods at every opportunity. He rarely discussed his most perilous adventure in the wilderness. Sometimes, when seated before a campfire, he shared stories from the expedition. But he didn't talk about the hard times, the conflicts, or the frustrations.

Hunt set up as a general practitioner on remote Swan's Island in the 1950s, when he was in his mid-seventies. This rocky, tree-covered dot was as beautiful as it was remote—exactly the kind of place Hunt liked. He made his rounds by motorized canoe because the island had no daily ferry service. Lobstermen recognized the gentle giant in the red plaid jacket. Whenever they saw him putt-putting along on his way to a case, they clutched their radio telephones so they could call for help in case of a mishap.

In 1960 Hunt returned to Bangor, where he lived out his final years. He died of viral pneumonia in 1967, at the age of eighty-nine.

The insecure, self-important Fitzhugh Green merits his own section, which is exactly how he would have wanted it. His public persona as a consummate navy lifer concealed a rolling stone who hurled himself down any hill that might have a pot of gold and an interviewer waiting at the bottom. He was just as the expedition revealed him to be: charming, industrious, reliable, selfish, erratic, and unstable.

Green thrived despite Knud Rasmussen's exposure of his role in Piugaattoq's death. In certain circles, the scandal made him more seductive. By the mid-1920s Green was a member of the Knickerbocker Club, the Explorers Club (which named him its honorary president in 1929), the Newspaper Club, the Army–Navy Club, and the American Geographical Society. He produced a regular feature for *Popular Science Monthly* called "Thrills I Never Had," which related exciting tales from the world of exploration. He was the general manager of the George Matthew Adams newspaper syndicate. He contributed features to the *New York Times*. He wrote books. He practiced the accordion and played golf. And, somehow, he was still in the navy.

Green saw himself balancing two jobs: "writing and conniving." Most of his conniving involved figuring out how to draw a paycheck from the navy without getting his feet wet. He churned out mediocre novels and a gushing biography of Robert Peary (*Peary: The Man Who Refused to Fail*). His imperious mother egged on his futile quest for literary fame, telling her son that he was the second coming of Victor Hugo. "It is the work of a scholar and a gentleman," she said of *Peary*. "It would have been impossible for any other to write it. Its technique is almost perfect."

Green's moment of decision, what he called "The Big Crisis," came in 1927. The navy promoted him to commander, then ordered him to the Pacific. Green was "frustrated, baffled and bewildered" that the service would exile such a valuable asset, especially one who had carved out a comfortable existence in New York City. "In the Navy there isn't a single prospect that is worth even sneezing at," he told his father. The idea of living "without a couple of bathrooms, a car, a cook, and so on" depressed him so much that he retired, exchanging his naval uniform for a business suit.

One of Green's peers from Annapolis was the famous pilot and explorer Richard Byrd, who introduced him to the lions of the daring world of aviation. Rene Fonck, Floyd Bennett, and Amelia Earhart joined the ex-navy man's social circle. Green became Byrd's publicist, feeding the press stories about his client's attempt at the Orteig Prize, a $25,000 award for the first nonstop flight between New York and Paris. Byrd came up short, but Green had also ingratiated himself with the winner, Charles Lindbergh. He penned a fawning postscript for Lindbergh's quickie autobiography, *We.*

Green was living the dream. He wrote more books and hobnobbed with the rich and famous. For a time he operated a nebulous business offering "guidance and general business assistance for any expedition or enterprise, ashore, afloat, or aloft, bound to any spot on the globe." As he explained, with himself in mind, "the modern explorer faces the most difficult problem in the world. He has to be a military leader, a business executive, writer, technician and publicist. At the same time, he is often temperamentally a genius." Green's job was connecting these geniuses with the best available financing, equipment, supplies, and publicity men.

In 1933, one week after his wife Natalie filed for divorce, Green married Margery Durant, the daughter of General Motors founder William C. Durant. It was her fourth marriage. The Great Depression eroded the Durants' fortune, but not enough to prevent the newlyweds from living in style. The couple maintained one home on Long Island and another in Palm Beach. Mediterranean cruises became a staple of their life. When in London they stayed at the Ritz. They toured Africa together. They crossed the Khyber Pass. Life was good. During World War II Green rejoined the navy and oversaw construction of ordnance plants. In 1942 a medical board declared him unfit for service because of a dislocated shoulder and high blood pressure and granted him an honorable discharge.

The Green family's charmed existence collapsed in March 1947, when Margery was arrested for possession of narcotics. She checked into the Hartford Institute for Living, a private psychiatric facility. Six months later, police charged the couple with operating a drug-smuggling ring. The details were as sordid as they were depressing. Both Fitzhugh and Margery were longtime drug abusers, probably of morphine and heroin. Margery's addiction predated their wedding. Over the years they blew at least $75,000 on drugs, a small fortune.

The Greens had been relying on a network of shady doctors to sell them drugs. Extended hospital stays—Margery for a gall-bladder operation and Fitzhugh for chronic heart problems—cut them off from their usual providers. While recuperating in an upscale sanitarium, they met a physician who hooked them up with a shady South American diplomat who, in turn, promised to deliver a steady stream of opiates to the couple. The Greens gave their contact $13,000. He gave them nothing. Desperate for their fix, they acquired drugs from a former private detective named Clemens Deisler.

Police found "a large quantity" of narcotics in the Greens' home. Green pleaded not guilty and was released on bail. Margery's frail mental state kept her out of court for the moment. Green switched his plea to guilty when the case went to trial. A federal judge gave him five years' probation for violating the Narcotics Act.

Green spiraled downward. On December 1, 1947, his children dragged him from his home to a care center for alcoholics. It was too late. Three hours after checking into Easy Acres he was transferred to a hospital, where he died three days later. His official obituary cited "chronic heart condition and lung congestion" as the cause of death. This is plausible. One family associate, however, later said that Margery had stumbled in on her husband canoodling with a nurse. They argued, and Green tumbled down a flight of stairs. Doctors never revived him.

Whatever the cause of his death, Green lived a double life. Confident and successful on the outside, his inner demons overwhelmed him in the end. His hometown paper, the *St. Joseph News*

Press, offered a gentle assessment of one of its favorite sons. "Let the curtain lower gently on Fitzhugh Green," an editorialist wrote. "After life's fitful fever may he sleep well. . . . He was a hero once. Let us in the charity that covers all, remember him only now as he was then."

Donald MacMillan entered a steep physical decline in the late 1960s. His movements became tentative and his gait shuffling. The man who had backflipped from the roof of Borup Lodge lost his balance with alarming regularity. None of his tumbles resulted in broken bones. "You're made of iron, admiral," his doctor marveled.

The explorer accumulated awards from the National Geographic Society and other prominent institutions. Massachusetts observed Rear Admiral Donald B. MacMillan Day on August 24, 1967. On that same day, he received the Boston Museum of Science's Bradford Washburn Award in honor of his lifetime of educating the public on scientific matters. Previous recipients included National Geographic Society president Melville Bell Grosvenor and oceanographer Jacques Cousteau. It has since been given to Neil Armstrong, Jane Goodall, Carl Sagan, and other luminaries.

The program for the event captured MacMillan's contribution to the worlds of science and exploration. "He is the last and gallant survivor of America's most thrilling era of terrestrial geographical discovery," it read, "an era when the first great secrets of the Arctic were wrested from nature by men inching northward, by ship and by dog team, with nothing but their own courage, ingenuity, and infinite patience to reward them with success."

There were no more adventures for MacMillan. He devoted most of his good hours to organizing and cataloging his massive collection of Arctic artifacts. Worcester Academy—he was still technically on leave—received his kayak and other items. Bowdoin would get most of the rest. Whenever he was too tired to work, he reminisced with Miriam about his "boys," the dozens of young men he brought north on the *Bowdoin* over the decades.

Miriam cared for Mac until his final days, when she transferred him to Cape End Manor, a local assisted-living center. By then he was too befuddled to understand where he was. It was a sad fate for a man whose life had depended on knowing his precise location.

Donald MacMillan died on September 7, 1970, ninety-five years, nine months, and twenty-seven days after his birth. In lieu of flowers, he asked mourners to make donations to Bowdoin College's Peary–MacMillan Arctic Museum.

Today his remains lie in Provincetown's rustic cemetery, marked by a small, flat, rectangular stone. "Donald B. MacMillan," it reads. "Rear Admiral USNR World War I & II." There is nothing indicating his long career in the north, no evidence of his onetime status as "the most distinguished living Arctic explorer." No carvings of polar bears or walruses, no pretentious renderings of ship's wheels.

Except for one thing. Time has aged the granite marker to a ruddy brown ringed with a speckled, greyish-white fringe. Taken as a whole, the colors in the tableau suggest a snow-swept plateau on a foggy Greenland afternoon. In a way, then, the Arctic will forever surround MacMillan's name. It's a romantic interpretation, but MacMillan was an incurable romantic when it came to the north. "The North!" he once wrote, "it was calling. . . . Men had died of the cold, of fatigue, of scurvy, of starvation . . . but they had sacrificed their lives for a purpose, a noble purpose namely, to add just one bit to the sum total [of] human knowledge."

"To me," one admirer said, "Mac was the epitome of everything that built America, and that an American ought to be. He was a dauntless pioneer with no limit to his courage and initiative. Yet he never lost the common touch, nor humility."

MacMillan's adventurous spirit outlasted his physical capacity for adventure. During his waning years, he lived vicariously through other pioneers. He loved watching American astronauts extend the limits of humanity to the stratosphere and beyond. When Alan

Shepard, the first American in space, asked Mac whether he was up for a trip to the moon, the ninety-four-year-old explorer replied, "Damn right!"

Mac never made that trip, but he was watching on television when Neil Armstrong took those historic first steps in July 1969. Mac turned to Miriam.

"I'd like to be there with them."

MYSTERIES SOLVED

THE END OF THE CROCKER LAND EXPEDITION did not mean the end of Crocker Land. "There can be little doubt . . . that there is a large land mass or a conglomeration of many islands in the unmapped regions," the *New York Sun* opined in January 1918. Mac-Millan himself insisted that "land must exist somewhere in the vast unexplored region beyond the point where we turned back. MacMillan's post-expedition report to the museum cited the gathering of "evidence of the existence of new land far to the west of our last camp on the Polar Sea" as one his party's most important accomplishments. The science was still good. Currents divided in odd ways, tides didn't behave as they should—*something* was causing these anomalies.

For almost everyone else, dreams of lost continents awaiting discovery were like the Edgar Rice Burroughs novels so popular at the time. Both were worth about a nickel and belonged on a shelf alongside other fantasies. Americans were scarred by the war and disillusioned by an inconclusive peace that offered no clear explanation of what they had fought for. People turned inward, focusing on domestic affairs rather than far-flung corners of the earth. In 1920, an undistinguished senator from Ohio named Warren Harding swept into the White House promising a "return to normalcy."

His victory reflected Americans' withdrawal from the kind of idealism MacMillan projected. Better to focus on our own country, they said, than to endanger our lives searching for new ones.

But MacMillan couldn't let go of the dream. Crocker Land drove him to do things foreign to his upright character. Yearning for another northern trip but bereft of funds, he enticed potential donors with false claims that he had seen land—real land—in the distance right before he and Green turned back. Crocker Land was again on the horizon, just out of reach. From the moment his young niece christened the *Bowdoin* in 1921, one of the ship's primary missions was to find the "lost Atlantis of the north." There must be *something* filling the triangle of empty white sprawling from Alaska, across Canada's north coast, and up to the North Pole. "It seems almost incredible that land is not there in that waste of a million square miles," a *New York Times* editorialist exclaimed after interviewing MacMillan.

Neither MacMillan nor subsequent adventurers found the place that must be there. Both Richard Byrd and Roald Amundsen made Arctic flights hoping to find Crocker Land (Lincoln Ellsworth, a finalist for Borup and MacMillan's original expedition, accompanied Amundsen in 1925). Australian Sir Hubert Wilkins, who had piloted a submarine, the *Nautilus*, through Arctic waters in 1931, used the mystery to pitch his 1937 plan to pilot a submarine from Norway to the North Pole, then into the Bering Sea. "If Crocker Land exists it will be Canadian territory, and of particular value when north polar flying is established," he told the Canadian Geographical Society. Wilkins never made his trip, but in 1938 former navy pilot Ike Schlossbach flew a Waco biplane over the area northwest of Ellesmere Island. He found nothing.

Schlossbach's aerial survey ended any realistic chance of there being an undiscovered Arctic continent. A search that began right before World War I sputtered to an end a year before Hitler's invasion of Poland began World War II. Crocker Land did not exist.

In retrospect, it is easy to explain why Crocker Land wasn't where Peary said it was—the commander's own notes, diaries, and other writings answer that question. But why wasn't it somewhere else? What of Dr. Rollin A. Harris, the government oceanographer whose analysis of ice patterns, tides, and currents lent scientific credibility to the myths and oral histories describing an unknown Arctic land? There is no reason to think that he was being dishonest. Instead, more than a century of research conducted since he published his provocative argument shows that Dr. Harris, Mac-Millan, and everyone else who believed in Crocker Land fell victim to confirmation bias, interpreting a few scraps of data in a way that verified what they already thought to be true.

The Arctic Ocean is a wickedly complex body of water. Present-day oceanographers with access to advanced computer models, satellite imagery, and far more data than their predecessors are still figuring out exactly how it functions. If present-day scientists resemble the proverbial six blind men touching an elephant ("The Sixth no sooner had begun / About the beast to grope, / Than, seizing on the swinging tail / That fell within his scope, / 'I see,' quoth he, 'the Elephant / Is very like a rope!'"), Harris was like a person who receives a piece of paper with two dots on it and is told to determine whether a straight line, a circle, or a shapeless squiggle connects the points. He had heard the old Inuit stories, and he interpreted what little he knew about the Arctic—and he knew as much as anybody—in such a way that those legends explained his data.

Considering the lack of reliable records at his disposal, Harris was right about an impressive number of things. Arctic tides are in fact narrow compared with those in other oceans. Thick, old ice does accumulate above Alaska and the Yukon. Currents do diverge in unexpected ways. Unfortunately for him, and for MacMillan's team, these oceanographic quirks can be explained without a massive island causing them.

Harris credited a mysterious landmass for the unusual tides in the western and eastern Arctic, and along Alaska's North Slope. But many forces influence the ocean's rise and fall, not just the presence of either land or open sea. Prevailing winds, currents, and eddies affect tides and sea levels, as does the shape of the coastline and the ocean floor, both of which can either stimulate or retard tides. How far water rises and falls at a given place, and the timing of that oscillation, depends on the geometry of the entire Arctic basin.

Harris had almost no data on any of these factors. At best, he could offer only an educated guess about the Arctic's currents. By plotting the paths of icebound ships, he correctly identified two of the ocean's main currents, one passing through the Bering Strait and along Canada's north coast, and the other emerging from near the same location before veering along the Siberian coastline. Today, oceanographers call these the Alaska Coastal Current and the Transpolar Drift.

Harris's mistake was imagining a significant landmass driving apart these two currents. This bold if reasonable leap of faith explained what his charts were telling him while placing an inordinate amount of trust in hazy rumors and third-hand stories about distant islands.

The real culprit was not Crocker Land. It was the Beaufort Gyre, a massive system located squarely between the Alaska Coastal Current and the Transpolar Drift, right where Crocker Land was supposed to be. The prevailing winds in the gyre blow surface ice, and the water beneath it, around and around in a clockwise rotation. Only a relative trickle of seawater gets ejected from the gyre into one of the currents that empty into the Atlantic near Greenland. The gyre, the exact mechanics of which remain subject to further scientific inquiry, explains the blank space on Harris's map. Ships drifted on the currents above or below the gyre without crossing what was in essence an enormous eddy, so that part of the sea remained a mystery until the maturation of airplane travel opened it to human eyes. The gyre also explains the appearance of old ice in the western Arctic. Ice can't escape the gyre to flow into warmer waters.

Rollin A. Harris was no liar, but neither was he the scientist MacMillan and others wanted him to be. His data tables are meticulous and his conclusions are offered in a sober, reasonable tone. But Harris was a dreamer, as are so many people who ponder the extreme north. Like the movie audiences who roared at *Conquest of the Pole*'s angels and giants, he believed with all his heart that there were secrets left to unlock in the Arctic, and that he was on the verge of unlocking them. Calling his conclusions optimistic is a generous assessment, but they did explain his fragmentary data within the context of how early-twentieth-century scientists understood the Arctic.

There is a final story to tell, a personal one. Just as the mystery of Crocker Land consumed MacMillan, Borup, Green, Hovey, and others, one mystery consumed me ever since I began researching the Crocker Land expedition. In May 2013, while standing midway between Peary Drive and MacMillan Drive, a few blocks from the Bowdoin College campus in Brunswick, Maine, I hoped I was close to an answer—literally.

Bowdoin is everything a guy from the Midwest expects from a New England campus. Where I'm from, when colleges get old, they just get *old*. But on that grey and drizzly day, Bowdoin looked venerable. Majestic spires, a graceful chapel, and squat dormitories spoke of untold generations of students, of genteel rituals, of great ideas. I imagined white-bearded professors hustling about in academic robes. I understood why MacMillan loved the place so much.

Unlike Mac, I couldn't spend four years here. There was much work to do, and little time. Both Mac and Miriam donated their personal correspondence to Bowdoin. Captain Bartlett also donated some materials. Although I had a general sense of what was in those collections, the only way to extract anything useful from them was to start turning pages.

The documents yielded a wealth of information about the Crocker Land expedition and its leader. MacMillan's journals were everything a researcher could hope for even if, Mainer that he was, he refrained from revealing too much about his inner feelings—he knew people would read those volumes some day. But something nagged at me as I perused boxes of material. I hadn't found the one piece of paper I wanted most of all.

Susan Kaplan and Genevieve LeMoine, the director and curator of Bowdoin's Peary–MacMillan Arctic Museum, saved the day. At their invitation, I wandered from the library over to the museum. It's a lovely redbrick building, studded with fine stonework that gives it a sense of weight without being ponderous. High, ribbed ceilings and tiled floors greeted me inside, along with large portraits of the museum's two namesake explorers and an imposing stuffed polar bear. No, I couldn't touch the bear—its fur might poison me because it had been treated with arsenic.

That was the last request my hosts denied. When I explained what I wanted, they led me up a grand staircase to the second floor, then up a narrow, winding one to the third. No elevator, they explained. That was fine with me—MacMillan wouldn't have used one, and long days in an archive make a researcher eager for any chance to stretch their legs.

There's nothing a historian loves more than a locked room, especially when your guide is holding the key. Opening a door marked with all the standard warnings about authorized personnel only, Susan and Genevieve waved me into a restricted area housing some of their off-exhibit items. It was a smallish space, with exposed pipes crisscrossing the ceiling and exotic artifacts piled everywhere. It resembled the stereotypical crazy grandmother's attic, only this crazy grandmother had a fantastic eye for Arctic memorabilia. One of Josephine Peary's fur suits was hanging in a dry-cleaning bag. Marie Peary's fur muff sat in a box. Rows of film cans, sealskin boots, and bearskin pants lined the shelves. MacMillan's camera looked like it weighed about 50 pounds. Ekblaw's binoculars were inside a cabinet, never to be misplaced again.

Susan and Genevieve dug around in the back for what I wanted and then placed it in my hands.

The envelope was yellow with age. Decades-old coffee stains ringed its surface. Across the front, in neat, confident, cursive writing, read "For You, To be opened when every thing's gone dead wrong. Hope you'll never have to open it!"

It was sealed. In fact, not only was the seal intact, the envelope was encased within a solid inch of Lucite. It would take a hammer and chisel to release its contents.

For years Miriam had begged Mac to open the letter. He refused. It was his good-luck charm. He took it with him every time he went north, and never once had everything gone dead wrong. Breaking the seal might break whatever spell kept him safe through countless life-threatening situations. When Mac died, Miriam suppressed her curiosity and respected his wish that it remain unopened. Neither she nor anyone else will ever learn who wrote that letter, or what sentiments it contains.

I held the block of plastic for as long as I could. I even lifted it to the light in the foolish hope that the envelope was translucent. My initial disappointment resolved into resigned acceptance. In a small way I felt like MacMillan did when Crocker Land evaporated into *pujoq*. Perhaps this was for the best. MacMillan unraveled one of the great mysteries of the twentieth century. It is only fair that he leave a small one for the twenty-first.

Crocker Land is gone. It never was, really. But the Crocker Land expedition has left us with an enduring uncertainty. We can only guess whether that envelope contains inspirational poems, a message of hope, good-hearted advice, or a silly joke. Because we do not know, MacMillan's superstition frees us to dream. Whatever that anonymous supporter wrote, it can't be as comforting, encouraging, or liberating as the words we write in our imaginations.

"I'd like to be there with them," MacMillan had said a half century earlier, when a man walked on the moon. My thoughts crept north to Etah as I handed over the target of my quest and watched my guides lock the door that separated me from the treasures of an alien world. As I left the building and returned to my researcher's table, I found myself thinking the same thing.

ACKNOWLEDGMENTS

THE MEN OF THE CROCKER LAND EXPEDITION all endured
the pain of long separation from friends and loved ones. Though
writing a book can be a solitary venture, I was fortunate to have
stalwart companions standing alongside me every step of the way.
Their support, advice, and good cheer brightened my years working on *A Wretched and Precarious Situation* far more than they will
ever know. Because of them, I never endured the researcher's
equivalent of the long, dark Arctic night.

My colleagues in the history department at the University of
Central Arkansas went out of their way to back this project from
the moment I began buttonholing people in the halls to ask
whether I could tell them a story I was thinking about turning
into a book. Ken Barnes, my former department chair, and Wendy
Lucas, my current chair, have been staunch advocates of my work
for years, as has Maurice Lee, the dean of the college of liberal arts.
Michael Rosenow did me the honor of critiquing an early draft of
the manuscript. I am also grateful to UCA's University Research
Council for supporting this project with a URC travel grant.

Many dedicated archivists went above and beyond on my behalf.
At the top of the list is Mai Reitmeyer, who guided me through
the research library of the American Museum of Natural History
and answered countless questions. Annette Springer and Gregory Raml also provided invaluable help. I am indebted to Eleanor
Schwartz, a volunteer who cataloged the museum's Crocker Land

collection. Colin Woodward digitally scanned original negatives from the collection for use as illustrations.

Scott Taylor assisted me with the Fitzhugh Green papers in Georgetown University's special collections library. His "by-the-way" revelation that Green kept private diaries during the expedition changed the direction of this book. Cathleen Miller at the University of New England photocopied the correspondence between George Borup and Marie Peary for me. Robert Michael Jaeger at the University of Wisconsin–Milwaukee answered numerous queries and tracked down one of Peary's old cairn notes. The entire staff at the College Park branch of the National Archives provided their usual extraordinary service. Gene Morris proved particularly helpful, as he always does. Thanks also to Alexis Hill, who digitized Robert Peary's 1906 diary for me the moment it returned to the archives from a two-year loanout. Waiting so long to read those crucial pages was agonizing, but worth it in the end. Kathy Peterson and everyone else at Bowdoin College's special collections library helped me navigate the Donald and Miriam MacMillan papers.

I'd like to give special thanks to the staff of the Peary–MacMillan Arctic Museum, a lovely facility on the Bowdoin College campus. Amy Hawkes, Susan Kaplan, Genevieve LeMoine, and Anne Witty treated me as one of their own during my time there. Susan and Genny have not only devoted themselves to the museum but are also talented archeologists who know more about the Crocker Land expedition than anyone else on the planet. They answered all my questions, even the dumb ones, with kindness. I cannot thank them enough.

Traveling to archives can get lonely, but a number of friends, some old and some new, made life on the road more bearable. Neils and Susan Aaboe took me in, listened to me complain about LaGuardia Airport, and directed me to the best scone I've ever eaten in my life. Chris and Karen Elzey provided shelter and companionship in Washington DC. Matt Klingle, a brilliant environmental historian at Bowdoin College, gave me a fine dinner and a marvelous tour of Brunswick.

Arctic historian Bob Bryce shared his wisdom with me many times over the past few years. Jerry Kobalenko described various Arctic landmarks he has visited and provided valuable insights into Arctic travel and survival. Luc Rainville at the University of Washington explained the mysteries of Arctic currents and tides to a perfect (and persistent) stranger. Kenn Harper is a treasure of a man who corrected my laughable attempts at rendering Inughuit names and Inuktun words, and who passed along a few fantastic stories about MacMillan. And Mardi Thompson George, a simply amazing woman, spent two afternoons reminiscing about her grandfather, Dr. Hal Hunt.

Mike (Sterno) Keckhaver created the frontispiece to this book, basing it on a map published around 1912. The inclusion of Crocker Land and Peary Land, which appeared on the original, is intended to create an image of the Arctic as MacMillan understood it when he left for the north.

The good people at W. W. Norton did a remarkable job of shepherding this project from manuscript to book. John Glusman was an enthusiastic supporter and a fount of good advice. Editorial assistant Alexa Pugh kept me on task and kept the project moving forward. Both deserve my most profound thanks, and much more. Ingsu Liu and Pete Garceau produced a striking cover design. Thanks also to production manager Anna Oler. Copyeditor Allegra Huston did magnificent work with the manuscript.

My agent—no, my superagent—Ann Rittenberg believed in this project from the start. Her enthusiasm is infectious, and every one of our lengthy chats (which, admittedly, sometimes strayed off topic) improved the book in some way. Camille Goldin and Rosie Jonker at the Ann Rittenberg Literary Agency also performed prodigious labors.

Lastly, and most important, my family deserves more thanks than I can ever express. My wife, Ali, endured my time away on research trips and my stories about musk oxen and Inughuit mythology. A gifted editor, she also read portions of an early draft of the manuscript. Our wonderful children, Jude and Kate, never read a word of this, and perhaps never will, but their presence has made the years spent writing this book so much better. And I very much appreciate their unwavering commitment to never, ever mess with Daddy's notecards.

NOTES

Complete references for the published books and articles cited below can be found in the bibliography, along with my abbreviations for archival sources.

Key
    DBM: Donald B. MacMillan
    EE: Elmer Ekblaw
    EOH: Edmund Otis Hovey
    FG: Fitzhugh Green
    GB: George Borup
    GS: George Sherwood
    HDB: Henry Dana (H. D.) Borup
    HFO: Henry Fairfield Osborn
    HJH: Harrison J. Hunt
    MP: Marie Peary
    REP: Robert E. Peary

A Note on Diaries

Donald MacMillan and Fitzhugh Green both produced multiple sets of writings about their day-to-day life in the Arctic. MacMillan kept many small field notebooks ("DBM field notebook"), the most important of which are at the American Museum of Natural History. He expanded and rewrote those notes in four large, hardbound books that serve as a diary of his entire stay in the north. Those diaries are housed in Bowdoin College's Special Collections Library and are referenced here as "DBM diary." Later, he typed out a copy of those diaries, adding in passages from other Arctic narratives and expanding his thoughts and descriptions at various moments. Those typewritten sheets are also at Bowdoin. I reference them as "DBM typescript diary."

Fitzhugh Green was even more prolific. His field notebooks ("FG field notebook") are part of Bowdoin's Donald B. MacMillan collection. He also kept a more formal diary at different times during the expedition. This diary ("FGD") is in the American Museum of Natural History. A typed diary ("FG typescript diary") is in Green's personal papers at Georgetown University, as is a three-volume set of personal journals ("FG private diary"). The latter, which was an outlet for Green's unstructured musings, includes no dates and makes no attempt to provide a day-to-day accounting of the expedition. Green also wrote stories in several bound, undated notebooks ("FG notebooks") that are housed at Georgetown.

Introduction: "Mine by the Right of Discovery"

   3 **April 21, 1906:** Unless otherwise noted, details of Peary's 1906 bid for the North Pole come from Peary, *Nearest the Pole.*
   5 **"hell-born music":** Ibid., 126.
   5 **"cut the margin":** Ibid., 135.
   6 **"It was the first":** Ibid., 141.
   6 **Retreat became:** Ibid., 166, 168; Dick, *Muskox Land,* 246.
   6 **"The attainment of the Pole":** Quoted in Herbert, *The Noose of Laurels,* 191.
   6 **"To think that":** Peary, *Nearest the Pole,* 168.
   7 **"Surely he is":** Dr. Louis Wolf, expedition journal, June 2, 1906, REPC Diaries.
   7 **"I am very much":** REP diary, June 7, 1906, REPC Diaries.
   8 **"What I see":** Ibid., June 17, 1906.
   8 **"As fine":** Ibid., June 24, 1906.
   8 **"The view was":** Peary, "Nearest the North Pole" (March 1907), 504.
   9 **"Twenty years":** REP diary, June 28, 1906, REPC Diaries.
   10 **"heart leaped":** Peary, "Nearest the North Pole" (March 1907), 506.
   10 **"Out of my new":** REP diary, July 10, 1906, REPC Diaries.
   11 **Peary climbed back:** Herbert, *The Noose of Laurels,* 198.
   11 **"Name the —— Sea":** REP diary, [1906], REPC Diaries.
   11 **He thought of:** Dick, *Muskox Land,* 241.
   11 **undiscovered landmass:** McCannon, *A History of the Arctic,* 66, 70; Lopez, *Arctic Dreams,* 16–17; Ramsay, *No Longer on the Map,* 172.
   12 **most extraordinary myths:** Ramsey, *No Longer on the Map,* 111–16.
   12 **"We know less":** Prentiss, *The Great Polar Current,* 107.
   14 **"a large tract":** Harris, "Some Indications of Land in the Vicinity of the North Pole," 255.
   14 **"the last great geographical":** Hovey, "In Search of Crocker Land," 85.

Chapter 1: The Tenderfeet

   20 **"If you are":** My reconstruction of this event comes from DBM unpublished autobiography, 77, MMC b. 8, f. 7; DBM to REP, May 26, 1908, REPC Letters Received b. 33, f. Donald B. MacMillan.
   20 **"Biscuits of compressed":** REP diary, [1906], REPC Diaries.
   20 **"Certain it is":** Peary, *The North Pole,* 11.
   20 **"I *must* have":** Quoted in Holland, *Farthest North,* 169.
   21 **"You will note":** REP to George Crocker, April 16, 1907, REPC Letters Sent b. 9, f. C 1907.

21 **"I am sorry"**: George Crocker to REP, April 17, 1907, REPC Letters Received b. 28, f. G.

23 **"This book is"**: Kane, *Arctic Explorations*, ii.

23 **"I'll see you"**: DBM unpublished autobiography, 77, MMC b. 8, f. 7.

23 **"Thrilled"**: Ibid., 1, MMC b. 8, f. 11.

24 **"Take this woman"**: Ibid., 107, MMC b. 8, f. 11.

25 **"Don't wait"**: DBM diary, [n.d., 1902], DBMC Diaries and Journals v. 1. MacMillan was paraphrasing the popular inspirational writer Orison Swett Marden.

26 **"stood there"**: DBM unpublished autobiography, 112, MMC b. 8, f. 11.

27 **"Sorry, but unable"**: Ibid., 72a, MMC b. 8, f. 7.

27 **MacMillan visited Portland**: DBM diary, June 26, 1905, DBMC Diaries and Journals v. 2.

27 **"My interest in"**: DBM to REP, [December 1906], REPC Letters Received b. 27, f. M 1906.

27 **"Will gladly meet"**: DBM to REP, May 10, 1907, REPC Letters Received b. 30, f. M 1907.

28 **Peary was studying**: MacMillan describes this meeting in DBM unpublished autobiography, 77–78, MMC b. 8, f. 7. Peary described his evaluation process and the roles his subordinates played in *Secrets of Polar Travel*, 44–57.

28 **"young men"**: Peary, *Secrets of Polar Travel*, 51.

28 **"wiry"**: Ibid., 52.

29 **"the success of"**: Ibid., 46.

29 **"MacMillan"**: DBM unpublished autobiography, 77, MMC b. 8, f. 7.

29 **"a veritable curiosity shop"**: Ibid., 78-B, MMC b. 8, f. 7.

29 **"I'm going to"**: Ibid., 18, MMC b. 8, f. 8.

30 **"might entirely change"**: *Deseret (UT) Evening News*, May 9, 1908.

30 **"with light"**: REP to DBM, June 21, 1908, REPC Letters Sent b. 11, f. D. B. MacMillan 1908.

30 **"You are doing good"**: REP to DBM, June 26, 1908, DBMC b. 1, f. 4.

30 **"Young Geo. Borup"**: REP to DBM, June 28, 1908, MMC b. 2, f. 15.

31 **He raised George**: W. A. Altenburg to HDB, October 3, 1906, REPC Letters Received b. 28, f. B2; "Brother George Borup," 379.

31 **"My son"**: HDB to REP, April 4, 1907, REPC Letters Received b. 28, f. B2.

32 **Sensing George's intelligence**: REP, "George Borup, the Explorer," [1912], REPC Manuscripts b. 17, f. Documents Regarding George Borup.

32 **"My father went"**: GB to REP, June 14, 1908, REPC Letters Received b. 30, f. B 1908.

32 **"Glad to have"**: REP to GB, June 14, 1908, REPC Letters Sent b. 11, f. George Borup.

32 **"to obey"**: GB to Peary Arctic Club, June 26, 1908, REPC Arctic Expeditions b. 21, f. Contract, PAC-1908.

33 **Peary's foresight**: Peary, *Secrets of Polar Travel*, 62–72; Herbert, *The Noose of Laurels*, 217.

33 **"These things may"**: Ibid., 72.

34 **"I have seen"**: Henson, *A Negro Explorer at the North Pole*, 16.

Chapter 2: The Best Year

35 **On July 6**: *New York Times*, July 7, 1908; Peary, *The North Pole*, 25–26.

35 **"Surely no ship"**: Peary, *The North Pole*, 26.

36 **"It's ninety or nothing"**: *New York Times*, July 8, 1908.

36 **"Good-bye captain"**: Ibid.

36 **"Good luck, Peary"**: Robert A. Bartlett, "Theodore Roosevelt's Visit to the *Roosevelt*," [1934], RABP, Clippings, b. 7.

36 **"a HIT"**: Borup, *A Tenderfoot with Peary*, 1.

36 **Borup's stomach heaved**: GB to MP, July 31, 1910, MAPP b. 2, f. 84; Borup, *A Tenderfoot with Peary*, 2.

36 **"Come back soon"**: Peary, *The North Pole*, 29.

37 **"If you fellows"**: Borup, *A Tenderfoot with Peary*, 4.

37 **"The lure of the North"**: Peary, *The North Pole*, 10.

37 **"He was not especially"**: DBM unpublished autobiography, 22, MMC b. 8, f. 8.

37 **Chamber of Horrors**: DBM tribute to Borup, [1912], DBMC b. 6, f. 30.

37 **"the cabin was so"**: *New York Times*, February 18, 1912.

38 **Mac's natural reserve**: DBM, "North Pole Expedition," [n.d.], 57, MMC b. 11, f. 19.

38 **In November 1883**: Unless otherwise noted, my reconstruction of Mac-Millan's early years comes from MacMillan's unpublished autobiography in MMC b. 8, and the *Boston Sunday Post*, June 7, 1925. Cod tongues—actually a muscle in the cod's neck—are a Norwegian delicacy and a traditional snack food among Newfoundlanders.

38 **"He's lost"**: DBM unpublished autobiography, 47, MMC b. 8, f. 11.

40 **"a man of good character"**: William DeWitt Hyde, letter of recommendation, July 6, 1898, DBMC b. 8, f. 13.

40 **As the *Roosevelt* slid past Newfoundland**: MacMillan discusses the importance of this moment in "North Pole Expedition," [n.d.], 57, MMC b. 11, f. 19.

40 **"Land!"**: DBM, "With Peary in the Arctic," [1910], MMC b. 7, f. 23.

40 **"It was almost impossible"**: Borup, *A Tenderfoot with Peary*, 14.

41 **"*Kissa Tikeri-Unga!*"**: Malaurie, *The Last Kings of Thule*, 234.

41 **"smell 'em"**: Borup, *A Tenderfoot with Peary*, 18–19.

41 **"Men, women, and children"**: Malaurie, *Last Kings of Thule*, 234.

41 **"a declining"**: Kane, *Arctic Explorations*, 338.

41 **"the Almighty had"**: Peary, *Secrets of Polar Travel*, 179.

41 **"On the whole"**: Peary, *The North Pole*, 50.

42 **"his wife and two children"**: REP quoted in Dick, *Muskox Land*, 337.

42 **"everything she had"**: Ibid.

42 **"his dogs and sledges"**: Ibid.

43 **"as bad as whale meat"**: GB to HDB, August 1, 1908, GBC f. 1.

43 **"I imagine they are"**: Ibid.

43 **"Look out"**: DBM, "North Pole Expedition," [n.d.], 99, MMC b. 11, f. 20.

43 **"If an infuriated walrus"**: Ibid., 98.

43 **They closed to 50 yards:** My reconstruction of this hunt comes from DBM, "North Pole Expedition," 97–102; and Borup, *A Tenderfoot with Peary*, 31–36.

44 **"the dividing line"**: Peary, *The North Pole*, 40.

44 **"Everywhere is historic"**: DBM to C. A. Towle, August 10, 1908, DBMC b. 1, f. 42.

45 **"Rip 'em"**: Peary, *The North Pole*, 105.

45 **"*Qanoq atinga*"**: DBM, "North Pole Expedition," [n.d.], 218, MMC b. 11, f. 21.

47 **"The influence of"**: Kane, *Arctic Explorations*, 91.

47 **"In the darkness"**: Ibid., 89.

47 **"uncontrollable nightmares"**: Peary quoted in Dick, *Muskox Land*, 56.

47 **"Very tender"**: DBM North Pole Diary, August 30 and December 18, 1908, MMC b. 16, f. 2.

47 **On Christmas day:** Unless otherwise noted, my reconstruction of the expedition's time at Cape Sheridan comes from Robert A. Bartlett, "The Conquest of the Pole," [n.d.], RABP b. 5, f. 1; DBM North Pole Diary, MMC b. 16; Borup, *A Tenderfoot with Peary*, 61–127; and Peary, *The North Pole*, 117–212.

49 **"When you say"**: Borup, *A Tenderfoot with Peary*, 145.

50 **MacMillan nearly torpedoed:** DBM North Pole Diary, March 7, 1909, MMC b. 16, f. 2; Herbert, *The Noose of Laurels*, 229.

51 **"This was one"**: Peary, *The North Pole*, 231.

51 **"a running broad jump"**: DBM North Pole Diary, March 8, 1909, MMC b. 16, f. 2.

51 **"I am finding"**: Ibid., March 7, 1909, MMC b. 16, f. 2.

52 **"You are to go"**: Ibid., March 14, 1909, MMC b. 16, f. 2.

52 **"*Amici usque*"**: Borup, *A Tenderfoot with Peary*, 173.

52 **"did not affect"**: Peary, *The North Pole*, 236.

52 **"the men"**: Ibid., 243.

53 **"I would have given"**: Borup, *A Tenderfoot with Peary*, 179.

53 **"all bum ones"**: Ibid., 181.

53 **"Prof D. B. MacMillan"**: GB to DBM, March 20, 1909, DBMC b. 1, f. 4.

53 **"Marvin gone"**: Borup, *A Tenderfoot with Peary*, 202.

54 **"a darned old"**: Ibid., 214.

54 **"worse than what Sherman"**: Ibid., 211.

54 **"Mac would tell"**: Ibid., 212.

54 **"George, this is"**: DBM, "North Pole Expedition," 309, MMC b. 12, f. 1.

54 **"Yes, Mac"**: Ibid.

55 **"Arrived on board"**: REP to DBM, April 28, 1909, DBMC b. 1, f. 4.

55 **"We were going"**: DBM, "North Pole Expedition," 324, MMC b. 12, f. 1.

55 **"I do not know"**: Ibid., 335.

56 **Fort Conger:** My recounting of MacMillan's Fort Conger trip is based on DBM, "North Pole Expedition," 366, MMC b. 12, f. 2; and DBM North Pole Diary, June 10, 1909, MMC b. 16, f. 3. The newspaper clippings and other ephemera MacMillan brought home are in DBMC b. 6, f. 26.

57 **"Close the pores":** DBM, "North Pole Expedition," 430, MMC b. 12, f. 3.

57 **"Wait for me!":** Ibid.

57 **"Mr. Mac *pivlerortoq*":** Ibid.

57 **"We had always":** Ibid.

57 **MacMillan awoke:** My reconstruction of this incident comes from DBM North Pole Diary, August 11 and 13 and September 18, 1909, MMC b. 16, f. 3; Henson, *A Negro Explorer at the North Pole*, 170; and DBM to C. A. Towle, September 12, 1909, DBMC b. 1, f. 42.

58 **"Gee, whiz!":** *New York Times*, September 20, 1909.

58 **"the best year":** DBM to Jessie MacMillan, September 6, 1909, DBMC b. 1, f. 4.

Chapter 3: "I Wish I Were There Now"

59 **"Well, well!":** Robert A. Bartlett, "The Conquest of the Pole," [n.d.], 376, RABP b. 5, f. 8.

59 **"Why, Harvard has":** Ibid. Harvard defeated Yale 4–0 on November 21, 1908. MacMillan was unhappy, too, as Harvard had defeated Bowdoin 5–0 two months earlier.

60 **"bughouse":** *New York Times*, September 20, 1909.

60 **"It is hard":** *New York Times*, October 1, 1909.

60 **"Death is a factor":** *New York Times*, September 20, 1909.

60 **"I don't know":** *New York Tribune*, October 1, 1909.

61 **"Bully!":** *New York Times*, October 1, 1909.

61 **"best characterized":** GB to MP, [1910], MAPP b. 2, f. 84.

62 **"I am not after":** DBM to REP, October 8, 1909, REPC Letters Received b. 36, f. M.

62 **"whatever you think":** Ibid.

62 **most modern researchers:** The literature on the Cook–Peary dispute is vast and contentious. Bryce, *Cook and Peary*, provides the most comprehensive and authoritative dissection of both explorers' cases, and finds both lacking. Herbert, *The Noose of Laurels*, also undercuts Peary's claims. Avery, *To the End of the Earth*, offers a contrary perspective.

62 **"Damn Cook!":** DBM to C. A. Towle, October 4, 1909, DBMC b. 1, f. 42.

62 **"He lied":** *New York Tribune*, October 16, 1909.

64 **"Lonely as hell":** GB to DBM, [1909], MMC b. 1, f. 13.

65 **"seemed like fairy characters":** *New York Times*, January 30, 1910.

65 **"Touchdown!!":** GB to MP, [1910], MAPP b. 2, f. 84.

65 **"You have got to":** H. W. Feilden to GB, February 4, 1910, GBC f. 3.

65 **"The man who":** H. W. Feilden to GB, March 28, 1910, GBC f. 3.

66 **"You know you can":** REP to Robert Bartlett, December 6, 1910, REPC Letters Sent b. 14, f. B 1910.

66 **"This Museum seems":** "George Borup—In Memoriam," *American Museum Journal* 12 (May 1912): 157.

67 **"He calls the outfit":** GB to DBM, October 1, 1910, MMC b. 1, f. 13.

68 **"By the great hornspoon":** GB to MP, July 31, 1910, MAPP b. 2, f. 84.

68 **"Here were three men":** DBM, "Labrador Trip in 1910," [n.d.], MMC b. 10, f. 21.

69 **"large, concrete observatory":** DBM to REP, November 15, 1910, REPC Letters Received b. 40, f. MacMillan.

69 **"Rasmussen is going":** Ibid.

69 **"Look here":** GB to DBM, October 1, 1910, MMC b. 1, f. 13.

69 **"old times":** DBM to REP, [December 1910], REPC Letters Received b. 40, f. MacMillan.

69 **"new species":** DBM to REP, February 28, 1911, REPC Letters Received b. 45, f. M 1911.

70 **"I have plans":** DBM to HFO, February 19, 1911, CLEP b. 1, f. 2.

70 **"the last important work":** Ibid.

70 **"This work should":** Ibid.

70 **"I am going to give":** DBM to Clifton A. Towle, February 21, 1911, DBMC b. 1, f. 44.

70 **"I am, as you know":** HFO to DBM, February 23, 1911, CLEP b. 1, f. 2.

71 **"Borup and myself":** DBM to REP, February 28, 1911, REPC Letters Received b. 45, f. M 1911.

71 **"Make use":** H. W. Feilden to GB, May 8, 1910, GBC f. 3.

71 **"very nice":** Peary quoted in ibid.

71 **"the Great Discoverer":** HDB to REP, March 6, 1911, REPC Letters Received b. 44, f. B 1911.

71 **"As you know":** Ibid.

71 **"MacMillan and he":** Ibid.

71 **"nothing to fall back on":** Ibid.

71 **"When this damned":** Ibid.

71 **"this wretched folly":** Ibid.

72 **"a dandy way":** GB to EOH, [March 1911], CLEP b. 1, f. 2.

73 **May 13, 1911:** *New York Times,* May 14, 1911.

74 **"Come on Dan":** GB to DBM, [1911], MMC b. 1, f. 13.

Chapter 4: Commander Borup?

75 **"the 'kid'":** *New York Sun,* April 8, 1911.

75 **"You feel all":** *Newark Call* quoted in *New York Times,* April 12, 1911.

78 **"all possible credit":** EOH to GB, May 27, 1911, CLEP b. 1, f. 2.

78 **"Crocker Land offers":** EOH to HFO, June 6, 1911, CLEP b. 1, f. 2.

78 **"make the expedition":** Ibid.

79 **"largely geographical":** HFO to EOH, June 7, 1911, CLEP b. 1, f. 2.

79 **"What are we":** EOH to HFO, November 13, 1911, CLEP b. 1, f. 3.

79 **"We can have":** Ibid.

79 **"Hurray!":** GB to MP, [November 1911], MAPP b. 2, f. 88.

80 **"We cannot have":** HFO to EOH, November 28, 1911, CLEP b. 1, f. 3.

80 **The leadership issue:** My reconstruction of this meeting comes from GB to MP, December 4, 1911, MAPP b. 2, f. 88; "Conference Notes," December 8, 1911, CLEP b. 1, f. 4; GB to MP, [December 1911], MAPP b. 2, f. 89; DBM to HFO, December 24, 1917, MMC b. 2, f. 13; and "Agreement," December 9, 1911, CLEP b. 1, f. 4.

81 **"We were just":** GB to MP, [January 1911], MAPP b. 2, f. 91.

82 **"I respect him":** GB to MP, January 25, 1912, MAPP b. 2, f. 92.

82 **"I must win":** Ibid.

83 **"You're everything":** GB to MP, [January 1912], MAPP b. 2, f. 92.

83 **"Do you love me":** GB to MP, February 6, 1912, MAPP b. 2, f. 94.

83 **"I only wish":** GB to MP, January 23, 1912, MAPP b. 2, f. 92.

84 **"Not only would I":** Ibid.

84 **"It was some event":** GB to MP, December 21, 1911, MAPP b. 2, f. 90.

84 **"scientific men":** Roosevelt's endorsement appeared in *Princeton (MN) Union*, February 29, 1912, and other outlets.

85 **"There is a little pride":** Harry Balfe to EOH, March 20, 1912, CLEP b. 1, f. 14.

86 **"a vague idea":** William H. Crocker to GB, December 30, 1911, GBC f. 2.

86 **a masterpiece:** *New York Times*, February 18, 1912.

86 **"the serious minded":** Walter James to HFO, February 19, 1912, CLEP b. 1, f. 9.

86 **"to take into consideration":** EOH to HFO, February 20, 1912, CLEP b. 1, f. 9.

86 **"This expedition of ours":** *Boston Herald*, March 24, 1912.

87 **"the last considerable mass":** *Tensas (LA) Gazette*, April 19, 1912.

87 **"MAY DEFINE AMERICA":** *New York Tribune*, February 14, 1912.

87 **A balmy New York evening:** My reconstruction of this event comes from HFO to REP, 7 and 29 March 1912, REPC Letters Received b. 47, f. American Museum of Natural History; REP, Address, April 5, 1912, REPC Manuscripts b. 13, f. Lectures 1912; Osborn, "Geographical Exploration and the Museum," 165; and GB to MP, December 19, 1911, MAPP b. 2, f. 90.

89 **"disloyalty", "treachery":** GB to MP, [February 12, 1912], MAPP b. 2, f. 95.

89 **"strong, energetic":** *New York Times*, February 18, 1912.

89 **"a formal application":** HDB to EOH, March 7, 1912, CLEP b. 1, f. 12.

89 **"It is useless":** HDB to HFO, April 14, 1912, CLEP b. 2, f. 3.

89 **"power of command":** HFO to HDB, April 9, 1912, CLEP b. 2, f. 3.

89 **"Gadzooks":** GB to MP, [February 1912], MAPP b. 2, f. 95.

89 **"this d—— expedition":** GB to MP, January 20, 1912, MAPP b. 2, f. 92.

90 **"mysterious incantations":** GB to MP, January 24, 1912, MAPP b. 2, f. 92.

90 **"I've been working":** GB to MP, February 5, 1912, MAPP b. 2, f. 94.

90 **"I need you":** GB to MP, March 24, 1912, MAPP b. 2, f. 98.

90 **"Would that count":** GB to MP, March 30, 1912, MAPP b. 2, f. 98.

90 **"I was and am":** GB to MP, January 15, 1912, MAPP b. 2, f. 91.

90 **a boating trip:** My reconstruction of this trip comes from "Brother George Borup," 380; *Middletown (CT) Penny Press*, April 29, 1912; *New Haven (CT) Evening Register*, April 29, 1912; *New York Times*, April 30, 1912; *New York Tribune*, April 30, 1912; *New York Sun*, April 29, 1912; and the *Norwich (CT) Bulletin*, April 25–30, 1912.

Chapter 5: A Fine Fellow

93 **"a friend who":** DBM, handwritten note, [April 1912], MMC b. 1, f. 13.

93 **"My God":** REP to HDB, April 29, 1912, REPC Letters Sent b. 19, f. B 1912.

93 **"It's too awful":** MP diary, April 29, 1912, http://blog.une.edu/mwwc/2013/10/07/george-borups-correspondence-with-marie-peary-friendship-love-and-tragedy/.

95 **"Of course you":** REP to EOH, June 3, 1912, REPC Letters Sent b. 19, f. H 1912.

95 **"is a fine fellow":** HFO to EOH, May 3, 1912, CLEP b. 2, f. 9.

96 **"The staff of":** *New York Tribune*, May 7, 1912.

96 **"I confess":** REP to HFO, May 29, 1912, REPC Letters Sent b. 20, f. O 1912.

96 **"I cannot think":** Herbert Gregory to EOH, May 13, 1912, CLEP b. 2, f. 11.

96 **"could not do":** REP quoted in EOH to HFO, May 2, 1912, CLEP b. 2, f. 9.

96 **MacMillan sensed:** DBM to C. A. Towle, May 16, 1912, DBM b. 1, f. 44.

96 **"invite unfavorable remark":** Herbert L. Bridgman to HFO, May 14, 1912, b. 2, f. 11.

96 **"that the expedition":** AMNH Board of Trustees, "Resolution," May 15, 1912, CLEP b. 2, f. 11.

97 **"I miss George":** DBM to REP, May 23, 1912, REPC Letters Received b. 48, f. Donald B. MacMillan 1912.

97 **"Am making no plans":** DBM to EOH, May 22, 1912, CLEP b. 2, f. 13.

97 **"God damn country":** DBM Labrador diary, September 9, 1912, DBMC Diaries and Journals v. 10; MacMillan, *I Married an Explorer*, 26.

98 **"The expedition is":** HDB to EOH, July 29, 1912, CLEP b. 3, f. 2.

98 **"Your military training":** EOH to HDB, July 10, 1912, CLEP b. 3, f. 4.

98 **"I am obliged":** Ibid.

98 **"The Committee":** EOH to DBM, October 29, 1912, CLEP b. 3, f. 9.

98 **"I can simply promise":** DBM to EOH, October 30, 1912, CLEP b. 3, f. 9.

101 **Successful as:** FG, "Who Is Fitzhugh Green?", December 15, 1925, FGP b. 5, f. 9.

101 **"I understand to":** FG to EOH, July 14, 1912, FGP b. 9 scrapbook.

101 **"no authority":** Ibid.

101 **"I believe that":** FG to EOH, October 9, 1912, FGP b. 9 scrapbook.

102 **"a means to":** FG to Dick Elliot, December 25, 1912, FGP b. 9 scrapbook.

102 **some gentle retrofitting:** FG to Bureau of Medicine and Surgery, October 25, 1912, FGP b. 8 scrapbook; FG to Edwin Denby, [1922], FGP b. 4, f.

6; *Prescott (AZ) Weekly Journal-Miner*, April 3, 1912; and Chief of Bureau to FG, June 22, 1912, FGP b. 8 scrapbook.

103 **"To have gotten":** FG to Dick Elliot, December 25, 1912, FGP b. 9 scrapbook.

103 **Fitzhugh Green dominated:** For the conference and the participants' reactions to it, see EE to EOH, November 1, 1912, CLEP b. 3, f. 10; FG to EOH, November 12, 1912, CLEP b. 3, f. 11; Commander W. W. Phelps to FG, November 8, 1912, FGP b. 9 scrapbook; EOH to FG, November 13, 1912, FGP b. 9 scrapbook.

103 **"I have worked":** FG to EOH, November 12, 1912, CLEP b. 3, f. 11.

103 **"Oh why was":** FG, "Written in a Bitter Moment," May 25, 1911, FGP b. 7, f. 23.

104 **"Murder in Rage":** FG, "Murder in Rage," [May 1911], FGP b. 7, f. 23.

104 **"Don't you see":** FG, "My Conscience," May 30, 1911, FGP b. 7, f. 23.

Chapter 6: The Boys

105 **"I think that":** EOH to DBM, December 5, 1912, CLEP b. 3, f. 13.

106 **"This is a clean":** Ibid.

106 **"If I am overstepping":** FG to DBM, January 22, 1913, FGP b. 9 scrapbook.

107 **"the more publicity":** FG to EE, January 24, 1913, FGP b. 9 scrapbook.

107 **"Greetings":** Capelotti, *By Airship to the North Pole*, 128.

108 **"The idea of being":** Hovey, "The Personnel of the Crocker Land Expedition," 182.

108 **"such as the word":** FG to DBM, April 8, 1913, FGP b. 10 scrapbook.

108 **"I am beginning":** DBM to FG, April 9, 1913, FGP b. 10 scrapbook.

108 **"the mediocre routine":** Jerome Allen to FG, March 13 [1913], FGP b. 10 scrapbook.

109 **"I must ask you":** FG to E. P. Edwards, May 18, 1913, FGP b. 11 scrapbook.

109 **"Just think of":** Mike Kelly to FG, March 19, 1913, FGP b. 9 scrapbook.

112 **"I am up against it":** DBM to Dr. Townsend W. Thorndike, May 6, 1913, CLEP b. 5, f. 10.

113 **"He just had to":** Author interview with Mardi Hunt Thompson, January 15, 2014.

113 **"See that Hunt":** DBM to EOH, [May 1913], CLEP b. 6, f. 6.

113 **"Hunt is certainly":** DBM to C. A. Towle, June 3, 1913, DBMC b. 1, f. 45.

Chapter 7: Goodbye

115 **Six of the Crocker Landers:** My reconstruction of the crew's visit to the *Diana* and the loading of equipment is based on FG private diary, July 1 and 2, 1913, FGP b. 10, f. 5; *New York Tribune*, June 30 and July 1 and 3, 1913; Green, "Arctic Duty" (September 1917), 1953; EOH to W & S Job Bros., July 5, 1913, CLEP b. 7, f. 3; "Symbols of Crocker Land Expedition," March 18, 1913, FGP b. 10 scrapbook; *New York Sun*, June 29, 1913; EOH

to Tom Fraser, May 9, 1913, CLEP b. 5, f. 12; and "Weights of Scientific
Equipment," [1913], FGP b. 11 scrapbook.

117 **"the Eskimos are":** *Washington Herald*, July 20, 1913.

117 **"There has never":** FG to EE, February 1, 1913, FGP b. 9 scrapbook.

117 **"If there be land":** *New York Sun*, July 6, 1913.

118 **"We thought we":** *New York Tribune*, June 27, 1913.

118 **They all kept their problems:** My reconstruction of this event is based
on the *New York Tribune*, July 2, 1913; and "Dinner Program," [June 1913],
FGP b. 11 scrapbook.

119 **Hunt, who was stinging:** Hunt and Thompson, *North to the Horizon*, 9.

119 **Green awoke:** My reconstruction of Fitzhugh Green's morning and the
scene at the *Diana* is based on FG private diary, July 2, 1913, FGP b. 10,
f. 5; *New York Times*, July 3, 1913; *New York World*, July 3, 1913; and MacMillan, *Four Years in the White North*, 3.

119 **"all personal risks":** "Contract," July 1, 1913, MMC b. 23, f. 1.

120 **"Crocker Land expedition":** *New York World*, July 3, 1913.

120 **MacMillan and Hovey went over:** EOH to DBM, July 7, 1913, MMC b.
1, f. 51; DBM to EOH, July 9, 1913, CLEP b. 7, f. 4; DBM to EOH, July 12,
1913, CLEP b. 7, f. 5.

121 **mulled their chances:** FG private diary, July 4 and 5, 1913, FGP b. 10, f. 5.

121 **"Goodluck and Bon Voyage":** REP to DBM, [July 1913], REPC Letters
Sent b. 21, f. L–M 1913.

121 **"Goodbye":** Isabelle Green to FG, July 2, 1913, FGP b. 1, f. 10.

Chapter 8: A True Leader

123 **"Should I lose":** EE to EOH, July 9, 1913, CLEP b. 7, f. 5.

123 **"Make burial":** FG to DBM, July 11, 1913, FGP b. 1, f. 14.

123 **"helpless . . . too scientific":** DBM to EOH, July 12, 1913, CLEP b. 7, f. 5;
DBM to EOH, July 23, 1913, CLEP b. 7, f. 7.

123 **"done about all":** DBM to Jerry Look, July 8, 1913, MMC b. 1, f. 65.

124 **"When things are":** DBM, "North Pole Expedition," 310, MMC b. 12, f. 1.

125 **"As usual":** DBM typescript diary, July 12, 1913, MMC b. 16.

125 **Captain Wayte hugged:** For the expedition's time in Sydney, see DBM
diary, July 8–13, 1913, MMC; FG private diary, July 8–13, 1913, FGP b. 10,
f. 5; FGD, July 8–13, 1913; MacMillan, *Four Years in the White North*, 5–6;
Hunt and Thompson, *North to the Horizon*, 10; *New York Tribune*, July 8 and
September 28, 1913.

126 **"It looks now":** DBM diary, July 15, 1913, MMC.

126 **"She went well up":** DBM to C. A. Towle, July 22, 1913, DBMC b. 1, f. 45.

126 **"deathlike stillness":** MacMillan, *Four Years in the White North*, 8.

126 **"Is that the bottom?":** Ibid.

126 **"Her back is busted":** Ibid.

126 **"Where's the captain?":** Green, "Arctic Duty" (September 1917), 1955.

126 **"Back her":** MacMillan, *Four Years in the White North*, 8.

126 **"If you do":** Ibid.

126 **"It'sh a bit":** Green, "Arctic Duty" (September 1917), 1956.

126 **"knowledge of Arctic waters":** Ibid., 1955.

126 **"The crew lost":** FG to HFO, August 30, 1913, REPC Letters Received b. 50, f. O 1913.

127 **"What in hell":** Green, "Arctic Duty" (September 1917), 1956.

127 **"Float her off":** Ibid.

127 **"I realized how pitifully":** MacMillan, *Four Years in the White North*, 8.

128 **"within a reasonable time":** DBM, handwritten contract, July 16, 1913, CLEP b. 7, f. 5.

128 **"All that we had":** FG private diary, July 16, 1913, FGP b. 10, f. 5.

129 **"impatient to examine":** DBM to C. A. Towle, July 22, 1913, DBMC b. 1, f. 45.

129 **"non-dictionary words":** Ibid.

129 **"I didn't even":** MacMillan, *Four Years in the White North*, 12.

129 **"I frankly believe":** FG to HFO, August 30, 1913, REPC Letters Received b. 50, f. O 1913.

129 **July 17, 1913:** Information on Osborn's conversation with the reporter comes from *New York Tribune*, July 18, 1913.

131 **"Conditions for northern work":** DBM to EOH, July 18, 1913, CLEP b. 7, f. 6; DBM to EOH, July 20, 1913, CLEP b. 7, f. 7.

131 **"perfect":** DBM to EOH, July 18, 1913, CLEP b. 7, f. 7.

131 **"must think that":** EOH to HDB, July 23, 1913, CLEP b. 7, f. 7.

132 **"It was now late":** MacMillan, *Four Years in the White North*, 13.

132 **"If they won't":** *New York Tribune*, August 1, 1913.

132 **"She was more roomy":** Green, "Arctic Duty" (September 1917), 1957.

133 **"Clean grit":** DBM to Jerry Look, August 4, 1913, MMC b. 1, f. 65.

133 **"We have had":** DBM to EOH, July 28, 1913, CLEP b. 7, f. 8.

Chapter 9: Blocked

134 **"the Bergy Hole":** MacMillan, *I Married an Explorer*, 108.

134 **"the breaking-up yard":** Lopez, *Arctic Dreams*, 217.

135 **"like a fevered eye":** Green, "Arctic Duty" (September 1917), 1959.

135 **"This is a land":** EE to HFO, August 29, 1913, CLEP b. 7, f. 10.

135 **"I firmly believe":** DBM to Jessie Fogg, August 14, 1913, MMC b. 2, f. 4.

136 **"Ah-gei-teq":** Green, "Arctic Duty" (September 1917), 1960.

136 **"His oleaginous coat":** MacMillan, *Four Years in the White North*, 18.

136 **"like a monkey":** Green, "Arctic Duty" (September 1917), 1960.

136 **"white-man fashion":** Ibid.

136 **"I have never seen":** FG private diary, August 15, 1913, FGP b. 10, f. 5.

136 **"Among themselves":** Cook, *My Attainment of the Pole*, 452.

137 **"desirable men":** MacMillan, *Four Years in the White North*, 20.

139 **"bawling lustily":** FGD, August 24, 1913.

139 **"Over timid":** FG to HFO, August 30, 1913, REPC Letters Received b. 50, f. O 1913.

140 **"To remain here":** Ibid.

140 **"Another great disappointment"**: DBM to HFO, August 30, 1913, CLEP b. 7, f. 10.

140 **"On no condition"**: *New York Times*, February 18, 1912.

141 **"buoyant optimism"**: FG to HFO, August 30, 1913, REPC Letters Received b. 50, f. O 1913.

141 **"we are all optimistic"**: EE to HFO, August 29, 1913, REPC Letters Received b. 50, f. O 1913.

142 **"After we bid"**: MacMillan, "Crocker Land Expedition," 265.

142 **He was afraid:** Author interview with Mardi Thompson George, January 31, 2014.

142 **"My Own True Love"**: HJH to Marion Hunt, August 25, 1913, reprinted in Hunt and Thompson, *North to the Horizon*, 12.

143 **"I'm mighty glad"**: *New York Tribune*, September 28, 1913.

Chapter 10: Home

144 **"We are done"**: FGD, August 30, 1913.

145 **Taking a deep breath:** My reconstruction of this event comes from JAD, September 5, 1913; FGD, September 5, 1913.

146 **"When a man has"**: FG private diary, [1913], FGP b. 10, f. 5.

149 **"the most palatial"**: DBM to HFO, January 10, 1914, CLEP b. 8, f. 3.

151 **"How do you"**: Green, "Arctic Duty" (September 1917), 1973.

151 **"The little cords"**: Ibid.

152 **"Thus far"**: DBM typescript diary, October 22, 1913, MMC b. 16.

153 **"I suppose"**: FG typescript diary, January 7, 1914, FGP b. 2, f. 4.

154 **"You may hear"**: DBM to Jerry Look, January 11, 1914, MMC b. 1, f. 65.

Chapter 11: Arctic Living

155 **"It is snowing"**: FGD, October 24, 1913.

156 **"Milton or Dante"**: Kane, *Arctic Explorations*, 300.

156 **"when the stars"**: Peary, *The North Pole*, 163.

156 **"The darkness is"**: Freuchen, *Ice Floes and Flaming Water*, 90.

156 **"A gloom descends"**: Cook, *My Attainment of the Pole*, 93.

156 **"A subtle sadness"**: Ibid.

157 **"In the darkness"**: Kane, *Arctic Explorations*, 89.

157 **"A night like"**: DBM to Jerry Look, January 11, 1914, MMC b. 1, f. 65.

157 **"A Tropic Moonlight"**: FG, "A Tropic Moonlight," March 14, 1911, FGP b. 7, f. 23.

157 **"This black monster"**: FG typescript diary, November 21, 1913, FGP b. 2, f. 4.

157 **"He cannot enter"**: Ibid.

157 **"The horrors of"**: FG to Charles Green, January 11, 1914, CLEP b. 8, f. 3.

158 **"It is strange"**: FG typescript diary, December 4, 1913, FGP b. 2, f. 4.

158 **"not going out"**: DBM to Lettie Fogg, January 10, 1914, CLEP b. 8, f. 3.

158 **"My quarterback"**: *Washington Times*, September 14, 1917.

158 **"They had a fine disdain"**: Ibid.

158   **"our rules":** FG typescript diary, November 13, 1913, FGP b. 2, f. 4.

159   **"I laughed so hard":** FG typescript diary, November 22, 1913, FGP b. 2, f. 4.

159   **"It is a happy life":** FG to Charles Green, January 11, 1914, CLEP b. 8, f. 3.

159   **"Bowdoin! MacMillan!":** My reconstruction of MacMillan's birthday party comes from Alice Munson to DBM, [1913], MMC b. 1, f. 23; DBM typescript diary, November 10, 1913, MMC b. 16; FG typescript diary, November 10, 1913, FGP b. 2, f. 4; and Hunt and Thompson, *North to the Horizon*, 38.

160   **"unbelievable quantities":** FG typescript diary, November 27, 1913, FGP b. 2, f. 4.

160   **"in order to draw":** Green, "Arctic Duty" (October 1917), 2208.

161   **"glorious":** DBM typescript diary, December 25, 1913, MMC b. 16.

161   **"absolutely essential":** Ibid.

162   **"Clothing made from":** Peary, *Secrets of Polar Travel*, 160.

164   **"it would be":** MacMillan, *Four Years in the White North*, 48.

164   **"Eskimos control":** Hunt and Thompson, *North to the Horizon*, 26.

164   **"If they could ever":** Quoted in Wilkinson, *The Ice Balloon*, 202.

165   **"The Eskimo polar dog":** Peary, *Secrets of Polar Travel*, 202.

165   **"and when he":** Ibid., 243.

166   **"one of the sturdiest":** Peary, *The North Pole*, 69.

166   **Minik:** For biographical information on Minik, see Harper, *Give Me My Father's Body*.

167   **"I guess not":** FG typescript diary, December 1, 1913, FGP b. 2, f. 4.

168   **"If you expect":** Quoted in Harper, *Give Me My Father's Body*, 117.

168   **"a fine fellow":** HJH to Marion Hunt, January 9, 1914, CLEP b. 8, f. 3.

168   **"It seems very funny":** JAD, December 1, 1913.

169   **"broken Eskimo":** Ibid., January 21, 1914.

169   **"anthropological and ethnological":** DBM typescript diary, December 1, 1913, MMC b. 16.

169   **sign up the best:** DBM to HFO, January 10, 1914, CLEP b. 8, f. 3.

169   **"He wants the south":** FG typescript diary, December 1, 1914, FGP b. 2, f. 4.

Chapter 12: Reaching Out

171   **"Our attack":** DBM typescript diary, December 6, 1913, MMC b. 16.

172   **"comparatively easy":** FG typescript diary, December 8, 1913, FGP b. 2, f. 4.

173   **"These men":** FG typescript diary, December 11, 1913, FGP b. 2, f. 4.

173   **"It sounds like":** FG to Charles Green, January 11, 1914, FGP b. 1, f. 8.

173   **"greasy barbarians":** FG typescript diary, December 13, 1913, FGP b. 2, f. 4.

174   **"a white man":** Ibid.

174   **"The return trip":** Green, "Arctic Duty" (October 1917), 2206.

174   **"the climate of"**: Hovey, "The Personnel of the Crocker Land Expedition," 182.

174   **"strong, fearless"**: *New York Times*, April 27, 1913.

175   **"moral character"**: William DeWitt Hyde to EOH, May 26, 1913, CLEP b. 6, f. 5.

175   **"Hunt is a"**: DBM to EOH, August 4, 1913, CLEP b. 7, f. 9.

176   **"one of the most"**: HJH diary, January 27, 1913, quoted in Hunt and Thompson, *North to the Horizon*, 43.

176   **"Brought to them"**: Ibid.

176   **"I would like"**: FG typescript diary, December 31, 1913, FGP b. 2, f. 4.

177   **"They did not ask"**: Hunt and Thompson, *North to the Horizon*, 29.

177   **"We will disrupt"**: Ibid.

177   **"While I am here"**: HJH diary, December 27, 1913, quoted ibid., 43.

177   **"This is not in"**: Ibid.

177   **"Oftentimes I wonder"**: HJH diary, October 27, 1913, quoted ibid., 35.

177   **"I would a thousand"**: HJH diary, January 1, 1914, quoted ibid., 44.

178   **"I am of Scandinavian"**: EE to EOH, October 20, 1912, CLEP b. 3, f. 8.

178   **"Will we take"**: EE to DBM, December 7, 1912, CLEP b. 3, f. 13.

178   **"I wish I might"**: EE to EOH, January 16, 1914, CLEP b. 8, f. 3.

179   **"civilized savage Eskimo"**: Rasmussen, *The People of the Polar North*, vii.

179   **"a gentleman"**: EE to EOH, January 16, 1914, CLEP b. 8, f. 3.

180   **"minor plagues"**: MacMillan, *Four Years in the White North*, 49.

180   **Within this sturdy exterior**: FG typescript diary, January 7, 1914, FGP b. 2, f. 4.

181   **"The wonderful expressiveness"**: FG typescript diary, November 24, 1913, FGP b. 2, f. 4.

181   **"that her husband"**: Ibid.

181   **"the prettiest woman"**: FG typescript diary, December 26, 1913, FGP b. 2, f. 4.

181   **"Her eyes"**: Ibid.

181   **Green was hardly**: Years later, Peter Freuchen connected Green with the beautiful Aleqasinnguaq, the mother of Peary's Inughuit children. A group of elders told researcher Kenn Harper the same thing in the 1980s. Documentary evidence neither proves nor disproves their assertion. If true, Green never mentioned the liaison in any of his diaries even though he discussed his love for Avianngorneq on many occasions. See Freuchen, *Ice Floes and Flaming Water*, 129; and Kenn Harper, "Taissumani: A Day in Arctic History," 28 April 2006, available at: http://www.nunatsiaqonline .ca/archives/60428/opinionEditorial/columns.html, accessed April 2, 2014.

181   **"quite enamored"**: FG typescript diary, January 16, 1914, FGP b. 2, f. 4.

181   **"the belle of"**: REP quoted in Harper, *Give Me My Father's Body*, 175.

182   **"after all is said"**: Nansen, *Eskimo Life*, 174.

182   **"I am crazy"**: FG typescript diary, December 18, 1913, FGP b. 2, f. 4.

182   **"They are not"**: FG typescript diary, January 24, 1914, FGP b. 2, f. 4.

183 **"I find"**: FG typescript diary, December 26, 1913, FGP b. 2, f. 4.

183 **"Never in my life"**: FG typescript diary, January 6, 1914, FGP b. 2, f. 4.

183 **"The keen difference"**: Ibid.

183 **"Can one of us"**: FG private diary, [1913], FGP b. 10, f. 5.

184 **"Our gang"**: JAD, February 4, 1914.

184 **On first sighting**: Kobalenko, *The Horizontal Everest*, 7.

184 **"Make our home"**: DBM to Jot Small, February 11, 1914, CLEP b. 8, f. 5.

185 **"I am looking"**: DBM to HFO, January 10, 1914, CLEP b. 8, f. 3.

185 **"The evil spirit"**: Ibid.

Chapter 13: The Evil Spirit

187 **"Existence of land"**: *New York Times*, October 13, 1913.

187 **"She will never"**: Robert Bartlett to REP, July 16, 1913, REPC Letters Received b. 49, f. Bartlett 1913.

187 **"I would love to"**: Ibid.

188 **"Popular interest"**: Talman, "The Outlook in Polar Exploration," 187.

188 **"the era of pole-hunting"**: Ibid., 179.

188 **"Vikings' sons"**: *New York Times*, July 10, 1913.

189 **"distinguished Arctic explorer"**: This story is told in Frederick G. Jackson, *A Thousand Days in the Arctic* (London: Harper & Brothers, 1899), 1:205.

190 **"The evil spirit"**: *New York Tribune*, May 26, 1914.

190 **"and cold feet"**: DBM diary, February 7, 1914, DBMC Diaries and Journals v. 16.

191 **"All of the skin"**: DBM diary, February 6, 1914, DBMC Diaries and Journals v. 16.

191 **"Too quick"**: DBM typescript diary, February 6, 1914, MMC b. 16. In *Four Years in the White North*, MacMillan insisted that the Inuk understood the markings and blamed the incident on Tautsiannguaq grabbing the wrong can because the room was dark (50).

191 **"We fully expect"**: FG to Isabelle Green, January 24, 1914, CLEP b. 8, f. 4.

192 **"something which Green"**: DBM diary, February 8, 1914, DBMC Diaries and Journals v. 16.

192 **"like the Devil"**: DBM diary, February 10, 1914, DBMC Diaries and Journals v. 16.

193 **"blissfully ignorant"**: MacMillan, *Four Years in the White North*, 43.

194 **"Friday the 13th!"**: DBM field notebook, February 13, 1914.

194 **"Can't discover"**: Ibid.

195 **"I am glad"**: DBM typescript diary, February 13, 1914, MMC b. 16.

195 **"gloomy and dirty"**: DBM field notebook, February 14, 1914.

195 **"If Peary remained"**: Ibid.

195 **"Never again"**: DBM typescript diary, February 15 and 16, 1914, MMC b. 16.

196 **"The song of the sea"**: *Annual Report of the Secretary of War*, vol. 4, *Report*

of the Chief Signal Officer (Washington, DC: Government Printing Office, 1884), 626.

197 **"That is too bad"**: DBM, "Religion of the Primitive Polar Eskimos," [1920s?], MMC b. 13, f. 5.

197 **More than 200 species**: Thomas, *Frozen Oceans*, 69–126.

198 **"A bit too close"**: DBM field notebook, February 17, 1914.

199 **"I could feel Ek"**: HJH diary, February 12, 1914, quoted in Hunt and Thompson, *North to the Horizon*, 48.

200 **"with nothing to do"**: HJH diary, February 14 and 15, 1914, quoted ibid.

200 **The ensign had not expected**: FG field notebook, February 15, 1914, DBMC Diaries and Journals v. 24.

201 **"I have come"**: DBM typescript diary, February 17, 1914, MMC b. 16.

201 **"The hirelings"**: FG to Josephus Daniels, "Preliminary Report of the Crocker Land Expedition," [September 1916], FG Jr. b. 4, f. 40.

201 **"chicken-hearted"**: MacMillan, *Four Years in the White North*, 54.

201 **"Young Eskimos"**: Ibid.

202 **"It would not be"**: JAD, February 13, 1914.

202 **"They thought that"**: DBM typescript diary, February 19, 1914, MMC b. 16.

203 **"looked like it"**: JAD, February 20, 1914.

203 **"Storm"**: FG private diary, [1913], FGP b. 10, f. 5.

203 **"It is pretty flat"**: FG typescript diary, February 23, 1914, FGP b. 2, f. 4.

203 **"They were ugly"**: HJH diary, February 19, 1914, quoted in Hunt and Thompson, *North to the Horizon*, 49.

203 **"whopping big blisters"**: HJH diary, February 21, 1914, quoted in ibid., 50.

Chapter 14: Slaughter Ground

205 **"Few but the dweller"**: Osborn, ed., *Discovery of the North West Passage*, 161. The *Investigator* was trapped in the ice for almost three years. McClure abandoned the ship in June 1853. For years it provided the Inughuit with a source of copper and iron. Canadian scientists discovered the ship in 2010. Sir John Franklin probably died on King William's Island in 1847. His remains have never been found.

206 **"It is so late"**: FGD, February 24, 1914.

207 **"be treated as"**: DBM to HJH, March 11, 1914, loose insertion in HJH field notebook.

207 **"Again we are started"**: DBM field notebook, March 11, 1914.

207 **"Rather a rough day"**: Ibid.

208 **"the most extreme place"**: Kobalenko, *The Horizontal Everest*, 3.

209 **"Impossible"**: DBM field notebook, March 17, 1914.

210 **"The geology"**: Green, "Arctic Duty" (October 1917), 2212.

211 **"I have considered"**: DBM typescript diary, March 16, 1914, MMC b. 16.

212 **"Make it fast"**: Green, "Arctic Duty" (October 1917), 2213.

212 **"Who will ever"**: DBM typescript diary, March 17, 1914, MMC b. 16.

212 "I feel that": DBM typescript diary, March 18, 1914, MMC b. 16.

212 "[Minik] decided": DBM field journal, March 18, 1914.

213 "Did you know?": MacMillan, *Four Years in the White North*, 57.

213 "two deserters": DBM field notebook, March 18, 1914.

213 "[Tautsiannguaq's] wife": Green, "Arctic Duty" (October 1917), 2214.

213 "His wife": MacMillan, *Four Years in the White North*, 57.

213 "If they will": DBM field notebook, March 19, 1914.

214 "Frozen cheeks": MacMillan, *Four Years in the White North*, 58.

214 "It is only": DBM field notebook, March 20, 1914.

214 "Living high": DBM field notebook, March 21, 1914.

214 "He is clean grit": DBM to HJH, March [23?], 1914, HJH field notebook.

215 "Green": FG, "Account of Oil Party," [1914?], FGP b. 2, f. 6.

215 "Am lonesome tonight": DBM field notebook, March 22, 1914.

215 "fine, faithful fellows": Ibid.

216 "I am anxious": DBM field notebook, March 23, 1914.

218 "I hunted them": Peary, *Secrets of Polar Travel*, 228.

218 "In this way": Ibid., 228–29.

218 **Green stood atop:** My reconstruction of Fitzhugh Green's supply run comes from FG, "Account of Oil Party," [1914?], FGP b. 2, f. 6; Green, "Arctic Duty" (October 1917), 2216–21; and FG field notebook, DBMC Diaries and Journals v. 25.

218 "filled with the beauty": Green, "Account of Oil Party," [1914?], FGP b. 2, f. 6.

219 "Their life": Green, "Arctic Duty" (October 1917), 2217.

219 "Mine was a cruel": Ibid.

220 "the cultured": Ibid.

220 "like three giant": Ibid., 2218.

220 **Legend held that:** Millman, *A Kayak Full of Ghosts*, 23.

220 "One-two-three": Green, "Account of Oil Party," [1914?], FGP b. 2, f. 6.

220 "I cannot explain": Ibid.

220 "Take a bone": Lewis Carroll, *Through the Looking Glass* (1872; New York: Penguin, 1962), 322–23.

221 "Two forlorn": Green, "Account of Oil Party," [1914?], FGP b. 2, f. 6.

221 "philosophical stoicism": Ibid.

221 "I always thought": Ibid.

221 "Powerfully built": Ibid.

222 "I think we had": Ibid.

222 "My teeth chattered": Green, "Arctic Duty" (October 1917), 2219.

222 "I couldn't keep warm": Ibid.

222 "He became": Green, "Account of Oil Party," [1914?], FGP b. 2, f. 6.

222 "The meat": Ibid.

223 "I explained": Ibid.

223 "A great day!": FG field notebook, April 6, 1914, DBMC Diaries and Journals v. 25.

223   **"My team"**: FG field notebook, April 10 and 11, 1914, DBMC Diaries and Journals v. 25.

224   **"Thank heavens"**: FG field notebook, April 12, 1914, DBMC Diaries and Journals v. 25.

224   **"Thank God"**: DBM field notebook, April 12, 1914.

224   **"grand, good work"**: Ibid.

224   **"The Lord"**: DBM field notebook, March 25, 1914.

224   **"We are certainly"**: Ibid.

224   **"Like savages"**: MacMillan, *Four Years in the White North*, 67.

225   **"This is one"**: DBM field notebook, April 8, 1914.

225   **"Nothing to do"**: Ibid.

225   **"The day is over"**: Ibid.

225   **"Again we get it"**: DBM field notebook, April 10, 1914.

225   **"The worst day"**: Ibid.

226   **"We plan to leave"**: FG field notebook, April 14, 1914, DBMC Diaries and Journals v. 25.

227   **"We are here"**: DBM to HJH, April 14, 1914, loose insertion in HJH field notebook.

Chapter 15: On the Ice
228   **"All kinds"**: DBM field notebook, April 15, 1914.

228   **"Many are under"**: Peary, *Secrets of Polar Travel*, 289.

228   **"indescribable chaos"**: Ibid., 291.

229   **"Much water"**: MacMillan, *Four Years in the White North*, 75.

229   **"Will not freeze"**: Ibid.

229   **"Almost impossible"**: FG field notebook, April 16, 1914, DBMC Diaries and Journals v. 25.

229   **"Good God!"**: Green, "Arctic Duty" (October 1917), 2195.

229   **"I hate to see"**: DBM diary, April 15, 1914, DBMC Diaries and Journals v. 17.

230   **"wondered what the Arctic"**: DBM field notebook, April 17, 1914.

230   **"apparently around"**: MacMillan, *Four Years in the White North*, 76.

231   **hunter encountered a polar bear**: This story and all quotes within come from Millman, *A Kayak Full of Ghosts*, 33.

231   **"I had carried"**: DBM diary, April 17, 1914, DBMC Diaries and Journals v. 17.

231   **"a pall-bearer"**: MacMillan, *Four Years in the White North*, 77.

232   **"He will never"**: Ibid., 78.

232   **"For a white man"**: FG, "Second Polar Trip," [1914], FGP b. 2, f. 4.

232   **"Most of the time"**: Malaurie, *The Last Kings of Thule*, 32.

233   **"They are people"**: Peary, *Secrets of Polar Travel*, 183.

233   **"real children"**: Ibid., 180.

233   **"not qualified"**: DBM, "Hunting Walrus with the Polar Eskimo," [n.d.], MMC b. 10, f. 10.

233   **"In general":** Malaurie, *Last Kings of Thule*, 45.

233   **Native legends:** Rasmussen, *The People of the Polar North*, 104.

234   **"the best Eskimo":** MacMillan, *Etah and Beyond*, 71.

234   **"Our best man":** MacMillan, *Four Years in the White North*, 128.

234   **"loyal, capable":** EE, "On Unknown Shores," quoted in ibid., 335.

234   **"my son":** DBM, "Names" [1915?], DBMC Diaries and Journals v. 58.

235   **English–Inuktitut dictionary:** Arthur Thibert, *Eskimo (Inuktitut) Dictionary* (New York: Hippocrene, 1997), 78.

235   **"She was struggling":** FG typescript diary, November 13, 1913, FGP b. 2, f. 4.

236   **"a calm and":** Knud Rasmussen to Reverend Dean C. Schultz Lorenzen, January 6, 1921, FG Jr. b. 4, f. 40.

236   **"the peaceful one":** Malaurie, *Last Kings of Thule*, 161.

236   **a small picture:** Peary, *Nearest the Pole*, 348.

237   **"the belle":** REP quoted in Harper, *Give Me My Father's Body*, 175.

237   **MacMillan called him:** DBM, "Census of Smith Sound Eskimos," [1913], DBMC Diaries and Journals v. 58.

238   **"We hope":** FG field notebook, April 19, 1914, DBMC Diaries and Journals v. 25.

238   **"Four days more":** DBM field notebook, April 21, 1914.

238   **The domed snow house:** Kirk, *Snow*, 153–57.

240   **"fairy-land":** MacMillan, *Four Years in the White North*, 69.

Chapter 16: Pujoq

241   **"We've got it!":** DBM to HFO, August 23, 1914, CLEP b. 8, f. 12.

241   **"We have it":** MacMillan, *Four Years in the White North*, 80.

241   **"There it was":** DBM field notebook, April 21, 1914.

241   **"Hills, valleys":** Ibid.

242   **"*Pujoq*":** DBM to HDB, November 28, 1914, CLEP b. 8, f. 14.

242   **"Could Peary":** MacMillan, *Four Years in the White North*, 80.

242   **"clear as a bell":** DBM field notebook, April 22, 1914.

242   **"was not going back":** DBM diary, April 22, 1914, DBMC Diaries and Journals v. 17.

243   **"the worst sledging":** DBM field notebook, April 24, 1914.

243   **"We were on":** DBM diary, April 23, 1914, DBMC Diaries and Journals v. 17.

243   **"It was absolutely":** FG field notebook, April 24, 1914, DBMC Diaries and Journals v. 25.

243   **"a crushed up":** DBM to HFO, August 23, 1914, CLEP b. 8, f. 12.

243   **"a great meadow-land":** FG to EOH, August 1, 1914, CLEP b. 8, f. 12.

243   **"will-o'-the-wisp":** MacMillan, *Four Years in the White North*, 81.

244   **"I have done":** DBM diary, April 24, 1914, DBMC Diaries and Journals v. 17.

244   **"Disappointment is":** Green, "Arctic Duty" (October 1917), 2223.

244   **"A great feeling":** DBM field notebook, April 23, 1914.

245 **"We have done"**: DBM diary, April 23, 1914, DBMC Diaries and Journals v. 17.

245 **"We should get home"**: *Red Cloud (NE) Chief*, July 3, 1913.

246 **"It might mean"**: DBM diary, April 25, 1914, DBMC Diaries and Journals v. 17.

246 **"In their characteristic"**: MacMillan, *Four Years in the White North*, 84.

246 **"The trail must be"**: Ibid., 84–85.

247 **"grinned and said"**: Ibid., 85.

247 **"I thought he"**: DBM diary, April 25, 1914, DBMC Diaries and Journals v. 17.

247 **"That day's work"**: MacMillan, *Four Years in the White North*, 85.

247 **The Red Queen**: FG field notebook, April 25, 1914, DBMC Diaries and Journals v. 25.

248 **"frightfully thin"**: MacMillan, *Four Years in the White North*, 86.

248 **"It was so much like"**: FG field notebook, April 27, 1914, DBMC Diaries and Journals v. 25.

248 **"We are unable"**: DBM typescript diary, April 27, 1914, MMC b. 16.

248 **"Land again!"**: FG field notebook, April 28, 1914, DBMC Diaries and Journals v. 25.

249 **"No one knows"**: MacMillan, *Four Years in the White North*, 87.

249 **"outlined against"**: Ibid.

249 **MacMillan now had**: For MacMillan and Green's state of mind during this climb, see ibid; and Green, "Arctic Duty" (October 1917), 2223.

250 **his own message**: DBM field notebook, April 28, 1914. German explorer Hans Krüger recovered this note during his 1930 Arctic expedition but died in the field. His body has never been found, so MacMillan's original cairn note is lost. In 1933, Harry Stallworthy of the Royal Canadian Mounted Police found Krüger's copy of MacMillan's note in the cairn.

250 **"move, and move"**: MacMillan, *Four Years in the White North*, 89.

Chapter 17: Crocker Land

252 **"Strange is the power"**: Nansen, *Eskimo Life*, 2.

252 **"living in the beautiful"**: *Pittsburgh Post* quoted in Wilkinson, *The Ice Balloon*, 163.

253 **Enormous pans of ice**: Gosnell, *Ice*, 206–7.

254 **Arctic conditions produce**: For more on Arctic mirages, see Kirk, *Snow*, 115; Gosnell, *Ice*, 17; and Lopez, *Arctic Dreams*, 23–24.

255 **"It becomes a nervous thing"**: Osborn, ed., *Discovery of the North West Passage*, 53–54.

255 **"a continuous line"**: Ibid., 82.

255 **"We were forced"**: DBM diary, April 21, 1914, DBMC Diaries and Journals v. 17.

255 **"one of the most"**: Cook, *My Attainment of the Pole*, 244.

256 **Iggiannguaq and Ulloriaq**: DBM to Jerry Look, July 19, 1914, MMC b. 1, f. 65.

256 **"A day of comfort":** REP diary, June 24, 1906, REPC Diaries.

256 **"Here Jesup Land":** Ibid.

256 **"no land visible":** Ibid.

256 **"We went on up":** REP diary, June 28, 1906, REPC Diaries.

256 **"With the completion":** Ibid.

257 **"Peary, June 28":** MacMillan, *Four Years in the White North*, 87. This note is at the American Geographical Society's archive at the University of Wisconsin–Milwaukee. Author email correspondence with Robert Michael Jaeger, July 1, 2014.

257 **"Arrived here noon":** REP cache note, June 30, 1906, REPC Arctic Expeditions b. 19, f. Cache Notes, 1906.

257 **"Have been west":** REP cache note, July 5, 1906, MMC b. 2, f. 15.

257 **"Commander reached ship":** Robert Bartlett, "Log of 'Roosevelt' during the Commander's Absence from June 3rd–July 30th, 1906," REPC Diaries.

258 **"Commander arrived":** Dr. Louis Wolf, "Expedition Journal," July 30, 1906, REPC Diaries.

258 **"new land":** Peary, *Nearest the Pole*, 195. For more on Meighen Island, see Bryce, *Cook and Peary*, 1111–12.

258 **Peary Arctic Club:** *New York Times*, December 13, 1906.

258 **Hubbard Medal:** REP, "Speech Accepting the Hubbard Medal," December 15, 1906, REPC Manuscripts b. 13, f. Speech Accepting Hubbard Medal.

258 **Delta Kappa Epsilon Association:** *New York Times*, January 17, 1907.

258 **1907 lecture tour:** Slide List [1907], REPC Manuscripts b. 13, f. 1907.

259 **"snow-clad summits":** Peary, "Nearest the North Pole" (March 1907), 506.

259 **A typed rough draft:** REP, "Draft: Nearest to the Pole," [1906], REPC Manuscripts b. 10, f. Drafts—Nearest to the Pole.

259 **"faint white summits":** Peary, "Nearest the North Pole" (March 1907), 504; Peary, *Nearest the Pole*, 202.

260 **"it must therefore":** "The Non-Existence of Peary Channel," *Geographical Review* 1 (June 1916): 449.

262 **"[you] would not care":** REP to George Crocker, April 16, 1907, REPC Letters Sent b. 95, f. C 1907.

Chapter 18: Panic

267 **"We plan to separate":** FG field notebook, April 28, 1914, DBMC Diaries and Journals v. 25.

268 **"All the adventurous blood":** Green, "Arctic Duty" (October 1917), 2223.

268 **"long-delayed storm":** MacMillan, *Four Years in the White North*, 89.

268 **"Good-by, Piugaattoq!":** Ibid.

268 **"Again we get it":** DBM field notebook, April 29, 1914.

268 **"Old Torngak":** Ibid.

269 **"the most uncomfortable night":** DBM field notebook, April 30, 1914.

269 **"Impossible!":** MacMillan, *Four Years in the White North*, 90.

269 **"We can't stand this"**: DBM diary, April 30, 1914, DBMC Diaries and Journals v. 17.

270 **"so full"**: DBM field notebook, May 1, 1914.

270 **"Will be glad"**: DBM field notebook, May 3, 1914.

270 **"He certainly is energetic"**: DBM diary, May 2, 1914, DBMC Diaries and Journals v. 17.

270 **"good luck"**: DBM field notebook, May 2, 1914.

271 **"Mac"**: Ibid.

271 **Ensign Fitzhugh Green:** My reconstruction of these days comes from FG field notebook, April 29–May 4, 1914, DBMC Diaries and Journals v. 25; FG private diary, [1914], FGP b. 11, f. 7; and Green, "Arctic Duty" (October 1917), 2223–24.

272 **"We were a mess"**: FG field notebook, April 30, 1914, DBMC Diaries and Journals v. 25.

272 **"Black as night"**: Ibid.

273 **"absolutely refused"**: FG field notebook, May 1, 1914, DBMC Diaries and Journals v. 25.

274 **"sullenly refused"**: Green, "Arctic Duty" (October 1917), 2224.

274 **"away from me"**: FG field notebook, May 1, 1914, DBMC Diaries and Journals v. 25.

275 **"ran up"**: Ibid.

275 **East Greenland Inuit:** Millman, *A Kayak Full of Ghosts*, 81.

276 **"We do not believe"**: Rasmussen, *The People of the Polar North*, 123.

276 **"The soul"**: Ibid., 106.

277 **"*Sinnepah tima*"**: Green, "Arctic Duty" (November 1917), 2458.

277 **"The situation"**: FG field notebook, May 1, 1914, DBMC Diaries and Journals v. 25.

277 **"Here I am"**: Ibid.

278 **"The Esquimo"**: "Extract from the Journal of Fitzhugh Green," May 2, 1914, FGP b. 2, f. 8.

278 **"Providence has watched"**: FG field notebook, May 1, 1914, DBMC Diaries and Journals v. 25.

278 **"Good God, Green"**: DBM field notebook, May 4, 1914.

278 **"Yes, Piugattoq"**: MacMillan, *Four Years in the White North*, 92.

278 **"splitting [the Inuk's] head"**: DBM diary, May 4, 1914, DBMC Diaries and Journals v. 17.

278 **"I would much rather"**: DBM typescript diary, May 4, 1914, MMC b. 16.

278 **"a deliberate murder"**: Ibid.

278 **"halting Eskimo"**: Ibid.

280 **"Look!"**: Green, "Arctic Duty" (November 1917), 2471–72.

280 **"unlucky day"**: FG field notebook, May 15, 1914, DBMC Diaries and Journals v. 25.

281 **"deep in grief"**: DBM typescript diary, May 21, 1914, MMC b. 16.

281 **"Of course it was"**: FG typescript diary, May 21, 1914, FGP b. 2, f. 4.

281 **"Not an ache"**: Ibid.

281 **"Toquvoq":** DBM typescript diary, May 21, 1914, MMC b. 16.

281 **"did not consider":** Hunt and Thompson, *North to the Horizon*, 56–57.

281 **On June 29:** DBM typescript diary, June 29, 1914, MMC b. 16. One year later, Fitzhugh Green recorded Peter's first birthday in his diary. It was the only time he ever made such an observation.

Chapter 19: Sundown

282 **writing letters:** DBM discusses this day in DBM diary, July 1, 1914, DBMC Diaries and Journals v. 17.

284 **"Playing little awks":** FG private diary, [1913], FGP b. 10, f. 5.

285 **"a garden":** DBM lecture notes, "A Garden on Top of the Earth," [n. d.], MMC b. 7, f. 8.

285 **"a little fruit":** EE, "The Summer at North Star Bay," in MacMillan, *Four Years in the White North*, 324.

286 **Hungry natives:** My reconstruction of this summer comes from ibid., 323–32.

286 **"Peter apparently":** Ibid., 328.

286 **"Never have I":** Ibid., 326.

286 **"botanizing":** DBM diary, August 11, 1914, DBMC Diaries and Journals v. 17.

287 **"pretty well starved":** DBM to HFO, August 23, 1914, CLEP b. 8, f. 12; MacMillan, *Four Years in the White North*, 114–15.

287 **"When are we":** MacMillan, *Four Years in the White North*, 115.

287 **"Right now":** Ibid.

287 **"without one regret":** EE, "The Summer at North Star Bay," in MacMillan, *Four Years in the White North*, 332.

288 **"We are all":** EOH to REP, November 19, 1914, REPC Letters Received b. 52, f. H 1914. Hovey's letter contains lengthy quotes from Ekblaw's original letter.

288 **"I have had":** Ibid.

288 **"Mac has said":** EE to EOH, August 29, 1914, CLEP b. 8, f. 12.

288 **"Green and Mac":** Ibid.

288 **"on Polar Sea":** Ibid.

288 **"a wild sea":** Ibid.

288 **"A day of days!":** FGD, August 30, 1914.

288 **"We should have":** EOH to DBM, June 8, 1914, MMC b. 1, f. 51.

289 **"Allen is not":** Ibid.

290 **"He put both kites up":** FGD, October 26, 1914.

290 **"Our wireless":** DBM diary, November 17, 1914, DBMC Diaries and Journals v. 17.

290 **"This summer":** FG to EOH, August 1, 1914, CLEP b. 8, f. 12.

290 **"a moiety":** FG typescript diary, July 1914, FGP b. 2, f. 4.

290 **"Still sane":** FG private diary, [1914], FGP b. 11, f. 7.

290 **"The black winter":** Ibid.

290 **"all sense of proportion":** Ibid.

290 **"I am doomed":** Ibid.

290 **"I have yet":** FGD, November 1, 1914.

290 **"insufferable life":** FG private diary, [1914], FGP b. 11, f. 7.

291 **"As a rule":** FGD, November 20, 1914.

291 **"I have my books":** FGD, November 9, 1914.

291 **He quoted Byron:** FG private diary, [1914], FGP b. 11, f. 7. Green slightly misquoted Byron's "Childe Harold's Pilgrimage." I have amended his quote for clarity.

291 **"Thoreau's house":** Ibid.

291 **"It is very":** FGD, November 13, 1914.

291 **"in space":** FGD, December 11, 1914.

291 **"not meant for man":** FGD, November 11, 1914.

291 **"back and forth":** FGD, October 5, 1914.

292 **"Some people would find":** FGD, December 7, 1914.

292 **"but I get":** Ibid.

292 **"Dearest":** FG to [Anna], August 8, 1914, FGP b. 1, f. 31.

292 **"Do you wonder":** FG to Anna, January 1, 1915, FGP b. 1, f. 31.

293 **"Of course I owe":** FG to Anna, [1914?], FGP b. 1, f. 31.

293 **"We are like children":** FG to Anna, December 21, 1914, FGP b. 1, f. 31.

293 **"A very happy season":** DBM to C. A. Towle, October 30, 1914, DBMC b. 1, f. 45.

293 **"Moonlit nights":** DBM diary, October 18, 1914, DBMC Diaries and Journals v. 17.

294 **"I ask your forgiveness":** HJH to Marion Hunt, December 20, 1914, quoted in Hunt and Thompson, *North to the Horizon*, 62.

294 **"the Nimrod":** DBM diary, June 2, 1914, DBMC Diaries and Journals v. 17.

294 **"As everyone is":** HJH diary, May 19, 1914, quoted in Hunt and Thompson, *North to the Horizon*, 54.

294 **Although he liked Mac:** Author interview with Mardi Thompson George, January 15, 2014.

295 **"How easy is it":** FGD, December 4, 1914.

Chapter 20: Mail

295 **Fitzhugh Green administered ether:** FGD, December 20, 1914; and DBM diary, December 19, 1914, DBMC Diaries and Journals v. 17. Hunt had performed a real operation a few weeks earlier when he sawed open the frozen corpse of an Inughuit woman to retrieve a cancerous tumor. He hung the tumor, which resembled a piece of liver, in the storeroom of Borup Lodge. That night a dog crashed through the window and ate the tumor, horrifying the natives.

296 **"When you read this":** C. A. Towle to DBM, June 24, 1913, MMC b. 1, f. 23.

296 **"a fine fellow":** DBM typescript diary, October 22, 1914, MMC b. 16.

296 **"My plan":** FGD, December 23, 1914.

297 **"I don't suppose":** Ibid.

297 **"absolutely helpless":** DBM typescript diary, December 29, 1914, MMC b. 16.

298 **"I felt":** Freuchen, *Ice Floes and Flaming Water*, 38.

298 **"We have reached something":** DBM diary, January 9, 1915, DBMC Diaries and Journals v. 17.

299 **"With no food":** DBM diary, January, 10, 1915, DBMC Diaries and Journals v. 17.

299 **"Dey are eating":** DBM diary, January 12, 1915, DBMC Diaries and Journals v. 17.

300 **"I have never":** MacMillan, *Four Years in the White North*, 134.

301 **"I expect a ship":** DBM to EOH, January 16, 1915, CLEP b. 9, f. 1.

301 **"poor cooking":** DBM diary, February 7, 1915, DBMC Diaries and Journals v. 17.

301 **"He is made":** EE to EOH, March 20, 1915, CLEP b. 9, f. 3.

Chapter 21: The World Beyond

304 **"It was a magnificent display":** Quoted in Davis, *Into the Silence*, 36.

304 **"I am constantly finding":** HDB to EOH, September 23, 1913, CLEP b. 7, f. 11.

304 **"I want him":** Ibid.

304 **"One thing is sure":** EOH to HDB, September 25, 1913, CLEP b. 7, f. 11.

305 **"little brown men":** *New York Tribune*, September 28, 1913.

305 **"By the time":** Ibid.

305 **"are enthusiastic":** *New York Tribune*, May 17, 1914.

305 **"just as happy as ever":** *New York Tribune*, May 26, 1914.

305 **"fraught with much adventure":** *New York Tribune*, May 27, 1914.

305 **"a howling success":** *New York Tribune*, June 2, 1914.

305 **"the horrors":** Ibid.

306 **"Our lot is nothing":** Ella Hunt to EOH, August 23, 1914, CLEP b. 8, f. 12.

306 **"It would be":** Victoria Allen to EOH, June 8, 1914, CLEP b. 8, f. 10.

306 **"far more of a luxury":** Ibid.

307 **"no Crocker Land":** EE to EOH, August 29, 1914, CLEP b. 8, f. 12.

307 **"In justice to MacMillan":** EOH to HFO, November 23, 1914, CLEP b. 8, f. 14.

307 **"Of course it is":** Ibid.

308 **"Undoubtedly":** *New York Tribune*, November 25, 1914.

308 **"has either melted":** *Ibid*.

308 **"Crocker Land has disappeared":** *New York Sun*, November 25, 1914.

308 **"The fact that it":** *Kansas City Times* quoted in *Monroe City (MO) Democrat*, December 17, 1914.

308 **"Crocker Land is not":** *Washington Times*, December 1, 1914.

308 **"Five years ago":** *Philadelphia Evening Public Ledger*, November 25, 1914.

308 **"I still prefer":** Cook, *My Attainment of the Pole*, 559.

308 **"I believe I sighted":** *New York Tribune*, November 25, 1914.

308 "It is almost": *New York Times*, November 26, 1914.

309 "there is no danger": *Philadelphia Evening Public Ledger*, November 25, 1914.

309 "either deceived by": *New York Sun*, November 30, 1914.

309 "Are you planning": Victoria Allen to EOH, February 15, 1915, CLEP b. 9, f. 2.

309 "About when will": Mrs. W. C. Fogg to EOH, February 18, 1915, CLEP b. 9, f. 2.

309 "the present stirring events": Augusta Krieger to EOH, February 14, 1915, CLEP b. 9, f. 2.

310 "The terrible war": EOH to Knud Rasmussen, November 23, 1914, CLEP b. 8, f. 14.

310 "I wish you were": GS to EOH, March 11, 1915, CLEP b. 9, f. 3.

311 "The fact that": L. A. Baver to GS, February 27, 1915, CLEP b. 9, f. 2.

311 "There is plenty": EOH to GS, April 29, 1915, CLEP b. 9, f. 4.

311 "and thus I should": Ibid.

311 "seriously in debt": EOH to Zenas Crane, May 25, 1915, CLEP b. 9, f. 6.

312 "circumstances": REP to HFO, June 1, 1915, CLEP b. 9, f. 6.

312 "Our year's work": DBM to Charles Brainard, August 25, 1914, DBMC b. 1, f. 7.

312 "In a way": Ibid.

312 "How Pee-ah-wah-to": DBM to HFO, August 23, 1914, CLEP b. 8, f. 12.

312 "extremely valuable": HFO to GS, June 21, 1915, CLEP b. 9, f. 8.

312 "they did see": DBM to HFO, August 23, 1914, CLEP b. 8, f. 12.

312 "We have reason": HFO fundraising circular, June 30, 1915, CLEP b. 9, f. 9.

313 "I think that she": EOH to H. C. Pickels, June 4, 1915, CLEP b. 9, f. 6.

313 "Greatly disturbed": EOH to H. C. Pickels, July 6, 1915, CLEP b. 9, f. 10.

313 "The days are slipping": EOH to GS, July 22, 1915, CLEP b. 9, f. 11.

314 "If this should be": Edith Demerell to EOH, July 9, 1915, CLEP b. 9, f. 10.

Chapter 22: Disintegration

315 "Boston": DBM diary, March 6, 1915, DBMC Diaries and Journals v. 17.

316 "is not at all": DBM diary, February 17, 1915, DBMC Diaries and Journals v. 17.

316 "Our meat supply": DBM diary, February 16, 1915, DBMC Diaries and Journals v. 17.

316 "one of the hardest": DBM to HFO, August 23, 1914, CLEP b. 8, f. 12.

318 "I could have hugged": EE, "On Unknown Shores," in MacMillan, *Four Years in the White North*, 342.

318 "as grand as": Ibid., 354.

318 "one of the dreariest": Ibid., 355.

318 "good-by messages": Ibid., 360.

319 "I was glad": Ibid., 368.

319 **"unsociable atmosphere":** FG typescript diary, May 1915, FGP b. 2, f. 4.

319 **"adequate":** FG, "Outline Report of Relief Party," FGP b. 2, f. 5.

319 **"Says he cannot":** DBM diary, June 20, 1915, DBMC Diaries and Journals v. 18.

319 **"is easily my best":** DBM to EOH, January 16, 1915, CLEP b. 9, f. 1.

320 **"I wish I were":** DBM diary, May 22, 1915, DBMC Diaries and Journals v. 18.

320 **Violent summer snowstorms:** DBM diary, July 11, 1915, DBMC Diaries and Journals v. 18.

320 **"give us a part":** DBM diary, June 18, 1915, DBMC Diaries and Journals v. 18.

320 **an independent nation:** Freuchen's vivid imagination warped even his fragmentary awareness of the war's course. For a time that summer he argued that the Dutch had opened their dikes and drowned an entire invading German army.

321 **"strongly tempted":** DBM diary, May 3, 1915, DBMC Diaries and Journals v. 18.

321 **"By God!":** Green, "Arctic Duty" (November 1917), 2493.

321 **"Jerome [Allen]":** DBM diary, May 3, 1915, DBMC Diaries and Journals v. 18.

322 **"We are expecting":** FGD, August 9, 1915.

322 **"As far as I am concerned":** DBM diary, August 10, 1915, DBMC Diaries and Journals v. 18.

322 **"who stood by us":** DBM diary, June 18, 1915, DBMC Diaries and Journals v. 18.

322 **"I have seen them":** Ibid.

Chapter 23: In a Pickel

323 **"Umiak-suah!":** DBM diary, September 5, 1915, DBMC Diaries and Journals v. 18.

324 **"general assistant":** DBM diary, September 1, 1915, DBMC Diaries and Journals v. 18.

324 **"This was mutiny":** Hunt and Thompson, *North to the Horizon*, 71.

324 **"Dr. Hovey is here!":** DBM diary, September 15, 1915, DBMC Diaries and Journals v. 18.

324 **"How is it":** Ibid.

324 **The *George B. Cluett's* departure:** Unless otherwise noted, my reconstruction of this trip comes from EOH, "Crocker Land Expedition Relief," HMM; and GCD, July 2-September 15, 1915.

326 **"There was nothing":** EOH, "Crocker Land Expedition Relief," 65, HMM.

326 **"the appearance of":** Ibid., 69.

326 **"Are you":** Freuchen, *Vagrant Viking*, 103.

326 **"Oh, thank goodness":** Ibid.

326 **"When they polish":** Ibid.

326 **"I could not understand":** Ibid.

327 "a wretched and precarious situation": EOH, "Crocker Land Expedition Relief," 84, HMM.

327 "Dr. Hovey is with me!": Ibid., 86.

327 "If Mac does not": EE to HJH, September 15, 1915, CLEP b. 9, f. 13.

329 "Well, Hunt": MacMillan, *Four Years in the White North*, 201.

329 "They've all gone": Hunt and Thompson, *North to the Horizon*, 73.

329 "Dr. Hovey has": MacMillan, *Four Years in the White North*, 201.

329 Resentment: Hunt and Thompson, *North to the Horizon*, 73.

329 MacMillan sensed: DBM diary, September 27, 1915, DBMC Diaries and Journals v. 18.

329 "like a stray cat": DBM diary, October 2, 1915, DBMC Diaries and Journals v. 18.

330 "Mac's attitude": Hunt and Thompson, *North to the Horizon*, 75.

330 "Unwise use": Ibid.

330 "no bad feeling": Ibid.

330 a strong-minded man: Author interview with Mardi Thompson George, January 15 and 31, 2014.

331 "And the men?": MacMillan, *Four Years in the White North*, 204.

331 "Oh, they are all": Ibid.

331 "like a squashed tomato": DBM diary, November 4, 1915, DBMC Diaries and Journals v. 18.

331 "My two year plans": Ibid.

331 "Well Mac": EOH to DBM, September 17, 1915, CLEP b. 9, f. 13.

332 "lazy, good for nothing": EOH, "Crocker Land Expedition Relief," 96, HMM.

332 "without delay": Ibid.

333 "The ship is going": EOH to DBM, November 18, 1915, CLEP b. 10, f. 2.

333 Pickels nearly killed: GCD, November 11, 1915; EOH, "Cluett, 1915," HMM.

333 "How *could* you": EOH to DBM, September 28, 1915, CLEP b. 9, f. 13.

333 "I cannot tell you": Ibid.

333 "for the sake of": EOH to Peter Freuchen, September 28, 1915, CLEP b. 9, f. 13.

333 "If you can only": Ibid.

333 "Mr. Freuchen": Ibid.

334 "From what I have heard": EOH to DBM, October 12, 1915, CLEP b. 10, f. 1.

335 "looking to be": DBM diary, December 28, 1915, DBMC Diaries and Journals v. 18.

335 "no severe physical exercise": Ibid.

335 "remove any stigma": EOH to DBM, December 31, 1915, CLEP b. 10, f. 5.

335 "I'm afraid they will be": DBM diary, December 28, 1915, DBMC Diaries and Journals v. 18.

336 "I feel that I am": DBM diary, January 4, 1916, DBMC Diaries and Journals v. 18.

336 **"Where's the ship?":** Augusta Krieger to GS, November 4, 1915, CLEP b. 10, f. 2.

336 **"I do not think":** GS to Mrs. W. C. Fogg, October 8, 1915, CLEP b. 10, f. 1.

336 **"All the scientific data":** Mrs. W. C. Fogg to GS, October 14, 1915, CLEP b. 10, f. 1.

337 **"I am hoping":** Marion Hunt to Edith Demerell, December 8, 1915, CLEP b. 10, f. 3.

337 **"It does seem hard":** Ibid.

337 **"We [are] not a happy party":** EOH, "Some Sledging Experiences in Arctic Greenland," 3, HMM.

337 **"sold it to the crew":** GCD, November 23, 1915.

337 **"unwise and extravagant":** EOH to HFO, December 27, 1915, CLEP b. 10, f. 4.

337 **"consistent and cooperative":** Ibid.

337 **"absolutely incompetent":** DBM to HFO, January 3, 1916, CLEP b. 10, f. 6.

337 **"put new land":** Ibid.

338 **"absolutely necessary":** Ibid.

338 **"just right":** EOH, "Some Sledging Experiences in Arctic Greenland," 5, HMM.

338 **"Personally, I advise you":** HJH to EOH, December 29, 1915, CLEP b. 10, f. 5.

338 **"jeopardize the safety":** DBM to EOH, January 3 and 4, 1916, CLEP b. 10, f. 6.

338 **"there are so many":** Ibid.

339 **"Godspeed":** EE to EOH, January 15, 1916, CLEP b. 10, f. 8.

339 **"At first the trail":** Ibid.

339 **"I am feeling very fit":** EOH to DBM, January 1, 1916, CLEP b. 10, f. 5.

Chapter 24: Flight

340 **"Tired but happy":** EOH, "Some Sledging Experiences in Arctic Greenland," 8, HMM.

340 **"Cheer up, doctor":** Ibid., 9.

341 **"hand of steel":** EOH, "Cluett, 1915," 43, HMM.

342 **"Nature's laws":** Ibid., 45.

342 **"This year has been":** EOH to Frederic Lucas, January 19, 1916, CLEP b. 10, f. 9.

342 **"The prospect is":** EOH to GS, January 18, 1916, CLEP b. 10, f. 9.

342 **"her ability to get":** EOH to Frederic Lucas, January 19, 1916, CLEP b. 10, f. 9.

342 **"has turned the object":** Ibid.

342 **"I shrank from":** EOH to HFO, February 21, 1916, CLEP b. 10, f. 11.

342 **"Now the Museum":** Ibid.

343 **"the salvation of":** EOH to HFO, February 7, 1916, CLEP b. 10, f. 10.

343 **"excellent on the trail":** Ibid.

343 **"they will necessarily":** Ibid.

343 **"had enthusiasm for":** Ibid.

343 **"absence of system":** Ibid.

344 **"He is an impossible man":** EOH to EE and HJH, April 25, 1916, CLEP b. 10, f. 13.

344 **"You have caused me":** H. C. Pickels to EOH, April 24, 1916, CLEP b. 10, f. 13.

344 **"tobacca":** Ibid.

344 **"Melville Bay in January":** Green, "Arctic Duty" (December 1917), 2806.

344 **"No landmarks":** Ibid.

344 **"Alas":** Ibid., 2807.

344 **"We [are] idiots":** FG, "Rough Notes," January 26–28, 1916, FGP b. 2, f. 9.

345 **"I am Itué":** Green, "Arctic Duty" (December 1917), 2814.

345 **"Not yet":** Ibid.

346 **"Life was once more":** FG, "Rough Notes," February 8–9, 1916, FGP b. 2, f. 9.

346 **"This intermarriage":** Green, "Arctic Duty" (January 1918), 78.

346 **"but besides slightly elevating":** Ibid.

346 **"who had risen above":** Freuchen, *Vagrant Viking*, 106.

346 **"I was relieved":** Ibid.

348 **"Food supply inadequate":** EOH to AMNH, May 18, 1916, CLEP b. 11, f. 1.

348 **"reliable steamer":** Ibid.

348 **"realizing seriousness":** Maurice Tanquary to AMNH, May 16, 1916, CLEP b. 11, f. 1.

349 **"I am in daily training":** HDB to HFO, March 17, 1916, CLEP b. 10, f. 12.

349 **When Sherwood checked:** "Crocker Land Expedition Fund Account," May 31, 1916, CLEP b. 11, f. 3.

349 **"The emergency":** "Plans for Relief of Crocker Land Expedition," June 6, 1916, FG Jr. b. 4, f. 40.

349 **"Hovey relief expedition":** John M. Clarke to HFO, June 8, 1916, CLEP b. 11, f. 5.

349 **"It is a very":** Edmund James to HFO, May 24, 1916, CLEP b. 9, f. 6.

350 **H. D. Borup died:** *New York Sun*, June 6, 1916.

Chapter 25: Discovery and Disappointment

351 **"What gluttons":** DBM field notebook, April 10, 1916.

351 **"Everything was an uncertainty":** Ibid.

352 **"He is now":** DBM field notebook, April 17, 1916.

352 **"King Christian Island":** DBM field notebook, April 19, 1916.

353 **"We are putting":** DBM field notebook, April 28, 1916.

354 **"Thank goodness":** DBM field notebook, May 15, 1916.

354 **"His father was lost":** DBM diary, August 31, 1916, DBMC Diaries and Journals v. 19. Captain George Comer observed that Sammie was "a boy about 14 who is Peary's son a fine looking boy." GCD, January 28, 1916.

354 **"Boat coming!":** DBM diary, August 17, 1916, DBMC Diaries and Journals v. 19.

354 **"Nothing good comes":** DBM diary, July 14, 1916, DBMC Diaries and Journals v. 19.

355 **"temporary heart weakness":** HJH to EOH, February 2, 1916, CLEP b. 10, f. 10.

355 **"I do not approve":** Ibid.

355 **"destructive and wasteful":** GCD, February 8, 1916.

356 **"The natives seem":** GCD, March 18, 1916.

356 **"The Gramophone":** GCD, April 7, 1916.

356 **"unprotected and in the hands":** Ibid.

357 **"MacMillan can not be sure":** Vilhjalmur Stefansson to REP, January 11, 1916, REPC Letters Received b. 58, f. 5.

357 **Stefansson was closer:** Stefansson, *The Friendly Arctic*, 528–31. Stefansson emerged safely from the Arctic in 1918.

358 **"They went leaving":** DBM to REP, November 11, 1916, REPC Letters Received b. 57, f. M 1916.

358 **"I shall be living":** DBM diary, September 4, 1916, DBMC Diaries and Journals v. 19.

358 **"the hours":** DBM diary, August 28, 1916, DBMC Diaries and Journals, v. 19.

358 **"Three or four days":** Ibid.

Chapter 26: Waiting

359 **"somewhat offensive":** FG notebook, [June 1916], FGP b. 2, f. 10.

359 **"Months of *not much*":** Ibid.

359 **"I don't want":** FG journal fragment, [September 1915], FGP b. 2, f. 11.

360 **"If there is a divine":** Ibid.

360 **"monotonous drudgery":** FG manuscript, April 26, 1916, FGP b. 7, f. 1.

360 **"Bah!":** Ibid.

360 **"Why not take truth":** FG manuscript, [May 1916?], FGP b. 7, f. 21.

361 **"the *best* [time]":** FG notebook, [July 1916], FGP b. 2, f. 10.

361 **"Rain all the time":** Ibid.

361 **"I hope Tanq":** Jerome Allen to FG, June 30, 1916, FGP b. 1, f. 2.

361 **"highly distasteful":** FG notebook, [July 1916], FGP b. 2, f. 10.

361 **"I seem to have done":** FG to EOH, July 26, 1916, CLEP b. 11, f. 8.

362 **"Best wishes":** Ibid.

362 **"I feel quite certain":** GS to Isabelle Green, August 16, 1916, CLEP b. 11, f. 9.

362 **"some action of":** Isabelle Green to GS, August 27[?], 1916, CLEP b. 11, f. 10.

362 **"I wonder if":** Isabelle Green to GS, June 19, 1916, CLEP b. 11, f. 5.

362 **"Where is *Danmark*?":** AMNH to W. S. Nyeboe, August 16, 1916, CLEP b. 11, f. 9.

362 **"Has Green or Allen":** Ibid.

362 **"We are at a loss":** GS to HFO, August 30, 1916, CLEP b. 11, f. 10.

363 **"It was Ensign Green":** *New York Tribune*, August 23, 1916.

363 **"Green persisted"**: *Washington Times*, August 23, 1916.

363 **"He felt that he"**: *New York Sun*, August 23, 1916.

363 **"Heat is unendurable!"**: FG notebook, [September 1916], FGP b. 2, f. 10.

363 **"I was sure I saw"**: *New York Tribune*, September 6, 1916.

364 **"It will be charged"**: *Washington Times*, September 9, 1916.

364 **"It may be"**: *New York Tribune*, August 26, 1916.

364 **"carries with it"**: FG to L. C. Palmer, September 7, 1916, FGP b. 4, f. 3.

364 **"the professional advantage"**: Ibid.

364 **"We had a"**: FG to REP, September 20, 1916, REPC Letters Received b. 57, f. G 1916.

365 **"I am delighted"**: FG to GS, October 2, 1916, CLEP b. 11, f. 13.

365 **"In the greatest"**: Bridgman, "Three Polar Expeditions," 291.

365 **"I suppose if"**: HFO to Herbert L. Bridgman, September 7, 1916, CLEP b. 11, f. 11.

366 **"the management of"**: HFO to EOH, September 8, 1916, CLEP b. 11, f. 11.

366 ***"extremely important"***: HFO to DBM, September 8, 1916, CLEP b. 11, f. 11. Emphasis in original.

Chapter 27: Reunion and Separation

367 **MacMillan sat on a hill:** DBM describes this event in DBM diary, February 12, 1916, DBMC Diaries and Journals v. 18.

368 **"They are the spirits"**: DBM, "Religion of the Eskimos," [1917?], MMC b. 13, f. 5.

369 **"false"**: Egede, *A Description of Greenland*, 188.

369 **"I am not"**: DBM diary, September 8, 1916, DMBC Diaries and Journals v. 19.

369 **"quite variable"**: GCD, August 28, 1916.

369 **"All lack confidence"**: Ibid.

370 **the grizzled captain:** Frederic Newcomb to GS, December 12, 1916, CLEP b. 12, f. 3. After some pleading, George Sherwood advanced Julia Comer enough money to get by.

371 **"slightly putrid"**: DBM to Jerry Look, November 7, 1916, MMC b. 1, f. 65.

371 **"[do] not taste bad"**: GCD, October 12, 1916.

371 **"blows his nose"**: GCD, December 19, 1916.

371 **"Great heavens"**: DBM to C. A. Towle, November 7, 1916, DBMC b. 1, f. 45.

372 **"A third ineffectual attempt"**: Ibid.

372 **"Our relief"**: DBM to HFO, November 16, 1916, CLEP b. 12, f. 2.

372 **"Relief must come"**: EOH to Frederic Lucas, November 9, 1916, CLEP b. 12, f. 1.

372 **"We shall be unable"**: EOH to HFO, November 14, 1916, CLEP b. 12, f. 1.

372 **"It is of great"**: EOH to GS, November 16, 1916, CLEP b. 12, f. 2.

373 **"Where is it?"**: Augusta Krieger to GS, October 12, 1916, CLEP b. 11, f. 13.

373 **"I am greatly"**: GS to Herbert L. Bridgman, November 10, 1916, CLEP b. 12, f. 1.

374 **"rather difficult":** EE to HFO, [1916], FGP b. 1, f. 7.

374 **"I am not":** Christian Jansen to EOH, November 4, 1916, CLEP b. 12, f. 1.

374 **"Why couldn't they":** Hunt and Thompson, *North to the Horizon*, 78.

374 **"Already I am so":** EE to EOH, October 15, 1916, CLEP b. 11, f. 13.

374 **"exceedingly monotonous":** EE to EOH, December 3, 1916, CLEP b. 12, f. 3.

374 **"We assume":** EE to HFO, [1916], FGP b. 1, f. 7.

374 **"These means":** Ibid.

374 **"How I wanted":** Hunt and Thompson, *North to the Horizon*, 77.

Chapter 28: Off the Map

376 **"I fully realize":** Marion Hunt to GS, February 18, 1917, CLEP b. 12, f. 5.

376 **"they just *must*":** Marion Hunt to GS, March 15, 1917, CLEP b. 12, f. 6. Emphasis in original.

376 **Elmer Ekblaw's mother:** K. J. T. Ekblaw to GS, January 6, 1917, CLEP b. 12, f. 4. The German submarine *U-79* sank the cargo ship *Danmark* on December 30, 1916, after allowing the crew to depart in lifeboats. There were no casualties.

377 **Christmas Eve:** Elmer Ekblaw, "Two Christmases in the Far Arctic," *Illinois Magazine*, December 1917, 107; DBM, "North Pole Expedition," 306, MMC b. 12, f. 1; EE to EOH, January 9, 1917, CLEP b. 12, f. 4; HJH field notebook, December 13 and 15, 1916; Hunt and Thompson, *North to the Horizon*, 79–82.

378 **"Hal":** Hunt and Thompson, *North to the Horizon*, 82.

378 **"Don't worry":** Ibid.

378 **"you have been sleeping":** Ibid.

378 **"I know where":** Ibid., 82.

378 **"We'll be at":** Ibid., 82–83.

378 **Uutaaq:** Peter Freuchen later reported that Uutaaq was suffering from a case of gonorrhea that he had gotten from his wife, who in turn had contracted it from a crewman on the *Cluett* when she had sex with him in exchange for a small piece of tobacco. Peter Freuchen to EOH, [January 1917], CLEP b. 12, f. 4.

378 **"Call off the dogs!":** Hunt and Thompson, *North to the Horizon*, 83. In EE to EOH, January 9, 1917, CLEP b. 12, f. 4., Ekblaw places their arrival at the Cape Seddon settlement on December 31. Hunt's notebook records their arrival on December 30. Ekblaw is likely correct. Hunt had not made any entries since December 21 and had spent at least one lengthy period asleep since then. He later realized his journal was two days off but wasn't exactly sure when he had lost the time.

379 **"I had lost":** EE, "Across the Ice-Fields of Melville Bay," in MacMillan, *Four Years in the White North*, 378.

379 **blood brother:** Hunt and Thompson, *North to the Horizon*, 84, 80.

380 **"I was determined":** Ibid., 85.

381 **Hunt and his guides:** My reconstruction of this period comes from HJH

field notebook, February 14–June 6, 1917; and Hunt and Thompson, *North to the Horizon*, 86–92.

381 **"We have just":** Hunt and Thompson, *North to the Horizon*, 91.

381 **"I had seen":** Ibid.

381 **"Feathers under me":** Ibid.

382 **"the worst year":** HJH field notebook, March 10, 1917.

382 **"They surely expect":** HJH field notebook, March 14, 1917.

384 **"not in good practice":** HJH field notebook, April 24, 1917.

384 **"He was a":** Hunt and Thompson, *North to the Horizon*, 102.

384 **"Had I fought":** Ibid.

385 **the Kaiser's U-boats:** In 1916 the British navy detained the *Hans Egede* on both its outgoing and incoming legs.

385 **"This may prevent":** HJH field notebook, May 12, 1917.

385 **"MacMillan Comer Small":** *New York Tribune*, May 30, 1917.

386 **"I am so happy":** Marion Hunt to GS, May 29, 1917, CLEP b. 12, f. 9.

386 **"Even should she":** *New York Sun*, November 23, 1916.

386 **"We have grave fears":** GS to Sir Cecil Arthur Spring-Rice, March 17, 1917, CLEP b. 12, f. 6.

386 **"Our gravest anxiety":** GS, "Report to the Executive Committee on the Status of the Crocker Land Expedition," March 21, 1917, CLEP b. 12, f. 6.

387 **"I am rather":** GS to Hugh Smith, February 12, 1917, CLEP b. 12, f. 5.

387 **"In spirit":** Albert T. Gould, "Captain Robert A. Bartlett," *Among the Deep Sea Fishers* 44 (July 1946): 46.

388 **The paradoxes:** F. Burnham Gill, "New Look at Bob Bartlett," November 23, 1972, RABP b. 6, f. 65; and Gould, "Captain Robert A. Bartlett," 46.

388 **"I am fit":** Robert Bartlett to REP, [1916], REPC Letters Received b. 56, f. Bartlett 1916.

388 **"This price":** GS to Robert Bartlett, April 10, 1917, CLEP b. 12, f. 7.

389 **"I confess":** Hunt and Thompson, *North to the Horizon*, 104.

390 **"for the advertisements":** Ibid.

390 **"It is always":** Hunt quoted in W. S. Nyeboe to GS, July 23, 1917, CLEP b. 13, f. 3.

390 **going home:** Hunt's decision to switch ships proved lucky; a German destroyer searched the *Hans Egede* for Americans when it traveled between Copenhagen and Oslo. GS to EOH, June 27, 1917, CLEP b. 13, f. 1.

390 **"I'll always know":** Hunt and Thompson, *North to the Horizon*, 105.

391 **martial air:** *American Museum Journal* 17 (May 1917): 354, 355, 359.

391 **"From the scientific":** *New York Times*, June 21, 1917.

391 **"the best equipped":** Ibid.

392 **"It is difficult":** Ogden Reid to HFO, June 5, 1917, CLEP b. 12, f. 11.

Chapter 29: Last Days

394 **Small was walking:** My reconstruction of this story comes from DBM diary, June 3, 1917, DBMC Diaries and Journals v. 22; DBM typescript diary, June 3, 1917, MMC b. 16.

394 **"To hell with it"**: DBM typescript diary, June 3, 1917, MMC b. 16.

394 **"The sum total"**: DBM diary, June 30, 1917, DBMC Diaries and Journals v. 19.

394 **"mostly sung"**: DBM diary, December 23, 1916, DBMC Diaries and Journals v. 19.

395 **"I want the day"**: DBM diary, October 1, 1916, DBMC Diaries and Journals v. 19.

395 **"The loss of Sunday"**: Ibid.

395 **"Of course the natives"**: GCD, February 18, 1917.

395 **"During our three"**: DBM diary, January 25, 1917, DBMC Diaries and Journals v. 19.

395 **"Some of the dogs"**: DBM diary, January 27, 1917, DBMC Diaries and Journals v. 19.

395 **"undoubtedly our next"**: DBM diary, January 11, 1917, DBMC Diaries and Journals v. 19.

397 **"The sun"**: DBM diary, February 17, 1917, DBMC Diaries and Journals v. 19.

397 **"next to northern Greenland"**: Markham quoted in MacMillan, *Four Years in the White North*, 282.

397 **"I decided"**: MacMillan, *Four Years in the White North*, 282.

398 **"Now that he"**: GCD, March 24, 1917.

398 **"I had a fine"**: EOH to J. C. Small, April 1, 1917, CLEP b. 12, f. 7.

398 **"a surprisingly"**: EOH to George Comer, April 1, 1917, CLEP b. 12, f. 7.

398 **MacMillan wasn't at the lodge**: My reconstructions of these two trips come from DBM field notebook, March 25–May 17, 1917; DBM diary, March 25–May 17, 1917, DBMC Diaries and Journals v. 19; and MacMillan, *Four Years in the White North*, 281–304.

399 **"broke up"**: GCD, May 25, 1917.

399 **"After four years"**: MacMillan, *Four Years in the White North*, 306.

399 **"Poor George"**: DBM diary, July 10, 1917, DBMC Diaries and Journals v. 22.

400 **"One Smith Sound"**: DBM typescript diary, May 22, 1916, MMC b. 16.

400 **"It is my ambition"**: DBM to HFO, January 20, 1915, CLEP b. 9, f. 1.

400 **"What has become"**: EOH to DBM, January 7, 1916, CLEP b. 10, f. 7.

400 **"One can't get away"**: DBM field notebook, May 4, 1917.

401 **"A little strain"**: GCD, July 22, 1917.

402 **"Not yet"**: MacMillan, *Four Years in the White North*, 313.

402 **"*Umiarsuaq!*"**: Ibid.

402 **"Is that you"**: Ibid.

402 **"Of course!"**: Ibid.

403 **"They are all"**: DBM diary, August 3, 1917, DBMC Diaries and Journals v. 22.

404 **"Bring back only"**: HFO to DBM, June 25, 1917, CLEP b. 13, f. 1. Emphasis in original.

Chapter 30: No Hero's Welcome

405 **"So many"**: DBM diary, August 5, 1917, DBMC Diaries and Journals v. 22.

405 **"The world"**: Ibid.

406 **"good luck"**: *New York Tribune*, August 27, 1917.

406 **"A taste of real bread"**: Ibid.

406 **"It was a wonderful image"**: Ibid.

406 **"tell only the good"**: HFO to EOH, June 25, 1917, CLEP b. 13, f. 1.

407 **"valuable mineral deposits"**: *New York Tribune*, August 27, 1917.

407 **"Month after month"**: *New York Sun*, September 2, 1917.

407 **"The expedition was"**: *El Paso Herald*, August 27, 1917.

407 **"What was your"**: *New York Sun*, September 3, 1917.

407 **Kane's hat lining:** One of MacMillan's favorite artifacts, the lining disappeared in early 1918. George Sherwood speculated that someone in the AMNH's Department of Public Education mistook it for packing material and threw it away. See GS to HFO, March 16, 1918, CLEP b. 14, f. 5.

408 **"Secret military work"**: Jerome Allen to GS, August 25, 1917, CLEP b. 13, f. 4.

408 **"when the cops"**: Jerome Allen to FG, February 22, 1917, FGP b. 1, f. 2.

409 **"playing golf"**: FG to Jerome Allen, May 16, 1917, FGP b. 1, f. 2.

409 **"For a man"**: DBM to HFO, September 23, 1917, CLEP b. 13, f. 5. The *Naval Institute Proceedings* published five installments of "Arctic Duty" despite Green's many assurances that he would end the series after one or two entries.

409 **"not a success"**: DBM to HFO, October 25, 1917, CLEP b. 13, f. 9.

409 **"was not at all"**: DBM to HFO, October 24, 1917, CLEP b. 13, f. 9.

409 **"There is nothing"**: DBM to HFO, October 25, 1917, CLEP b. 13, f. 9.

409 **Hal Hunt:** Judging by surviving correspondence, Hunt enjoyed cordial relations with the other Crocker Landers, although it is unclear whether he saw or even corresponded with any of them again. He had a pleasant reunion with Minik when the Inuk passed through Bangor with a plan to start a lumber business in the Maine woods.

409 **"The pleasure of meeting"**: HJH to HFO, November 14, 1917, CLEP b. 16, f. 3.

409 **"a National disgrace"**: HJH to HFO, October 30, 1917, CLEP b. 13, f. 9.

410 **"for the good"**: Ibid.

410 **"I am not convinced"**: HJH to HFO, April 12, 1918, CLEP b. 14, f. 6.

410 **"He was terribly homesick"**: EOH to HFO, January 9, 1918, CLEP b. 14, f. 1.

410 **"Do not draw"**: George Comer to GS, January 22, 1918, CLEP b. 14, f. 2.

411 **The museum kept:** Roy Chapman Andrews to GS, December 27, 1917, CLEP b. 13, f. 13; GS to HFO, August 4, 1920, CLEP b. 14, f. 14; and *Boston Globe*, [1921], undated clipping in MMC b. 18a, f. 4. MacMillan's Bowdoin bear now stands outside a workout room in the college's Morrell Gymnasium.

411 **"to make it possible":** GS to HFO, October 17, 1917, CLEP b. 13, f. 9.

412 **"replete with thrills":** MacMillan, *Four Years in the White North*, 207–8.

412 **"fairly crawling":** Ibid., 257.

412 **"faithful helpers":** Ibid., 313.

413 **"The story":** Ibid., 92.

413 **"magnanimously":** FG, "Arctic Duty" (October 1917), 2223.

413 **"All the adventurous blood":** Ibid.

413 **"From this":** Ibid.

413 **"He sullenly refused":** Ibid.

413 **"pumped in":** Ibid.

414 **"As I stood":** Ibid., 2456.

414 **"At last I tasted":** Ibid.

414 **"At my question":** Knud Rasmussen to Reverend Dean C. Schultz Lorenzen, January 6, 1921, FG Jr. b. 4, f. 40.

415 **"most certainly":** Ibid.

415 **"In telling [Ittukusuk]":** DBM to HFO, May 4, 1921, FG Jr. b. 4, f. 40.

415 **"for trade monopoly":** Ibid.

416 **"It is quite true":** Ibid.

416 **"but the brown native":** Ibid.

416 **"fits of despair":** Ibid.

416 **"You have no idea":** DBM to Jerry Look, May 30, 1918, MMC b. 1, f. 65.

417 **"No joking":** DBM to Jerry Look, September 7, 1918, MMC b. 23, f. 27. Richard Byrd claimed to have made this trip in 1926, although many doubt he reached ninety north.

418 **"very unsatisfactory":** DBM to HFO, June 6, 1921, MMC b. 2, f. 13.

418 **"Though he is going":** EE to GS, October 19, 1920, CLEP b. 14, f. 14.

418 **MacMillan laid two additional items:** Cowan, *Captain Mac*, 93.

419 **"I hold it that we should":** *New York Tribune*, July 19, 1921.

Chapter 31: Endings

420 **The house on Commercial Street:** MacMillan, *I Married an Explorer*, xiii, 24; Miriam MacMillan to F. L. Slattery, August 26, 1971, MMC b. 3, f. 19; Miriam MacMillan to Melville Grosvenor, November 5, 1970, MMC b. 3, f. 19; Miriam MacMillan to Herman Friis, May 8, 1969, MMC b. 1, f. 15.

421 **"I'll be Donald MacMillan":** MacMillan, *I Married an Explorer*, 16.

421 **"Miriam has grown":** The Looks to DBM, July 8, 1913, DBMC b. 1, f. 6.

421 **Aglaliortok:** MacMillan wrote this as "Ag-lalior-tok," which appears to be his interpretation of an Inuktitut (Labrador Inuit) phrase. In Inuktun it would appear as Allaliortoq.

422 **"Who was Mr. Crocker":** DBM to Melville Grosvenor, April 7, 1966, MMC b. 2, f. 9.

423 **"A medal":** *New York Times*, May 26, 1945. George Borup, John Goodsell, Matthew Henson, and Ross Marvin also received medals, Borup and Marvin posthumously. Goodsell was an invalid and did not attend.

Newspaper reports do not indicate why Henson, who was well and living in the Bronx, was not present.

424 **"He likes thrills":** H. B. Parks, "Some Prominent Men in Texas," *Beekeeper's Item* 5 (November–December 1921): 343.

424 **"With his natural talent":** *Provincetown (MA) Advocate*, June 12, 1952.

426 **"writing and conniving":** FG to John Stapler, April 9, 1925, FG b. 4., f. 9.

426 **"It is the work":** Isabelle Green to FG, [1923?], FGP b. 1, f. 10.

426 **"It would have":** Ibid.

426 **"frustrated, baffled":** FG, "The Big Crisis," [n.d.], FGP b. 7, f. 2.

426 **"In the Navy":** FG to Charles Green, February 21, 1926, FGP b. 1, f. 8.

426 **"without a couple":** Green, "The Big Crisis," [n.d.], FGP b. 7, f. 2.

427 **"guidance and general business":** *New York Herald-Tribune*, May 29, 1927.

427 **"the modern explorer":** Ibid.

427 **The Green family's charmed existence:** My reconstruction of the Greens' drug use and arrest comes from Madsen, *The Deal Maker*, 277–80; and *New York Times*, September 27, October 25, and December 3, 1947.

428 **"large quantity":** *New York Times*, September 27, 1947.

428 **"chronic heart condition":** *New York Times*, December 4, 1947.

428 **One family associate:** Madsen, *The Deal Maker*, 280. Margery Durant died in 1969, allegedly of a heroin overdose.

429 **"Let the curtain":** *St. Joseph (MO) News Press*, December 3, 1947.

429 **"You're made of iron":** Miriam MacMillan to Stub, January 5, [1971], MMC b. 3, f. 19.

429 **"He is the last":** "Program," August 24, 1967, DBMC b. 8, f. 18.

430 **"the most distinguished":** Harry Hansen to E. F. McDonald, February 17, 1953, DBMC b. 1, f. 25.

430 **"The North!":** DBM unpublished autobiography, 29, MMC b. 8.

430 **"To me":** George Pierrot to Miriam MacMillan, September 9, 1970, MMC b. 3, f. 19.

431 **"Damn right!":** *New York Times*, September 8, 1970.

431 **"I'd like to be there":** Miriam MacMillan to Richard Nixon, September 22, 1970, MMC b. 3, f. 19.

Epilogue: Mysteries Solved

433 **"There can be":** *New York Sun*, January 6, 1918.

433 **"land must exist":** *Washington Times*, August 31, 1917.

433 **"evidence of the existence":** MacMillan, *Four Years in the White North*, 321.

434 **"lost Atlantis of the north":** *New York Times*, April 12, 1925.

434 **"It seems almost incredible":** *New York Times*, June 22, 1925.

434 **"If Crocker Land exists":** *New York Times*, March 13, 1937.

435 **a wickedly complex body:** My discussion of Arctic oceanography comes primarily from my interview with Luc Rainville, February 2, 2015.

435 **"The Sixth":** John Godfrey Saxe, "The Blind Men and the Elephant," in *The Poems of John Godfrey Saxe* (Boston: James R. Osgood, 1873), 260.

SELECT BIBLIOGRAPHY

Archival Sources
American Museum of Natural History, New York, New York (AMNH)
    Crocker Land Expedition Papers (CLEP)
    Donald B. MacMillan Field Notebooks (DBM field notebook)
    Edmund Otis Hovey, Manuscript Material on the Crocker Land
        Expedition (HMM)
    Fitzhugh Green Diary (FGD)
    George Borup Collection (GBC)
    George Comer Diaries (GCD)
    Harrison J. Hunt Field Notebooks (HJH field notebook)
    Jerome Allen Diary (JAD)
    Roy Chapman Andrews Collection
Bowdoin College Special Collections Library, Brunswick, Maine
    Donald B. MacMillan Collection (DBMC)
    Miriam MacMillan Collection (MMC)
    Robert A. Bartlett Papers (RABP)
National Archives, College Park, Maryland
    Robert E. Peary Collection (REPC)
        Biographical Materials
        Family Correspondence
        Letters and Telegrams Received (Letters Received)
        Letters and Telegrams Sent (Letters Sent)
        Manuscripts, Published Writings, and Lectures (Manuscripts)
        North Pole Diaries, 1886–1909 (Diaries)
        Papers Relating to Arctic Expeditions
        Photographs Relating to the Life and Career of Robert E. Peary
Georgetown University Special Collections Research Center, Washington DC
    Fitzhugh Green, Jr. Papers (FG Jr.)
    Fitzhugh Green, Sr. Papers (FGP)
University of New England, Maine Women Writers Collection, Josephine
    Abplanalp Library, Portland, Maine
        Marie Ahnighito Peary Papers (MAPP)

Published Sources

Allen, Everett. *Arctic Odyssey: The Life of Rear Admiral Donald B. MacMillan.* New York: Dodd, Mead, 1962.

American Museum of Natural History. *The Crocker Land Expedition: Geographical Exploration in Its Connection with the American Museum of Natural History.* New York: AMNH, 1912.

"Back from the Arctic." *The Independent*, September 15, 1917, 415.

Balch, Edwin Swift. *The North Pole and Bradley Land.* Philadelphia: Campion, 1913.

Berton, Pierre. *The Arctic Grail: The Quest for the Northwest Passage and the North Pole, 1818–1909.* McClelland & Stewart, 1988.

Borup, George. *A Tenderfoot with Peary.* New York: Frederick A. Stokes, 1911.

Brandt, Anthony. *The Man Who Ate His Boots: The Tragic History of the Search for the Northwest Passage.* New York: Anchor, 2010.

Bridgman, Herbert. "Three Polar Expeditions, 1913–1916." *The American Museum Journal*, May 1916, 291–94.

"Brother George Borup." *The Circle of Zeta Psi*, May 1912, 379–80.

Bryce, Robert M. *Cook and Peary: The Polar Controversy, Resolved.* Mechanicsburg, PA: Stackpole, 1997.

Cabot, William B. *In Northern Labrador.* Boston: Gorham Press, 1912.

Capelotti, P. J. *By Airship to the North Pole: An Archeology of Human Exploration.* New Brunswick, NJ: Rutgers University Press, 1999.

"Captain Bartlett to the Rescue." *Travel*, July 1917, 39.

"Captain Bartlett to the Rescue." *Travel*, September 1917, 38–39.

Cook, Frederick A. *My Attainment of the Pole.* New York: Polar Publishing, 1911.

Cooley, Austin. "With MacMillan to the Arctic." *Radio Broadcast*, April 1927, 551–54.

Cowan, Mary Morton. *Captain Mac: The Life of Donald Baxter MacMillan, Arctic Explorer.* Honesdale, PA: Calkins Creek, 2010.

"The Crocker Land Expedition." *Bulletin of the American Geographical Society*, March 1912, 189–93.

"The Crocker Land Expedition." *Bulletin of the American Geographical Society*, May 1913, 371–72.

"The Crocker Land Expedition." *Bulletin of the American Geographical Society*, June 1913, 449–50.

"The Crocker Land Expedition." *Bulletin of the American Geographical Society*, October 1913, 753–56.

"The Crocker Land Expedition." *Science*, June 15, 1917, 609–10.

"The Crocker Land Expedition." *Science*, June 29, 1917, 655–56.

"Crocker Land Expedition to the North Polar Regions (George Borup Memorial)." New York: Irving Press, 1913.

"Crocker Land Expedition under the Auspices of the American Museum of Natural History and the American Geographical Society." *Science*, March 15, 1912, 404–8.

"Crocker Land Party Safe." *American Museum Journal*, May 1917, 346.

Davis, Wade. *Into the Silence: The Great War, Mallory, and the Conquest of Everest.* New York: Vintage, 2011.

"Death of George Borup, Revised Plans of the Crocker Land Expedition." *Bulletin of the American Geographical Society,* June 1912, 429–31.

Deniker, Joseph. *The Races of Man: An Outline of Anthropology and Ethnology.* New York: Charles Scribner's Sons, 1912.

Dick, Lyle. *Muskox Land: Ellesmere Island in the Age of Contact.* Calgary: University of Calgary Press, 2001.

Diubaldo, Richard. *Stefansson and the Canadian Arctic.* Montreal: McGill–Queens Press, 1999.

Egede, Hans. *A Description of Greenland.* Rev. ed., London: T. & J. Allman, 1919.

Ekblaw, W. Elmer. "The Danish Arctic Station at Godhavn." *American Museum Journal,* November 1918, 581–99.

———. "The Ecological Relations of the Polar Eskimo." *Ecology,* April 1921, 132–44.

———. "The Material Response of the Polar Eskimo to Their Far Arctic Environment." *Annals of the Association of American Geographers,* 1927, 147–98.

Ellis, Richard. *On Thin Ice: The Changing World of the Polar Bear.* New York: Alfred A. Knopf, 2009.

Ellsworth, Lincoln. *Beyond Horizons.* Garden City, NY: Doubleday Doran, 1938.

"Equipment and Purposes of the Crocker Land Expedition." *Science,* July 25, 1913, 120–21.

Fleming, Fergus. *Ninety Degrees North: The Quest for the North Pole.* New York: Grove, 2001.

Freuchen, Peter. *Ice Floes and Flaming Water: A True Adventure in Melville Bay.* New York: Julian Messner, 1954.

———. *Peter Freuchen's Adventures in the Arctic.* New York: Julian Messner, 1960.

———. *Vagrant Viking: My Life and Adventures.* New York: Julian Messner, 1953.

"Geographical Record." *Bulletin of the American Geographical Society,* May 1913, 365.

Goodsell, John W. *On Polar Trails.* Austin, TX: Eakin Press, 1983.

Gosnell, Mariana. *Ice: The Nature, the History, and the Uses of an Astonishing Substance.* New York: Alfred A. Knopf, 2005.

Greely, A. W. "The Discoverers of the North Pole." *Munsey's Magazine,* November 1909, 290–96.

———. "The Stefansson Expedition and Other Arctic Explorations." *American Museum Journal,* December 1913, 347–49.

Green, Fitzhugh. "Arctic Duty with the Crocker Land Expedition." *United States Naval Institute Proceedings* 43, nos. 9–12, and 44, no. 1 (September 1917–January 1918).

———. "The Crocker Land Expedition." *Natural History,* 1928, 463–75.

———. *Peary: The Man Who Refused to Fail.* New York and London: G. Putnam's Sons, 1926.

Guttridge, Leonard F. *Ghosts of Cape Sabine: The Harrowing True Story of the Greely Expedition*. New York: G. P. Putnam's Sons, 2000.

———. *Icebound: The Jeannette Expedition's Quest for the North Pole*. Annapolis, MD: Naval Institute Press, 1986.

Hall, Clarence R. "George Borup." *Independent*, September 30, 1909, 732–33.

Harper, Kenn. *Give Me My Father's Body: The Life of Minik, the New York Eskimo*. South Royalton, VT: Steerforth, 2001.

Harris, Rollin A. *Arctic Tides*. Washington, DC: Government Printing Office, 1911.

———. "Evidences of Land Near the North Pole." *Report of the Eighth Geographical Congress Held By the U.S*. Washington, DC: Government Printing Office, 1905: 397–406.

———. "Some Indications of Land in the Vicinity of the North Pole." *National Geographic*, June 1904, 255–60.

———. "Undiscovered Land in the Arctic Ocean." *American Museum Journal*, February 1913, 57–61.

Harrison, A. H. "In Search of an Arctic Continent." *Geographical Journal*, March 1908, 277–87.

Henderson, Bruce. *Fatal North: Adventure and Survival Aboard USS* Polaris: *The First U.S. Expedition to the North Pole*. New York: New American Library, 2001.

Henson, Matthew. *A Negro Explorer at the North Pole*. New York: Frederick A. Stokes, 1912.

Herbert, Wally. *The Noose of Laurels: Robert E. Peary and the Race for the North Pole*. New York: Anchor, 1990.

Holland, Clive, ed. *Farthest North: A History of North Polar Exploration in Eyewitness Accounts*. New York: Basic, 1999.

Holtved, Erik. *The Polar Eskimos: Language and Folklore*. Copenhagen: Med. On Gronl., 1951.

Hovey, Edmund Otis. "Child-life among the Smith Sound Eskimos." *American Museum Journal*, May 1918, 361–71.

———. "George Borup: A Brief Biographical Sketch." *American Museum Journal*, May 1912, 156–58.

———. "News from the Crocker Land Expedition." *American Museum Journal*, December 1914, 309–10.

———. "The Personnel of the Crocker Land Expedition." *American Museum Journal*, April 1913, 179–82.

———. "The Reorganized Crocker Land Expedition." *American Museum Journal*, December 1912, 309.

———. "In Search of Crocker Land." *American Museum Journal*, March 1912, 83–88.

Hunt, Harrison J., and Ruth Hunt Thompson. *North to the Horizon: Searching for Peary's Crocker Land*. Camden, ME: Down East Books, 1980.

"Is the Crocker Land Party Living Like Eskimo?" *The American Museum Journal*, February 1916, 121–23.

Kane, Elisha Kent. *Arctic Explorations in Search of Sir John Franklin*. Boston: T. Nelson & Sons, 1890.

Kirk, Ruth. *Snow*. Seattle: University of Washington Press, 1998.

Kobalenko, Jerry. *The Horizontal Everest: Extreme Journeys on Ellesmere Island*. New York: Soho, 2002.

Loomis, Chauncey. *Weird and Tragic Shores: The Story of Charles Francis Hall, Explorer*. New York: Modern Library, 2000.

Lopez, Barry. *Arctic Dreams*. New York: Scribner, 1986.

MacDonald, John. *The Arctic Sky: Inuit Astronomy, Star Lore, and Legend*. Toronto: Royal Ontario Museum, 1998.

"MacMillan Arctic Expedition Sails." *National Geographic*, August 1925, 224–26.

MacMillan, Donald B. "Crocker Land Expedition." *American Museum Journal*, October 1913, 263–65.

———. *Etah and Beyond: Or, Life Within Twelve Degrees of the Pole*. New York: Houghton Mifflin, 1927.

———. "Food Supply of the Smith Sound Eskimos." *American Museum Journal*, March 1918, 161–76.

———. *Four Years in the White North*. New York: Harper & Brothers, 1918.

———. "Geographical Report of the Crocker Land Expedition, 1913–1917." *Bulletin of the American Museum of Natural History*, May 1928, 379–435.

———. *How Peary Reached the Pole: The Personal Story of His Assistant*. New York: Houghton Mifflin, 1934.

———. "In Search of a New Land." *Harper's Magazine*, October 1915, 651–65.

———. "In Search of a New Land." *Harper's Magazine*, November 1915, 921–30.

———. "Scenes from the Eastern Arctic." *American Museum Journal*, March 1918, 177–92.

"MacMillan in the Field." *National Geographic*, October 1925, 473–76.

MacMillan, Miriam Look. *Green Seas and White Ice*. New York: Dodd, Mead, 1948.

———. *I Married an Explorer*. London: Hurst & Blackett, 1951.

Madsen, Axel. *The Deal Maker: How William C. Durant Made General Motors*. New York: John Wiley & Sons, 1999.

Malaurie, Jean. *The Last Kings of Thule: With the Polar Eskimos, As They Face Their Destiny*. New York: E. P. Dutton, 1982.

Markham, Clements. "On the Next Great Arctic Discovery." *Geographical Journal*, January 1906, 1–15.

———. *The Threshold of the Unknown Region*. London: Sampson Low, Marston, Searle, & Rivington, 1876.

Maxtone-Graham, John. *Safe Return Doubtful: The Heroic Age of Polar Exploration*. London: Constable, 1988.

McCannon, John. *A History of the Arctic: Nature, Exploration and Exploitation*. London: Reaktion, 2012.

McClintock, Francis Leopold. *The Voyage of the "Fox" in the Arctic Seas: A Narrative of the Discovery of the Fate of Sir John Franklin and His Companions*. London: John Murray, 1859.

McConnell, Burt M. "With Stefansson in the Arctic." *American Museum Journal*, March 1915, 123–27.

Millard, Bailey. "Where the Map Is a Blank." *Technical World*, August 1913, 819–26+.

Millman, Lawrence. *A Kayak Full of Ghosts: Eskimo Folk Tales*. Santa Barbara, CA: Capra, 1987.

Nansen, Fridtjof. *Eskimo Life*. London: Longmans, Green, 1893.

———. *Farthest North: The Epic Adventure of a Visionary Explorer*. New York: Harper & Bros., 1897.

———. *In Northern Mists: Arctic Exploration in Early Times*. New York: Frederick A. Stokes, 1911.

———. "On North Polar Problems." *Geographical Journal*, November 1907, 469–87.

———. "On North Polar Problems." *Geographical Journal*, December 1907, 585–601.

"News from the Crocker Land Expedition." *American Museum Journal*, December 1915, 415–16.

Niven, Jennifer. *The Ice Master: The Doomed 1913 Voyage of the Karluk*. New York: Hyperion, 2001.

Osborn, Henry Fairfield. "Geographical Exploration and the Museum." *American Museum Journal*, May 1912, 164–65.

Osborn, Sherard, ed. *Discovery of the North West Passage*. London: Longman, Brown, Green, Longmans, & Roberts, 1857.

Peary, Marie Ahnighito. *Snow Baby*. London: Routledge, 1935.

Peary, Robert Edwin. "Arctic Exploration and the New Stefansson Expedition." *Scientific American Supplement*, May 3, 1913, 276–77.

———. "Arctic Exploration and the New Stefansson Expedition." *American Museum Journal*, February 1913, 51–54.

———. "The Crocker Land Expedition." *American Museum Journal*, May 1912, 159–63.

———. "Nearest the North Pole." *Harper's*, February 1907, 335–50.

———. "Nearest the North Pole." *Harper's*, March 1907, 497–510.

———. *Nearest the Pole: A Narrative of the Polar Expedition of the Peary Arctic Club in the S. S. Roosevelt, 1905–1906*. London: Hutchinson & Co., 1907.

———. *The North Pole: Its Discovery in 1909 under the Auspices of the Peary Arctic Club*. New York: Frederick A. Stokes, 1909.

———. *Secrets of Polar Travel*. New York: Century Company, 1917.

"Peary's New Expedition." *Scottish Geographical Magazine*, September 1908, 496–98.

Poe, Edgar Allan. *The Narrative of Arthur Gordon Pym of Nantucket*. 1838. Reprint, New York: Penguin, 1975.

Prentiss, Henry Mellen. *The Great Polar Current*. Cambridge, MA: Riverside Press, 1897.

Preston, Douglas J. *Dinosaurs in the Attic: An Excursion into the American Museum of Natural History*. New York: St. Martin's Griffin, 1993.

———. "The Search for the Arctic Atlantis." *Natural History*, November 1983, 112–17.

"Proposed Expedition to Crocker Land." *Scientific American Supplement*, March 16, 1912, 164–65.

Ramsay, Raymond. *No Longer on the Map: Discovering Places That Never Were.* New York: Viking, 1972.

Rasmussen, Knud. *Greenland by the Polar Sea.* London: W. Heinemann, 1921.

———. *The People of the Polar North.* London, Kegan Paul, Trench, Trübner & Co., 1908.

Reed, William. *The Phantom of the Poles.* New York: Walter S. Rockney, 1906.

"The Reorganized Crocker Land Expedition." *Bulletin of the American Geographical Society*, February 1913, 137.

"The Returned Arctic Expedition." *New Outlook*, September 5, 1917, 9.

Richardson, John. *The Polar Regions.* Edinburgh: Adam & Charles Black, 1861.

Riffenburgh, Beau. *The Myth of the Explorer: The Press, Sensationalism, and Geographical Discovery.* London: Belhaven, 1993.

Rink, Hinrich Johannes, *Tales and Traditions of the Eskimo.* Edinburgh and London: William Blackwood & Sons, 1875.

Robinson, Michael F. *The Coldest Crucible: Arctic Exploration and American Culture.* Chicago: University of Chicago Press, 2006.

"Scientific News and Notes." *Science*, March 30, 1917, 305–6.

Sherwood, George H. "Note on the Crocker Land Expedition Ship." *American Museum Journal*, April 1915, 195–96.

Simmonds, P. L. *Polar Discoveries During the Nineteenth Century.* London: Routledge, Warne & Routledge, 1860.

"Society's Hubbard Medal Awarded to Commander MacMillan." *National Geographic*, April 1953, 563–64.

Steensby, Hans P. "The Polar Eskimos and the Polar Expeditions." *Fortnightly Review*, November 1, 1909, 891–902.

Stefansson, Vilhjalmur. "The Eskimo and Civilization." *American Museum Journal*, October 1912, 195–204.

———. *The Friendly Arctic: The Story of Five Years in Polar Regions.* New York: Macmillan, 1922.

———. "Misconceptions about Life in the Arctic." *Bulletin of the American Geographical Society*, January 1913, 17–32.

———. "The Technique of Arctic Winter Travel." *Bulletin of the American Geographical Society*, May 1912, 340–47.

———. *Unsolved Mysteries of the Arctic.* New York: Macmillan, 1938.

Talman, Charles Fitzhugh. "The Outlook in Polar Exploration." *American Review of Reviews*, February 1914, 179–88.

Thomas, David N. *Frozen Oceans: The Floating World of Pack Ice.* London: Firefly, 2004.

Towle, Clifton. "Donald B. MacMillan." *Independent*, September 30, 1909, 730–31.

Vaughan, Richard. *Northwest Greenland: A History.* Orono, ME: University of Maine Press, 1991.

Warner, C. B. "Concerning the Crocker Land Expedition." *Official Bulletin of the National Dental Association*, March 1914, 24.

Wilkinson, Alec. *The Ice Balloon: S. A. Andrée and the Heroic Age of Arctic Exploration*. New York: Alfred A. Knopf, 2011.

"The Week." *Nation*, August 30, 1917, 213.

Wright, Helen S. *The Great White North: The Story of Polar Exploration from Earliest Times to the Discovery of the North Pole*. New York: Macmillan, 1909.

INDEX